SOCIAL WORK
AN INTRODUCTION

MARY WIRTZ MACHT
Chairperson, Wisconsin State Public Defender Board

JEAN K. QUAM
University of Minnesota

FREDRICK W. SEIDL, Consulting Editor
State University of New York at Buffalo

Charles E. Merrill Publishing Company
A Bell & Howell Company
Columbus Toronto London Sydney

To Tim and Teddi

Published by Charles E. Merrill Publishing Co.
A Bell & Howell Company
Columbus, Ohio 43216

This book was set in Garamond.
Production Editor: Anne Daly
Cover Design Coordination: Cathy Watterson
Text Designer: Rodelinde Albrecht
Cover Photo: Ralph Carr

The excerpt on p. 193 from "Unequal Education and the Social Division of Labor," by Samuel Bowles was first published in the *Review of Radical Political Economics* 3, no. 4 (Fall–Winter 1971), pp. 38–66. Reprinted by permission of the Union for Radical Political Economics.

Photo Credits: Mary Hagler for Charles E. Merrill, pp. xviii, 132, 180, 260; Social Welfare History Archives, University of Minnesota, p. 58; David S. Strickler, p. 309; Department of Housing and Urban Development, 372. Excerpt, pp. 312–317, from *Ethnic Sensitive Social Work Practice* (St. Louis: Mosby, 1981), 214–218. © 1981 C.V. Mosby Co., © 1985 Charles E. Merrill Publishing Co., Columbus, Ohio. Reproduced by permission of Charles E. Merrill.

Library of Congress Catalog Card Number: 85–63036
International Standard Book Number: 0–675–20324–4
Printed in the United States of America
3 4 5 6 7 8 9 — 91 90 89 88 87

Preface

"Social workers should and will continue to experiment and debate many issues. They should cherish their diversity. Diversity will not split the profession if all social workers are clear about their shared interlocking perspective, purpose, and values. Diversity can create innovation, knowledge building, and new approaches."[1]

The authors of this text met as students in the doctoral program at the University of Wisconsin—Madison. While our experiences in that program were quite different, we learned at least two things in common: that diversity should be cherished and that faculty and students can learn from each other. As doctoral students we observed faculty who taught conservative approaches often associated with casework, behavioral techniques, radical social work, task-centered methods, cognitive-behavioral models of intervention, "macro" and "micro" approaches to both policy and practice, and, of course, a strong general systems framework. The faculty also divided themselves according to fields of practice—child welfare, mental retardation, health, rural social work and aging. It would have been easy to look around and say, "What is social work?" "Who's teaching social work?" The reality was that everyone was teaching social work and that, in fact, social work is diversity.

In this text we have attempted to emphasize the importance of looking at some of the diversity in the social work profession. We begin by examining political perspectives. Social work practice and social welfare policy are shaped by ideology and values. Three orientations—conservative, liberal and radical—are presented throughout the text. While the goal of social work is to strengthen people's ability to cope with life's tasks while promoting improvements in the environment, the specific ways social workers will attempt to achieve this goal depend significantly on their political orientation and practice perspective. The diversity of possible responses is well illustrated in the various chapters.

This text is divided into seven parts. The first part defines the political components of practice, the ideology of the profession, and the generalist framework as a model of practice. Unique to this text, is an historical analysis of the profession in Part Two that is also developed from the three political perspectives. Though a relatively young profession, social work has diverse historical roots. Of special interest are the discussions of the role of women in what has been called a woman's profession and the history of black social work that has frequently remained unrecorded in social welfare histories.

Parts Three and Four define the profession of social work. Social work has a knowledge base and a value base that also vary depending upon the social worker's political orientation. The National Association of Social Work's Code of Ethics is compared to the Radical Code of Ethics, various professional social work organizations are discussed, and a comparison is made between social work and other professions. The knowledge base includes an understanding of social functioning, human behavor, social policy, and organizational theory. Though including a chapter on organizational theory may be somewhat unusual, the authors feel strongly that effective social work practice requires the ability to understand and work effectively with organizations.

The theme of diversity is continued in the last three parts of the text. Certainly, social work finds great variety in its fields of practice (family welfare, communities, health care and criminal justice) as well as the clients it serves (minorities, women, the elderly, Vietnam veterans, and gays and lesbians). The social work profession, again depending on the prevailing political orientation at the time, has historically contributed to the oppression of these client groups. Only recently has social work education moved toward being more proactive in suggesting the inclusion of material on women, minorities, and gays and lesbians. Part Seven looks at possible futures for the social work profession. While there exist overwhelmingly frightening futures such as nuclear war, there is also reason to believe that social workers will recognize many opportunities to work with new client groups using innovative methods. The potential of a computerized profession, for example, holds many exciting possibilities. We have seen how the diversity of social workers has shaped our past into a rich heritage of promoting change. Now, social workers have the opportunity to shape the future.

We are grateful to many people who have contributed in countless ways to the development of this textbook. First and foremost is Lucy Rowley who has contributed extensively to the practice material in this text. While she may not totally agree with the final product, her initial work has left an indelible imprint on the final material. Anne Minahan, teacher and colleague to both authors, has also had a marked effect on this book even though she has not seen any of the preliminary work. Anne's dedication to teaching and social work has indeed been an inspiration to the authors.

All of the material contained in this text has been tested on students in Professor Macht's classes. Janet Williams, Toby Ferrell, and Ron Cross, contributors to this text, are just some of the many students who have profoundly affected this book. Without the excitement and challenge of students this task would never have been completed.

Our colleagues at Charles E. Merrill Publishing Company, Vicki Knight, Anne Daly, and our consulting editor Fredrick Seidl, have all provided valued assistance. Various copies of the manuscript were read by Alan Siman (San Diego State University), David Biegel (University of Pittsburgh), K. Jean Peterson (Portland State University), Julia Watkins (University of Maine), Ray Price (University of Kansas), Jack Finley (Portland State University), Ruth McRoy (University of Texas at Austin), Mavis Spencer (Wayne State University), and Edward Brown. Their input has been invaluable.

A final thank you to our families for providing the caring atmosphere that allows creative activity to take place—Phil, Tim, and Teddi Macht, Ted and Grace Wirtz, Lois Partenheimer Quam, and Frederick W. Quam.

Reference

1. Anne Minahan, "It Was the Best of Times, It Was the Worst of Times," *Social Work* 27, No. 4 (July 1982): 291.

Foreword

The profession of social work seeks to reduce suffering and to improve the quality of life for individuals, families, groups and communities. In implementing this broad mandate, social workers have been in the forefront of program and policy development and have delivered services to literally millions of people and communities. They have done this through publicly funded and privately supported agencies, as individual practitioners and as members of multidisciplinary teams. Social workers have worked in such fields as child and family welfare, mental health, rehabilitation, the juvenile and criminal justice systems, aging, poverty and income maintenance and others. The profession has had a particular historical commitment toward the elimination of racism and sexism.

To carry out this mandate, social workers have had to combine expert knowledge of social problems and effective interventions, commitment to positive social values and creativity in problem solving. Professional practice is based on an intricate combination of knowledge, skill, values, and creativity. This book will give the reader, student and practitioner alike, a fresh look at the mix that makes up social work in terms of these and other components.

While not scrimping on description, Professors Macht and Quam provide us with an analytical view of many professional themes and issues. While many, if not all, overviews of the field provide only one ideological frame of reference, usually liberal or occasionally radical, Macht and Quam provide three ways of looking at the ideology of the profession of social work. Examining the profession from different ideological perspectives fits neatly with the overall generalist systems view of social work that is described as the unifying framework. What is particularly joyful about this approach is that the student is not told what to believe, but is provided with alternatives which stimulate his thinking.

Because the reader is not told what to believe but provided with a framework for analysis, the section of the book on the historical development of social work is an exciting addition to the literature. Here we can see that the development of social welfare systems is reflected in the politics, economics and culture of the times. There were significant and important differences among social workers themselves as to how best to proceed, for example, since social workers also reflect their times and social positions. Indeed, the very objectives of social work are examined in the contradicting orientations of the settlement houses, which developed group work, and the Charity Organization Societies, which developed casework. The story is followed to the present day. History, presented this way, takes on a dynamic and exciting character, a welcome antidote for many previous presentations which have tended to view history as "over" and its study as expository and bland.

Macht and Quam bring us more than a history book. Their examination of the profession encompasses both the sociology of professions and some of the particulars of the social work profession; both social work professional organization and comparisions with other professions. These comparisions of social work with sociology, psychiatry, psychology, counseling and law will be particularly helpful to the student interested in making career choices among related professions. In examining the knowledge base for social work, the authors make good use of the generalist model of practice in clarifying the importance of each of the various components. These components are also those found in the courses that follow the typical social work curriculum and represent areas considered essential by the Council on Social Work Education, the accrediting body for both baccalaureate and graduate social work education. Thus, this material, as well as other material for that matter, will provide a good introduction for students who continue to study social work as a major.

Part Five reviews social work in four illustrative fields of practice: family welfare, communities, health care and criminal justice. The book concludes with an examination of social work with special populations and issues; minority people, women's issues, the elderly, Vietnam veterans and homosexuality. The addition of material on Vietnam veterans and homosexuality is new to introductory texts in social work and a welcome addition. They have been neglected topics. The addition of these fields and topics makes the book a comprehensive overview of social work and social welfare. This review, coupled with the analytical perspectives provided, will hold the student in good stead as an introduction to the field of social work.

Fredrick W. Seidl

Contents

PART I

AN OVERVIEW OF SOCIAL WORK PRACTICE

"The forces shaping human relationships and thus practice relationships . . . reflect tension, change, and crisis. Rigid, impersonal, formal organizations and mindless, regressive social and political protests sit like threatening giants on each side of the narrow gate to a humane social future . . . Through history there have always been threatening giants . . . but people of tolerance, compassion, and vision have worked, struggled and persisted toward a better life for their fellow human beings."[1]

Almost every introductory social work text states that social work practice reflects the social, political, and economic environment in which it exists. Having given lip service to that reality, authors tend to launch into descriptive essays about social work practice that either ignore or discount the political and economic contingencies shaping practice. This text not only suggests that the political and economic environment affects practice but also asserts that it is the major determinant of the form professional practice assumes.

The social worker's ideological perspective is the foundation on which social work practice is based. Her frame of reference, interpreted through her unique ideological perspective, then determines the professional knowledge, values, and skills that will guide the social work intervention. Perhaps a figure best illustrates the whole process.

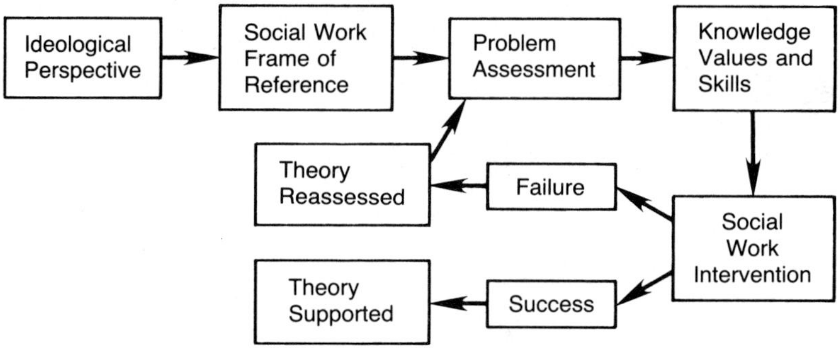

Figure 1

Feedback from the system alters other components of the system, but the ideological base and the social work frame of reference tend to remain stable. Individual practitioners may become more liberal, conservative, or radical with experience, but the degree of change is rarely significant. Their frame of reference remains consistent; their analysis of the components varies only with changes in their ideological perspective.

The social work frame of reference guides the problem assessment, which in turn identifies the knowledge and skills needed to solve the problem. The intervention leads either to a resolution of the problem (success) or a reassessment of the problem and reformulation of the intervention strategy. A successful intervention confirms the social worker's operating theory base.

Part One lays the foundation for an analytical approach to social work practice. The first chapter defines social work practice, asserts the importance of the ideological perspective, and identifies the social work frame of reference.

Chapter Two examines in depth each of the ideological perspectives that shape practice; it identifies the preconceptions on which our "social reality" is constructed. A typology of perspectives (liberal, conservative, and radical) is presented along with a special category identified as the social work perspective. Two social problems, drug abuse and juvenile delinquency, are analyzed to illustrate the relationship of ideology to practice.

The ideological perspective and the social work frame of reference having been identified, Chapter Three presents the generalist model of practice that addresses the three final components depicted—in Figure 1, problem assessment; knowledge, values, and skills; and intervention. In addition this chapter addresses the attributes of a model of practice; the roles, relationships, and functions of social workers; the problem solving process; and the four systems model of problem assessment. Part One as a whole develops the conceptual framework that structures the rest of this book.

Reference

1. Thomas Keefe and Donald Maypole, *Relationships in Social Service Practice* (Monterey, Calif.: Brooks/Cole Publishing Co., 1982), 242.

CHAPTER ONE

Understanding Social Work Practice

Beginning a discussion of social work practice brings to mind the fable of the blind men who had never experienced an elephant. "What is it like?" asked the first. "Like a big hose!" replied the second, who was holding the elephant's trunk. "No, no!" cried the third. "It's like a tree trunk!" He was feeling the feet and legs. "You're all wrong!" exclaimed the fourth who was holding the tail. "An elephant is like a piece of rope!"

Each had provided accurate information about the part of the elephant he was experiencing, but none could grasp the whole image. In its own way social work practice is like the elusive elephant. Grasping a picture of the whole, a gestalt of what it is about in our world today with its diverse fields of practice and philosophical orientations, is a difficult and demanding task. Like the blind men we are setting out in this chapter to provide you with an appreciation for the gestalt of social work practice by describing some of its parts.

The most relevant question in an introductory social work text may be: What do social workers do? Woody Allen offers one explanation when he describes an Introduction to Social Work Course.

> A course designed to instruct the social worker who is interested in going out in the field. Topics include: how to organize street gangs into basketball teams and vice versa; playgrounds as a means of preventing juvenile crime; and how to get potentially homicidal cases to try the sliding pond; discrimination; the broken home; what to do if you are hit with a bicycle chain.[1]

A serious study of the field suggests the almost limitless range of activities encompassed in social work practice. The attempt to capture the breadth of practice in an introductory text may at times resemble the shopping list approach used by Woody Allen.

Definitions of social work

Social work practice describes what social workers do, and how they apply professional knowledge and values to the many problem situations they encounter. Social workers provide direct and indirect services to individuals, families, and groups, with the objective of achieving mutually established goals to improve the quality of life, prevent breakdown, and solve problems. Social work is planned, purposeful intervention based on professional knowledge, value, and skills and aimed at individual and social change.[2]

Social work practice comprises three major methods: casework, group work, and community organization. These methods are discussed in Chapter 6.

Given the diversity of practice, it is predictable that definitions will abound, each with distinctive characteristics. Yet, the consensus is that the practice of social work occurs at the interface between people and their environment and involves goal-centered change.[3] Defining social work therefore requires identifying the goals and boundaries of social work practice. Those goals provide meaning for the actions the social worker undertakes. Some of the most frequently cited definitions of social work practice incorporate the activities, boundaries, and goals of practice.

> Social work seeks to enhance the social functioning of individuals, singularly and in groups, by activities focused upon their social relationships which constitute interaction between individuals and their environments. These activities can be grouped into three functions: restoration of impaired capacity, provision of individual and social resources, and prevention of social dysfunction.[4]

There is still considerable debate within the profession about how to define social work. Several different definitions are presented here.

> Social work is the professional activity of helping individuals, groups, or communities enhance or restore their capacity for social functioning and creating societal conditions favorable to that goal.[5]

> Social work practice (is) a goal-oriented planned change process.[6]

> Social work is concerned and involved with the interactions between people and the institutions of society that affect the ability of people to accomplish life tasks, realize aspirations and values, and alleviate distress. These interactions between people and social institutions occur within the context of the larger social good.[7]

The consensus among these definitions is that the goal of social work practice is to strengthen people's ability to cope with the tasks and problems they face in life and to promote improvements in the environment to more adequately meet human needs. This description of the goals of social work reflects the mainstream professional values identified in the NASW Code of Ethics. Not all social workers subscribe to these goals to the same degree. The specific ways individual social workers strive to strengthen coping capacities and achieve environmental change varies with her political or ideological ori-

The NASW Code of Ethics (1979) and the Radical Code of Ethics appear in Chapter 7.

Jane Addams (1860–1935), founder of Hull House and winner of the Nobel Peace Prize in 1931, helped to define social work as a profession of social reform and social action. Photo courtesy of Social Welfare History Archives, University of Minnesota.

entation and perspective. Therefore the first step in analyzing social work practice is identifying the political components of practice, the frame of reference, and the way these variables interact to affect problem assessment and intervention.

The political components of practice

Problem definition is greatly influenced by the practice perspective as well as the political orientation of the social worker.

The practice perspective can be determined by first looking closely at the definition of the problem and then the specified frame of reference. Problem definitions direct attention to the interplay between people and their environment. The identified locus of the problem varies depending upon the social worker's perspective. One social worker may stress the person as the appropriate target of change; another may see the environment as the primary target of change. The professional's ideological orientation determines the knowledge and values she selects to guide her activities; it speaks not only to the nature and function of the interplay between people and environments but also to the particular makeup of each. Political orientation influences each component of the social work frame of reference. It determines whether the problem will be viewed as a private trouble or a public issue, whether a system's improvement or system's design approach will be implemented, and whether or not (or to what degree) the environment is seen as the cause of the problem.

Moderate orientation to practice

Pincus and Minahan, for example, focus on people in interaction with resources, yet with the view that it is not " . . . *who* has the problem, but how the elements in the situation (including the characteristics of the people involved) are interacting to frustrate people with their tasks."[8] Carel Germain, on the other hand, asserts that

Most social workers have a moderate or liberal orientation to practice. This is further explained in Chapter 2.

> . . . practice is directed toward improving the transaction between people and environment in order to enhance adaptive capacities and improve environments for all who function within them. Knowledge required to understand the complexities of people, environments, and the nature of their transactions draws upon evolutionary biology, environmental psychology, ethnology, and organizational theory as well as disciplines more familiar to social workers.[9]

In addition to a moderate political orientation Pincus, Minahan, and Germain share an eclectic view of practice.

Radical orientation to practice

In contrast to Pincus and Minahan, Galper's political orientation emphasizes the broader struggle for socialist transformation within the social welfare sector of our society.[10] In a similar vein Peter Leonard stresses that social work practice must be based on " . . . a radical social systems theory; a unified approach to work with individuals, families, groups, communities, residential institutions, and organizations; and on an approach to the development of critical consciousness."[11] Holding with this political perspective an East coast collective of social workers contends that traditional social work practice is counterproductive to the attainment of the profession's goals of a humanistic and egalitarian society. They emphasize the importance of the socioeconomic system as a source of people's problems instead of looking to intrapersonal explanations.[12] In contrast to those social workers who emphasize the social determinants of behavior, others tend to see behavior in almost purely intrapsychic terms.

See Chapter 2 for an extended explanation and examples of the radical perspective.

Conservative orientation to practice

Psychodynamic theories, for instance, signal different substantive domains for inquiry and intervention than ecological or political-economic theories. Psychodynamic views emphasize family dynamics, family structure, sexual pas-

Variations on the conservative perspective are presented in Chapter 2.

sions, valences, and rivalries implicit in the problems the individual is experiencing. Political ideologies enter into the practice of individual social workers in varying degrees.

Frame of reference

A basic frame of reference guides social work practice.

Even this brief discussion of the impact of political orientations on individual practice might lead one to overlook the consistencies of practice, but in fact a basic format or frame of reference guides all social work practice. That frame of reference incorporates three areas of knowledge:

1. the "private troubles of people in social situations and the public issues which bear on them,"[13]
2. general systems theory including orientation toward either system improvement or system design,[14, 15] and
3. the interaction of people with their environmental resource systems.[16]

Private troubles and public issues

Historically, the social work profession has debated on whether to focus on private troubles such as intrapsychic problems or on public issues affecting many people.

Historically social work has been concerned with difficulties people have within their social situations.[17] The locus of such difficulties has been seen at various levels or systems depending on the particular point in time and orientation of the profession. C. Wright Mills offers an assessment that suggests these difficulties generally fall into one of two categories: "troubles" that are difficulties occurring within the character of the individual and within the range of immediate relations with others, and "issues" that are difficulties going beyond the individual and reflecting the society as a whole and the ways its various institutions interact and overlap.[18]

Unemployment is an example of both a private trouble and a public issue.

Consider, for example, the difficulties of unemployment. To the individual and her family day-to-day problems (inadequacies in food, shelter, transportation, and health care) add to the psychological stress of unemployment. The pressure to provide, with little if any opportunity to do so, may lead to emotional difficulties within individuals as well as strained relationships within the family. As long as few individuals are unemployed, unemployment is a private trouble. When these private matters are open to personal experience and activity and societal resources are available to solve the problem, the intervention is logically limited to solving personal problems.

However, unemployment may be a public issue, too, particularly when the private sector does not provide enough jobs to support the work force. Our present economic system functions properly only when approximately 7 percent of the work force is unemployed. But when 7 percent of the population has no means of support, unemployment becomes a public issue—not only because an individual family is suffering but also because the entire system is jeopardized by the alienation and frustration of the unemployed. Complex public issues like unemployment require a societal response. The fabric of social integration essential to social functioning can break down unless the government or some sector of society responds to needs not being met in the marketplace.

When confronted with an unemployed client a social worker faces two concerns, the private trouble and the public issue, both of which must be addressed for a satisfactory resolution to the client's difficulties. Private troubles and public issues are inextricably intertwined.

Divorce can also be seen as a private trouble and, increasingly, as a public issue.

Divorce is another difficulty traditionally perceived as a private trouble, but as the divorce rate grows, divorce too is increasingly perceived as a public issue. When private troubles become viewed as public issues, society tends to develop structural responses to the difficulty; with unemployment the structural change may entail making the government the employer; with divorce it may entail changes in family policy. For social workers these private trouble and public issue questions are basic ingredients in all problem assessments. Any social worker working with divorced or unemployed clients will address the private trouble/public issue dichotomy.

The ideological perspective of the social worker doing the assessment will influence whether she sees unemployment as a predictable outcome of a capitalistic society (The cause of unemployment is primarily structural.) or as a personal problem that can be solved only by changing the individual (Unemployment is a moral not a societal flaw.). Designated by society to deal with these problems, social work must balance societal and individual needs. Therefore, whether the emphasis is on individual or structural causes of the problem, neither component can be ignored.

General systems theory

Systems theory has greatly influenced social work practice and has been incorporated into practice models since the late 1960s.

Systems theory as used by social workers is descriptive rather than explanatory. It does not contain prescriptions for practice, but instead it serves as a tool for analyzing a situation and suggesting points of intervention. Generalist practice incorporates many assumptions of general systems theory.

A basic idea of systems theory is that components of a system do not exist in isolation but in interaction with each other. "Any unit we wish to analyze—physical, biological, or social—exists within a context which affects it and which it, in turn, affects . . . . A system is both a part and a whole."[19] A family, a neighborhood, departments in a university, or the planets in the solar system—all are typical examples of systems consisting of interdependent and interacting parts, together creating a whole greater than the sum of the individual parts. A change in one part of the system creates a change in the other parts of the system.

To understand the concept of the whole being greater than the sum of the parts, you might consider experiences you have had solving problems. If you have a problem to solve and each of five people comes up with independent solutions to the problem, you are unlikely to have either the quality or quantity of solutions you might have had if the five people had worked together. Hence the sum of the group's ideas is greater than the sum of all the individual solutions.

General systems theory provides a way of analyzing, understanding, and explaining the complex interactions of a system. The initial work of von Bertalanffy serves as the point of departure for this analysis.[20, 21] Systems theory prods one to take a different view of individuals. People are seen as individual physical systems and as elements in a larger social system. Systems theory stresses the importance of boundaries. Since the systems are limitless, it is necessary to determine some kind of limits for what will be considered in assessment and intervention.

One variable that determines those boundaries is the social worker's political perspective. Although systems theory inclines a person to consider the interaction among all systems, it does not preclude emphasizing one system over another nor does it determine what systems must be included. In fact some theorists suggest that even psychodynamically-oriented casework is guided by systems theory. This psychodynamic view of systems theory is more circumscribed than the one adopted by generalist social workers who see the boundaries of the system as open and permeable.

Feedback is another element of systems theory. Systems must receive both positive and negative feedback; accurate feedback provides both warnings and reassurance. Open social systems maintain themselves by a constant flow of material (energy and information). At its simplest an open system maintains itself by adapting to changes, moving, and growing in keeping with the exchanges and interrelationships of its environment.

Open systems generally have several unique characteristics: structural characteristics, and functional or behavioral characteristics. Structural characteristics include boundaries, hierarchy (the way the system is organized), and centralization (the way it makes decisions). Functional characteristics include the communication processes, the division of labor (how the system differentiates or specializes its activities), and adaptive mechanisms (the way it adapts to environmental transactions).

Systems need to be dynamic and flexible and yet stable enough to endure; all systems must maintain an equilibrium. Systems function in generally predictable ways. The way systems process the energy and information needed to carry out their tasks can be depicted with a flow chart.

Figure 1–1

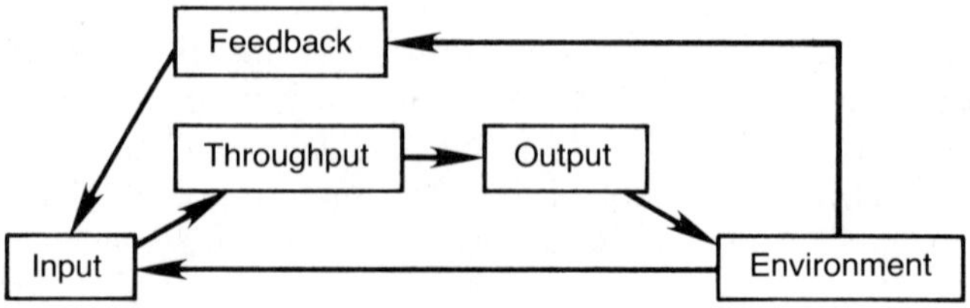

As the system works in this loop process, it monitors itself and gains information about changes within and without and in the relationships to other systems in the environment. If the response to the system's activities is positive, growth results. Negative responses encourage change so the system will continue. Feedback modifies the system so it can continue to take in and use the energy needed to move toward its goal.

Throughout the entire process the system must remain in relative balance (equilibrium) with itself and the other systems in its environment. Since change in one part of the system in time produces changes in other parts, the better the feedback system the more constant the equilibrium. If a system is too unchanging and rigid, it may fail to respond to innovation. If a system is too unstable, chaos may occur.

A final concept from systems theory important to generalist practice is equifinality. Equifinality implies more than one possible interpretation of the nature and locus of the problem and therefore more than one way to achieve the desired outcome. An example that illustrates equifinality could be the intervention with a truant teenager. After a thorough problem assessment, one social worker may feel the locus of the problem is the teenager. Based on this assessment the worker could proceed to set up a behavior modification program. Possibly this intervention would successfully decrease the teenager's truancy. Another social worker might analyze the same situation and decide that family dynamics are the source of the problem. Working with the family to improve communications may also lead to a decrease in truancy. Given the same problem, different diagnoses and interventions could be generated. The goal-oriented change process could produce the same results in spite of the diversity of interventions.

Equifinality is illustrated in the variety of interventions used with a truant teenager.

On another level systems theory allows diverse goal identification. For example, in analyzing a dysfunctional family one can begin by assuming that difficulties like child abuse arise because of the way the particular family lives and works. The orientation that emphasizes an attempt to change the way the individual family lives and works is one of "systems improvement"—" . . . the process of ensuring that a system performs according to expectations. It implies that the design has been set and is established." Here, improving the system refers to tracing the causes of departures from established norms . . . —the design . . . is not questioned.[22]

Such an assumption contrasts with a structural approach that suggests the family's difficulties result from a norm of family structure established by our society. A structural analysis of abusive parents would begin with the assumption that a family's difficulties spring from the societal design of the family system. " . . . The systems approach is basically a methodology of design and as such it questions the very nature of the system and its role in the context of the larger system."[23]

In essence, systems' characteristics and principles can provide social workers with tools of analysis needed for virtually all practice situations. By providing a way of organizing information about people, their difficulties, and the interactions taking place within their environments, systems theory facilitates the understanding necessary for day-to-day social work. By accommodating conflicting approaches systems theory also accommodates a broad and diverse political base. Until the profession develops a better understanding of the cause or causes of social problems, their effective resolution is more likely if social workers do not limit inquiry and intervention to one system.

Environmental resource system interaction

Environment in social work practice includes all the variables affecting the problem: physical, social, cultural, and interpersonal. Germain describes the physical environment as comprising the "natural world and the built world."[24] The social environment consists of the

> . . . network of human relations at various levels of organization. Both the physical and social environment are affected by the cultural values, norms, knowledge, and beliefs that pattern social interaction and determine how we use and respond to the physical environment.[25]

Similarly Pincus and Minahan discuss environment in terms of "people in interaction with their resource system."[26] Their view suggests problems cannot be attributed solely to the person or people involved: people's problems are an outcome of the wider social situation.

The history of the development of social work methodology is reviewed in Chapter 6.

Debate about whether the focus of practice should be individual change or social change is of long duration. Historically, social work has conceived of its work based on some type of person-situation formulation. Consequently it has continually had to develop ways to implement a dual focus and a unitary frame of reference compatible with this focus. The paucity of empirical knowledge has made it difficult to achieve this aim; practice has been based on weakly organized and untested bodies of practice knowledge.

In the last thirty years psychological and sociological information about people and their interactions has expanded to the point that specific practice principles based on this knowledge are being developed. Ways of working with individuals to effect personal change have outdistanced the knowledge generated to deal with environmental issues. But in spite of recent gains considerable work remains to be done in developing an understanding of individuals, social environment, and the interactive effects of each.

One of the newest social work practice models is the ecological or life model of social work practice.

Unifying paradigm

In the 1970s some theorists saw an ecological view of social work as a potentially unifying frame of reference. Carel Germain explained this approach in the following way:

> Ecology is a form of general systems theory; ecologists have always been systems thinkers concerned with the relations among living entities and between entities and other aspects of their environment . . . [Systems theory] rests on an evolutionary, adaptive view of human beings (and all organisms), in continuous transactions with the environment. As a metaphor for practice, the ecological perspective provides insights into the nature and consequences of such transactions both for human beings and for the physical and social environment in which they function. The perspective is concerned with the growth, development, and potentialities of human beings and with the properties of their environments that support or fail to support the expression of human potential. By clarifying the structure of the environment and the nature of its adaptive influence, the perspective appears to be admirably suited to the task of developing concept and action principles for intervening in the environment . . . . In an ecological view practice is directed toward improving the transactions between people and environments in order to enhance adaptive capacities and improve environments . . . .[27]

Within this ecological perspective the concepts of adaptation, determinism, diversity, autonomy, identity, social network, time, space, and stress are prerequisite to understanding person and environment and the transactional area between them. Instead of being a new approach to practice the ecological perspective reemphasizes the importance of the environment.

Since the resources social workers need to assist people are contained within the environment, it has been suggested that they analyze three types of environmental interactions: those among people within a resource system, those between people and resource systems; and those between resource systems.[28]

Having identified the distinct elements of the social work frame of reference and the impact of political orientation on practice, the next logical step is to illustrate these concepts with practical examples. The chosen cases all address a common social work concern: mental health and its affect on family functioning. But though each case exemplifies the social work frame of reference, practitioners adopt different ideological perspectives that lead to different applications of the frame of reference and practice knowledge.

The case of Bobby Ramirez clearly illustrates a dual focus on the private troubles of Bobby and the public issue of needed change in the juvenile justice system. Systems theory helps us understand how tradition, ethnicity, and social class are all important parts of this family system. The environmental resource system is important both in terms of economic impact on the family and lack of opportunity for Bobby.

The Case of Bobby Ramirez*

WYNETTA DEVORE AND E.G. SCHLESINGER

Bobby is 15 years old, the fourth of five sons in the family of Luis and Berta Ramirez. He was referred to the child welfare agency by the family court after episodes of delinquent behavior. The charges included truancy and automobile theft. On one occasion he stole a truck and demolished it. He is believed to be incorrigible at home, having little regard for the expectations set forth by his father. It is the expectation of the court that the child welfare agency will find a place for him outside the community: a foster home or, as a last resort, a residential treatment center.

The Ramirez family is Mexican American. Mr. Ramirez was born in Mexico but came to the United States as an infant; his wife Berta was born here but her parents were born in Mexico. Their eldest son, age 23, is self-supporting and lives outside of their home. The second son lives at home but is partially dependent upon his parents. The work that he finds is of an unskilled nature and does not provide him with an income essential for living. The other sons at home besides Bobby are 17 and 13; both attend school.

Mr. and Mrs. Ramirez have completed high school and are employed. Luis is a sanitation worker for the city; Berta is a domestic worker. They live with their sons in a two-bedroom house, which they rent. At one time they owned a house but lost it when they were unable to keep up the payments. There is never enough money to save for the down payment on another house, even though that is their wish.

They have barely enough money for clothing. In order to stretch the food budget, their diet often includes rice and beans prepared in the Mexican way. There is no money for recreation and so leisure time is spent with friends and family. Parties are often spontaneous. Friends, whose circumstances are similar, bring food and beer. There is dancing, drinking, eating, and a great deal of happiness in just being together.

Bobby Ramirez's route to the social worker was totally coercive; it is the decree of the court, which has also suggested a solution. In addition, he is in a state of dual marginality, that involving his ethnic minority status on the one hand and adolescence on the other (Long and Virgil 1980): the universal tasks of coping with puberty and a growing sexual awareness, seeking for independence from parents, and developing the skills for that independence are compounded by his ethnicity. Exposure to the Mexican American and Anglo worlds may well have produced pressures which force him to make a choice rather than make a decision; internal ambivalence develops. Garcia (1971) suggests the kinds of questions which confront Bobby and many other Mexican American youth and which may generate ambivalence: Should I reject my parents and accept the culture, ideals, and aspirations of the Anglos? If I do, will my family reject me? But, if I claim my cultural identity will I eliminate the possibility of admission to the Anglo world that offers success and escape from poverty? The temptation is to choose the Anglo way.

This beginning knowledge of Bobby's adolescent dilemma comes from the layers of understanding focused on a (1) general knowledge of human behavior and (2) an awareness of the ethnicity of others. The problem identified by the court is juvenile delinquency—a place must be found for him. As the worker begins this task, the model for ethnic sensitive practice aids in developing insights that may make this transition less painful for all involved. Although the parents seem to concur with the decision of the court there is pain, for Bobby has brought the honor of the family into question.

Although Bobby has ignored the authority of his father by breaking the family rules (a major transgression among Mexican Americans), Luis as the head of his household will nevertheless take part in the planning for Bobby's future. Some Mexican

*From *Ethnic-Sensitive Social Work Practice,* W. Devore and E. Schlesinger, © 1981 C. V. Mosby Co., © 1986 Merrill Publishing Company. Reproduced by permission of Charles E. Merrill.

American fathers feel so shamed by this kind of behavior on the part of their sons that they will offer no support (Murillo 1976). Failure in the adult policing roles does not deny him the role of representing the family in the community and in association with other systems, in this instance the child welfare department. The roles of policing and representing the family are among the activities associated with *machismo.*

In his analysis of *macho,* the masculine role, Paz (1961) sees it as one which incorporates superiority, aggressiveness, insensitivity, and invulnerability subsumed under one word—*power.* The history of this position of honor, strength, and masculinity lies in associations which lead back to a history of the "warring, sacrificing Aztecs and their medieval Spanish conquerors" (Queen and Haberstein, 1974). In the present, *machismo* calls for an aloof authoritarian head of the family who directs its activities, arbitrates disputes, polices behavior, and represents the family in the community and society.

The social worker may expect Mrs. Ramirez to be devoted to her husband and children, including the eldest son who has moved away. Children, family, and a few friends are the core of life for Mexican American women (Murillo 1976). Even though she works as a domestic, she does not do this every day; she must leave some time for her family responsibilities.

Her employment, along with that of her husband, provides barely enough income for the family to survive. Domestics and sanitation workers clean up after others. They carry out the most menial of tasks. The completion of high school has not provided access to higher positions; racism and discrimination have limited their opportunities. Although all family members speak English fluently, their surname and physical appearance provoke attitudes which diminish them in stature and attack their self-esteem.

A smaller family would require fewer resources but a smaller family would deny a tradition which supports large families. This tradition, however, serves to diminish the opportunity to attain the ordinary material rewards of American life. Mexican Americans are much more marginal in this respect than most other populations (Moore 1970); they have few new clothes, a limited diet, and little recreation. The ethnic reality involves a life of near poverty, but at the same time there is much pride in their ethnic heritage; this is certainly true for the adults. Support comes from ethnic associates, who in an informal way share resources. This activity is not limited to the parties mentioned earlier but may be a regular occurrence, in respect to daily needs.

The decree of the court gives the social worker and the Ramirez family little choice; Bobby must be placed outside of the home. The court, however, is representative of those macro systems which appear to be blind to the needs of those most vulnerable: the poor, ethnic minority families. To remove Bobby from the community protects automobile owners from his larceny; it does nothing to address his adolescent conflict as he is trapped between two cultures of almost equal force.

The ethnic-sensitive worker has a heightened awareness of the need to promote change in the judicial system which will recognize the larger world of Bobby Ramirez and others like him. Perhaps efforts may be made to seek out *compadres* (godparents) of offenders, as a matter of policy, to assess their ability to lend support to their godchildren and become part of the process in planning for their care. The community in which the Ramirez family lives has few recreational resources for children and teenagers, a complaint that has often been expressed by the Ramirez boys and their friends. A study of the community will determine the accuracy of their statement. If their claim is indeed true, what efforts may be made to organize the various kinship groups in the area so that together they may press for funds from the city recreation budget to provide the supervised recreation needed by all of the children in this poor ethnic neighborhood?

The model for ethnic-sensitivity practice focuses the social worker's attention on how ethnicity and social class impact on the daily life of families. Bobby's acting out behavior has led him to a social worker, who with patience and greater awareness may begin to change his life and the lives of other young Mexican Americans with similar problems. In so doing the worker also takes into account the unique family dynamics involved.

In the second example, Tucker addresses mental health on a community level, specifically how social structure leads to mental illness for blacks—"to be black and well-adjusted under current social circumstances is to be emotionally disturbed."[29] Tucker's dual focus stresses the public issues aspect of mental illness and suggests effective intervention cannot ignore the structural/societal components of the problem. A broad system intervention with changes in environmental resources is necessary for healthy development of the black family.

Minority Issues in Community Mental Health*

SAMUEL TUCKER

I must constantly remind myself that the peculiar relationship of blacks to American society is constantly in flux, and any statement today could have no relevance under different social circumstances tomorrow. However, I will mention in passing that racism, historically practiced and institutionalized, is the social atmosphere by which majority rule has justified minority status and roles in society. And, it is the black psyche that has suffered this peculiar adjustment.

In popular community language—"to be black and well adjusted under current social circumstances is to be emotionally disturbed."

The basic theoretical frame is social structural conceptualization formulated by the 19th-century French sociologist, Émile Durkheim (1951). The selection of social structure conceptualization emanates from this writer's perception of the black community as an "internal colony." While I recognize the radical characterization Stokely Carmichael and Charles Hamilton gave the concept of *internal colonialism* (Blauner, 1968), in their book *Black Power* (1967), Kenneth Clark in his book, *Dark Ghetto* (1965), demonstrated the colonial nature of Harlem in good acceptable sociological form.

* Reprinted with permission from *Social Work Processes* by Beulah Compton and Burt Galaway (Homewood, Ill.: Dorsey Press, © 1984), 168–170.

Clark (1965, p. 38) describes the situation as follows:

> The community can best be described in terms of the analogy of a powerless colony. Its political leadership is divided, and all but one or two of its political leaders are short-sighted and dependent upon the larger political power structure.
>
> Its social agencies are financially precarious and dependent upon sources of support outside the community. Its churches are isolated or dependent. Its economy is dominated by small businesses which are largely owned by absentee owners, and its tenements and other real property are also owned by absentee landlords.
>
> Under a system of centralization, Harlem's schools are controlled by forces outside the community. Programs and policies are supervised and determined by individuals who do not live in the community.

While Harlem is not typical of all black communities, the nature of external control differs only slightly. While internal colonialism is not a precise conceptualization, it has sufficient implications to merit serious research and testing as a valid model.

Community mental health practice in minority, and particularly black, communities must be characterized by a different orientation. This orientation requires additional information in problem indentification, problem and need assessment, and a social system approach to causation and solution. To implement, such practice would require knowledge and skill in the areas of social structural change, positive assessment of community and cultural life, social structural support, community management, social structural building, and a needs and maintenance approach.

This should not be assumed to indicate a limit on knowledge and skills, but an additional dimension added to existing knowledge and skills. While this presentation will not deal with psychodynamic conceptualization, past personal experiences of individuals, individual support on the ego level, agency service, rehabilitation, problems, and treatment, it should be understood that these are necessary and important treatment activities in mental health. Community mental health is an added interventive arm of the mental health body.

SOCIAL STRUCTURE CHANGE

The notion of social structural change is rooted in the elementary ideas of one of the founders of modern sociology, Émile Durkheim. However, the works of Peter M. Blau (1976), Lewis A. Coser (1956), Ralph Linton (1936), Robert K. Merton (1968), Ernest Nagel (1967), and Talcott Parsons (1951) have legitimized the concept of social structure in theory. The basic idea of social structure change consists of a change in the combination of statuses or roles which make up the structure or change the types of people who occupy that structure. When this concept is applied to the black community, described earlier as having many aspects of an internal colony, it is clear that the social relationship is such that one cannot change the colony without some change in the colonist—or more specifically—"colonial interest." Social work practice must enter such systems, being fully aware that the residual model is not appropriate, if the residual model is practiced, it must be perceived as a means of maintaining "colonial domination" or, to put it more mildly, a means of protecting the status quo.

Under such a social arrangement—internal colonialism—the mental health problems cannot be separated from the economic, political, and social life of the individual in such a relationship. The luxury of such separation is in itself traumatic to the black psyche and lends itself to the sick reality that "a well-adjusted black person in such a social system," is mentally ill.

Consequently, problem identification in a colonial social system requires that we add to community assessment a careful look at external power influences in black communities including:

1. Land ownership;
2. Housing;
3. Business;
4. Employment control;
5. Church affiliation and support;
6. Composition of boards in control of institutional policy that affect local community conditions. This includes social agencies, schools, city councils, political parties, labor unions, and financial institutions.

All of these forces must be looked at in terms of their influence on the health and well-being of local residents. Their actions must be weighed in direct proportion to their power and be credited with their share of the community climate that creates the atmosphere of emotional chaos—frustration, insecurity, lack of recognition, negative self-image, powerlessness, pessimism, double standard experiences of moral, legal, economic, and political behavior measures.

For example, the worker must be aware of the frustrations and mental agony suffered by minority communities over policy decisions to build roads, expressways, warehouses, halfway houses, drug abuse centers, and junk yards in black areas, rationalized by nonownership or cheap land, while attractive office buildings, universities, and hospitals are by necessity located elsewhere . . . while deliberate or expedient, black communities are constantly devalued . . . in a social atmosphere that determines the "self-image" on physical appearances.

POSITIVE ASPECTS OF BLACK COMMUNITY LIFE

The assessment process in such a system by necessity should take into account the odds by which the local social structure must function. The functioning of the black institutions, such as the family, church, and community cannot start with identification of the problem but must first begin with an assessment of the strengths.

For example, the black family has managed to fulfill its socializing function to the society even more successfully in many cases than their white counterpart, given the proclaimed societal values (Olson, 1976) of the "work ethic, freedom, local autonomy, equal opportunity, and land ownership." In spite of the circumstances of a colonial system that limits the access of blacks to the fulfillment of those values, blacks unquestioningly hold these in high esteem.

The black family has functioned exceptionally well in spite of the exploitative labor practices committed against black males and the destructive social environment created for black women and children. The black family has functioned in spite of institutionalized dependency of the welfare system (National Advisory Commission on Civil Disorders, 1968) and an educational process that intimidates the black child and the family with opportunities that, in fact, can never exist under racism.

The black church, in spite of its unstable financial base, its often secondhand, converted buildings, its poor attempt at imitating Western rituals has produced from its shabbiness, moral leadership unmatched by the white churches. And, at a time when national morality is in a church, the white church has appeared to "leave the driving to us."

The black community has survived in spite of its segregated character. It has survived in spite of the violation of its privacy by police, bill collectors, "Johns," research surveys, and social workers. The community survives in spite of its unprotected residents who have been left powerless by a majority rule, handcuffed by an economic system based on free enterprise, and demoralized by a social system that teaches democracy and practices colonialism.

But, the black community has survived as a symbol of common goals, language, and experiences that are so nationally profound that "brother and sister" from every social class, geographic region, and age understands and are bound by the common heritage. This again, I suspect, has qualities unparalleled in the majority community.

If the assessment does not begin with strength, a sense of weakness and failure can be fed into the community and solutions on such bases become accommodations to weakness and failure.

SOCIAL STRUCTURAL SUPPORT

In this model of practice, intervention begins at the level of community social structure. The support has to be deliberately designed to support the family structures as they exist; observing functions as a measure of adequacy rather than design. Those aspects of family function that provide biological needs, emotional needs, and support for acceptable values and goals, rather than the process by which they are achieved.

For example, the father role may be played by a grandfather, who enjoys, accepts, and is enhanced by the role. The child loves, accepts guidance, and turns to him for protection and help. The record should reflect this, rather than a long social monolog on illegitimacy, loose morals, absentee father, and weak parental involvement. The state of the family functioning must be reflected and supported.

The role of the black church and its influences must be recognized, accepted, and worked with to broaden its social structural involvement. Its institutional posture has historically evaded overt colonial interference to the degree that it has survived as a perpetuated institution over time. Since the interference with it is more pronounced and reacted to, it stands as a monument in the black community. Community mental health efforts must be tied to the spiritual and moral needs of the black community.

The third example illustrates a system-oriented framework that differs from the first two in its emphasis on private troubles. Satir deals with the family; public issues and environmental resources are incorporated into her practice only to the degree that they interfere with family communication patterns. The family is basically the system.

An Analysis of Virginia Satir's Approach to Family Therapy

CHARLES ZASTROW

Satir stresses clarification of family communication patterns in her work; hence she is considered among the school of communication theorists. Satir notes, in particular, that communication patterns among troubled families tend to be vague and indirect. In other words, rather than speaking clearly for themselves, the marital pair tends to avoid talking with one another about their needs and desires; or, they talk to each other about what they want through their children. Children are thus maneuvered into the stressful position of speaking for, and therefore in alliance with, one parent or another, precipitating of loss of the other parent.

In Satir's view, indirect communication in the troubled family begins with courtship of the married pair (if not before), due to the low self-esteem of the individuals involved. Each spouse-to-be feels worthless, but hides the feeling of worthlessness by acting confident and strong. Neither person talks about these feelings of worthlessness, for fear of driving the potential mate away. So each sees in the other a strong person who will take care of him or her, and essentially marries to gain an extension of the self, but a stronger self who will be able to meet all felt needs; in other words, each marries to "get" (Satir, 1967, pp. 8–10).

Unfortunately, after marriage some of the illusions must fall away. Each spouse is forced to realize at some level that the other spouse is not just an extension of the self. One insists on using a separate toothbrush, for example, while the other wants to share the same one. Such incidents force perceptions of difference, and difference is experienced as bad because it leads to arguments. A desire for fusion and to be cared for conflicts with the other's different felt needs. Facing difference feels frightening—it might lead to arguments and that could result in the other's leaving.

Hence each frightened spouse with low self-esteem and high need for the other tries to mask differences as much as possible, attempting to please the other on one level to keep him or her, while yet fearing and resenting expressed needs from the other which may be experienced as undesirable. Since both spouses are in the same uncomfortable position of resenting differences yet needing the other, interpersonal communication gradually becomes more and more indirect. Rather than risk a clear statement such as "I'd like to get a dog," the spouse desiring a pet might state something like "Aunt Matilda likes dogs." The hope will be that the other spouse will mind read the intended message of the speaker, and that he or she will then spontaneously agree to get a dog for the family. However, the receiver of this particular message will more likely communicate a return response dealing wtih Aunt Matilda, bringing disappointment to the speaker. The speaker isn't able to negotiate the desired dog with this type of communication, and is left with angry feelings toward the spouse and a sense of unfulfilled needs, but this state of affairs is experienced as being preferable to risking a pointblank denial. Meanwhile, the receiver of the message may become aware of the disappointment or anger of the speaker through nonverbal channels, but have no idea what he or she has done to cause it, if anything. If he/she is also afraid to deal with conflict, s/he will not ask the reason for the apparent upset. So the misunderstanding and tension builds.

Satir also notes that communicating involves far more than the literal meaning of any words used.

Reprinted with permission from *The Practice of Social Work* (Homewood, Ill.: Dorsey Press, © 1985), 171-173.

First of all, she notes that much communication is nonverbal—gestures, facial expressions, voice tone, posture, and the like. If nonverbal communication matches the meaning of any words used (if, for example, the words "I am sad" are accompanied by tears and a downturned mouth), then Satir considers the communication "congruent." The receiver is not likely to misunderstand the meaning of this message because the verbal and nonverbal components agree. However, messages sent are often incongruent. For example, the statement "I am sad" may be accompanied by a grin. Which message should the receiver believe, the words or the facial expression? The receiver is likely to make a mistaken interpretation unless he or she explicitly asks the sender to explain. But the person who feels safe only with indirect communication is not likely to ask. Moreover, the sender who becomes skilled at sending incongruent communication for self-protection may even be unaware he or she is doing it, and will be unable to explain if asked. Satir believes that incongruent communication can lead to a good deal of misunderstanding in troubled families. Mother, for example, may say to her spouse in words, "I am angry with you." However, since she fears rejection if she sends this message too forcefully, she smiles sweetly as she says it. The spouse may then choose to believe the smile, not to take his spouse's words seriously, and continue the very behavior that made her use the word "angry." This is likely to make her angrier, but she may not feel safe enough to express the feeling more congruently; and the communication driving the spouses apart goes on.

While incongruent communication is one example of a double message, another type of double message may place the receiver in a "double bind," where no matter how one responds, the sender will criticize. This type of situation can occur in a family where father says, on the one hand, that all good children should keep their toys picked up, and yet on the other tells his son that all "real" boys are messy. The boy who receives both these messages will be unable to please father whether he keeps his toys neat or messy. He may solve the problem by refusing to listen at all. At the extreme, he may pull away from reality to such a degree that he may develop a severe emotional disturbance.

Satir's therapeutic goals and techniques are based on her assumption that people have the inherent ability, even drive, to grow, to mature. She feels that people can choose to take responsibility for their own lives and actions, and that the mature person will:

a. Manifest himself clearly to others.
b. Be in touch with signals from his internal self, thus letting himself know openly what he thinks and feels.
c. Be able to see and hear what is outside himself as differentiated from himself and as different from anything else.
d. Behave toward another person as someone who is separate and unique.
e. Treat the presence of differentness as an opportunity to learn and explore rather than as a threat or signal of conflict (Satir, 1967, p. 921).

To help the members of a troubled family differentiate from one another and learn to own their special unique beings, Satir patiently teaches each person to speak for him or herself, to send "I messages."[3] She serves as an active, directive loving role model. She teaches that differentness is normal and should be viewed as a catalyst for growth. She points out incongruent messages and double binds, and teaches family members to send clear, congruent messages instead. She uses touch and other nonverbal means such as family sculpturing to help illustrate to families the unverbalized assumptions they operate by, and in this way takes the burden of labeling off the identified client and reveals his or her symptomatic behavior as a product of the family system as a whole. She analyzes rules in the family and helps clarify them in the context that rules may be bad, but the people setting or bound by them are not. She teaches that bad rules can be changed, and has the family members negotiate new ones as she insists that each member be heard in her presence, thus teaching respect for each person and point of view.

Clearly, then, Satir views the family as a system and works with the family as a whole as the means

[3] "I-messages" are described in Chapter 20.

of relieving the distress of the identified client, or of the family itself due to the previous dysfunctional behavior of the identified client. Her major emphasis in intervention wtih the family as a system is to clarify the family communication patterns and to help them become direct and congruent. Basically, Satir's therapeutic goal of improving methods of communication involves three outcomes: (1) Each member should be able to report congruently, completely, and obviously on what he or she sees and hears, feels and thinks about himself or herself and others. (2) Each person should be related to in his or her uniqueness so that decisions are made in terms of exploration and negotiation, rather than in terms of power. (3) Differentness should be openly acknowledged and used for growth.

Summary

This chapter suggests the diversity of social work practice assessments and interventions can be traced to the social worker's frame of reference and ideological perspectives. While ideology has the most profound effect on practice, this chapter only briefly identifies the ideological variable and concentrates on social work's unique frame of reference. Understanding social work's frame of reference is necessary for understanding how ideological perspective affects this frame of reference.

Therefore, this chapter has outlined the social work frame of reference in terms of the dual focus—private troubles vs. public issues, the effect of the environmental resource system, and the importance of a general systems theory in problem assessment. Case examples drawn from major social work texts illustrate the components of the frame of reference and how they are affected by ideology. Chapter Two will further develop the ideological perspectives inherent in social work practice.

References

1. Woody Allen, *Getting Even* (New York: Random House, 1966).
2. Mabel G. Wells, "The Classroom Teaching of Social Work Practice," *Journal of Education for Social Work* 20, no. 3 (Fall 1984): 58–65.
3. Harriet Bartlett, *The Common Base of Social Work Practice* (New York: NASW, 1970).
   William Schwartz, "On the Case of Groups in Social Work Practice," in *The Practice of Group Work,* ed. William Schwartz and Serapio Zalba (New York: Columbia University Press. 1971), 3–24.
   William Gordon, "Basic Constructs for an Integrative and Generative Conception of Social Work," in *A Holistic Conception of Social Work* (New York, CSWE, 1969): 5–11.
4. Werner Bollim, "The Nature of Social Work," *Social Work* 3, no. 2 (April 1958): 18.
5. National Association of Social Workers, Standards for Social Service Manpower (Washington, D.C.: NASW, 1973), 4–5.
6. Allan Pincus and Anne Minahan, *Social Work Practice: Model and Method* (Itasca Ill.: Peacock, 1973), xii.
7. Betty Baer and Ron Federico, *Educating the Baccalaureate Social Worker* (Cambridge, Mass.: Ballinger, 1978), 68.
8. Alan Pincus and Anne Minahan, *Social Work*

Practice: Model and Method (Itasca, Ill.: Peacock, 1973), 11, 14.

9. Carel Germain, *Social Work Practice: People and Environments. An Ecological Perspective* (New York: Columbia University Press, 1979), 8.
10. Jeffrey Galper, *Social Work Practice: A Radical Perspective* (Englewood Cliffs, N.J.: Prentice-Hall, 1980), 11.
11. Peter Leonard, "Towards a Paradigm for Radical Practice," in *Radical Social Work* ed. Mike Brake and Roy Bailey (New York: Pantheon Books, 1975), 47.
12. Galper, *Social Work Practice,* 8–9
13. Pincus and Minahan, *Social Work Practice,* 13.
14. John P. Van Gigch, *Applied General Systems Theory* (New York: Harper and Row, 1978), 4.
15. Robert Berger and Ronald Federico, *Human Behavior: A Social Work Perspective* (New York: Longman, 1982), 40.
16. Germain, *Social Work Practice.*
17. Pincus and Minahan, *Social Work Practice,* 105.
18. C. Wright Mills, *The Sociological Imagination* (New York: Oxford University Press. 1959), 8.
19. Berger and Federico, *Human Behavior,* 41.
20. Ludwig von Bertalanffy, *General System Theory Yearbook for the Society for General Systems Research,* ed. L von Bertalanffy, Fol. 1 (Bedford, Mass.: Society for General Systems Research, 1956), 11; and *General Systems Theory* (New York: Braziller, 1968).
21. Frederick Bates and Clyde Harvey, *The Structure of Social Systems* (New York: Gardner Press, 1975), 29–30.
22. Van Gigch, *Applied General Systems Theory,* 4.
23. Ibid.
24. Germain, *Social Work Practice,* 13.
25. Ibid.
26. Pincus and Minahan, *Social Work Pracice,* 11.
27. Germain, *Social Work Practice,* 7–8.
28. Pincus and Minahan, *Social Work Practice,* 13.
29. Samuel Tucker, "Minority Issues in Community Mental Health," in *Social Work Processes,* by Beulah Compton and Burt Galaway (Homewood, Ill.: Dorsey Press, 1984).

CHAPTER TWO

Social Work Values and Ideology

"It does make a difference in human existence whether the highest value is moral excellence or the possession of wealth; whether value standards are strictly applied or whether a general permissiveness is the order of the day; or whether the stress is placed upon human beings as the supreme value or upon profit and economic utility. What men regard as worthy of their best efforts, individually and collectively, determines the value pattern of their times and gives meaning and relevance to their general world view.[1]"

As a profession social work has a knowledge base and a value base.

Social work practice and policy are shaped by ideology and values—beliefs held about people, their nature, and what is desireable. Although unproven, values are powerful guides to action that can be tracked through the day-to-day practice of a social worker. An ideology is a value system characteristic of a group; it is tied to political and economic interests.[2]

Assumptions about what constitutes "good" for the individual and society are important, but the ideology that groups adopt has an even more powerful effect on practice. By addressing the different theories of humans and society, it is possible to expand on these assumptions and consider in more depth how these value systems relate to political and economic interests.

The most widely accepted ideology is directly reflected in social welfare policy, which in turn sets the parameters of publicly supported social work practice. Furthermore, society's rejection of more extreme ideologies makes practice difficult for practitioners adopting those perspectives.

Social work practice is shaped by the belief systems of individual workers. These social workers are protesting at a Mother's Day March for Peace. Photo by Michelle Lesley.

Social construction of reality

The importance of ideology is that it shapes our social construction of reality. What may be presented as an objective description of reality is replete with implications for the social priorities of certain groups. Ideologies are instruments of group interest; they justify and rationalize inequality and legitimate group power.[3] The same ideology cannot serve the interests of both capital and labor.[4]

It is important to understand how an individual's beliefs and values affect his actions—in policy and in practice.

To move beyond accepting value-laden assumptions as objective reality, it is necessary to make manifest the preconceptions on which such assumptions are based. To understand various approaches to social work practice and texts or policies and policymakers requires recognition of fundamental assumptions that underlie policy and practice. Whether or not the author, policymaker, or practitioner is consciously aware of his own ideology, it does affect his actions. How different social workers choose to answer certain basic questions helps clarify specific differences among ideologies.

1. What is the stated or unstated preconception about individuals and how individuals relate to one another in our society? What motivates individuals? What controls do they require? What is their potential and how can it be maximized?
2. What role does the state play in the welfare of people? What role is appropriate for the state?
3. What assumptions do they make about the present economic and political systems? How would they envision an "ideal" political and economic state? What is their vision of an "ideal" society?

Since parsimony is an essential component of any useful analytical scheme, it is necessary to develop a typology from these questions. But in addition to losing some of the richness of the analysis, naming typologies also presents conceptual and operational complications. This chapter does not aim to develop a new approach to the perspectives inherent in social work literature, but rather it aims to clarify what is already present. Studying the assumptions basic to the ideology of the profession leads to a better understanding of social work practice.

A typology is a simplification of a complex set of characteristics.

Comprehending the relationship of ideology to practice is contingent upon understanding the relationship of practice to the social welfare institution. The institution of social welfare is society's response to meeting human needs. It is a formal system that supplements informal systems such as family, friends, and church. The social welfare institution brings the societal resources to bear on meeting human needs. It encompasses social welfare policy and laws, the social service delivery system, and several professions. Social work is one of these professions, and therefore the societal approach to social welfare sets both the limits and potential of social work practice.

An example of a formal social welfare system is a state hospital. An example of an informal welfare system is the family.

One early typology developed by Wilensky and Lebeaux identified two dominant conceptions of social welfare—the residual and the institutional—still frequently cited in current literature.[5] The institutional conception of social welfare was expanded by writers such as Romanyshyn and Kahn to include a developmental approach.[6,7] More recent authors, Gordon and Galper among others, have incorporated the residual, institutional, and developmental conceptions into the conservative and liberal perspectives and have expanded the typology to encompass a radical perspective.[8,9] Ryan combines these perspectives somewhat differently into a fair shares vs. fair play schema.[10]

A residual service is provided only to someone in crisis who is qualified to receive help (e.g., AFDC). An institutional service is a part of our everyday functioning (e.g., schools).

Typologies described in this book will bear the labels conservative, liberal, and radical since these terms are the most inclusive and the most common in the current literature. The analysis will begin with a discussion of social work's guiding ideology that research suggests is consistent with assumptions of the liberal perspective. Having drawn the parallel, the liberal perspective will be further analyzed. Conservative and radical perspectives will then be compared to the mainstream perspective.

While three different perspectives are presented in this text, the guiding ideology in social work is the liberal perspective.

The social work perspective

Chapter 1 introduces the importance of political perspectives.

The assumptions underlying the liberal perspective are generally assumptions that structure the majority of social work literature and practice. Ephross and Reisch surveyed the most widely used social work introductory texts and found that none adopted a conservative or radical stance; all clustered within the liberal perspective.[11] Their findings situate clusters on the Left—"which relate most directly to public issues and views social work as fundamentally related to social change"[12] (similar to Kahn's developmental view)[13]; Centrist—"which acknowledges clearly the connections between social work clients and societal forces and events, but does not deal with the need for political, social, and economic changes"[14]; and Right—"which views societal forces as part of the field within which individuals and families exist but stresses this connection largely for the purpose of understanding how to work better with individuals and families (It avoids questions about social change)."[15]

Ephross and Reisch's findings illustrate that liberalism and conservatism are best described as being on a continuum. In spite of real differences, the consistencies appear greater than the distinctions.

But perhaps more revealing than the liberal perspective these texts have in common is the equivocating answers the authors generate to the questions they ask. In discussing methodology Ephross and Reisch say they will address certain basic questions.

1. What assumptions does the book contain about the political-economic structure of society?
2. What assumptions does the book contain about the nature of social class and social class relationships?
3. What assumptions does the book contain about the nature of social change? In addition, general implications for a definition of social work practice were noted for each book.[16]

In the end the authors do not seem to answer the very questions they identify as critical. What class interest is served by the ideology presented in the text? Nor do they analyze the political-economic structure in any depth or address class issues. In other words Ephross and Reisch never really address the question of a benign or hostile political-economic environment.

Since Ephross & Reisch studied only influential texts, their findings reflect the most widely held perspectives in current social work education. Their article provides considerable evidence that a liberal perspective permeates the literature assigned to social work students. Mendelsohn's observation—that as social work became more committed to increased professionalism it became important to define an area of expertise—at least partly explains the lack of critical analysis.

> The new professionals certainly recognized that social problems were more than manifestations of individual malaise. Social problems were rather manifestations

> of the social, economic, and political system. The question became whether to work to correct the system or to work with the victims of the system. The professional field opted to work with the victims primarily, and both the quality and the content of professional social work training were influenced by this decision.[17]

Although analysis shows the "system's" contribution to social problems, society funds social work, and since social work depends on public funds the

> profession of social work must reflect the prevailing values, assumptions, and attitudes of the social system. As a consequence, the practice of social work is basically concerned with helping the victim rather than alleviating the causes of the problems.[18]

See Chapter 6 for an historical account of the profession's development.

The state of the art in social work practice is limited by the reality that social workers are agents of society and practice is basically designed to change or assist victims rather than remove societal causes of their problems.

It may be helpful to review the definitions of social work in Chapter 1.

The liberal perspective

From a liberal perspective the present economic system is basically a benevolent one and the reason that most Americans enjoy a high standard of living. However, liberals see social problems as a natural dysfunction of industrialization. Merton and Nisbet typify this approach in their widely-used text *Contemporary Social Problems.* They assume our economic and political structure is good because it has produced an

> imposing command of physical resources, high standards of private consumption, effective maintenance of public order and security, freedom from the uncertainties of life that plagued our ancestors, and relatively high levels of humanitarianism. . .[19]

But in addition to these advantages, industrialization has also led to social problems.

> There are also, of course, squalid slums . . . sudden eruptions of violence and bigotry . . . people for whom the struggle for food and shelter remains obsessing and precarious. Thus, we are not free of social problems, and some of them seem to grow almost in direct proportion to our affluence.[20]

If one accepts Merton and Nisbet's implication that along with the high standard of living comes certain social problems, then social welfare becomes a legitimate function of the government and industrialized society. This analysis suggests the state's involvement in social welfare is consistent with the liberal conception as defined by Wilensky and Lebeaux.

> Social welfare becomes accepted as a proper legitimate function of modern industrial society in helping individuals achieve self-fulfillment. The complexity of modern life is recognized. The inability of the individual to provide fully for himself or to meet all his needs in family and work settings, is considered a "normal" condition; and the helping agencies achieve "regular" institutional status.[21]

Liberals recognize society's responsibility to provide for those unable to care for themselves in a capitalistic society.

Liberals assume the basic values of capitalism (individualism, acquisitiveness, and competitiveness) automatically serve the best interests of society. However, preserving freedom does not necessitate preserving every feature of capitalism. Liberals wish to modify capitalism, to intervene in the process, and to minimize the number of people not benefiting from the system, but not to fundamentally change the economic system itself. The welfare state evolves from the altruistic progressive forces innate in human beings. The social welfare institution is a basically desirable way to meet human needs and organize society to respond to the problems of industrialization and urbanization.[22]

But, though liberals are committed to decreasing inequality, they also fear true equality would decrease productivity and efficiency. People must be motivated by want or need to be productive. Recognizing the potential dysfunctions of a system based on acquisitiveness and individualism, liberals see government as the proper instrument for correcting the deficiencies of the marketplace as long as the availability of workers is not threatened.[23] The developmental view (within the liberal perspective) assumes it is desirable for a society to set up a social welfare institution simply to make living better and to fulfill human development—not only to solve a problem.[24] Liberalism is also committed to civil liberties. Liberals believe the abridgement of civil rights is a much greater threat to our society than the crimes possibly prevented by the reckless pursuit of law and order. Liberals vigorously oppose preventive lockup of potential criminals and involuntary commitment of mental patients.

These ideas are applied to the specific examples of drug abuse and juvenile delinquency at the end of this chapter.

An example compares conservative and liberal perspectives.

An example may clarify concepts developed thus far. In 1981, NATO voted to ban sale of certain infant formula to underdeveloped countries in response to evidence presented by the World Health Organization that these formulae had been instrumental in the malnutrition and death of numerous children.[25] The United States was the lone dissenting vote on this boycott. Consistent with the free market perspective of the Reagan Administration, the United States delegate suggested this ban interfered unnecessarily with free trade. The conservative view holds that if the product is not good, people will not buy it. The liberal perspective asserts that the advertising techniques used in these underdeveloped countries corrupt the mechanisms of the marketplace. Theoretically, the institutional or liberal perspective assumes that it is appropriate for government to protect the people from misleading advertising; in fact this assumption did lead to at least two trials of companies producing the baby formula.[26] The developmental approach finds it acceptable and desirable for the government to intervene and stop the inappropriate sale of baby formula simply for the good of society in spite of the loss of profit to the private sector; the developmental approach assumes a society makes decisions based on what will increase the quality of life and does not assume this is the same as increasing profit. Developmentalists see it as a proper role of government to provide such protection.

Morales and Sheafor suggest that anyone desiring to become acquainted with social work should start in the "mainstream," and once they master its perspective, then they can explore the tributaries.[27] The "mainstream" in this case is the liberal analysis of social work, and it must be hoped that this discussion has provided an understanding, if not a mastery, of the typical social work perspective. Nonetheless professional education should not be limited to the liberal social work perspective; our analysis examines the tributaries as well. A broader framework to understand practice also has potential benefits; the consensus view of practice can be comforting for the student but frustrating for a practicing social worker. To provide a fuller view of practice we need to examine the conservative and radical perspectives too.

Conservative perspective

Just as it is possible to observe variations within the liberal perspective, so is it possible to observe them in the conservative perspective. Nonetheless conservatives respond to the basic analytic questions with considerable consistency.

While the liberal perspective blames the economic system for social problems, the conservative perspective blames the individual.

The basic assumption of the conservative perspective is that free enterprise (the market system, capitalism) is good. The more capitalism is allowed to develop uninhibited by government, the better off everyone will be. Welfare is an attempt to subordinate the individual to the state—to destroy individual initiative. Conservatives believe strongly in private property—welfare confiscates property from one person or group and gives it to another. Senator Barry Goldwater, a long-time spokesperson for the conservative ideology, suggests that welfare transforms the individual from a "dignified, industrious, self-reliant spiritual being into a dependent animal.[28] While present day conservatives like Goldwater would not go as far as Herbert Spencer and the Social Darwinists and suggest the poor be allowed to starve, they would limit welfare to private voluntary charity. Private charity is acceptable because it grows out of the generosity of the donor rather than the right of the receiver. Conservatives stress the unlimited potential and free will of every human being; the individual is capable of overcoming economic and personal problems. In sum, the conservative perspective suggests the causes of social problems are located in the moral character of the individual: the economic system (capitalism) is blameless. The only appropriate role of government is as a protector from aggressors, whether those aggressors be other countries infringing on territorial sovereignty or other individuals infringing on the property rights of own-

Conservatism is discussed from an historical perspective in Chapter 5.

ers. Therefore since all societies need rules, government must rightfully provide a means to modify the rules, mediate differences in interpretations, and enforce compliance. Government is necessary because of human imperfections.

While conservatives believe government should stay out of the welfare business and leave private enterprise to operate with minimal restraint from government, many are also willing to legislate what some claim are personal decisions for women and children. Two recent examples are the push by some conservatives (notably Jerry Falwell and the Moral Majority) to mandate prayer in the schools and limit abortion. Liberals claim that conservatives are less concerned about protection of civil liberties and value them less than protection of the "common good." A recent report from the conservative Heritage Foundation suggests ending restrictions that ban mail openings by the F.B.I., require prior approval from the Attorney General before the F.B.I. can conduct break-ins, and permit investigation of political groups only when suspected of criminal activity. Furthermore, the report suggests that while civil liberties are legitimate concerns, they are secondary to the requirements of national security and internal civil order. The report argues that serious surveillance of dissident groups requires "such standard intelligence techniques as wiretapping, mail monitoring, informants and at least occassional illegal entries." The Heritage Foundation listed the communist party, radical and New Left groups, "anti-defense and anti-nuclear" lobbies, and white racist groups like the Ku Klux Klan among groups that should be under higher surveillance.[29]

Social workers operating from the conservative perspective reinforce much of the modern apparatus of "social control"—strict eligibility supervision for welfare benefits, supervision of work-welfare projects, and prisons. Such an approach to social work is consistent with the residual conception as outlined by Wilensky and Lebeaux.[30] The residual formulation assumes two natural channels through which the individual's needs are met—the family and the market system. Only when these institutions do not function adequately is the welfare structure expected to strengthen the family or economic system and then to withdraw as soon as possible. Social welfare is seen as a temporary substitute and benefits carry the stigma of the "dole."

Residual services is defined in Chapter 1.

The 1980s have produced a new upsurge of the assumptions underlying the conservative perspective. "Reaganomics," for example, is replete with conservative assumptions. *Wealth and Poverty,* distributed by President Reagan's budget director to thirty top employees in the Office of Budget and Management, presents as fact conservative assumptions about individuals, the state, and the economic system.[31] Profit and economic utility take precedence over economic security. Maximization of human potential is predicated on competition rather than cooperation. This move toward conservatism does not bode well for social workers committed to income redistribution, social change, and client empowerment. As this ideology carries over into our social programs, there is renewed emphasis on social control through punishment and individually oriented treatment modalities.

The example at the end of this chapter suggests that, from a conservative perspective, the best cure for juvenile delinquency is punishment.

The radical perspective

Although radicals too come in many varieties, one assumption they all hold in common is that the present economic system does not operate in the interest of the common person. Radicals believe the economic system benefits the ruling class and the state and is designed to maintain the privileges of the ruling class. Webber describes the state in the following manner:

The radical heritage of social work is presented in Chapter 5.

> The state is a product and manifestation of the irreconcilability of class contradictions. The state arises where, when, and to the extent that class contradictions cannot be reconciled. And, conversely, the existence of the state is an organ of class rule, an organ for the oppression of one class by another; it is the creation of "order" which legalizes and perpetuates the classes.[32]

Piven and Cloward view the social welfare system and particularly the relief system as an important component in maintaining class privilege. In *Regulating the Poor* they cite historical evidence to support the following position:

> The key to understanding of relief-giving is in the functions it serves for the larger economic and political order, for relief is a secondary and supportive institution. Historical evidence suggests that relief arrangements are initiated or expanded during the occasional outbreaks of civil disorder produced by mass unemployment and are then abolished or contracted when political stability is restored. We shall argue that expansive relief policies are designed to mute civil disorder and restrictive ones to reinforce work norms."[33]

In their more recent book, *The New Class War,* Piven and Cloward suggest that relief has become so embedded in a general structure of income support programs for such a wide range of constituencies that subsistence programs have been replaced by a variety of permanent income-maintenance entitlements.[34] A fundamental change has taken place in our society—"working people who once looked to the marketplace as the arena for action on their economic grievances and aspirations now look more often to the state.[35]

Webber's analysis of the role of the welfare institution, consistent with the earlier Piven and Cloward thesis, suggests that capitalists gain the most with welfare programs. In addition to the grants businesses receive every welfare penny goes immediately into the hands of landlords, supermarkets, and utility companies.

> It is common knowledge that programs involving money transfers to "low income" families and individuals are at levels far below need—even by the state's own determination of poverty lines. Moreover the welfare services are granted as privileges, that are paid for by the ordinary working people who bear the burden of taxation, and they are withdrawn or cut back depending on the fluctuation needs and dictates of capital.[36]

An analysis of casework from a radical perspective is presented in Chapter 6.

In addition to differing with liberals and conservatives on their view of the state, radicals see individuals and their relation to one another in a different light. Whereas liberals and conservatives believe true equality would be detrimental to motivation and productivity, radicals believe human beings achieve their full potential when they produce without being compelled by the physical necessity of selling themselves as a commodity.[37] Radicals suggest it is in the best interest of society and the individual that everyone be allowed and required to contribute to society. Galper expresses this idea succinctly.

> In every society it takes the efforts of the majority of us, working with our hands and minds to produce the goods and services on which the physical maintenance of life depends. Making society work is a collective effort.[38]

The radical view implies that capitalism, based on possessiveness and competition, distorts the best impulses of human beings. The present economic system is irrational since it produces for profit rather than social need, it requires inequality and exploitation, it distorts the value and meaning of human life, and it contains inherently anti-democratic features.[39]

Visions of an ideal economic system vary among radical theorists. One recent proposal for restructuring the economic system is contained in the Carnoy and Shearer work: *Economic Democracy*. The two fundamental reforms they suggest for the United States today are the shift of investment control from corporate domination to the public and the reconstruction of economic decisionmaking through democratic and worker/consumer controlled production.[40] Carnoy and Shearer argue for structural reforms in the American economy that would make periodic fights to preserve welfare benefits unnecessary. These structural reforms can and must be based on American ideals of individual freedom and rights, not on the perceptions of "foreign ideologies." Further, people must be convinced that the prescribed reforms will result in a more, not less, humanistic society, an extension of democracy, and an increase in material well-being. For reform to happen, it must be based on American ideals of economic and political democracy. But political democracy remains a myth until people can construct an economic democracy that allows the common person power to make economic decisions—not just earn wages. Until that power is wrested from the few and returned to the many, political democracy remains an illusion.

In summary, the radicals see people as basically good and willing to contribute to society when provided the opportunity. Individual productivity and potential is maximized by removing want and insecurity. The welfare state is a limited attempt by government to ameliorate the most blatant injustices of capitalistic development.[41] Corporations that require increased government services for defense cause budget deficits. Military buildup is necessary so corporations can expand abroad and welfare services at home are necessary to control and pacify the unemployed when the economy does not provide enough domestic jobs to maintain civil order.[42]

Radicals suggest the nature and application of welfare programs have worked to maintain the continuity of corporate capitalist development under politically difficult conditions. While welfare does improve the relative income position of the poor, it does so in a way that reinforces their low status and forces them to feel vulnerable to the changes in the economic system.[43]

On a practice level, Gwen Gilbert criticizes the profession for facilitating the oppression caused by our present economic arrangement. She sees this problem as so pervasive that the basic content of social work education would have to be changed to prepare students to work for human liberation rather than oppression. Educational requirements necessary for nonoppressive (radical) practice include

The influence of radical social work on the development of a common social work methodology is discussed in Chapter 6.

1. appropriate knowledge for analysis of the economic, political, and social structures that perpetrate oppression,
2. appropriate concepts for understanding the devasting impact of these structures on the lives of the oppressed; and
3. direction for the formulation and use of new and diverse strategies for change in response to the resultant goals of survival, liberation, and being.[44]

She also points out that the nonoppressive practitioner must have a knowledge of himself (value clarification), and particularly how his behavior contributes to oppression or liberation. Gilbert's critique of social work practice underscores the dilemna of social work as identified by Mendelsohn—"who pays for the service?" Certainly few who choose to enter the field of social work want to support oppression. While the difficulty of practicing liberating social work in traditional settings is obvious, there are social workers who have found radical liberating practice possible. By and large social workers have been limited by skill and resources to helping clients cope and adjust to difficult situations and have not been able to make the far reaching societal changes necessary for the liberating practice Gilbert desires.

Ideologies summarized

The values and ideologies that shape social work are complex. But however enumerated or elaborated, those values do not exist in a vacuum. Instead values exist within a large and diverse societal context, and the profession makes a selection from the premises available that it can support and build upon. Recognizing that the liberal perspective is the primary perspective, an understanding of the conservative and radical ideologies explains some of the directions in which the profession is pulled. Social work is in the uncanny position of being criticized from both sides. The radicals criticize the profession for facilitating oppression. The conservatives criticize the same actions for creating dependencies. While some educators suggest it is desirable to have students master the liberal perspective of social work before exploring the tributaries, this book adopts the approach that it is better to educate students for practice by providing a broader analytic framework. To provide one perspective on practice, which is a common approach in social work education, does not prepare students for the dissonance they will experience as they encounter attacks on their chosen profession. By getting a grasp of three very different perspectives on social work practice, students will then have increased capability to withstand the demoralizing effects of destructive criticism and to experience professional growth from constructive criticism.

Self-awareness as related to practice

Realistically, it may also help the student to understand some of the conflicting values he may experience within himself. As long as values remain abstractions, agreement tends to be high. Just how these general values are put into day-to-day practice, however, can be a source of considerable disagreement among professionals as well as between the practitioners and the communities they represent and serve. Investigating personal values and being self-aware are important parts of developing plans and specific actions in work situations. In this ongoing translation of abstract principles into specific activities, understanding differences in value applications from person to person is essential. Value differences are the source of strong disagreements and very different choices of specific activities to be undertaken. Frequently when there is marked disagreement on how to proceed, it is brushed off as a value difference. If values are as compelling as has been asserted, then it is a disservice to pass off lightly issues that may require resolution if the work being done is to succeed. Furthermore, it is assumed that an integral part of professional education is the socialization of the individual into the norms, values, and culture of the profession. Value clarification should be at the center of professional education.

The exercise presented at the end of the chapter may help to clarify the different values inherent in the three perspectives.

The process of value clarification helps develop understanding of what is happening so that people can work together to accomplish specific goals even though there may be a "difference in values." It is to be hoped that this comparison of ideologies within the profession will help students make an informed choice about entering the profession.

Those who think the liberal perspective most closely frames their reality will experience little or no difficulty in accepting social work values. The Code of Ethics, the major texts, the professional culture, and social work methodology are all consistent with a liberal ideology. The liberal practitioner's sense of frustration will come from the larger society that does not fully subscribe to the same degree of liberalism.

Students who hold conservative values will find only a few areas in social work practice in accord with their value base. Only a limited number of the special populations will fit into the conservative conception of "deserving." The literature and practice in the field will probably create value conflicts within the conservative practitioner. A conservative needs to analyze the NASW Code of Ethics closely to make certain the profession's ideology does not conflict with his sense of morality.

The NASW Code of Ethics and the radical Code of Ethics can be found in Chapter 7.

Radicals students, like conservative students, will frequently disagree with the social work profession. Since they will be sensitive to the oppressive as well as the beneficial aspects of social programs, they will probably find agency or program restrictions problematic. Since it is unlikely that the radical social worker will have access to better programs, it is especially important that they follow the rules and regulations necessary to assure clients receive the benefits that are available. Orthodox radicals argue that since the present services only protect the status quo, radical social workers should not work within these settings. Should an individual worker also hold this view, it would be important for him to work only in alternative settings. While the present benefit programs have obvious shortcomings, they are frequently the only means clients have to meet basic needs. Unless the radical worker has an alternative way to meet clients' needs, the poor should not be further deprived as the ideologues plan the "revolution" to bring about equality.

When radicals are willing to work within the present structures of the service delivery system, they make important contributions to both policy and professional practice. A radical critique of our present system keeps in the forefront the structural causes of social problems and the potentially oppressive features of treatment programs and social welfare policies.

Ideology, policy, and practice

The importance of ideology is best illustrated by its affect on policy and therefore practice. Two examples show how ideological perspectives affect analysis, policy, and practice in interventions with drug abuse and delinquency.

A practical example: Drug abuse

Liberal. From a liberal perspective drug abuse is the result of social disorganization, and addiction is a physical or mental disease. A combination of social (such as workplace alienation, family dislocation, marital problems), psychological, and biological elements cause the disease. And though the disease may be an individual problem, the individual is not responsible for the social conditions that may have contributed heavily to the disease and should not be punished. Identifying drug abuse as a disease is one way liberals attempt to remove the stigma from drug addiction. Narcotics Anonymous is a treatment program that makes the same assumption. Consistent with this assumption, intervention is individually oriented: it attempts to make the individual "well." Since liberals are more attuned to the social causes of drug addiction, they see it as appropriate that society should assume the responsibility for both treatment and prevention programs.

Conservative. From the conservative perspective drug abuse becomes a problem when it threatens existing institutions. An individual has the right to take medication (in whatever dosage) prescribed by a physician as long as that medication increases his ability to meet role expectations. If a person takes drugs to the extent that he cannot function appropriately, then drug usage becomes a problem. The drug user is weak or inadequate in his ability to face reality or cope with everyday life. The conservative response to drugs overuse is punishment. For an upper class abuser punishment may be limited to stigmatization if he has the financial ability to compensate for potential role deficiencies without threatening the status quo. Members of the lower class tend to be channelled into the correctional system.

Until drug usage interferes with social roles it is not a problem. Whatever the social class, drug abuse is an individual problem or crime to be dealt with by negative sanctions. Since the problem lies within the individual, intervention can only be helpful at an individual level. This intervention generally aims to control the individual through punishment.

Radical. Radical analysts see drug usage as an important component in controlling oppressed groups. They suggest a clear contradiction in the policies of a government that impedes importation and distribution of "illegal" drugs and at the same time promotes the legal use of similar drugs. Some feminists, for example, are concerned about overprescription of drugs to control women. Recent reports claim 45 percent of American women take mood-altering drugs. Only half as many men receive such prescriptions. Traditionally, women have been portrayed as hypochondriacs whose pains are a manifestation of emotionalism rather than illness or justifiable dissatisfaction.[45] For example, a woman died of cancer following psychiatric hospitalization for psychosomatic stomach pain; another woman died of a brain tumor while being treated for psychosomatic head and neck pain.* Another example of pharmacological social control is the sedation or medication of highly active children. One pediatrician stated, "If a mother can't handle the kids, we just have to medicate them."* In reality the medication is frequently being prescribed at the request of the school rather than the mother.

Radicals contend our social response to drug abuse merely protects the status quo, and that the definition of abuse itself is politically motivated. If a substance is used by a professional to control an individual who may upset the status quo, it is not abuse. This supply channel (the licensed professional) is also open to people who can afford to be legally addicted to drugs as long as their behavior is not disruptive. Drug use becomes "abusive" or criminal when lower class individuals go outside of the law to obtain relatively the same drugs the wealthy purchase legally.

*examples taken from author's practice experience.

Summary. A basic value question that lacks societal consensus is: Is drug abuse a crime, an illness, or a choice? Varying attitudes lead to diverse answers to a related question: Is the individual responsible for his behavior or acts he commits under the influence of drugs? If drug abuse is a crime or a choice, the answer is yes. If it is an illness, the answer is no. Since we do not yet know from empirical evidence whether drug addiction is a crime or an illness, these various answers remain value judgments. Because certain theorists hold strongly to their value-laden assumptions does not make their assumptions fact.

A second example: Juvenile delinquency

Liberals. The liberal perspective suggests a complex relationship between the individual and society. Although crime is irrational behavior, social problems usually push the individual toward the irrationality of crime. It is a problem with the system as well as the individual. Liberals have considerable faith in rehabilitation programs and feel if society would just put enough value (and money) into studying the problem, the causes of delinquency could be understood and the problem solved. Liberals stress the cause of the problem as social rather than individual origin.

Some of these ideas are discussed further in Chapter 17 on the criminal justice system as a field of practice.

Conservative. The conservative perspective has a less complex view of delinquency. The individual (not the system) is diseased with little or no hope of rehabilitation. All delinquents should be punished regardless of any mitigating social conditions. Since delinquency is a threat to society, delinquents should be removed from society. The greatest hope for decreasing delinquency is to increase the severity and length of punishment. Intervention in delinquency is defined as more police and equipment, longer sentences, and, if necessary, preventive lock-up. This perspective is reflected in the "law and order" or "get tough on crime" mentality.

Liberals and conservatives agree on a number of points: both view the social order as rational and the violators as irrational, both feel the individual needs to change either through punishment or treatment, and both see urban crime as the most threatening because it is the most violent.

Radical. Radicals suggest that understanding juvenile delinquency requires understanding that crime is rooted in the structure of American political and economic institutions. Society emphasizes urban crime because it is lower class crime and it threatens the property of the upper class. The purpose of the justice system or the state is to protect the ruling class. The very act of determining a certain behavior is criminal is structured by ruling class interest. Any act can become criminal by fixing a penal sanction to it and processing it through the judicial machinery. For example, different times and different societies have viewed certain acts as criminal or legal—possession of marijuana, heroin addiction, abortion, and poverty.

Radicals see juvenile delinquency as a rational response to the goals of a capitalistic society. Capitalistic societies value acquisitiveness and competitiveness. Therefore, if lower class juveniles are rational and attempt to maximize on societal goals, and if they cannot achieve financial success legally, they will create for themselves opportunities to achieve this success illegally. In actuality, it may be more rational for many juveniles to take the illegal route than it would be to delude themselves they can "make it" legally.

A radical framework makes intervention difficult since radicals believe the insecurity and competitiveness required by capitalism cause crime. Therefore, the solution—removal of the inequality and racism necessary to capitalism—would in essence be changing the economic structure. Realistically, the radical perspective does not contribute immediately applicable intervention techniques to decrease crime, but it does make a persuasive argument for understanding criminal behavior as a rational act. Radicals refuse to blame social workers for high recidivism rates. The social workers are scapegoats for an ineffective system that ignores the structural causes of juvenile delinquency.

In contrast to the liberal and conservative views, radicals suggest crime is rational in a capitalistic society, and the judicial machinery protects the ruling class and controls the lower class. It is not more of the present array of social services juvenile delinquents need, but rather the opportunity to participate in and benefit more equitably from society.

Summary. A critical analysis of a problem like juvenile delinquency can be disconcerting. Historically society has experienced cycles of dealing with delinquency from a conservative perspective (punishment) and a liberal perspective (treatment). But in spite of the different approaches, the incidence of delinquency remains relatively stable at intolerable levels. The radical perspective, which suggests the answer to juvenile delinquency is a basic restructuring of societal values and the economic system, is unlikely to be tested. Neither individual social workers nor the profession is prepared to take on such a monumental task.

In summary it can be said that the kinds of social work interventions we undertake are determined by our value system rather than empirically supported knowledge of the cause and effect of juvenile delinquency. If the conservative attitude toward delinquency prevails, the intervention will be swift, harsh, and certain punishment. Liberals will continue to fight for development of prevention and treatment programs. Radicals will work to overcome the oppression that they see as the cause of juvenile delinquency. No one knows how to cure the problem but many will work to eliminate it, each guided by his own personal and professional values.

Fill in the blanks following the definitions of the conservatives, liberals, and radical perspectives as defined in this chapter.

	Assumptions about Individuals	View of the Present Economic System	Present Role of the State	Normative Role of the State	Cause of Social Problems	Outcome of Present Services or Programs
Conservative						
Liberal						
Radical						
Issues:	a. Inherently good or evil/potential b. What motivates human beings	a. Who benefits the most b. How does it apply to society	a. Whose interests are served b. Who benefits from social welfare programs	a. Whose interest "should" be served b. Who "should" benefit from welfare programs	a. Individual b. Social system c. Economic system d. Political system	a. Liberation of lower class b. Greater economic security c. Weakening of individual d. Oppression of lower class

References

1. W. H. Werkmeister, *Historical Spectrum of Value Theories* (Lincoln, Nebraska: Johnsen Publishing Co., 1970), 1: xii.
2. George T. Martin, and M. N. Zald, *Social Welfare and Society* (New York: Columbia University Press, 1981).
3. Jean Anyon, "Ideology and U.S. History Textbooks," *Harvard Educational Review* 49, (August 1979): 361–383.
4. Marlene Webber, "Abandoning Illusions: The State and Social Change," *Catalyst* 6 (1980): 41–66.
5. H. L. Wilensky, and C. N. Lebeaux, *Industrial Society and Social Welfare* (New York: Free Press, 1958), 138–47.
6. John M. Romanyshyn, *Social Welfare: Charity to Justice* (New York: Random House, 1971).
7. Alfred J. Kahn, *Social Policy and Social Services* (New York: Random House, 1979).
8. David Gordon, *Problems in the Political Economy* (Lexington, Mass: Health, 1977).
9. Jeffry H. Galper, *The Politics of Social Services* (Englewood Cliffs, N.J.: Prentice-Hall, 1974).
10. William Ryan, *Equality* (New York: Pantheon, 1981).
11. P. H. Ephross, and M. Reisch "The Ideology of Some Social Work Texts," *Social Service Review* 56 (June 1982): 273–291.
12. Includes texts by Romanyshyn, *Social Welfare;* Ruth R. Middleman and Gale Goldberg, *Social Service Delivery: A Structural Approach to Social Work Practice* (New York: Columbia University Press, 1974); David Macarov, *The Design of Social Welfare* (New York: Holt, Rinehart, and Winston, 1978); Allan R. Mendelsohn, *The Work of Social Work* (New York: New Viewpoints, 1980).
13. Alfred Kahn, *Social Policy*.
14. Includes texts by Allen Pincus and Anne Minahan, *Social Work Practice: Model and Method* (Itasca, Ill.: Peacock, 1973); Carol Meyer, *Social Work Practice* (New York: Free Press, 1970); Frank Loewenberg, *Fundamentals of Social Work Intervention* (New York: Columbia University Press, 1977); Beulah Compton and Burt Galaway, *Social Work Processes* (Homewood, Ill.: Dorsey Press, 1975).
15. Includes texts by Walter Friedlander and Robert Apte, *Introduction to Social Welfare,* 4th ed. (Englewood Cliffs, N.J.: Prentice-Hall, 1974); Max Siporin, *Introduction to Social Work Practice* (New York: Macmillan, 1978); Howard Goldstein, *Social Work Practice: A Unitary Approach* (Columbia: University of South Carolina Press, 1973).
16. Ephross and Reisch, "Ideology of Social Work Texts."
17. Mendelsohn, *The Work of Social Work.*
18. Frances Lappi, and J. Collins, *Food First: Beyond the Myth of Scarcity* (New York: Ballantine, 1977).
19. Robert Merton, and R. M. Nisbet. *Contemporary Social Problems* (New York: Harcourt Brace and World, 1961).
20. Ibid., 4.
21. Wilensky and Lebeaux, *Industrial Society*.
22. Galper, *Politics of Social Service*.
23. Gordon, *Problems in the Political Economy*.
24. Ralph Dolgoff, and Donald Feldstein, *Understanding Social Welfare* (New York: Harper, 1980).
25. Lappi and Collins, *Food First*.
26. Ibid.
27. Armando Morales and Brad Sheafor, *Social Work: A Profession of Many Faces*, 2nd ed. (Boston: Allyn and Bacon, 1980).
28. Barry Goldwater, *Conscience of a Conservative* (New York: Manor Books, 1960).
29. *Milwaukee Journal* 16 November 1980.
30. Wilensky and Lebeaux, *Industrial Society,* 138–147.
31. George Gilder, *Wealth and Poverty* (New York: Basic Books, 1981).
32. Webber, "Abandoning Illusions."
33. F. F. Piven, and Richard Cloward, *Regulating the Poor* (New York: Pantheon Books, 1971).
34. ———, *The New Class War* (New York: Pantheon Books, 1982).
35. Ibid.
36. Webber, "Abandoning Illusions."
37. Galper, *Politics of Social Service*.

38. Ibid.
39. Ibid.
40. Martin Carnoy, and Derek Shearer, *Economic Democracy* (White Plains, New York: Sharpe, 1980).
41. Ibid.
42. Ibid.
43. Ibid.
44. Gwen Gilbert, "The Role of Social Work in Black Liberation," *The Black Scholar* 19 (December 1974):16–23. Reprinted in Morales and Sheafor, *Social Work,* 2nd ed.
45. Elinor Polansky, "Women and the Health Care System: Implications for Social Work Practice," in *Women's Issues and Social Work Practice*, ed. Elaine Norman and Arlene Mancuso (Itasca, Ill.: Peacock, 1980), 183–200.

CHAPTER THREE

The Generalist Model

"Professionals are paid for doing, for operationalizing, and not simply speculating on the nature of life. Their stock in trade is technique and society holds them responsible for their ability to perform their work with skills not available to the ordinary citizen. How-to-do-it is the bread and butter of the lawyer, the doctor, the engineer—and the social worker."[1]

A model is by definition an abstraction created to explain, analyze, and develop the reality it represents. Model cars, model airplanes, model homes, model cities, and mathematical models all represent desired outcomes in the day-to-day "real" world. A model can be quite abstract or quite specific. Anytime one constructs a model, however, consensus (or lack of consensus) is related to the model's specificity. The model of social work practice presented here is intended to be somewhat abstract yet with enough detail to provide direction for students and to engender controversy and contrasts with proponents of competing models.

Attributes of a model

Attributes of a model are explained here.

If a model of practice is to be considered seriously for either academic debate or practice, it must have five attributes.

1. It must provide for a way of dealing with *all* the people involved in a particular practice situation.
2. It must account for the physical and social environment that impinges on the situation of concern.

3. It must provide a way of understanding and affecting the interactions between and among the people and environments of concern.
4. It must provide a focal point for the social work practitioner to begin the necessary work.
5. It must be consistent with both the definition of practice and the frame of reference used for practice.

Historical models

The three traditional models of social work practice are casework, group work, and community organization.

In the past models of practice in social work have been developed to accommodate the number of people being served at any one time, i.e., individuals, families, groups, organizations, and communities. These models have been severely criticized on the grounds that they fragment problems and the services needed to bring about their solution; they tend to lead the social workers to respond with the intervention strategy they know best rather than what is most appropriate. Nor do they take into account the interrelatedness of contemporary life. As early as 1966 Helen Harris Perlman, a scholar involved in developing principles of practice for the caseworker suggested that

> . . . maybe the way to go about identifying social work practice activities is not within the traditional boundaries of casework, group work, and community work at all, but *across lines* [emphasis added] by asking ourselves what kinds of problems call for what kinds of services and actions.[2]

In 1973 Pincus and Minahan wrote *Social Work Practice: Model and Method* a book that presented their model of generalist practice.

In the early 1970s Pincus and Minahan carried this suggestion further, guided by the developing body of general systems theory. Their model of practice suggested that each social worker must decide what the purposes and relationships are that are involved in working with all the people that may be encountered. Social workers must also understand clearly who will benefit from the work to be done, who has provided the sanction for that work, who needs to be changed or influenced, and who needs to be counseled to achieve the desired outcomes.[3,4] Pincus and Minahan then defined the social work process as those steps taking place in social work practice regardless of the problem or size of system.

Problem-focus model

Thus the groundwork was laid for organizing a current model of practice around the particular problem or situation of concern within which a social worker may be called upon to act. A good deal of professional literature is directed at the problem, which is defined as "any question or matter involving doubt, uncertainty, or difficulty; a question proposed for solution or discussion."[5] This emphasis makes sense since social workers only become involved when people are experiencing difficulties, stress, or problems. Problems can be viewed from several perspectives: what type, whose they are, where they are located in time and space, etc. In addition to the problem, the other parts of the model include the social worker and the employing agency or organization (the social worker system); the people or person who asks for assistance, who will benefit from the efforts of the social worker, and with whom there is an established working agreement (the client system); the people, policies, or organization which must change if the work is to be successful (the target system); and those resources, people, and environmental systems that can be used to influence the target system to change (the action system). These concepts parallel those developed by Pincus and Minahan in 1973.[6] This problem-focus model may be illustrated with a diagram.

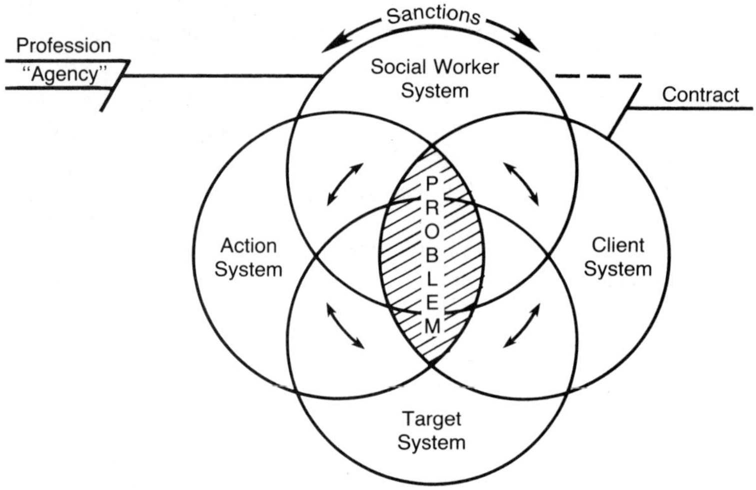

Figure 3-1

A case example using this model is presented at the end of this chapter.

But before we turn to a case example that demonstrates how this practice model works, four additional concepts must be introduced: social work roles, the professional relationship, function as it relates to social work practice, and introduction of the problem solving process.

Social work roles

We discuss social functioning in Chapter 10.

The sociological concept of role developed in an attempt to explain how people relate to one another. George Herbert Mead analyzed how the human self grows through social processes and relationships.[7] He stressed it was not possible to understand people without understanding the social context in which they lived; it was within the social context that certain patterns of behavior were imposed and learned, that attitudes and relationships became fixed and consistent. Now referred to as socialization, the imposition of social patterns on behavior, this powerful process defines expectations in nearly every situation, personal and professional.[8] A role reflects a society's expectations of behavior, attitudes, and values for a particular status or position acquired either by accident of birth or achieved later in life. Roles also involve age and sex. Joseph Anderson defines roles in the following words:

> Roles are defined in terms of role expectations. A role has certain privileges, obligations, responsibilities, and powers. When role incumbents put these obligations and responsibilities into effect, they are said to be performing their role. The expectations define what individuals should or should not do so long as they are the incumbent of a particular role.[9]

The mechanism by which socialization proceeds is meaningful interaction and identification with others. Over time identifiable patterns develop that illustrate how social roles involve consistent and reiterated patterns of conduct.[10]

Roles serve many functions in social work practice. Roles provide a comprehensive pattern for both behavior and attitudes and suggest particular strategies for dealing with recurring situations. Roles are defined as quite specific social entities even though they may be played out by any number of different individuals. Social role expectations provide a major means of identifying and placing people within their social context.

Professional roles have changed over time as has the focus of social work practice. For example, "advocate" is now considered an important role for social workers in addressing certain problems. Prior to the "Great Society" movement of the 1960s this was not the case; social workers were unlikely to "speak for the client by presenting and arguing the client's cause . . . in . . . the effort to win for the client."[11] The emphasis on human rights and civil liberties of the 1960s was reflected in this new social work practice role. Social work roles develop and are shaped and reshaped as the objectives of the profession, the mood of society, and the needs of clients develop and shift.

Historical roles that social workers performed are presented throughout Part II.

Role definition is a flexible and fluid process that corresponds with the assignment the profession receives from society to deal with certain social problems and tasks. The individual social worker meets the challenge of these societal assignments through using abilities, skills, and knowledge in relationships with all those involved in the change system. These relationships may be collaborative or conflictual. Specific roles used most frequently in direct practice and stressed in professional education are commonly termed broker, enabler, teacher, mediator, and advocate.[12] Indirect practice incorporates these roles as well as additional roles such as planner, supervisor, policy developer or analyst, and administrator.

The question of how many roles exist for social workers is unresolved.

As the social worker becomes involved with the members of the client, action, and target systems, the necessity of multiple roles becomes apparent. A frightened client seeking legal satisfaction in a child custody matter may need the social worker to be supportive, encouraging, calm, and reassuring. In dealing with the court, that same social worker may need to take on an adversarial, advocate role to help protect the client's right to make choices and be treated with respect.

Broker

In this role the social worker "serves as a linkage between the client and other community resources."[13] Acting as a broker requires a broad knowledge of the specific community and the operating procedures of the agencies, organizations, or services that may be needed. Like a real estate agent or stock broker, the social worker attempts to make connections and make things happen in an attempt to assist the client in achieving his goals. Because parts of the social service system may be complex and unresponsive, it is reasonable to suppose that the average person will not be able to navigate the process successfully. While assisting clients to find needed resources may not carry the prestige of doing psychotherapy, it is frequently the most important service a social worker can provide. Some examples of brokering might include finding a shelter for a battered woman, helping someone negotiate the paperwork process to receive public assistance, or helping a family find respite care for an elderly chronically impaired person.

The broker role may also include "case management" of a client's situation.

Advocate

The advocate role assumes very direct efforts on the part of the social worker.

Advocacy is a concept borrowed from the legal profession, but has taken on unique characteristics in social work. The legal advocate and the social work advocate roles are not equivalent. The legal advocate must be guided by the client's wishes. The social work advocate must be guided by the client's wishes but limited by the "best interests" of society.[14] As an advocate the social worker becomes the speaker for the client, presenting and arguing the client's cause when necessary. In this partisan representation of the client the goal is to win. The client system, of whatever size, may not in fact be directly involved. For instance, social workers may work with attorneys to bring a class action suit to benefit clients. They may also lobby their legislators on behalf of their client. The key to using this role is a firm and clear contract with the client. The terms and limits of the advocacy effort must be explicit and clearly understood.

Enabler

See the case example at the end of this chapter for a look at the social worker as enabler.

Enabler is the role most frequently associated with the social work profession. An enabler is one who assists clients to find strengths and resources within themselves to produce whatever changes may be needed or to accomplish the goals desired.[15] The social worker as enabler has the responsibility to facilitate change in a given situation by offering encouragement, support, and reassurance. This role incorporates many assumptions of Rogerian theory and is frequently utilized in dealing with individual problems. In this role the social worker "enables" the client to change or achieve the desired goal by concentrating on the client's own strengths and abilities and helping the client to apply them to the specific problem situation. The client is primarily responsible and the "responsibility of the worker is to facilitate or enable the client's accomplishment of a defined change."[16] Whether the source of the problem is identified as the individual or the environment, the worker helps the client find the inner strength to alter her own behavior or as much as possible, the environment.

Teacher

The teaching role is similar to the enabling role since it is directed toward strengthening the client's ability to effect change in the problem situation. The teaching role involves introducing additional information and resources into the situation. Education has long been seen in our society as a way of improving social position; it can also be a way for a client to learn how to overcome a difficult situation. Teaching can involve skills such as communication or parent effectiveness training; it can involve teaching clients and client groups how to become politically effective. Numerous situations can be improved by teaching clients new knowledge and skills.

One technique used by the social worker as teacher is role-playing or behavioral rehearsal. Chapter 11 describes behavioral techniques.

Mediator

> The social worker in the role of mediator will use techniques to try to bring about a convergence of the perceived values of both parties to the conflict, help each party recognize the legitimacy of the others' interests, assist the parties in identifying their common interests in a successful outcome, avoid a situation in which issues of winning and losing are paramount, break the conflict down to separate issues, and help parties identify that they have more at stake in continuing a relationship than the issue of the specific conflict.[17]

As a mediator the social worker acts to reconcile differences and to intervene between conflicting parties in order to promote reconciliation, settlement, or compromise. The conflict may occur in many arenas in which social work is involved; it might be a dispute between natural parents and foster parents, between parents and children, between teachers and parents, or between separated husbands and wives (divorce mediation is a recently developed specialty within social work). Whatever the arena, the social worker works to resolve disputes.

Relationships and social work practice

During our lifetime each of us has experienced the connectedness of emotion and intimacy with others that is called the 'human relationship' . . . The most critical characteristic of our humanity is that lives are lived within relationships to other people, thus 'relationships' do not originate for any of us within the social work process or the professional helping effort . . Nor can social work claim to have been the lone discoverer of this attribute of humanity or the only group interested in pursuing its investigation . . . However, social work can take pride in the fact that from its earliest beginnings it recognized the importance of human interaction and attempted to employ the concept of relationship in a conscious and deliberate way for the benefit of the people it served.[18]

A professional relationship is formed for a purpose. When that purpose is accomplished or ends, the relationship also ends. These relationships involve self discipline, self knowledge, and congruent use of self by the social worker as well as a knowledge of the people with whom the relationships are being formed.

Social workers form many relationships in their work. In the course of dealing with just one client, a social worker may have to contact a landlord, teachers, an employer, doctors, politicians or public servants, law enforcement personnel, various program administrators, neighbors, community groups, and fellow professionals. Within any of these contacts, the social work relationship has common elements that relate to the nature of the work to be accomplished.

The NASW Code of Ethics helps define the boundaries of a professional relationship with a client. See Chapter 7.

The most commonly identified components of social work relationships are concern for others, commitment, a sense of obligation, acceptance, positive regard, expectations, empathy, authority, genuineness, congruence, and goal orientation. "All social work relationships have purposes that have some common aspects because they embody the normative purposes and values of the profession."[19]

The amount of literature on social work relationships is considerable.[20] A common thread among these many references is that the key to understanding the nature of a relationship in social work practice is the purpose for which that relationship is developed. This purpose, linked directly to the assessment and definition of a specific problem and the desired goals, determines not only the parameters of the relationship itself, but also the specific interventive roles assumed by the social worker. It is from the analysis of the work actually done by social workers that the nature of the helping relationship, the professional roles and behaviors employed within the relationship have been identified.

Function

Function is defined as "the kind of action or activity proper to any person or thing; the purpose for which something is designed or exists."[21] A component is functional to a system if it enhances the functioning of the system.

Pincus and Minahan differentiated seven major functions of social workers in carrying out the purposes of the profession. Social work activities perform one or more of those functions.

1. Help people enhance and more effectively utilize their own problem-solving and coping capacities.
2. Establish initial linkages between people and resource systems.
3. Facilitate interaction and modify and build new relationships between people and societal resource systems.
4. Facilitate interaction and modify and build relationships between people within resource systems.
5. Contribute to the development and modification of social policy.
6. Dispense material resources.
7. Serve as agents of social control.[22]

Since this model of practice is based on an identified problem, the function then becomes one of solving problems or the process of bringing together resources to meet identified needs. This is ordinarily accomplished through the process of problem solving.

Problem solving process

The case study of Sharon Whitethunder at the end of this chapter illustrates the problem solving process.

The problem solving process (the social work process) consists of several phases.

1. The social worker and the client come to an agreement of what the problem is and what changes the client wants to achieve.
2. The social worker and the client reach a goal consensus and enter into a contract to reach the desired outcome of the intervention.
3. The social worker uses professional analytical skills and information from other systems to determine what resistances to change are impeding the desired outcome.
4. The social worker develops an intervention plan to overcome the resistance.
5. The client and the social worker agree on what specific actions are to be undertaken by each to implement the intervention plan.
6. The social worker and the client jointly evaluate how effective the interaction has been in solving the problem.[23]

The agreement between a client and a worker is called a contract.

The first step in the social work process is identifying the problem. Working together to solve the problem, the social worker and the client must agree about what the problem is and what changes the client wants to achieve. Depending on variables unique to each situation this agreement comes about in various ways and takes various forms. The step is most clearly reflected when a client desires services, knows what problem she would like to work on, and can clearly identify what kinds of help she needs. This is not the typical initial contact for a social worker; frequently social workers make the intitial contact based on a referral from another agency. The client may or may not identify the situation as problematic. If the client does not desire to work on the identified problem the client remains a "potential" client system until the social worker either determines that services are not needed or desired and that discontinuing services will not endanger anyone. If the social work process is to proceed, there must be consensus on the definition of the problem.

Once the social worker and client reach a consensus on what the problem is and determine that the client wishes to engage in a problem solving relationship (enter into a social work contract), then the client and social worker jointly identify a desirable outcome. For instance, a social worker working with a teenager in conflict with her parents over social activities may want to persuade her client's parents to become more lenient. The social worker cannot agree to work for a goal unless her professional assessment suggests such an intervention would be in the client's best interest.

Accurate assessment of a client's situation precedes intervention.

Having reached consensus on problem definition and desired outcome, the social worker then draws upon theoretical knowledge about individual behavior and the social environment, knowledge of community resources, knowledge of organizational structure, knowledge of policy, and knowledge of systems to assess why the problem behavior is occurring, what components of the environment are supporting this negative behavior, and what changes need to take place to alter the problem behavior. Frequently the social worker must deal with resistance at this stage—from the client, from relevant agencies or organizations, from the schools, from the community, or from the family.

After determining what is causing the negative behavior and what is impeding change, the social worker again uses theoretical knowledge to develop an intervention plan. Client and social worker develop the plan jointly (contract): they agree on specific actions each will take to implement the intervention plan. At this point both need to clarify expectations. The social worker needs to understand what the client expects from the worker and the agency. The client needs to understand the expectations she must fulfill. The social worker decides whether the expectations are clear and reasonable. Can the client accommodate the expectations? Does the social worker have the skills and power to fulfill the role expectations the client has developed?

The social worker must continue to evaluate the intervention plan at each step. Are all the activities the client and social worker engaging in functional to the agreed upon goal? Is the contract clear and agreed upon? Can the plan's effectiveness be increased by either the client or the social worker?

The final step in the social work process is termination. Since the relationship is professional, it ends when the goal is met, when the client and social worker agree the goal is not feasible, or when the client no longer desires services. At times professional relationships end because a client moves or the social worker changes jobs, retires, or becomes ill. When terminations can be anticipated, they should be planned. The final step in termination is a joint assessment of the effectiveness of the intervention.

The steps in the process then can be summarized.

An example of this process in working with the elderly appears in Chapter 20.

1. Problem identification. Client and social worker agree on a definition of the problem.
2. Goal Identification. The social worker and the client reach a goal consensus—the desired outcome of the intervention.
3. Solution Search. The social worker uses professional analytical skills and information from other systems to determine what resistances to change are impeding the desired outcome.
4. Development of Intervention Plan. The social worker develops an intervention plan to overcome the resistance.
5. Implementation of Intervention Plan. The client and the social worker agree on what specific actions are to be undertaken by each to implement the intervention plan.
6. Evaluation and Termination. The social worker and the client jointly evaluate how effective the intervention has been in solving the problem.

It is important to plan for termination with a client.

A case study designed to illustrate the application of the problem-solving method to an individual follows. Professional roles, functions, and relationships are all evident. The interventions were based on a liberal philosophy that determined how the social work frame of reference would be applied to the problem assessment and social work intervention.

A Case Example: Social Work With Individuals

Sharon Whitethunder, a sixteen year old native American of the Winnebago Tribe, was referred to Children's Services because she was not attending school. Sharon is in her junior year in high school. Until this year Sharon had been a B+ student and had caused no behavior problems. Although she is concerned about Sharon's absenteeism, the school counselor is even more concerned that Sharon is considering dropping out of school. The counselor feels Sharon is experiencing personal problems that are affecting both her motivation and the quality of her work. Sharon states she does not have a prob-

At an American Indian Center a worker takes time to listen to a young girl's concerns. Photo courtesy of Student Support Services Publication Center, University of Minnesota.

lem. She knows her attitude and goals have changed but does not see why anyone should care. Sharon appears angry but does not have a focus for her anger. While Sharon's behavior is not really disruptive, the school counselor feels Sharon needs someone to help her work out personal problems.

SOCIAL HISTORY

Sharon Whitethunder is an attractive, healthy, native American with above average intelligence. Her mother and father lived in a common law marriage that produced five children. They presently live in different midwestern states. Neither of the parents works steadily and each of them indulges quite heavily and frequently in alcohol. The children see their parents only at Indian powwows. Ranging in age from nine to sixteen, the children have lived with the maternal grandmother for the last eight years. The grandmother is in her late seventies. Although she is very loving, neither her temperament nor her health are conducive to supervision of children. As a result, Sharon has assumed many of the parental functions for her younger siblings. The grandmother receives Aid to Families with Dependent Children (AFDC) as a nonlegally responsible relative and is quite satisfied with the amount she receives. Mrs. Crow (the grandmother) was married for forty five years to the chief of the Winnebago tribe. She continues to be strongly committed to preserving Indian ways. She is not very happy that the social service department recently forced her to move into the city. She was much happier in her home on the cranberry marsh where she could cook in the ground and live among the Indians. Although she now has a ten room house, the family lives in three rooms. Mrs. Crow feels it is all right for the children to attend the white school but does not like some of the ideas they are taught. She would much rather they attend Indian school, but none is available in the state. Mrs. Crow and her family are descendants of Indians who were brought from South Dakota to harvest cranberries. The cranberry growers built small homes for the harvestors to live in, but when cranberry harvesting became mechanized some of the Indians stayed on in homes that the owners, however, no longer maintained. Because her home had no indoor plumbing or central heat, the social services department decided the home was unfit for the children. Although her family has lived in the Midwest for three generations, Mrs. Crow still feels her home is in South Dakota. It is very important to Mrs. Crow that she and her descendants return to South Dakota for certain religious holidays; all her family participate in the rituals at these celebrations.

INITIAL CONTRACT

Since Sharon was a minor, contact was made with both Sharon and her grandmother. It was clear that Sharon had a deep love for her grandmother, but that some of her grandmother's ideas were causing conflict within her. In the initial contact Sharon talked about her plans for the future. She wanted to become a medical technician, but her grandmother felt she had already gone to school long enough. During this first visit Mrs. Crow made frequent references to the "Indian" way. It soon became apparent that Sharon was torn between the two very different cultures in which she had been raised. Part of her related to her friends at school who were planning their futures in the working world; the other part of her related to grandma who wanted Sharon to stay close by and take care of her and the children. With Grandma's permission, it was agreed that Sharon would continue to meet with the social worker. While Grandmother did not view Sharon's behavior as a problem, she understood that the children must attend school or her right to custody might be questioned. Mrs. Crow had a basic fear of the social services department and was inclined to cooperate out of fear that she might lose the children. In spite of her agreement to the initial contract, however, she resisted Sharon being seen by the social worker; she frequently had Sharon do tasks for her when she was supposed to meet with the social worker. The social worker made frequent calls on Mrs. Crow to reassure her and gain her cooperation.

PROBLEM ASSESSMENT

The problem was not difficult to assess. Here was a sixteen year old girl caught between two cultures and three generations. At times Sharon wanted to break with her Indian culture and pursue a career. But when she would begin to work on this goal, she would experience guilt over her grandmother's reaction. As the professional relationship progressed, it became clear that neither consensus nor cooptation was going to be effective in changing the grandmother's attitude. If Sharon was to pursue her own goals, it would entail conflict with her grandmother's wishes and actually her entire value system.

SOLUTION SEARCH

The social worker initially engaged in a Rogerian based enabling intervention providing support for Sharon. The social worker felt it was not her role to direct Sharon but rather to provide a supportive empathetic relationship that would enable Sharon to make the decision that was right for her. In addition it seemed clear that Mrs. Crow would be the target of change. By working slowly and in a nonthreatening manner, it was hoped that Mrs. Crow would come to appreciate and value Sharon's decisions. However, changing Mrs. Crow's attitudes proved to be impossible. Mrs. Crow had already managed to "hang onto" three of her own children. These children all lived in the same city as Mrs. Crow, spent most of their waking hours, and probably their sleeping hours at her home. None were employed. Some had held part time jobs, but all three were receiving AFDC for unemployed parents. Mrs. Crow liked her children and grandchildren to be accessible and free to travel to powwows both in and out of state. Here was a very closed family system that seemed to operate in a manner personally satisfying to most of the family members; problems arose only when a member wanted to leave the "nest." Sharon's mother had created a precedent for breaking with this pattern when she had left the family; it seemed reasonable to assume that her departure was also traumatic.

Sharon needed help first to make the decision about her future. Which was more important to her, to maintain her strong family ties or to pursue a future of her own? Although it was clear she would have to make a choice, it was not predictable how long the alienation from her grandmother would last if Sharon went against her wishes.

INTERVENTION PLAN

Since Sharon's conflict was cultural, neither Rogerian nor behavioral or psychoanalytic theory seemed adequate to solve her problem. After working with Sharon over a frustrating and unhappy three months, the social worker realized that an action system had to be developed to aid and support Sharon in this life crisis. Since Sharon's mother, Angeline, had succeeded in breaking with her family, she was identified as a potential action system for Sharon. Sharon had difficulty viewing her mother in this role as she had never experienced a mother-daughter relationship with her; in fact, Sharon did not feel her mother would want to be bothered with her. After a good deal of hesitation Sharon agreed to let the social worker contact her mother. Even though Angeline lived over 300 miles away, she was very concerned and seemed to understand clearly what Sharon was experiencing; she gave up her apartment in Chicago and came home to stay. Sharon and Angeline developed a strong friendship resembling a peer relationship more than a parental-child relationship. Sharon seemed much happier and began attending school regularly; still, Sharon had not decided what to do about her future.

EVALUATION PHASE

On a short term basis the intervention was apparently successful. Her mother having been engaged in her problem, Sharon seemed happier. Her school attendance and performance improved. But just as the social worker was preparing to terminate the relationship with an offer of continued service on request, Sharon informed her that she was quitting school and moving to Chicago with her mother.

RENEGOTIATION OF CONTRACT

Fortunately, the story does not end there. Sharon went to live with her mother for one month. The living conditions she endured, however, furnished her with the personal resolve to improve her own lot in life; Sharon returned with a strong commitment to pursue her education. The social worker suggested the possibility of foster care, and Sharon accepted this option. After living in the foster home for two months Sharon decided she preferred to live with her grandmother, and she could do that without giving up her own goals. The social worker met with Sharon once a month for the next three months. Sharon was doing well in school and Mrs. Crow was not interfering with her school attendance. The professional relationship was then terminated.

In the case of Sharon Whitethunder the social worker applied many levels of knowledge. Her theory of practice was a generalist one. In addition she needed to understand how native American families are different from mainstream families. One important difference is that, as a group, native Americans reject the dominant values of acquisitiveness and competitiveness. Then too she had to deal with the grandmother's attitude toward appointments and time in general. In most instances she was careful to make appointments and not to drop in unannounced although the family did not mind if she did drop in. The family kept appointments if there was nothing else to do. They did not have a telephone, and they did not believe in changing their plans or informing the worker of conflicting commitments. The social worker at first hesitated to drop in casually because she felt she was invading the family's privacy. However, after working with a number of Indian families in the area, she realized their homes were much more open to visitors than the homes of white families; it was not unusual to observe friends dropping in unannounced. Having material possessions, getting ahead, or making an impression are not part of their value system. Family and sharing are two dominant values.

The social worker had to know the law as well. If she had not been familiar with the custody laws, she might have attempted to stop the mother from taking Sharon to Chicago. Should she have taken this approach, she would have found that she did not have the legal grounds to follow through, and she probably would have alienated the mother and Sharon.

Family structure in this group of native Americans was also different than that associated with middle-class white Americans. A large percentage of the Indian children in the community were cared for by their maternal grandmothers. This practice has been passed down for generations. The grandmother's mother had cared for her children. This was a source of conflict between some families and their social workers since the social workers felt it was the mother's responsibility to care for the children.

American Indians still tend to be more oriented to the collective than to the individual. When a social worker doesn't understand this commitment, she can cause problems for her client. To encourage Sharon to pursue her goals without recognizing her loyalty to the collective would have caused further trauma rather than growth.

This brief case example illustrates both the use of the four systems approach and the problem solving process. The model of practice used in this case has been referred to as the Four Systems Model of Social Work Practice,[24] a generalist model. Since the Four Systems Model involves several systems or subsets and is also a system itself, general systems theory guides its application. The worker, client, target, and action systems are in interaction with one another, and consequently a change in one will cause changes in the others. The system as a whole is in motion toward a goal. The goal is defined as resolution of the particular problem. As the system moves toward the goal, it must maintain some balance within itself as each specific activity is put into operation.

Summary

This chapter addressed social work practice by looking at what social workers do in their professional role. This discussion has interspersed abstract discussion of practice with concrete description and application of a model of social work practice. The complexity and diversity of practice has been illustrated by pointing out the impact of individual political orientation on the social work frame of reference. Without negating the tremendous diversity this creates in practice, we have underlined the consistent components of practice.

The emphasis on the interface of person and environment is an essential component of all social work practice. The view of practice as a problem-solving process is also widely adopted. Regardless of political orientation, all social workers operate from the social work frame of reference by addressing the dual focus, systems theory, and the impact of the environment.

The goal of this chapter has been to provide a preliminary answer to the question, "What do social workers do?" in a manner conducive to further discussion, study, and clarification. Subsequent chapters expand on specific aspects of social work practice.

The comprehensiveness of social work practice is both a strength and a weakness. When the professional organization lacks consensus on what model or political perspective to adopt, it is little wonder that practice takes diverse forms. Initially, this may create dissonance in the student. However, as the student begins to experience the richness provided by this openness of boundaries, it is predicted that she will welcome entry into a profession which allows her to utilize her unique attributes in new and creative ways.

References

1. William Schwartz, "Private Troubles and Public Issues. One Job or Two?" Lindeman Memorial Lecture (New York. National Conference on Social Welfare, 28 May 1969).
2. Helen Harris Perlman, "Social Work Methods: A Review of the Past Decade," *Social Work* 10, no. 4 (1965): 94–95.
3. Alan Pincus and Anne Minahan, *Social Work Practice: Model and Method* (Itasca, Ill.: Peacock, 1973), 11 ns.
4. Also see Carol Meyer, *Social Work Practice*, 2nd ed. (New York: Free Press, 1976), and Howard Goldstein, *Social Work Practice: A Unitary Approach* (Columbia, S. C.: University of South Carolina Press, 1973); Peter Leonard, "Towards a Paradigm for Radical Practice," in *Radical Social Work*, ed. Brake and Bailey (New York: Pantheon Books, 1975); and Jeffry Galper, *Social Work Practice: A Radical Perspective* (Englewood Cliffs, N.J.: Prentice-Hall, 1980), 11.
5. *Random House College Dictionary*, Revised ed. (New York: Random House, 1980), 1055.
6. Pincus and Minahan, *Social Work Practice*, 53–68.
7. George Herbert Mead, *Mind, Self and Society* (Chicago: University of Chicago Press, 1934).
8. Peter Berger and Brigitte Berger, *Sociology: A Biographical Approach* (New York: *Basic Books*, 1972), 55.
9. Joseph Anderson, *Social Work Methods and Processes* (Belmont, Cal.: Wadsworth, 1981), 112.
10. Berger, *Sociology*, 53.
11. Beulah Compton, and Bert Galaway. *Social Work Processes*, revised ed. (Homewood, Ill.: Dorsey Press, 1979), 342.
12. Ibid., 338.
13. Ibid., 339.
14. Ibid., 362.
15. Ibid., 340.
16. Ibid.
17. Ibid., 342.
18. Ibid., 159.
19. Ibid., 163.
20. See Felix Biestek, *The Casework Relationship* (Chicago: Loyola University Press, 1957); Karkhoff, *The Art of Helping: An Introduction to Life Skills* (Amherst, Mass.: Human Resource Development Press, 1973); Alan Keith-Lucas, *The Giving and Taking of Help* (Chapel Hill, N.C.: University of North Carolina Press, 1971); Carl Rogers, "The Therapeutic Relationship: Recent Theory and Research," in *The Human Dialogue*, ed. Matson and Montague (New York: Free Press, 1967), 246–259.
21. *Random House Dictionary*, 535.
22. Pincus and Minahan, *Social Work Practice*, 15.
23. Compton and Galaway, *Social Work Processes*.
24. Pincus and Minahan, *Social Work Practice*.

NATIONAL FEDERATION OF SETTLEMENTS
TENTH ANNUAL CONFERENCE
ROYCROFT INN SEPT 24-26th 1920

PART II

HISTORICAL DEVELOPMENT OF SOCIAL WORK

"Social work originated in late nineteenth-century England, where there was growing discontent with the kind of society that had been created by industrialization and by the political and economic practices of laissez-faire capitalism. The early ideas from which social work grew soon traveled to the United States. . . . Discontent within a society that was shaped by values and institutions of laissez-faire capitalism, a society whose industries and urban concentrations were destructive of many people, led to diverse ideas for change."[1]

Social work is a young profession tracing back only to the late 1800s. In its first century important social progress has been made in spite of occasional failures. Today social work continues to build on its strengths and learn from its errors. Our historical analysis of social work has three goals: to identify how tradition defines practice, to clarify the origins and consequences of our definition of deviance, and to recognize the limitations of our understanding of human behavior. We hope this brief discussion will help students recognize what activities are functional and dysfunctional to current social work goals, encourage them to guard against becoming oppressors of "deviants", make them aware of the current limitations of knowledge, and give them a personal resolve to expand the limits of that knowledge.

Analyzing history and how past practice reflected past times helps clarify how present practice reflects the present time. It introduces important questions. How much of what social workers presently do is dictated by tradition? How much "traditional" practice should be eliminated or modified? What new methods need to be developed to address our present times? Do present methods of intervention reflect current need? Do social workers respond to need or do they respond with the methods they know best regardless of their applicability to the problem?

A primary mandate social workers have from society is to deal with deviants—individuals who do not behave according to societal norms or do not accept the dominant values of society. In 1926 the Milford Conference Report stated:

> Social casework deals with the human being whose capacity to organize his own normal social activities may be impaired by one or more deviations from accepted standards of normal social life. . .[2]

If society had no poor, mentally ill, delinquents, or criminals there would be no social work profession. Social workers espouse maximizing human potential, but society would not support a profession for that purpose alone. People who are "different" must be kept from disrupting the functioning of society.

Political, social, and environmental constraints

The earliest forms of organized mutual assistance have advanced through the years from diverse and unrefined methodologies to the unifying paradigm of generalist practice and from loosely-knit professional groupings to a single national professional organization. As the profession developed, however, its goals and structure have always been shaped by current political, economic, and social conditions. The effect of the environment is reflected in the development of mainstream professional practice but is exemplified even more clearly in the black community's effort to meet human needs.

The history of the United States is a history of maltreatment of the black population. Individual citizens and social institutions have contributed to this injustice, and social work is no exception. From its earliest beginnings social work participated in the segregationist policies of the broader society; there were white settlement houses and "colored" settlement houses; white women's clubs and "colored" women's clubs; white fraternities and "colored" fraternities. Our history has made it clear: If blacks wanted to receive relief or aid of any kind they had to look to themselves.

The Axinn and Levin text, *Social Welfare: A History of the American Response to Need* illustrates this tendency. In their historical analysis veterans and blacks represent the two extremes of American attitudes about the worthy and unworthy poor.[3] Veterans were given special consideration for social welfare benefits because they had served in the armed forces. For minorities a different picture emerges. Blacks, in particular, have suffered the dual difficulties of class and color, racial discrimination and poverty. On the whole it can be said that social work has responded historically to the needs of poor Americans of European descent.[4]

An ideological framework for social work history

An historical perspective on social work will broaden the student's understanding of how ideology affects practice. Theories about poverty and deviance are not born in a vacuum. Nor is the effect of these theories neutral. History shows how theories about poverty evolved from specific economic, social, and political environments; it illuminates the different assumptions, values, and goals implied by various theories; it illustrates how these theories have been used by different individuals, organizations, and classes to promote their economic, social, and political interests; and it shows the influence of the past on contemporary theories and policies. In contrast the typical study of social work history identifies the Charity Organization Society as the precursor of casework, the settlement house and recreation movement as the progenitor of groupwork, and the civil rights movement, Saul Alinsky, and the United Way as the inspiration for community organization theory and practice.

The evolution of practice

While social work has been shaped by many historical forces, certain movements have more directly affected the philosophy and skills of social work practice: The Charity Organization Society and the settlement movement have been widely discussed in the social work literature. These movements reflect both the liberal and conservative strains in our history. Less frequently discussed is the contribution of the radical theorists (for example, the abolitionists, radical feminists, or unemployed councils) who represent the earlier political-economic approaches to alleviating social problems. While they were not social workers, they do reflect the philosophical base of radical social workers today. It is important to recognize the importance of the "fringe" element; their programs for social justice may not have won acceptance in their time, but their presence made less radical social work movements more acceptable.

The three major methodologies (casework, groupwork, and community organization) have now been conceptualized. Students now have a generalist model of practice that prepares them to work with different sizes of systems and different types of problems. This systematic approach to practice directs the social worker to intervene with the skill and intervention appropriate to the problem presented rather than to apply her specialization without regard to the problem.

Since social work practice is only a part of the social welfare system and has evolved from societal responses to social problems, Part Two will analyze early social welfare responses. Our goal is to develop a context for the growth of social work practice rather than to develop an extensive history of social welfare.

Summary

Part Two addresses the major sources of social work ideology and practice by outlining historically the assumptions about the cause of individual and social problems, the founding social welfare movements, early strategies, and subsequent methods that have evolved. The context for the evolution of professional practice is set with the presentation of the earliest forms of governmental response to social problems, beginning with England's Statute of Laborers in 1349. Study of early American responses show strong traces of English influence. As the United States became increasingly industrialized, the societal response to social problems became more formalized and professionalized. From these formal responses, social work emerged as a profession beginning in the late nineteenth century. The roots of professional practice are examined in significant social movements and the historical development of methodology.

The "proper" role of women is presented as a powerful influence on the profession of social work. Finally, parallel developments in service provision to minorities are presented. The history of black social work identifies an area where traditional methods of social work have failed. Black movements illustrate the larger society's response to minorities since blacks have historically been excluded from both the profession and the service delivery system. Part Two illustrates how values and ideologies have cut across the different sizes and types of client groups and interventions. Throughout history there have been liberals, conservatives, and radicals who have used casework, groupwork, and community organization skills for problem solving.

References

1. Gerald Handel, *Social Welfare in Western Society* (New York: Random House, 1982).
2. The Milford Conference, *Social Casework Generic and Specific: A Report of the Milford Conference* (Washington, D.C.: Reprinted by the National Association of Social Workers, 1974) 17.
3. June Axinn and Herman Levin, *Social Welfare: A History of the American Response to Need,* 2nd ed. (New York: Harper and Row, 1982).
4. Toby Ferrell, *Why Not Us? Blacks and Social Welfare* (Unpublished monograph, 1982).

CHAPTER FOUR

History of Relief for the Poor

"The goals of social welfare programs for the poor derive from the goals of the larger society for itself and from the view that society holds of itself and of its various members. In turn, decisions about who is needy and how the needy are to be helped bear upon economic development, political organization, social stability, and family integrity. . . . . . Because social welfare goals touch a core of ideologies, they tend to polarize Americans."[1]

Knowing the history of poor relief is essential to understanding social work practice and social welfare policy today. Poverty has existed throughout recorded history. The response to poverty has typically been a response to the needs of the economic system.

Middle Ages

The earliest social welfare institution was the church.

Prior to the fourteenth century, poverty in the Middle Ages (400 A.D. to 1500 A.D.) was treated quite differently than it is today. Religious motivation was the paramount incentive to relieving the suffering of the poor. A concern for "thy neighbor and thyself" pervaded religious teaching. Christians were admonished to "Do unto others as you would have them do unto you," and "Give, and it shall be given unto you . . . For with the same measure that ye mete withal it shall be measured to you again."[2] The church was the administrator of poor relief, and church canonists turned to biblical text as their guide to poor law construction. The culture respected the individual regardless of material possessions; in medieval poor law, the poor had a right to assistance and the better off had a duty to provide it. The only test of eligibility for assistance was evidence of need. Moreover, "In case of doubt it is better to do too much than to do nothing at all."[3]

Not only did the church assert the dignity of the individual, but also the economic system (feudalism) provided a subsistence to most of the population. Most people lived a rural life. People vulnerable to economic insecurity and attack surrendered their freedom and land to more powerful men. They exchanged a portion of what they produced for protection of the lord of the manor. In exchange these serfs received protection and gained the right to stay on the land.[4] The laborer exchanged his freedom for economic security.

End of feudalism

By the end of the fourteenth century feudalism was ending and a wage system was taking over. The laborer had increased freedom and decreased economic security. People made the most of their new freedom by travelling about seeking higher wages; their new mobility threatened the landowners who had previously dominated society. The new merchant class replaced the landowners in power and prestige. Still Christianity continued to influence the beliefs of the people. The merchant class was concerned with justifying its accumulated wealth in the eyes of God; merchants strove to achieve the best of both worlds: maximum accumulation of wealth in this world, and salvation in the hereafter. Through private charity merchants felt they could atone for the injustices that crept into their business dealings. One method of distributing charity adopted by the merchants was the funeral dole; when a merchant died his estate would distribute money and food to the poor. But doling out money at funerals contributed to the vagrancy problem in England. To combat this problem, merchants often left orders to distribute money only to the industrious poor, "not to those who were astute enough to stop working in order to live by the indiscriminate almsgiving that went on at funerals."[5]

Statute of laborers

In the fourteenth century the landowners faced new threats. Merchants were usurping the power and privilege of the propertied class. Laborers were increasingly moving about and demanding higher wages. As long as labor was plentiful, landowners had to be concerned only about looting. But between 1315 and 1321 England suffered a great famine; fewer laborers were available, and those who could work demanded higher wages. The problem became even more acute when the bubonic plague struck in 1348. England lost one third of its population. During the last half of the fourteenth century workers could demand high wages and good working conditions; employers had to

During this period England lost nearly one-third of its population to the plague within two years.

compete for labor. This was the first true taste of freedom for workers and competition for landowners. To regain their power the landowners had to decrease the power of labor.

King Edward III issued the Statute of Laborers in 1349.

It was under these circumstances that the Statute of Laborers was adopted. This statute was an attempt by the English landowner to assure a sufficient supply of agricultural workers at low wages. One paragraph has special significance.

> Because that many valiant beggars, as long as they may live of begging, do refuse to labor, giving themselves to idleness and vice, and sometime to theft, and other abominations; none upon the said pain of imprisonment, shall under the color of pity or alms, give anything to such, which may labor, or presume to favor them towards their desires, so that thereby they may be compelled to labor for their necessary living.[6]

This law set up certain conditions for the laborer. A maximum wage was set; landowners no longer had to compete for labor since they were allowed to pay only a certain wage and could be punished for paying more. The Statute of Laborers also permitted the landowner to choose his workers; the laborer's choice was not considered. In addition to setting these harsh conditions upon work, the law also provided penalties for begging or almsgiving. If anyone was inclined to provide assistance to a poor worker, he would be punished.

Controlling vagrancy

During this period we first see the distinction between the worthy and the unworthy poor.

As England progressed from feudalism to mercantilism to capitalism, labor statutes became progressively harsher. Begging, an acceptable and even honorable occupation for certain groups in the Middle Ages, became a crime. The first mention of special treatment for the "impotent to serve" was in 1388; these people were to have lesser punishment for begging, but they had to stay in their own communities. The Statute of Laborers in 1495 suggested that beggars would spend three days and nights in stocks, but pregnant women and the extremely ill would be punished less severely. In 1504 persons over sixty and the ill were added to the group receiving lesser punishment.[7]

The fifteenth century was relatively prosperous. While laborers lived poorly by present standards, they had the bare necessities of life, and relief was largely unnecessary. As the fifteenth century drew to a close, however, poverty began to increase. One reason for the growing impoverishment of workers was sheep raising. Sheep raising required many fewer workers and much more land than crops. The problem became so great that in 1534 Henry VIII tried to limit the number of sheep per estate to two thousand.[8]

The movement from serfdom to freedom created a whole new set of problems. Under feudalism life was stable; war and famine were the only major threats to the serfs' livelihood. As capitalism grew, individual freedom increased at the price of economic security. As England moved into industrialization, poverty became the concern of government. Once the economic system no longer provided security to individuals, the government was left to provide some means to assure security. Industrial society has since been baffled by the problem of how to provide people with the equivalent protection against sickness, old age, and unemployment—security that feudalism provided, however inadequately.

While the Statute of 1536 established public responsibility for the poor, it also threatened to punish them severely for begging.

Until the 16th century begging had been the societal response to poverty. Not only the poor, but also mendicant friars and university students lived by begging. Mercantilism changed the economic structure of society, and begging and private philanthropy were no longer able to handle the problems of poverty. The Statute of Laborers in 1531 was the first assumption of government responsibility for the care of the destitute. The introduction to the act made it clear that idleness was a vice to be punished, but it also recognized the necessity of helping those genuinely in need. The statute decreed that mayors, justices of the peace, and other local officials

1. Shall make diligent search and inquiry of all aged poor and impotent persons which live or of necessity be compelled to live by alms of the charity of the people.
2. Shall have power [to assign impotent persons limits within which they may beg] and to give in commandment to every such aged and impotent beggar that none of them shall beg without the limit to them so appointed.
3. Shall also register and write the names of every such impotent beggar in a bill or roll indented.
4. Shall make and deliver to every such impotent person by them enabled to beg, a letter containing the name of such impotent person, and witnessing that he is authorized to beg, and the limit within which he is appointed to beg.[9]

The major points of the statute were that beggars had to be registered and given a letter and a territory to beg in, parish constables were to search out impotents, and able-bodied beggars were to be punished more harshly. These may seem like no provisions at all, but actually they represent the beginning of the assumption by government of the care of persons in economic distress. In setting up eligibility requirements and certifying beggars, England had made important movement toward public administration of relief. However, even authorized begging was not adequate to provide for the poor. Therefore, the Statutes of 1536 provided a more comprehensive system of relief and harsher punishment for the able-bodied. Some elements of the Statute were as follows:

(1) All and every person or persons being whipped or sent unto their countries in form aforesaid, at the end of every ten miles shall repair unto the constable of

> any parish, being directly in his way towards the county and place whereunto he is so appointed, and upon sight of his letters given unto him at the time of his whipping . . . every of the said constables and others the King's subjects shall and may furnish him with competent meat, drink, and lodging for one night only or for one meal, and so he shall continue his daily journey of ten miles until such time as he shall come unto the hundred and place whereunto he is assigned to go.
> (2) Any of the aforesaid ruffelers, sturdy vagabonds, and valiant beggars . . . upon due examination and proof of the continuance of his said loitering, wandering and idleness, or vagabondage, shall eftsoon not only [be] whipped again . . . but also shall have the upper part of the gristle of his right ear clean cut off . . [if] having the upper part of the right ear cut off, as is aforesaid . . . and . . . found guilty . . . of continual loitering and idleness, then every such sturdy vagabond and valiant beggar . . . shall have judgment to suffer pains and execution of death as a felon and as enemies of the Commonwealth.
> (3) [The justice and other officers] shall have authority . . . . to take . . . children under the age of fourteen years and above the age of five years, in begging or idleness, and to appoint them to masters of husbandry or other crafts or labors to be taught, by the which they may get their living when they shall come of age.[10]

Parish relief was similar to contemporary local county relief for the poor.

This statute set out the nature of the provision, the method of administration, the government's responsibility for collecting contributions, and the administrative structure for relief. The parish became the unit of administration; for the first time a paid staff administered relief.

Poor laws of 1601

Except for a trend toward exceeding harshness in 1547, which said beggars should be branded with a V and if they still begged, branded with an S and enslaved forever, new laws followed the spirit of the 1531 and 1536 statutes. An economic depression in 1594 precipitated a famine and breadriots that lead to a revision of the statutes; the Poor Law of 1601, Elizabeth 43, was actually a revision of previous statutes. These new statutes are important because for the first time the total act was rewritten. Further, these laws were to stand with only minor changes until 1662.

The patterns that developed between 1531 and 1601 are still embodied in social welfare policy today.

Many of our current welfare practices are direct descendants of the English Poor Laws.

1. Relief is to be locally administered and financed. Both the General Revenue Sharing Act 1972 in the Nixon era and the State Federalism concept in the Reagan administration reflect this attitude.
2. The administrator is to be a public official. Before the Statutes of Laborers, parishes were empowered to raise taxes for relief.

3. The unemployed are categorized; both treatment and benefit are to be related to the individual's relationship to the work force. No able bodied person is to benefit by the relief system. Handicapped and elderly people who cannot work—the "worthy" poor—should be given help.
4. Families are to be responsible for themselves. With the Poor Laws grandparents were responsible for their children and grandchildren; adult children were responsible for the children and their parents. Present welfare policy states that parents are responsible for their minor children but are not financially responsible for their parents. Some states are presently considering a system whereby adult children would have to contribute to the care of their parents if they required nursing home care.
5. Children were to be given apprenticeships or training to ensure they would be productive members of society. This principle is less obvious currently because modern society prepares children for the workplace in the educational settings rather than through apprenticeships; nonetheless modern policy continues to reflect the importance of preparing poor children for the marketplace through the educational system.

Even though the Poor Laws set up the mechanism whereby relief was a legal right, the majority of relief funds still came from private charity. For two generations after the passage of Elizabeth 43 only about 7 percent of the relief came from public funds. Even so it is significant that, after two centuries of attempting to control the poor through repression, England recognized a positive obligation to the destitute.

1662 Law of settlement and removal

This law is similar to what is referred to in this country as residency requirements.

The Law of Settlement and Removal decreed that the overseer could remove anyone from the parish that he thought might become needy. The basis on which this was determined was whether the person paid more than 10 pounds per year rent. There was a belief present that many indigents were moving from local parishes to the more urban parishes because the assistance was more liberal. This law represented a return to serfdom; an individual belonged in the parish of birth. The law permitted repression; not only was the individual forced to work for whoever wanted him but at whatever price. In addition to these horrendous conditions local authorities were empowered to force the laborer back to his original place of residence. The law also provided a means of conveying the poor back to their parish of settlement. To further ensure available labor when needed a provision was made for "certificates of settlement" to be given if workers were needed in a certain area. The certificate of settlement allowed the laborer to go to the parish where he was needed during harvest and also ensured that his parish of settlement would take him back when he was no longer needed. This law was a significant victory of the landowners over labor. In 1795 the law was amended so that a person could not be removed unless he asked for assistance. (In the United States, similar residency requirements remained in effect until April 21, 1969; in the case *Shapiro vs. Thompson,* the Supreme Court declared considering residency a requirement for granting public assistance was unconstitutional.)

Workhouses: Indoor relief

Welfare provided to people in their own homes is outdoor relief. Institutional care and workhouses are examples of indoor relief.

At the same time that Parliament was passing punitive laws such as the Law of Settlement and Removal, a countermovement in England suggested that poverty could best be relieved by making all citizens, including children, productive. Andrew Yarranton was a proponent of this approach to poverty. Following a trip to Germany he wrote a report describing Germany's workhouses and suggesting that England could be more competitive commercially if it adopted this system. Yarranton's report (published in 1677) states that

> In all these parts there is no beggar, nor no occasion to beg; and in all towns there are schools for little girls, from six years old and upwards, to teach them to spin, and so to bring their tender fingers by degrees to spin very fine, which being young are thereby easily fitted by degrees to spin very fine, which being young are thereby easily fitted for that use. Whereas people overgown in age cannot so well feel the thread. Their wheels go all by the foot, made to go with much ease, whereby the action or motion is very easy and delightful. And in all towns there are schools according to the bigness, or multitude of the poor children.
>
> I will show you the way, method, rule, and order how they are governed. First, there is a large room, and in the middle thereof a little box like a pulpit. Secondly, there are benches built around the room as they are in our playhouses; upon the benches sit about two hundred children spinning, and in the box in the middle of the room sits the grand mistress with a long white wand in her hand. If she observes any of them idle, she reaches them a tap; but if that will not do, she rings a bell which by a little cord is fixed to a box, and out comes a woman; she then points to the offender, and she is taken away into another room and chastised. And all this is done without one word speaking. And I believe this way of ordering the young women in Germany is one great cause that the German women have so little of the twit twat. And I am sure it would be well were it so in England. . . .[11]

Yarranton's was an example of a positive, optimistic view of how the poor could serve society and lend strength to the nation. Cynical punitive proponents of workhouses, however, overshadowed Yarranton and his ideas. In

1722 the workhouse law was passed. Proponents of the workhouse argued that institutional care (indoor relief) would be less expensive than caring for people in their own homes (outdoor relief). Their plan was to make workhouses so horrible that people would go without rather than enter the workhouse.

All poor people were placed together in workhouses without medical help and in often unsanitary conditions.

Workhouses were usually managed by whoever would do it for the least amount of money. Since managers were paid according to the number of people they served, it was in their personal interest to spend as little as possible on the poor. Within ten years of the passage of the workhouse law (1722), over one hundred workhouses had been established in the London area. Workhouses were run like prisons even though people housed in them had not broken the law. Children suffered tremendously.

Charles Dickens wrote about life in a workhouse in *Oliver Twist* published in 1837.

Death rates of workhouse children under one year old were as high as 82 percent. In one workhouse only three of nineteen babies survived; in another not a single child survived; a third workhouse record showed only seven out of one hundred children survived over a three year period.[12] As the conditions and the cost of the workhouse became known, policies swung back toward outdoor relief.

One of the major concerns of social work has been the proper care of children. These children were playing in an early settlement house. Photo courtesy of Social Welfare History Archives, University of Minnesota.

The Speenhamland Act: A return to outdoor relief

The allowance given to supplement the wages based on the bread scale is similar to guaranteeing a minimum wage based on the cost of living.

By 1795 industry was becoming mechanized. Factories and power machines were replacing cottage industries and handwork. The commons were being enclosed for sheep farming; the poor were no longer able to engage in subsistence farming on common land. Prices were increasing; wages were decreasing; riots and looting were occurring. Rather than raising wages so laborers could meet the cost of living, the Justices of Berkshire (meeting at Speenhamland) proposed to use relief to make up the difference between what families earned and what they needed to subsist. This allowance was known as the bread scale; when a gallon loaf sold for 1 shilling, the parish supplemented a man's pay up to three shillings. Speenhamland had four methods through which able-bodied were aided without entering the workhouse. The most widely used was the allowance in support of wages or bread scale; the roundsmen system was similar. The allowance was used for people who were already working and the roundsmen system was for the unemployed. A report based on the Roundsmen plan (written in 1795) states

> In the winter and at other times, when a man is out of work he applies to the overseer, who sends him from house to house, to get employ: the housekeeper who employs him, is obliged to give him victuals, and 6d a day; and the parish adds 4d (total 10d a day) for the support of his family; persons working in this manner are called roundsmen, from their going around the village or township for employ.[13]

The third method used was the labor rate; landowners were responsible for the unemployed. The parish would determine wages and then distribute the unemployed among the employers who were required to provide employment or pay the difference in increased taxes. This system led to the displacement of workers already employed. The fourth and most infrequently used method of providing outdoor relief was employing poor laborers on public projects.

The effects of Speenhamland were disastrous for everyone. Wages went down, people on relief increased, the laborer's initiative and hope were destroyed, the landowner had no incentive to pay decent wages, the laborer's standard of living fell. A movement back to the workhouse ensued.

German response to poverty

In Munich, at about the same time, Count Rumsford (an American by birth) was charged with clearing that city of beggars. Instead of attempting to make people happy through virtue, his system proposed making people virtuous through happiness. The way to clear Munich of beggars was to adopt effective measures for maintaining and supporting the poor. He did not believe workhouses should be odious; in fact he felt work and relief should be provided in homes when possible. Under Count Rumsford's guidance, Munich developed the most thorough and comprehensive relief program of its time. Rumsford's system included not only relief, but also employment, aid to children, child placing, nurseries, and educational programs. Although it too reflected a doctrine of less eligibility, it did not make relief punitive.[14]

The doctrine of less eligibility means making relief less than what a person could earn if work was available.

Thomas Chalmers: Casework methodology

Reverend Thomas Chalmers (1780–1847) organized a system of private giving to the poor.

One other small scale operation developed at this time that did not have immediate widespread effect but reappeared fifty years later in the charity organization society movement. Reverend Thomas Chalmers, a minister of the Church of Scotland, objected to using church and public funds for relief. He thought the laity rather than the clergy should serve as almoners. He trained members of his parish to visit families and make a thorough study of their situations. Drawn from the wealthy families of the parish, these deacons used personal influence, attention, advice, civility, and good will (all enhanced by their elevated social status) to alleviate suffering in the parish. Chalmers raised all the money for his parish from collections, and he was such an excellent speaker that people traveled from many miles to hear him speak. He agreed to make no more referrals to the workhouse if he could keep the funds he raised in his own parish—St. John's in Glasgow—the poorest parish in the city. He believed each parish should take care of its own. Thomas Chalmers was at St. John's from 1819 to 1823. His success was largely attributable to his own fundraising abilities rather than the casework methodology that he developed.

Philosophy

Adam Smith proposed a gradual elimination of government involvement in poor relief.

Two philosophers also had considerable impact on the poor law thinking of the day: Adam Smith (1723–1790) and Reverend Thomas Malthus (1766–1834).

Adam Smith is widely recognized as the father of modern economics. He was an optimist, perhaps because his writings predate the misery that the Industrial Revolution would bring to England. In his model the best of all possible economic systems would result if each person was free to act in his own self-interest. Smith felt competition, not regulation, would limit the power of the businessmen. He assumed that there was a harmony of interests among all economic classes. *The Wealth of Nations* (1776) shows that he favored high wages to spur industriousness, population growth, savings, large markets, and a division of labor. Smith believed the difference between the classes was based on nurture not nature. His was an optimistic vision of all classes ascending together toward the road to prosperity.[15]

Malthus proposed an argument that we hear today: the poor will keep having children to receive more welfare.

This happy view was to be overridden by the negative view of the poor so prevalent in the work of Thomas Malthus. Malthus was an ordained minister who brought bad tidings to the poor. His *Essay on Population* (1798) set forth the law of population that said that if unchecked, population tends to outstrip the food supply. If there is no moral restraint to curb population growth, then famine, misery, pestilence, or war will do the job. The poor had only themselves to blame for their misery; poverty was the natural punishment for overbreeding. The poor should not be given relief since it would only encourage them to have more children; high wages would have similar consequences. Malthus saw poverty as useful and inevitable; it disciplined the poor, who would not work without the threat of starvation. His arguments justified low wages and terrible working conditions. The upper class movement to abolish relief gained strength from Malthus' argument. The Poor Laws of 1834 were the operationalization of the Malthusian approach to poverty.[16]

Poor law reform 1834

In 1832 a Royal Commission for Inquiring into the Administration and Practical Operation of the Poor Law was appointed to reform the Poor Law and to stop outdoor relief. This commission produced a 13,000 page study biased against the reliefer (pauper) and full of praise for the indigent independent laborer. Subjective reporting permeated this document, exemplified by this quotation.

> In the pauper's habitation you will find a strained show of misery and wretchedness; and those little articles of furniture which might, by the least exertion imaginable, wear an appearance of comfort, are turned, as it were intentionally, the ugliest side outward; the children are dirty, and appear to be under no control; the clothes of both parents and children in nine cases out of ten, are ragged, but evidently are so for the lack of the least attempt to make them otherwise; for I have very rarely found the clothes of a pauper with a patch put on or a seam made upon them since new; their mode of living, in all cases that I have known (except and always making the distinction between the determined pauper and the infirm and deserving poor, which cases are but comparatively few) is most improvident. Whatever provisions I have found, on visiting their habitations, have been of the best quality; and my inquiries among the tradesmen, as butchers, chandler's shopkeepers, etc., have all been answered with—"They will not have anything but the best."
>
> In the habitation of the laboring man who receives no parish relief, you will find (I have done so), even in the poorest, an appearance of comfort; the articles of furniture, few and humble though they may be, have their best side seen, are arranged in something like order, and so as to produce the best appearance of which they are capable. The children appear under parental control; are sent to school (if of that age); their clothes you will find patched and taken

> care of, so as to make them wear as long a time as possible; there is a sense of moral feeling and moral dignity easily discerned; they purchase such food, and at such seasons, and in such quantities, as the most economical would approve of.[17]

Rather than "burden" people with the whole report, the commissioners selectively reported findings. Their report implied that most recipients were able-bodied and that administration of relief was lax; its purpose was to eliminate outdoor relief. The commissioners also stressed less eligibility; paupers should not live better than the poorest workers. The report states that

> it is shown that in proportion as the condition of any pauper class is elevated above the condition of independent labourers, the condition of the independent class is depressed; their industry is impaired, their employment becomes unsteady, and its remuneration in wages is diminished. Such persons, therefore, are under the strongest inducements to quite the less eligible class of labourers and enter the more eligible class of paupers."[18]

This report led back to the policy of making the workhouse the only source of relief and making the conditions of the workhouse so bad that no one would want to enter. The Poor Laws of 1834 instituted a number of policy changes: outdoor relief was to be abolished, relief was to be supervised nationally, the poor were to be classified as worthy or unworthy and placed in separate portions of the workhouse, and less eligibility was to prevail. Workhouses were like penal institutions; England officially declared poverty was a crime.

Colonial history 1647–1776

Very different economic, social, and political conditions prevailed in colonial America. England had to deal with unemployed masses; America needed every possible laborer. Unemployment was not a problem but sickness, disability, and widowhood resulting from the difficult living conditions engendered considerable need for relief. Colonial Americans did not immediately distinguish between classes of poor—all problems were seen as economic problems. Rothman cites the example of the lunatic.[19]

Lunatics came to public attention not because they were afflicted with delusions or fears, but because they suffered from poverty. In this spirit a Massachusetts law (frequently copied elsewhere) established that "when and so often as it shall happen any person to be naturally wanting of understanding, so as to be uncapable to provide for him or herself" then the town in the absence of relatives and personal property, was to provide for their relief.[20] No one was willing to support the rogue or vagabond. This was not a great problem because everyone knew the people of his community, and there was strong community pressure to be productive.

Why then did a country with such different concerns adopt the English Poor Laws? Some suggest that colonial Americans had a strong sense of locality—everyone felt a duty to take care of his own. Others point to the fact that no private charity was organized to respond to problems of poverty so a public institution was compelled to address those problems. Finally, every laborer was needed, and the Poor Laws set up a mechanism to force everyone to work.

The Puritan ethic

The Puritans believed poverty and idleness were sins.

Calvinism and the Puritan ethic were also influential in the development of colonial poor law. Social status was a manifestation of predestined grace. This outlook justified a decrease in community ownership and an increase in private property. Poverty was part of God's design; it allowed suffering and benevolence. The wealthy were stewards of God and had a duty to protect God's wealth. While poverty was part of the natural design and public relief was necessary, it was not to be forgotten that the poor were morally flawed and should not be pampered.

Families

Colonial families were to provide for themselves; each member was to be a productive and contributing member of society. Public well being came before individual or family well being. If a child's family was not able to raise him in a manner appropriate to this end, the child was placed with a family that could. One state tested the fitness of a family by whether or not a child knew the alphabet at the age of six. If he did not, he was placed with another family to receive a decent and Christian education. Families that were not financially successful were dangerous, economically and morally. Children were bound out to be educated in honest and profitable trades and to learn and understand the principles of religion and law. It was important to protect children from the contagion of parental failures. Adult poor were also farmed out to the lowest bidder. As the colonies become more populous, workhouses were built to administer proper punishment and put the poor to work.[21]

Crime

All types of crime merited harsh punishment.

The colonial attitude toward crime reflected a belief in predestination. The identification of disorder with sin made it difficult for lawmakers to distinguish between major and minor infractions. Both were testimony to the natural depravity of man and the power of the devil—sure signs the offender was destined to be a public menace and a (literally) damned sinner. This attitude underlies the heavy-handedness of the 18th century code that set capital punishment as the sancton for crimes as different as murder and arson, horse stealing, and childish disrespect for parents. A passage from the writings of Reverend Benjamin Wadsworth reflects this belief.

> When children are disobedient to parents, God is often provoked to leave them to those sins which bring them to the greatest shame and misery . . . when persons have been brought to die at the gallow, how often have they confessed that disobedience to parents led them to those crimes?[22]

The standard theory of crime was that the family had failed to train its charges to their social and religious obligations and had left their depraved nature unchecked. Sin demanded retribution; whippings or harsh physical punishment would not rehabilitate but terrorize the guilty into good behavior.

Revolutionary War To Civil War

The early federal period witnessed many changes in the treatment of social problems particularly poverty, mental and physical illness, and crime. Poverty continued to be seen as an individual abberration rather than a social problem. Relatives were legally responsible for family members; relief was viewed as unnecessary. Local communities were the most important source of political decisions; state governments were distant, consisting of a group of legislators who met for two weeks every two years. Families and neighborhoods were self-sufficient. As industrialization progressed, state government became more significant and local government less so. Still it was up to the overseer to ensure that on one shirked his responsibility to work.

Farming out

The individual rights of someone who was poor were not considered during the federal period.

Methods of dealing with the poor varied from town to town. Some towns farmed out their poor; the overseer had to hire someone to take care of the poor person. Orphans and children whose parents were on relief were bound out to proper families. Some adults were auctioned off to the lowest bidder, and a few were sent out on the roundsmen system. Prevalent liberal economic theory suggested that what was spent for the poor decreased the amount available for capitalists and productive people. Poverty and relief were problems to study.

The study of poverty

In 1818 the New York Society for the Prevention of Pauperism set up a study to find the causes of poverty. This study found that ignorance, idleness, intemperance, want of economy, imprudent and hasty marriages, lotteries, pawn brokers, houses of prostitution, and charitable organizations were all causes of poverty.[23] In response to those findings, the society developed a plan whereby friendly visitors would advise families to save their money and encourage them to be productive. This plan was never really implemented.

The Quincy Report (1821) and the Yates Report (1824) led to growth in the establishment of almshouses and workhouses for the poor.

In 1821 a committee in Massachusetts led by Josiah Quincy found that outdoor relief was both expensive and injurious to morals. Quincy and his committee had studied homes where the children had been bound out and adults had been farmed out or auctioned. They found that the poor were treated with barbarity and neglect, the education and morals of the pauper children were almost wholly neglected, no adequate provision was made for employment, and little attention was given to the disbursement of public funds. According to the committee the almshouse was the only answer to these many shortcomings of outdoor relief. A few years later the Yates report concluded that workhouses would not only benefit children morally but would also help the economic system.

Prison: punishment and rehabilitation

Until 1790 jails were for poor and detainment of prisoners not punishment. Punishment until that time generally meant time in the stocks, whipping, flogging, branding, mutilation, and hanging. Cesar Beccaria's *Essays on Crime and Punishment* (1764) introduced the utilitarian approach to punishing crime. Beccaria argued that crime should be clearly defined, laws should be codified to allow defense, and punishment should fit the crime and be based not on vengeance but on instilling good citizenship. This approach based imprisonment on the offense committed; prisoners were put to constructive tasks.

The Quakers led the move for prisons as rehabilitative units. Inmates in Quaker prisons were not to associate with each other; they needed solitude to reflect on their evil ways; prisoners could read the Bible, but should not engage in any other activity. The goal of imprisonment was redemption.

Crime was then perceived as an exercise of free will, not predestination. The environment could be a source of temptation or inspiration. Constructive punishment could lead to a decrease in criminal behavior. Juveniles were placed in separate institutions called Houses of Refuge or Schools for Industry. Some juveniles were lawbreakers; some were just poor. Discipline was harsh, and didactic moralizing was an important part of the programs in these houses and schools.

Health care

In 1794 Bellevue Hospital in New York began as part of an almshouse.

The first half of the 19th century was a time for great breakthroughs in medicine. Bleeding, blistering, and purging had been the most common treatment for illness. Studies done in Paris showed that this type of treatment was actually detrimental to the health of the patient. Hospitals had traditionally been a form of poor relief. Infirmaries in almshouses became hospitals. American doctors were dependent on European medicine for many advances that were made as the United States did not allow medical students to work on cadavers. Illness had also been seen as a moral fault under principles of predestination. In contrast physicians were beginning to understand biological components of illness.[24]

Mental health and moral treatment

Treatment of mental illness advanced at the same time. Once perceived as demonic possession, mental illness was now sometimes associated with physical causes. Bleeding and blistering or the tranquilizer chair became popular treatments. Patients in straight jackets sat in the tranquilizer chair, and were spun about until they became calm. In colonial America the insane had almost always been kept at home in a cellar or shed and usually behind locked bars; now doctors began setting up private madhouses that began to prescribe "moral" treatment. Moral treatment was based on the theory that the brain was susceptible and malleable. Physical illness as well as the environment could affect the brain. The physician was to discover the source of the difficulty and correct it. To correct conditions and stimuli was to cure mental illness. Treatment usually involved separation from home or other pathological circumstances. Such was the origin of asylums.

Asylums provided the potential for a carefully controlled environment and restoration of patient's balance. But only the rich could afford moral treatment. Patients who could afford the treatments responded favorably; a certain Dr. Todd cured twenty-one of twenty-three patients in one asylum. In the 1840s there were nineteen asylums but only seven or eight good ones. There were over 17,457 reported cases of bizarre insanity. One in seven patients was under medical supervision; the rest were in attics, almshouses and jails.

Dorothea Dix was an important force in the mental health movement. Ms. Dix taught Sunday school in East Cambridge Jail. There she observed lunatics in unheated cells. She began visiting other places where the mentally ill were kept. She compiled case-by-case records of the misery and abuse she observed. She was responsible for founding or enlarging thirty-two mental hospitals here and abroad. Dorothea Dix was very impressed with moral treatment and tried to make it widely available.[25]

Dorothea Lynde Dix (1802–1887), despite poor physical health, spent her entire life lobbying for reforms in treatment of the insane.

Her program for the mentally ill contained three points: patients should receive humane care instead of neglect, isolation, and cruelty; special state institutions should receive financial aid because individuals, local governments, and private charity could not afford to run the institutions; and patients should receive medical care based on the moral treatment model. In 1848 Dorothea Dix asked Congress to designate five million acres for mental institutions. Congress doubled the amount of land and passed the legislation. President Pierce vetoed the bill because he said welfare domain belonged to the states, not the federal government.

Child saving movements

Charles Loring Brace (1826–1890) not only developed the idea of foster care but also helped to establish schools, lodging houses, summer camps, and shelters for vagrant children.

Children in the almshouses did not receive the care they needed. Amshouses tended to be undemocratic and anti-family; submission and obedience were stressed, and children were not allowed to develop as individuals. There were just too many children, and public education was taking away apprenticeship opportunities. One response to this problem was introduced by Charles Loring Brace. Brace was the director of the Children's Aid Society in New York City. He wrote *The Dangerous Class of New York* describing his work with the poor children of New York City. Brace felt the answer to poverty for children was foster care on Western farms that needed laborers and he believed in getting children out of the city. The only real resistance he got to his idea was from the Catholic Church as they were afraid he might be placing Catholic children in Protestant homes. Between 1853 and 1864 his agency placed 4,614 children on farms. Brace's work has been featured in a public television special entitled "Orphan Train."

Aftermath of the Civil War

Following the Civil War, the North and South developed differently and experienced different problems. The North experienced rapid economic growth, but even though the United States had become a leading manufacturer poverty continued to grow. There was increased polarization of economic classes; while some owners pursued wealth ruthlessly, workers and farmers lived precariously. The North suffered a serious unemployment problem from 1873–79, and labor unions lost much of their strength because of a large reserve labor force.

The Freedmen's Bureau, established by Congress in 1865, provided transportation home, distributed medical supplies, and helped establish schools, hospitals, and orphanages.

The South had to deal with devastated land, transportation systems, and financial institutions. The rural was particularly impoverished. Black codes that limited the property rights of ex-slaves and forbid them from working as artisans and mechanics were enacted to control ex-slaves. Blacks could work only in limited areas. Any unemployed black was subject to lease to farmers, and former owners had first chance to bid. The Freedmen's Bureau was the first federal welfare agency; it was housed in the War Department and was the major source of public welfare in the South. The Bureau dealt with the transient blacks and abandoned property. Townspeople opposed these programs and wanted blacks to work under former conditions; jobs created by the government interfered with this. General Otis Howard, the director of the bureau, was responsible for seeing that black educational institutions like Howard, Fisk, and Hampton Universities were built. Personnel problems within the agency and political pressures from without led to its demise after just seven years (1872).[26]

Summary

History illustrates how social work practice and social welfare policy have been shaped by the dominant values of the time. Today social welfare policy reflects the assumptions of the Statute of Laborers more closely than the religious motivation of the Middle Ages. With industrialization workers lost economic security, and became dependent on the economic cycle. The social welfare institution provided members of society with some sense of order in a rapidly changing economic system. Lack of security was partially compensated by the welfare system in a manner that did not threaten the economic system. When cheap labor was needed, the social welfare system insured its availability; when there was a surplus of labor, the social welfare system provided minimal subsistence for the unemployed. British and American poor laws have always reflected the needs of the economic system; religion and philosophy too have supported the social welfare institution as a stabilizing element in the economy.

Before the Civil War professionalization began to creep into the social services: jails were designed to redeem the sinner, mental health institutions were beginning to treat the insane, and children were being placed in foster care. The tragedy of the Civil War changed the complexion of the social welfare system. North and South were faced with different economic and social problems. The major problems in the North were related to immigration, industrialization, and urbanization. The charity organization societies and settlement houses were designed to respond to these problems. It is here in particular that one can discern the beginning of the social work profession. Since the worst poverty in the South was suffered by blacks, there was not the same societal concern about these problems. Blacks were left on their own to deal with their problems, and black responses often paralleled white services. Blacks, however, were generally limited to self-help groups that did not have the luxury of developing training schools for professionals and were limited to providing survival mechanisms to an impoverished, oppressed people who did not have the sponsorship of the wealthy.

These historical underpinnings of welfare illustrate the great diversity of responses a society can choose in dealing with poverty and other social problems. Differences in ideology and economic interests led England and Germany to different societal responses. Differences in economic base and racial make-up led to the development of different welfare systems in the North and the South. Obtaining a perspective on past societal choices provides insight for present choices. It also introduces the question of how much a profession can impact on society and how much society dictates the limits of professional practice.

References

1. June Axinn and Herman Levin, *Social Welfare: A History of American Response to Need*, 2nd ed. (New York: Harper and Row, 1982).
2. Blanche Coll, *Perspectives in Public Welfare: A History* (U.S. Printing Office).
3. Brian Tierney, *Medieval Poor Law: A Sketch of Canonical Theory and its Applications in England* (Berkeley and Los Angeles: University of California Press, 1959), 65; cited in Coll, *Perspectives,* 3.
4. Gerald Handel, *Social Welfare in Western Society* (New York: Random House, 1982), 51.
5. Ibid. 59.
6. 23 Edward III, The Statute of Laborers, 1349. For a more complete survey of early poor laws, see Karl de Schweinitz, *England's Road to Social Security* (London: University of Pennsylvania Press, 1947).
7. De Schweinitz, *England's Road*, 8.
8. Coll, *Perspectives.*
9. 22 Henry VIII, c. 12, An Act Concerning Punishment of Beggars and Vagabonds, 1531.
10. 27 Henry VIII, c. 25, 1536.
11. Andrew Yarranton, *England's Improvement by Sea and Land to Outdo the Dutch without Fighting, to Pay Debts without Moneys, to set at Work All the Poor of England with the Growth of Our Own Lands*, London, 1677, pp. 46–47.
12. Beulah Compton, *Introduction to Social Welfare and Social Work: Structure Function and Process* (Homewood, Ill.: Dorsey, 1980), 158.
13. Sir Frederic Morton Eden, *The State of the Poor: Or, An History of the Labouring Classes in England, From the Conquest to the Present Period*, Vol. 2, p. 384, London, 1797.
14. De Schweinitz, *England's Road*, 91.
15. Helen Ginsberg, *Poverty, Economics, and Society* (Washington, D.C.: University Press of America, 1981), 20.
16. Ibid. 30.
17. *The Report from His Majesty's Commissioners for Inquiring into the Administration and Practical Operation of the Poor Laws, Published by Authority*, 1834, 88–89.
18. Sidney Webb and Beatrice Webb, *English Local Government: English Poor Law History, Part I* (New York: Longman, Green, 1927), 417–418; cited in Coll, *Perspectives,* 61–62.
19. David Rothman, *Discovery of the Asylum* (Boston: Little, Brown, 1971), 4.
20. Ibid.
21. Axinn and Levin, *Social Welfare.*
22. Rothman, *Discovery*, 16.
23. Walter Trattner, *From Poor Law to Welfare State* (New York: Free Press, 1979).
24. James Lieby, *A History of Social Welfare and Social Work in the U.S.* (New York: Columbia University Press, 1978).
25. Ibid.
26. Axinn and Levin, *Social Welfare.*

CHAPTER FIVE

Societies, Settlements, and Social Justice

"Professional social work in the United States developed from an imperfect union between late-nineteenth century "scientific charity" movement, with its emphasis on friendly visiting and individual case diagnosis on the one hand, and the slightly younger social settlement movement, with its strong orientation toward social reform and social survey on the other. Leaders of the scientific charity movement sought to coordinate centrally all charity resources in a city, and volunteer "friendly visitors" investigated applications for assistance to determine how much aid they needed and the kind of help required. . . . In the early twentieth century, the social settlements not only provided clubs and classes for neighborhood residents, but collected descriptive and statistical data regarding neighborhood social conditions which they then utilized to agitate for social reform."[1]

Industrialization: Different races, different responses

During the late 1800's the problems associated with the industrial revolution brought about a need for massive delivery of services. People of all races flocked to the cities looking for work. As industrialization and urbanization increased so did unemployment.

Without denying that the Settlement and Charity Organization Movements deserve primary recognition for the development of professional practice, this chapter seeks to illustrate the many different movements that have contributed to the present shape of practice. The unifying professional organization (National Association of Social Work—NASW) has been in existence only since 1955. Before the chartering of the NASW numerous professional groups identified themselves with titles like the American Association of Group

Workers, American Association of Hospital Social Workers, American Association of School Social Workers, and the American Association of Psychiatric Social Workers.

COS and settlement movements

The first American Charity Organization Society (COS) opened in Buffalo in 1877.

The first settlement house (the Neighborhood Guild) opened in 1866 in New York.

The Charity Organization Society, the settlement house movement, and the less familiar social justice movements provide contrasting images of ideology shaping practice. Even though the Charity Organization Society (COS) and the settlement house movement developed at the same time in the United States their analysis and response to social problems differed sharply. The COS's "Four Pillar" approach of investigation, registration, cooperation, and coordination contrasted sharply with the settlement movement's "Three R's": residence, research, and reform. As these terms suggest the COS stressed personal fault, and the settlement workers stressed social and economic conditions as the prime cause of hunger and poverty. To the COS the problem was pauperism; to the settlement movement the problem was poverty. Because settlement workers assigned so much weight to the social causes of poverty, they believed an effective solution would be social rather than individual.

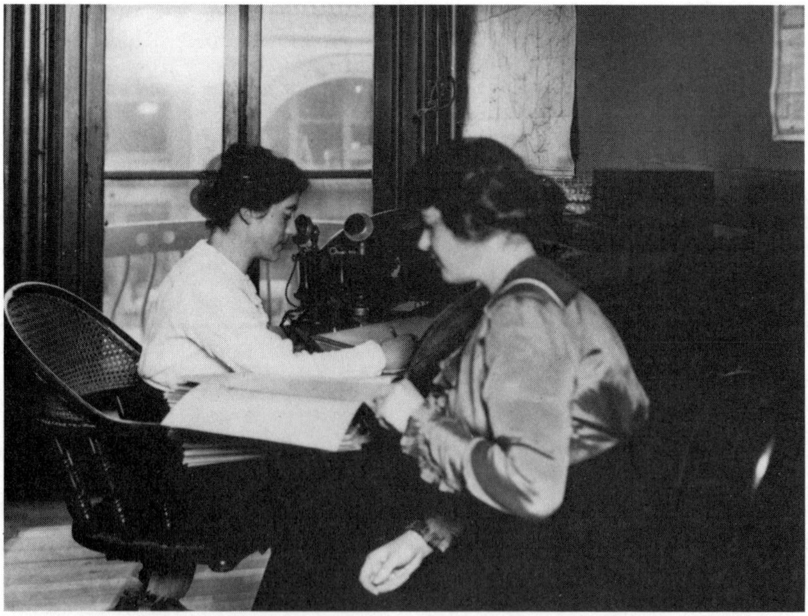

Charity Organization Society workers offered a conservative, scientific approach to investigating and helping the poor. Photo courtesy of Social Welfare History Archives, University of Minnesota.

Both movements felt the rich and poor would have to come together to deal with the problem. COS workers did "friendly visiting" to set an example and uplift the spirits of the poor. In the Settlement movement the rich actually moved to the slum areas and tried to bring culture and education to the neighborhoods.

In the early stages of development neither movement had much appreciation for the other. Settlement workers criticized COS workers for their limited view of poverty. COS workers criticized the settlements as being too sentimental and unscientific. As the movements matured the distinctions and suspicions decreased and mutual projects were undertaken. For instance the juvenile court project in Cook County was conceived by settlement workers who directed the project but depended upon the casework skills of the COS workers to make it a success.[2]

Data collection was important to both movements. COS workers investigated applicants for assistance to determine how much aid they needed and the kind of help required. Settlement workers collected descriptive and statistical data about social conditions and used these data to agitate for social reform.[3]

WOMEN IN THE CHARITY ORGANIZATION MOVEMENT

Josephine Shaw Lowell, director of the New York COS, gave primary importance to virtue, character, and morality. She said charity must tend to raise the character and elevate the moral nature:

Josephine Shaw Lowell (1843–1905) worked for reforms in the working hours of women and the conditions of almshouses and prisons. She was active and in promoting women's suffrage.

> The main instrument to be depended upon, to raise the standard of decency, cleanliness, providence and morality among them must be personal influence, which means that a constant and continued intercourse must be kept up between those who have a high standard and those who have it not, and that the educated and happy and good are to give some of their time regularly and as a duty, year in and year out, to the ignorant, miserable and vicious.[4]

Friendly visitors were committed to relieving distressed women and children and encouraging industry among the poor. Intervention was based on the assumption that the locus of the problem was the individual, and the individual must be the target of change. The one recognized social cause of poverty was undue generosity of the relief agencies.

In the early days of charity organization societies, the paid administrators were men; women did the volunteer work, primarily friendly visiting with clients. As this service became formalized many tasks originally done by volunteers were taken over by professional paid staff.

The practical goal of charity organization workers was to make productive citizens of the poor. From this conservative heritage sprang individually oriented models of casework, group therapy, and the social planning model.

Black organizations

One of the major Negro organizations, the National Urban League, emerged from several philanthropic groups in 1911.

The response of white Americans to the problems of industrialization can be learned by reading any United States history book, but little has been written about how blacks approached those problems. What became of the millions of blacks newly freed from slavery? How were they to live with no money and no land? Freedmen's Bureau, a federal program that lasted six years and provided education and jobs for poor southern whites and blacks, was a temporary answer. Ultimately the only solution for blacks was self-help.[5] Blacks had to rely on each other to survive.

The black self-help groups frequently organized into mutual benefit societies that provided for ill members and took care of burial and survivors when a member died. These societies included the Black Masons, the Knights of Pythias, Good Samaritan Societies,[6] Free African Society,[7] and the Brown Fellowship Society. By 1850 almost half the adult black population belonged to a mutual benefit society.[8]

After the Civil War the prevalence and the severity of black needs increased. In response cooperatives like the Farmer's Improvement Society of Texas were formed. One purpose of these organizations was to form cooperative buying and selling groups in the Oakland, Texas area.[9] Cooperatives worked to improve the homes of rural and village blacks and improve farming methods. This was in addition to the usual benefits of the mutual relief societies such as sick and death benefits to members and their families.

Views of the economic structure

The most important characteristic shared by the white settlement and charity movements was a belief in the basic economic and political structure. On the other hand, there were social reformers and revolutionaries of all races who believed that the social structure precluded equality. Instead of seeing society as open to all races and sexes, they suggested societal institutions ensured continued inequality. These men and women fought for social, political, and economic equality by pursuing a fundamental redistribution of power to overcome structured inequality. Since these reformers believed that inequality was structured into society, they believed societal transformation was necessary to overcome structured inequality.

While these groups are not frequently viewed as an integral piece of social work heritage, their work has significantly affected social work practice and might be considered forerunners of present day radical practitioners. The groups mentioned in the analysis will be radical feminists, abolitionists, Councils of the Unemployed, Black Labor Councils, the Rank and File Movement, the National Welfare Rights and Civil Rights Movements, and the Black Panther Movement.

Analysis of the conservative, liberal, and radical heritage of professional practice will be presented. Presentation of the underlying philosophies is designed to clarify the connections between each of the ideologies and the practice which has subsequently developed.

Conservative heritage

Charity Organization Society

The Charity Organization Society movement began in England in 1867 and is another example of an idea borrowed from England.

The Charity Organization Society movement is clearly the best known and most powerful source of conservative ideology in the profession. The COS solution to poverty was to investigate and register the poor, and to cooperate and coordinate with other relief agencies. These methods would overcome pauperism. The COS movement discounted the economic and social contributions to poverty and saw it instead as a "disease resulting from personal defect and evil acts—laziness, deceitfulness, intemperance, improvidence, inefficiency, extravagence, and sexual vices."[10] Charity was a necessary evil that provided material resources for the poor when they really needed spiritual sustenance. No principle of practice ranked higher in importance than coordinating relief to make certain no one received too much material assistance; too much charity was detrimental to character. Friendly visiting was a substitute for alms[11]; the friendly visitor was to show the poor how to be thrifty, moral, and industrious. Poverty was an evil which could only be overcome by the good influence of the rich. Even into the twentieth century mothers' pensions and allowances were fought earnestly and sometimes bitterly by COS leaders including Mary Richmond, Director of the New York COS. Richmond believed that sound relief practices could not be achieved under governmental auspices.[12]

Mary Richmond wrote about the methods of working with the poor in *Social Diagnosis* (1917).

Theory and Method. The COS movement was a response of the upper and middle class to the social dislocations of the post Civil War industrial city. Theirs was a scientific approach to poverty guided by social Darwinist assumptions. Contempt for the poor was at the heart of social Darwinism, which misapplied evolutionary concepts to human society.[13] The phrase *survival of the fittest* originated with Herbert Spencer (1820–1903) who actually drew his ideas from Thomas Malthus rather than Charles Darwin. In fact Spencer wrote about social selection almost ten years before the publication of Darwin's *Origin of The Species* (1859). Spencer argued that the poor were unfit and society would be better off if they were eliminated; welfare could only interfere with natural selection and perpetuate the weak. Survival of the fittest was a rallying cry against the poor. It was used to oppose social legislation and justify indifference to the terrible living conditions of the poor.[14] Spencer hypothesized that if relief practices supported dependency and misfits, then doling out relief would weaken the human species. The only appropriate assistance was work or spiritual guidance; the only remedy for poverty was self-help. "Protecting the ill-favored in the struggle for existence would only permit them to multiply and this could lead to no other result than a disastrous weakening of the species."[15]

National Urban League

To read about more contemporary issues in working with minority groups see Chapter 18.

Paralleling the white COS movement in method and goals was the National Urban League, the most outstanding example of blacks working with whites to gain equality in the deliverance of social services. Springing from the Committee on Urban Conditions Among Negroes (founded in 1910), the National Urban League was formed on October 16, 1911 and became the first black national social service agency. Its stated purpose was

> to carry on preventive and constructive social work among blacks, for improving their social and economic conditions in urban centers; to bring about coordination and cooperation between existing agencies working in interest of Negroes and to develop agencies where necessary; to secure and train Black social workers; to make studies in cities to carry out these objectives.[16]

During its early years the Urban League concentrated on what it termed scientific social work.[17] Its main focus was researching and collecting data to downplay the racial and class differences among people. It also searched for solutions to problems such as unstable families, poverty, and illiteracy.

One quality of the National Urban League missing in many black human service organizations is its ability to change and adapt to the needs of its constituents. For instance, during the World War I era the migration of blacks to the city and an increase in job availability prompted the Urban League to provide vocational training and guidance. After the war the Urban League was again called upon, this time to protect the rights of those same workers.[18] Once the war ended, the demand for workers decreased, and of course blacks were the most expendable.

While white America was experiencing the roaring twenties, blacks were singing the same old last hired first fired blues. One reason was the inability of blacks to get into the white labor unions. In 1925 the National Urban League created its Department of Industrial Relations to improve its associations with the American Federation of Labor.[19] This department also studied the job market so it could direct blacks to locations where jobs were available. This tactic served to distribute black workers and helped alleviate overcrowding.

With the 1940s the objectives of the National Urban League took on a broader perspective. The move was toward higher standards of social work technique, in fact suggesting all its departments and affiliates should be headed by social workers, sociologists, or somebody knowledgeable in matters of race relations.[20] The hunger, poverty, illiteracy, poor health, and lack of recreation blacks faced were all believed caused by segregation and discrimination based on white racism.[21]

So after thirty years of working with relatively conservative white groups the National Urban League came to a new assessment of the root of blacks' problems—white racism. It was then that the National Urban League became more than just a small time labor organization and became a full-fledged civil rights group. Currently it possesses the largest annual budget of any black civil rights organization.

The National Urban League has put its money to good use. By 1975 it had a National Skills Bank with a centralized computer system containing information on job openings throughout the country. A person can submit his qualifications into the skills bank and be matched to an appropriate job. A law enforcement and manpower project helps recruit black police in an attempt to combat police brutality. The League's Street Academies help dropouts finish high school. The list of projects and accomplishments goes on and on.

Throughout its history the Urban League has remained interracial in its make-up and social work-oriented in its objectives. It works to reform society, but it views the problems that blacks face not so much as capitalism, but as white racism within the capitalist framework that dispossess blacks.

Leaders in the Urban League met at the 78th Annual Forum of the National Conference on Social Welfare in Atlantic City in 1951. Photo courtesy of Social Welfare History Archives, University of Minnesota.

Social feminists and women's clubs

For some examples of contemporary issues facing women see Chapter 19.

The women active in the COS movement could be described as social feminists since they reflected the proper role of women. Their duty was to expand women's family role to the wider society; they had no desire to interfere in the work of men. A charter of the Charitable Society of St. Louis reflects this view of women.

> Women would yield to men the care of government for which they are better qualified . . . . it is hoped that women may claim (without danger of neglecting the dearer sense of duty which lies at home) the more humble field of benevolence as their sphere of action.[22]

Sheila Rothman described this role as "virtuous womanhood."[23] The woman was to develop her social, intellectual, and moral power in the most perfect manner to become a better mother, wife, and social reformer. She was to obtain the appropriate scientific and practical training for her distinct profession as housekeeper, nurse of infants and the sick, educator of children, trainer of servants and minister of charities. In the role of the virtuous woman, a wife had the awesome responsibility for both home and society; she was to tame her husband.[24] A contemporary woman made this comment:

> Few women understand at the outset that in marrying, they have simply captured a wild animal . . . the taming of which is to be the life work of the woman who has taken him in charge. . . . The duty is imposed upon her by high heaven, to reduce all these grand, untamed life-forces to order . . . to make them subservient to the behests of her nature, and to those vast undying interests which to these two and to their posterity center in the home.[25]

Rothman suggests that women had the mandate to "tame" society as well. Another quotation from that period suggested that women

> use their power to purify and amend society. If a woman be herself pure and noble-hearted she will come into every circle as a person does into a heated room who carries with him the freshness of the woods.[26]

Black women's clubs

Black churches and settlement houses alone could not handle the enormous needs of black people. Near the turn of the century a new idea began to take hold in the black community. Women's clubs started forming all over the country; denied entry into white clubs, black women formed their own. These clubs provided the same benefits to their members that benevolent societies and Mason-like organizations offered men. But in contrast to male organizations, women's clubs reached out to the community. The male organizations sought to maintain themselves first and foremost. The social orientation of the women's clubs was consistent with the proper role of women for that era; women were called upon to tame society.

By 1903 there were seven black women's clubs in Chicago alone.[27] The primary source of social welfare services available to blacks during the early 1900's, these clubs sponsored kindergartens, nursery schools, day care centers, and orphanages for young children. They also operated homes for elderly people and supported various educational institutions with fundraising activities.[28] Black women engaged in the same activities as white social reformers of the Progressive Era, but the movements were separate. Once educational institutions were developed many women used the buildings for community organizing as well. Emma J. Wilson, Cornelia Bowen, Lucy Lainey, Charlotte Hawkins Brown, Nancy Burroughs, and Mary McLeod Bethune were among the most active organizers.[29] These women raised financial support for schools and community buildings and in turn used them as centers or meeting places to conduct their social action activities.

The women's clubs of this period offered a wide range of activities. For instance the Tuskegee Women's Club organized in 1895 by Mary Margaret Washington gave advice on child care, home economics, gardening, and sewing—skills necessary for the housewife.[30] It also operated a missionary and a small library, and helped out at the local jail and nearest settlement house. It participated in women's suffrage and political activities as well.[31]

Ida B. Wells formed a different kind of club. Lynching and raping blacks was at an all time high in the late 1800's. Wells started a national anti-lynching crusade in 1892, and in 1893 the Ida B. Wells Club was formed.[32] Wells launched an all-out campaign to discourage lynching and raping. She spoke out against the white abuse of black women and in defense of black womanhood; she worked to eliminate police brutality and discrimination.

The medical profession

The medical profession was a powerful influence circumscribing the role of women. In spite of their great virtue women were weak. Menstruation was considered not only an illness but also temporary insanity. Women were instructed to take to bed for pregnancy and menstruation. By equating normal body functions with disease, the culture made even competent women unfit for extensive activity outside the home. Women were more virtuous, civilized, and moral but always susceptible to physical and mental derangement. Vassar, the first women's college (founded in 1865), treated women more like patients than students.[33]

Liberal heritage

The settlement house movement

Toynbee Hall was founded in 1884; Hull House and the Henry Street settlement followed in 1889 and 1893 respectively.

The settlement philosophy was very different from the scientific philanthropy of the charity organization society. The first settlement, Toynbee Hall in England, was organized by a group of university students and faculty attempting to practice Christian socialism in the London slums. The most well known settlements in the United States were Hull House in Chicago, established by Jane Addams after visiting Toynbee Hall in England, and Henry Street Settlement in New York, established by Lillian Wald.

The settlement houses embodied the neighborhood ideal—the desire to create a community among people living in the same area. Interdependence of social groups was important and necessary to cope with problems. Settlement workers believed that by helping individuals they actually helped the whole community.

Concepts underlying the movement were participation in small groups, a belief in the democratic ways of life and a two-way responsibility between the community and the individual. Settlement workers attempted to unite the scattered industrial and religious elements thrown together in the great cities; they did not confine their commitment to the poor but included the working class as well. They felt that by developing a truly democratic society, America could provide all people the means to develop fully and allow them to take their places as responsible members of the human race.

BLACK SETTLEMENT HOUSES

During this period the large scale migration of blacks to the North increased the need for settlement houses to help blacks adjust to life in the city. The White Rose Industrial Association was just such a place. It was organized in 1895 to train black girls and women to be self-sufficient and to live "right."[34] This association also set up settlement houses and offered aid to travelers in Norfolk, Virginia, and New York City for girls coming up from the South. In Chicago, Celia Parker Wooley established the Frederick Douglass Center in 1904.[35] The Frederick Douglass Center had a workshop and clubroom for boys, and held classes in manual training and domestic service. By today's standards these services may seem minor or unimportant, but at the time those were the only jobs open to blacks and such training represented a valuable opportunity for the unemployed.

THEORY AND METHOD

The primary settlement methodology followed John Dewey's "learning by doing" model. Like Dewey, settlement workers believed in informality and

One of the main goals of settlements such as Hartley House was to improve conditions for people living in the cities and to restore communication between the college-educated and the working class. Photo courtesy of Social Welfare History Archives, University of Minnesota.

starting where the group was. The first university group work course was taught in 1920 by Grace Coyle at Case Western Reserve. Settlement workers were much slower than caseworkers to teach their methods in a university setting. The conflict between settlement workers and friendly visitors continued between groupworkers and caseworkers.

Group work was the primary social work methodology used by settlement workers.

Group work practice by settlement house workers has been referred to as the "social reconstruction through political action" phase of welfare work. They were committed to a democratic and humane society, and their accomplishments reflect their goals. Participating in society was necessary to mental health and preservation of the democratic ideal.

PROFESSIONAL EDUCATION

While early settlement workers were not concerned with codifying their methods, academics (particularly Grace Coyle) eventually described and taught settlement methods.

Grace Longwell Coyle (1892–1962) is credited with defining the method of group work.

The first theoretical work on group work method, considered as significant for group work as *Social Diagnosis* was to casework, was written by Grace Coyle.[36] *Social Processes in Organized Groups* appeared in 1930, ten years after Professor Coyle had taught the first group work methods course at the School of Applied Social Sciences of Western Reserve University in Cleveland. Like the settlement house workers, Coyle envisioned working with groups to encourage growth of responsibility to the larger society. Democracy was to be enhanced and enriched by "socially intelligent citizens."[37] Group workers did not join the National Association of Social Workers until 1955.

THE SOCIAL GOSPEL

Settlement workers tended to be young single women and the first generation of women who were college-educated. But though educated, traditional male positions were not open to them. If they were to have meaningful careers, a new professional domain had to be developed.

> Women were marginal in the male-dominated public world of occupations. For them a professional qualification was a badge of competence, a symbol of their right to follow paid professional work. For men such work was merely a phase in life, not a career in itself. The identity of the male derived from his role as clergyman, or from his prospects in business or the major professions. Men from good social backgrounds who engaged in social work for any length of time tended to participate in an organizing or managing capacity. It was the women's settlements then which developed training for social work as a career.[38]

The tremendous suffering caused by heavy immigration, industrialization, and urbanization offered many women an opportunity to be socially useful. Then too settlement work was often attractive to these women because of their commitment to the "social gospel"; the social gospel was an attempt by conscientious ministers and priests to get their congregations to address problems of the poor. They wanted to establish the kingdom of God on earth through social reform. Washington Gladden, a Yale divinity professor warned that

> "unless the churches became thoroughly aroused by these issues and used their influence to promote fundamental reform, they would cease to be religious bodies and degenerate into institutions for the preservation of meaningless rites and superstitions."[39]

Influenced by the militant social gospel movement of the day, the women saw in settlement work "a sense of mission to God and to mankind that had been aroused and nurtured by the religion of their youth."[40] Instead of entering the ministry, which was closed to women, they chose a life of service to the poor.

Black churches

The black church also played a vital role in the relief of blacks. Released from slavery, blacks were left with the clothes on their backs and their religion. The church stood strong during this period of crisis. Besides establishing missions and giving out various forms of relief, the church also involved itself in labor disputes on behalf of its congregation. Reverend T.W. Walker, for example, pastor of a black church in Birmingham, Alabama helped organize local black women into a union in 1884. Many worked as maids in the homes of more prosperous whites; Reverend Walker showed them they were not getting adequate pay for their work. When the women approached their employers for better wages they were fired. Reverend Walker then united his church in a blacklisting of the employers; eventually the women were rehired and received the requested wage increases.[41] Walker also used his church to form a Christian Relief Society that aided blacks throughout Birmingham.

Chapter 4 discusses the early role of the church as a provider of social welfare. Here again, we see the importance of the church.

Southern blacks were not the only ones in need of services during this period; Northern blacks suffered hardships too, and the black church was there to lend a helping hand. St. Mark's Episcopal Church in New York City led by its pastor Dr. William H. Brooks aided blacks in Harlem, Brooklyn, and the Bronx by establishing social service missions in their communities.[42]

These examples are just two illustrations of how the black church responded to the needs of blacks in the late 1800s. From being advocates for their congregations to providing social services to those in need, black churches were the most prevalent source of social welfare available to blacks from the end of Reconstruction to the 1890s.[43]

Educated motherhood: Role of woman

The Progressive Era ushered in a new ideal for womanhood that Rothman labels "educated motherhood."[44] A new attitude toward children suggested children needed more than affectionate care; they needed mothers with sophisticated skills of management too. Educators suggested that mothers mold their children; suddenly women needed great preparation for the mothering task. The kindergarten was a societal response to this new perception, but settlement women also worked with individual mothers. Workers taught cleanliness and instilled American values. Settlement house workers were making home visits similar to the charity organization society ladies with several important differences—settlement house women were helping neighbors; they emphasized hygiene and child development instead of virtue, temperance, and frugality.[45]

The Progressive Era lasted from 1896 to 1916.

This service to the poor went far beyond the traditional boundaries. Settlement house workers developed playgrounds, improved housing, worked for housing legislation, organized neighborhood protests against destructive city regulation, helped immigrants negotiate with traditional agencies, and were peripherally involved in helping rural Southern blacks adjust to the city. Settlement house workers supported labor, fought against child labor, and protested political corruption.

Black Council for National Defense

Women have always dominated the social service field and black social welfare is no different from the mainstream in this regard. Because of segregation blacks were excluded from services available to whites; the burden of relief for blacks fell upon black women.[46] Organizations like the Tuskegee Women's Club, the Atlanta Neighborhood Union, and the Council for National Defense provided vital services for the black population. Women like Ida B. Wells and Mary Margaret Washington provided the leadership.

Blacks faced difficult years after Reconstruction and before World War I. Those who did not benefit from Reconstruction were left to fend for themselves; without the aid of black service organizations many would have perished. But the contributions of these groups did not stop with the black community. They also played a vital role in World War I. The Committee on Women's Defense Work of the Council for National Defense consisted mainly of black women.[47] It helped care for families of absent soldiers, gave comfort kits to the soldiers, helped conserve and enlarge the food supply, and formed canning clubs. The Committee also brought attention to the high infant mortality rate in this country.[48] It discovered a need for better community health services. To correct these problems the Council set up programs to weigh and measure infants and provide them with milk. In addition, the Committee sought to improve recreational facilities available to youth and pushed for nurse's training for black women. Medical personnel for black people had always been woefully inadequate; the committee compiled and circulated a list of hospitals where black women could be trained.

Summary

The liberal value assumptions inherent in the settlement house movement are reflected in ecological casework, social action models of groupwork, and the grass roots approach to community organization.

The characteristics of the more liberal settlement house and related movements were very different from the characteristics of conservative organizations like the Charity Organization Society. Their emphasis was on social action. They had little concern for scientific theories of poverty or human behavior. They used informal methods—they worked with the community rather than for the community. The poor were suffering because of social conditions, and the way to relieve the suffering was to change those conditions. They also felt that if the opportunity existed, the poor would become contributing members of society. Basic to their belief was that democratic participation of all citizens was in the best interests of both the individual and society.

People of color, feminists, gays, and youth declared that mainstream social work was too white, too middle-class, too patriarchal, and too identified with the bourgeoisie to be relevant to their needs. They created alternative self-controlled agencies: the Black Panther breakfast program, feminist health collectives and shelters for battered women. . . . Most of these were not staffed by professional social workers, although social workers sympathetic to the particular agency's ideology were sometimes employed.[49]

Radical heritage

Social justice movements

Both the liberal and conservative strains of social work have been highly visible and concentrated throughout history. Radical strains have been more diverse and less well organized. The visibility of radical practitioners has varied tremendously throughout the last century. Saul Alinsky, probably the most well known and articulate of radical theorists, identifies what he sees as the goal of community organization—an apt summary of the goals of most radical groups.

A classic text on radical social work practice is *Reveille for Radicals* by Saul Alinsky (1946).

> We are concerned with how to create mass organizations to seize power and give it to the people; to realize the democratic dream of equality, justice, peace, cooperation, equal and full opportunities for education, full and useful employment, health, and the creation of those circumstances in which man can have the chance to live by the values that give meaning to life. We are talking about a mass power organization which will change the world into a place where all men and women walk erect, in the spirit of that credo of the Spanish Civil War, "Better to die on your feet than to live on your knees." This means revolution. . . . There are people who say that it is not revolution, but evolution, that brings about change—but evolution is simply the term used by non-participants to denote a particular sequence of revolutions as they synthesized into a specific major social change.[50]

Taking a leadership role in radical social justice movements has been outside the professional experience and training of most social workers. Not until the War on Poverty released money to train social workers in community organization did social workers begin to specialize in that field. Between 1960 and 1969 the community organization majors rose from 1.5 percent to 9 percent of the social work majors.[51]

Radical approaches to casework, group work and community organization are described in Chapter 6.

Even though the number of community organization specialists has risen, few of these social workers would identify with a radical practice framework. And in fact not all radical practitioners choose to practice community organization; some are caseworkers and group workers. Radical practice can comprise major protest movements, organized action at a community level, or individual casework. Whatever the intervention, radicals view the redistribution of resources and power as the ultimate goal of social work practice. While radical strategies are varied and less clearly defined than those that have come out of the settlement and charity movement, history shows that social work has sometimes facilitated radical movements and sometimes been the target for change for these movements. While the rank and file movement is the only clearly social work movement, social justice movements in general are presented as the third important contribution to social work practice. The history of social justice movements also underscores the degree to which societal attitudes toward women have shaped both social work practice and social policy.

Radical feminists and abolitionists

In contrast to the social feminists involved in the charity organization societies and the social gospel adherents of the settlement movement, some groups, primarily of women, have perceived those reforms as inadequate to deal with the societal human oppression. They have been and continue to be committed to a redistribution of power in society.

The anti-slavery struggle is an important component of this history; a study of this struggle points up not only the oppression of slaves but also of women. Lucretia Mott and Esther Moore were influential members of the anti-slavery movement who helped organize the first anti-slavery convention in 1833. Shortly afterward, they were joined by the Grimke sisters, Sarah and Angeline, from South Carolina. Society became frightened at women's increasing power and influence. White churches, powerful societal institutions, attempted to crush that power and influence. The Orthodox Congregational Church, for example, the largest and most influential ecclesiastical body in Massachusetts, issued a pastoral letter in 1837 calling upon all "churches under their care to defend themselves by closing their doors against the abolitionists who had set aside the laws of God by welcoming women to their platforms and allowing them to speak in public."[52] This letter went on further to define the "proper role" for women.

It may be interesting to contrast this "proper role" for women with the ideal role presented earlier in this chapter.

> We invite your attention to the dangers which at present seem to threaten the female character with wide spread and permanent injury. The appropriate duties and influence of woman are clearly stated in the New Testament. Those duties and that influence are unobtrusive and private, but the source of mighty power. When the mild, dependent, softening influence of woman under the sternness of man's opinions is fully exercised, society feels the effects of it in a thousand forms. The power of woman is her dependence, flowing from the consciousness of that weakness which God has given her for her protection, and which keeps her in those departments of life that form the character of individuals and of the nation. There are social influences which females use in promoting piety and the great objects of Christian benevolence which we cannot too highly commend. We appreciate the unostentatious prayers and effort of woman in advancing the cause of religion at home and abroad; in Sabbath schools; in leading religious inquirers to the pastors for instructions; and in all such associated effort as becomes the modesty of their sex; and earnestly hope that she may abound more and more in these labors of piety and love.

This letter exemplifies how an institution sanctioned by God had sustained slavery of both women and blacks. Not only did women have no rights within the church, they did not even have civil rights in the early 19th century. They were chattels of men, legal minors until they married and civilly dead upon marriage. They were not allowed to attend college, do public speaking, or have legal custody of their children. Like the slaves, they had no part in making the laws that governed them.[53] The church and the state united to keep the Grimmke sisters silent; they were banned by the church from speaking and by legal decree from the city of Charleston. They were informed that if they should return to Charleston, they would suffer mob violence from which the state could not protect them. Church men also effectively blocked the participation of Lucretia Mott and Esther Moore in the World Anti-Slavery Convention in London (1840). They argued that to admit a women was to violate the ordinance of Almighty God.[54]

In 1848 Lucretia Mott and Elizabeth Cady Stanton called the first Equal Rights Convention in Seneca Falls, New York. This was the official beginning of the suffrage struggle. It was seen as an extreme movement because it went against the socially defined roles of women. The fruition of these efforts came seventy years later when the Nineteenth Amendment was passed and women's suffrage became a reality. But women's suffrage started out as a radical movement demanding rights for women *and* blacks; the Nineteenth Amendment did not pass until a much more conservative contingent joined in the struggle. In fact, one argument for passing the amendment was that if blacks (even more lowly than women) could vote, then women must be given the vote too.

This example illustrates the point that often "women's issues" and "minority issues" compete with each other for attention as well as resources.

Unemployed councils

More recent examples of organizing to redistribute power were the Unemployed Councils active during the depression. Groups of men out of work congregated at local relief offices and took over those offices until their demands were met. In Chicago, the Unemployed Council organized 5,000 men to march on relief headquarters demanding three meals a day, free medical attention, tobacco twice a week, the right to hold meetings, and the assurance of no discrimination against council members. They forced the city to rescind a fifty percent cut in relief funds.[55]

Black labor councils

Asa Philip Randolph is probably the most reknown black union organizer. He first came into the national prominence as the leader of the Brotherhood of Sleeping Car Porters. Black railroad porters were denied entrance into the traditional white unions so they were forced to form their own; they were not accepted as members of the American Federation of Labor until 1925.[56] Randolph gradually worked his way up through the ranks and attained a seat on the American Federation of Labor's Executive Board. Randolph was a constant agitator on issues concerning black labor in any form. It was this constant agitation that helped to produce Executive Order 8802, signed by President Franklin Roosevelt on June 6, 1941, banning discrimination in factories working on national defense contracts.[57] Many jobs opened up for blacks, but even this order was inadequate to deal with the problem of discrimination.

That same summer Randolph threatened to organize 50,000–100,000 blacks to march on Washington D.C. because of discriminatory labor practices. This threat prompted the formation of the Fair Employment Practices Commission (FEPC) to investigate these unfair dealings. This establishment of the FEPC was looked on as a great achievement at the time and might have had far-reaching effects, but it did not have the necessary power to punish the wrongdoers it found.[58] A. Philip Randolph was the foremost spokesman for black labor during this time. At a minimum, he forced America to sit up and take notice of blacks as a labor force and helped blacks recognize their latent power as a labor force.

The value of self-help organizations for blacks was emphasized earlier in this chapter.

But Randolph was not the first to attempt to organize the black labor force. Over sixty years before him, in December, 1869, Isaac Myers, a ship caulker, organized a Colored National Labor Convention in Washington.[59] Attended by clerks, ministers, and politicians for the most part, it focused on the economic problems blacks faced. The main resolutions brought from the convention were that workers should organize cooperative trade unions and that there should exist no conflict between labor and capital. This is a clear example of the fact that many years ago blacks recognized that self-help was their only recourse to achieving equality in the field of labor.

Rank and file movement in social work

The rank and file movement in social work was active in the 1930s and 1940s.

Between 1929 and 1942 a visible minority of social workers openly questioned the prevailing values of the American system. They disagreed with the reforms of the New Deal because they saw them as an evasion of the need for a planned society in which production decisions would be based on need not profit. They argued that the economic programs of the New Deal helped big business and big agriculture but not society as a whole.

This group managed to publish their own journal, *Social Work Today*. Its first issue stated the purpose of the journal: to meet "the need for a frank, critical analysis of basic social problems and their relation to social work." It promised to "promote an interest in the fundamental reorganization society must undergo to provide security for all" and to "support labor's struggle for a greater measure of control as the basic condition of reorganization."[60]

Bertha Capen Reynolds felt the philosophy of social work could not be separated from the philosophy and values of society as a whole.

In retrospect it is difficult to determine how much support the rank and file movement or *Social Work Today* had from the social work profession. A number of prominent social workers, including Bertha Capen Reynolds, allowed their names to be used as contributing editors. Individual chapters of the American Association of Social Workers were supportive, but the national organizations chose to remain silent.

May 1942 saw the last issue of *Social Work Today.* The reason for its demise is not totally clear, but it was very likely related to the Nazi invasion of Russia. The journal had taken a strong stand that America should remain neutral during the war. Once the Nazi invasion took place, the position of the journal changed; instead of advocating neutrality, editorials and articles emphasized how social work could contribute to the war effort. The editors of the journal along with the rest of American society decided basic structural change would have to wait for the coming of peace.[61] Not until 1978 did another radical social work journal (*Catalyst*) appear.

Black Panther Party for Self Defense

An excellent example of self-help in social welfare and social service delivery among blacks is the Black Panther Party. Founded in 1966 by Huey Pierce Newton and Bobby Seale, its full name is the Black Panther Party for Self Defense.[62] During their early years the Panthers used the gun as a temporary symbol to draw attention to themselves and show they were ready to defend themselves, but the role of the gun in Panther philosophy has been over-emphasized. It temporarily established the Panthers in the black community as a group that could defend itself by any means necessary against police brutality and harrassment.

Another early and temporary tactic was patrolling the police by riding around black neighborhoods armed with a gun, a law book, and a tape recorder. When they would come upon a black being arrested, they would supervise the proceedings and ensure that the matter was handled correctly. This practice caused many confrontations between Panthers and police, the result of which is well known.

The Black Panther Party (Self Defense was dropped in later years to better emphasize its political nature) has a plan upon which its programs and methods of service are based. Goals include

1. full employment of blacks,
2. the right to control politics of black community,
3. decent housing,
4. education that teaches black history,
5. exemption of blacks from military service,
6. release of all blacks in prison,
7. an end to police brutality,
8. trial by jury of peers, and
9. land, bread, housing, education, clothing, justice and peace.[63]

The Black Panther Party, as an organization, underwent a major change in its goals in the 1970s.

For a time the Panthers alienated themselves from the black community during the late 1960's by becoming an elitist organization, forming coalitions with white radical groups, and emphasizing violence. But as they matured, they began to place more emphasis on local service delivery.

From 1972–1975 the Panthers underwent a vast reorganization and change of emphasis. Survival programs and more locally and community oriented services became the focus. The Oakland Community School, for example, was founded during this period and still operates today.[64] It handles 150 children of nursery and elementary school age. Members help the elderly shop and provide guard details to escort them to the bank to cash their Social Security checks. Free legal aid, free rat and roach control, dances, and martial arts training are examples of other programs.[65] To supplement the inadequate services of hospitals they also operate a volunteer medical research clinic.[66]

Along with the move back to the community, the Panthers also became politically active. Bobby Seale ran for Mayor of Oakland in 1973; although he did not win, he received over 47,000 votes (37 percent) and forced a run-off with the incumbent mayor. Another Black Panther, Elaine Brown, twice ran for city council coming in second both times. She also served as a delegate for Jerry Brown at the Democratic convention.[67]

One facet of the Panthers' organization that did not change was the makeup of its membership. The Panthers began as a black organization and have remained one. One of the group's fundamental beliefs is that black people are primarily responsible for the work to be done in the black community. Self-determination must be a reality within the black community. Panthers believe that whites can help most effectively in their own communities.

During their history the Panthers have entered into alliances and coalitions with white organizations, but their membership has remained black. Upon returning to the black community, they received a warm reception simply because they were offering services the people needed and, just as important, they were bringing services to the people.

Even though evidence suggests that blacks are most effective when using self-help techniques, the dominant form of action taken by blacks has always been integrationist, as the longevity of organizations like the National Association for the Advancement of Colored People and the National Urban League prove. Black separatist organizations have tended to come on the scene in a flourish and then die down in popularity.

National Welfare Rights Organization

One organization that attempted to take advantage of the 1960s wave of self-determination was the National Welfare Rights Organization (NWRO). The National Welfare Rights Organization banded (though loosely) racial groups into an organization demanding rights for poor people. Its size reached as high as 75,000 families grouped in 300 local chapters in 150 cities.[68]

Some of the NWRO's methods were not always well accepted by the public. Many felt that it was much too radical and prone to violence. But the NWRO wanted to grant full citizenship to the poor, and to make this point, members demonstrated, lobbied, negotiated, picketed, boycotted, and did almost anything they thought was necessary to achieve their goals.

The NWRO consisted primarily of welfare recipients and social workers.

One of these goals was a Guaranteed Adequate Income plan. The NWRO wanted every American citizen to be guaranteed a decent, livable income. Another goal was to enroll all eligible people on the welfare rolls. Many people were eligible to receive local, state, or federal assistance but either did not realize they were eligible or were kept from applying by a false sense of pride.[69]

In many ways the NWRO taught welfare recipients how to become more involved in changing public policy.

Because the NWRO was composed of hundreds of local grassroots organizations, the vast majority of its activities concerned local business and survival techniques. Concerned Parents For Adequate Welfare in Queens, New York, for instance, established a program for welfare recipients to get credit at Montgomery Ward.[70] Until then people on public assistance were denied credit. They also pressured the Queen's General Hospital because of its deficiencies in caring for the poor. Some of their daily activities include helping welfare recipients shop and find apartments. They provided babysitting, helped burned out families find furniture, and went with clients to welfare hearings and court appearances.[71]

But radical demonstrations continued. During the late 1960s hundreds of people occupied welfare offices and refused to leave until more liberal benefits were given. At times they were successful.[72] In May of 1969 members of the National Welfare Rights Organization interrupted the meeting of the National Conference on Social Welfare and demanded 35,000 dollars from the delegates to fund the participation of the poor at the 1970 conference. They managed to collect 700 dollars at the meeting with a promise of the balance.[73]

Although their constant fight was for material gains, the National Welfare Rights Organization's greatest contribution was that it put an end, if only temporarily, to the apathy among welfare recipients.[74] No longer did the poor feel guilty when receiving services or shame when cashing their green checks at the supermarket. Now they felt they had a right to a decent living. The National Welfare Rights Organization also put all responsibility for achievement and progress upon the people themselves. It was formed by the people to benefit the people. It operated with a shoestring budget, and it was people that kept it going, not politicians.

By the early 1970s the NWRO was no longer active.

Summary

This chapter has identified the organizational sources of the various ideological perspectives which shape social work practice. The conservative and liberal philosophies of the charity organization and settlement movements have always been the dominant influence on practice. Radical social justice movements have been less influential but a continued presence.

In this chapter, the charity organization movement was introduced as the historical source of conservative practice. Just as conservative assumptions guided the friendly visitors of the 19th century, so do they guide some practitioners in the 1980s. The conservative point of view holds the client is the locus of the problem and hence the target of change. The poor and unemployed suffer because of personal shortcomings. The role of government should be limited; government assistance should go to the private sector to help stimulate the economy and create jobs. Social workers should get the poor to accept dominant values and become productive citizens. While the conservative philosophy is not the philosophy of the social work profession, its prominence in the 1980s shapes federal policy in a way that severely limits practice.

Liberals, like their forebears in the settlement house movement, view social problems as a predictable outcome of industrialization. Government is an integral mechanism designed to protect the poor and to control excesses of the market system. Liberal practitioners continue to seek increased opportunities for oppressed groups, increased control over corporations, and more liberal benefit programs. Liberals do not disregard individual weakness but are just as likely to see environmental causes of problems.

Radical philosophy has guided smaller groups of social workers who have worked for basic restructuring of the economic system. Radical philosophy has guided women, labor, and minorities in fighting for more equitable distribution of societal resources.

References

1. Steven J. Diner, "Scholarship in the Quest for Social Welfare: A Fifty-Year History of the *Social Service Review*," *Social Service Review* 51, no. 1 (March 1977): 3.
2. Diner, "Scholarship."
3. Ibid.
4. Josephine Shaw Lowell, *Public Relief and Private Charity* (New York: 1884), 111. Quoted in Rothman, *Woman's Proper Place*, 74.
5. Toby Ferrell, "Why Not Us?: Blacks and Social Welfare" (Unpublished monograph. 15 September 1982).
6. William Henry Katz, *Eyewitness: The Negro in American History* (New York: Pitman, 1967), 355.
7. Franklin E. Frazier, *The Negro in the U.S.* (Toronto: MacMillan, 1957), 368–369.
8. Benjamin Quarles and Leslie H. Fishel, Jr., *The Black American: A Documentary History* (Glenview, Ill.: Scott, Foresman, 1976), 161.
9. August Meier, *Negro Thought in America, 1880–1915* (Ann Arbor: University of Michigan Press, 1969), 123.
10. Helen Harris Perlman, *Social Casework: A Problem-Solving Process* (Chicago: University of Chicago Press, 1957).

11. Walter Trattner, *From Poor Law to the Welfare State* (New York: Free Press, 1974).
12. Ralph Pumphrey and Muriel Pumphrey, *The Heritage of American Social Work* (New York: Columbia University Press, 1961).
13. Helen Ginsberg, *Poverty, Economics, and Society* (Washington, D.C.: University Press of America, 1981), 89.
14. Ibid., 90.
15. Robert Bremner, *From the Depths* (New York: New York University Press, 1956).
16. Jesse Thomas Moore, Jr., *A Search for Equality: The National Urban League 1910–1961* (University Park: Pennsylvania State University Press, 1981), 47–49.
17. Ibid., 55.
18. Ibid., 59.
19. Ibid., 66.
20. Ibid., 96.
21. Ibid.
22. Susan T. Vandiver, "A Herstory of Women in Social Work," in Norman and Mancuso, op. cit.
23. Sheila Rothman, *Woman's Proper Place* (New York: Basic Books, 1978).
24. Ibid.
25. Ibid.
26. Ibid.
27. Gerda Lerner, "Early Community Work of Black Club Women," *The Journal of Negro History* 59, no. 3 (August 1978): 161.
28. Ibid., 159.
29. Ibid.
30. Ibid.
31. Ibid., 160.
32. Ibid.
33. Rothman, *Woman's Proper Place*.
34. Meier, *Negro Thought* 134.
35. Moore, *A Search for Equality*.
36. Grace Coyle, *Social Process in Organizing Groups* (New York: Harper, 1930).
37. Gerald Handel, *Social Welfare in Western Society* (New York: Random House, 1982), 226.
38. Noel Parry, Michael Rustin, and Carole Satyamurti *Social Work, Welfare, and the State* (Sage, 1982), 25.
39. Bremner, *From the Depths*.
40. Ibid.
41. Moore, *A Search for Equality*.
42. Ibid., 39.
43. Ferrell, "Why Not Us?"
44. Rothman, *Woman's Proper Place*.
45. Ibid.
46. Ferrell, "Why Not Us?"
47. William J. Breen, "Black Women and the Great War: Mobilization and Reform in the South," *The Journal of Southern History* 44, no. 3, (August 1978): 422, 435–436.
48. Ibid., 437.
49. Betty Reed Mandell, "Blurring Definitions of Social Services: Human Services vs. Social Work," *Catalyst* 4, no. 3 (1983): 5–21.
50. Saul Alinksy, *Rules for Radicals* (New York: Vintage, 1972), 3.
51. Rino Patti, *Social Welfare Administration* (Englewood Cliffs, N.J.: Prentice-Hall, 1983).
52. Matilda Joslyn Gage, *Woman, Church and State* (Watertown, Mass.: Persephone Press, 1980).
53. *Social Casework* 1976.
54. Ibid.
55. F. F. Piven, and R. Cloward. *Poor People's Movement* (New York: Pantheon, 1977).
56. Katz, *Eyewitness*, 295
57. Ibid., 434.
58. Ibid., 227.
59. Julius Jacobson, ed., *The Negro and the American Labor Movement* (Garden City, New York: Doubleday and Co., 1968), 28–30.
60. Jacob Fischer, "Social Work Today, 1934–42," *Catalyst* no. 5 (1980): 3–23.
61. Ibid.
62. Thomas R. Frazier, ed., *Afro American History: Primary Sources* (New York: Harcourt, Brace, and World, 1970), 467.
63. Ibid., 468–70.
64. "The Odyssey of Huey Newton." *Time* 112 (13 November 1978): 38.
65. Peter Goldman and Gerald C. Lebenow, "Huey Newton Comes Home," *Newsweek* 90 (11 July 1977): 27.
66. Gwendolyn Evans, "The Panthers' Elaine Brown," *MS.* 9, no. 8 (March 1976): 104–109.
67. Goldman and Lebenow, "Huey Newton," 7.
68. "Welfare Union Steps Up its Demands," *U.S. News and World Report* 66 (23 June 1969), 36.

69. Carolyn P. DuBose, "Champion of Welfare Rights," *Ebony* 25, no. 6 (August 1970): 33.
70. Richard Rogin, "Now It's Welfare Lib," *New York Times Magazine* (27 September 1970), 76.
71. Ibid., 31.
72. *U.S. News*, "Welfare Unions," 35.
73. Ibid., 36.
74. DuBose, "Champion," 33.

CHAPTER SIX

Ideology and Methods: A Developmental View

"In order to understand social work as it is conceptualized and practiced contemporarily, it is necessary to have some idea of how it developed. This is a part of the "why" of social work; contemporary practice is what it is in part because of the way the profession has developed. It is the product of a heritage of responses to need and concern in other times and situations. . . . Because the development of a systematic knowledge base is one of the important aspects of a profession, an understanding of the development of the practice theory enhances one's understanding of contemporary social work practice and theory."[1]

Without denying the continuity of evolution between the social movements of the 19th century and the social workers of the 20th century, one can make a distinction between the volunteer activity of the former and the professional activity of the latter. It is important not to equate charity work and workers with social work and social workers or professional social work thinking with social agency thinking.[2] This chapter analyzes the development of professional goals, roles, activities, techniques, and theory. Again the presentation will show the diversity of practice throughout history rather than attempt to present a monolithic profession.

Development of common methodology

Participants in the Milford Conference met annually from 1923 to 1929 to discuss the profession of social work.

Prior to the formation of the National Association of Social Workers in 1955, caseworkers, groupworkers, and community organizers tended to stress differences rather than commonalities of methodology. At the Milford Conference in 1929 the desirability of generic principles was first seriously debated. This group of distinguished social work educators suggested

> the most significant contribution of social casework to society is. . . . its increasing ability to deal with the human being's capacity for self-maintenance when it has become impaired by these and other deviations from accepted standards of normal social life.[3]

Although the conference originally aimed to identify generic skills, it ended up identifying a generic emphasis. Practitioners were to foster this self-maintenance through their chosen methodology. Not until the 1970s were generic practice skills codified.

One of the basic ideas of the problem solving model is that all social living is, in fact, a problem solving process.

The formation of a single professional organization provided a new impetus to look for commonalities in practice. Hence, in the 1960s it seems the problem solving process was acknowledged by caseworkers, groupworkers, and community organizers as the commonality. Helen Harris Perlman stated, "The casework process is a problem solving process in that it employs the orderly, systematic methods which are basic to any effective thinking and feeling toward action."[4] Helen Northern stressed the problem solving theme in *Social Work With Groups.*[5] Community organization theorists like Murray Ross stressed the problem solving process as an integral piece of community organization methods.[6]

See Chapter 3 for a discussion of the generalist model of social work.

However, the seminal work identifying the commonalities of casework, groupwork, and community organization was *Social Work Practice: Model and Method* by Allen Pincus and Anne Minahan.[7] The book's basic assumption is a common core of concepts, skills, tasks, and activities is essential to the practice of social work, regardless of the many forms that social work practice may take. Pincus and Minahan called their approach the generalist model and explained that their model building was guided by their view of social work practice as a goal-oriented planned change process.

The idea of problem solving and planned change as the key commonalities in social work practice is now commonly accepted. Picard summarizes this idea by stating: "It is important to recognize that differences in philosophy do not change the process of planned change."[8] But while the process of planned change remains consistent across philosophies, clearly the target of the change and the goal of the social work intervention varies with the ideological basis of the social worker's assessment of the problem.

Knowing the historical development of each method (casework, groupwork, and community organization) leads to an appreciation of the breadth of professional experience and expertise culminating in the generalist model and illustrates the effect of ideology on practice. An historical analysis exposes the richness of social work practice. Throughout the short history of the social work profession liberal, radical, and conservative practitioners have worked with individuals, groups, and communities. Historically these professionals identified themselves as caseworkers, groupworkers, and community organizers specializing in either micro or macro systems and direct or indirect practice. Today they would more likely identify themselves as part of the larger profession of social work.

Most social workers today identify with the liberal ideology, but conservatives and radicals also continue to practice. Ideology does not dictate methodology, but it does direct the problem assessment and ultimately the goal and target of the change process. History provides a wealth of examples of adherents to each ideological perspective engaging in each of the major methodologies. Let us trace the historical development of each methodology and how it came to be incorporated into generalist practice.

Casework:

Conservative framework

Most early caseworkers were employed by the Charity Organization Society; as a group they were the first to pursue professionalism. The first summer school training program was conducted in 1898 at the New York School of Philanthropy. Mary Richmond, director of the New York COS and later the Philadelphia COS, organized the first training program and wrote the first social work text *Social Diagnosis* (1917)—the first major presentation of the concepts underlying casework practice.[9]

The New York School of Philanthropy is now the Columbia University School of Social Work.

But in spite of her close association with the COS, Mary Richmond also had a profound interest in the importance of the social environment to casework practice. In *What Is Social Casework* (1922) she clarified the importance of the environment.

> . . . . Social casework . . . in addition to its supplementary value in these other tasks, has a field all its own. That field is the development of personality through the conscious and comprehensive adjustment of social relationships, and within that field the worker is no more occupied with abnormalities of the individual than in the environment, is no more able to neglect the one than the other. The distinctive approach of the caseworker, in fact, is back to the individual by way of his social environment, and wherever adjustment must be effected in this manner, individual by individual, instead of in the mass, there some form of social case work is and will continue to be needed. . . .
>
> To state this in a more formal way is to arrive at my tentative definition: Social case work consists of those processes which develop personality through adjustments consciously effected, individual by individual, between men and their social environment.[10]

Yet Richmond's book was adopted by many who minimized the importance of the environment and concentrated on internal functioning. One reason this occurred was that her book was published when Freudian theory was quite popular. Since Richmond's book presented an atheoretical methodology, Freudianism quickly became the theoretical base for practice.[11] By combining the casework methodology of Mary Richmond and the psychoanalytic theory of Freud, caseworkers felt they were now truly professionals with a unique method and atheoretical base.

Mary E. Richmond (1861–1928) published *Social Diagnosis* after over seventeen years of research and practice

Confident they had attained professional status, the caseworkers invited Abraham Flexner, the leading authority on professional education, to address their national conference in 1915. Flexner startled the young profession of caseworkers by announcing that social casework was not a profession since it did not have a unique method or theoretical base. Soon after Mary Richmond codified social work methods in her book *Social Diagnosis* (1917). Richmond's book provided social work's modus operandi but did not delineate its theoretical base. The lack of a theoretical foundation for this book led many caseworkers to adopt the inherently conservative Freudian theory. Then too, the social and political events of the 1920's pressured caseworkers to become both more conservative and more concerned with professional status.

Liberal framework

See Chapter 5 for more discussion of these issues.

Settlement house workers committed to helping immigrants fit into the American system also employed casework methods. While this required societal acceptance of the immigrants, it also necessitated adjustment counseling for individuals, especially immigrant women who not only had to adjust to the norms of a new country but also had to adjust again as these norms changed. The casework method used by settlement workers closely resembles the ecological casework practiced today.

1920s: The predominance of conservatism

In the wake of a serious economic depression the Progressive Era (1896–1916) reflected a systemic theory of poverty. World War I then overshadowed these social reform approaches to poverty as the entire country channeled its economic and social powers toward the war effort. The military victory of World War I was seen as an endorsement of the American economic system and the business community was idolized. It was not fashionable to rally against the conditions of the workplace or the unemployment produced by shifts in the market; to do so invited questions about one's patriotism. Once again individual weakness was perceived as the cause of poverty; the functioning of the economic system was above question. Furthermore, many Americans were afraid about what was happening in Russia; the fear of Bolshevism made efforts to initiate social reform suspect. In response to Russia's collectivism Americans strove for increased individualism.

> The process of professionalization and abandonment of overt social reform activity was hastened not only by calls to serve one's country, during the World War I crisis, but also by the law and order oppression of the postwar era.[12]

In addition, the country was weary from war. Life was in turmoil: veterans suffered from shell-shock, families struggled to readjust, and women held important positions in the work force. People wanted a return to normal routine, veterans needed treatment and jobs, and women needed to return to the home. Given these conditions, it is little wonder that caseworkers adopted Freudian theory—a theory that identified women as the weaker sex and explained social problems as unresolved complexes or inadequate development in the individual.

Psychiatric social work

In 1918 Mary Cromwell Jarrett organized the first formal training program for psychiatric social workers. Consistent with conservative principles, its purpose was to train social workers to help clients adjust to their social conditions. One target of change was working women who did not relinquish their positions in the work force. Freudian theory justified removing women from positions of power by identifying them as sexually deficient and biologically underdeveloped. Women were counseled to accept their inferior position and adjust to the status quo. Women who resisted were diagnosed as deviant and in need of adjustment-oriented casework.

Mary Cromwell Jarrett (1876–1961) is given credit for the term "psychiatric social worker."

Casework during the depression

With the onset of the depression caseworkers again looked at the social causes of poverty. Casework did not disappear but changed to a more liberal approach to problem assessment. The growing prevalence of poverty made it difficult to suggest its cause was individual weakness. Determining eligibility (let alone worthiness) was almost impossible. Necessity and obvious suffering led caseworkers to assume clients were honest in reporting need. Instead of providing psychiatric casework, caseworkers helped clients adjust to lower incomes. Caseworkers needed a working knowledge of housing conditions, rental rates, food costs, money management, homemaker and health services.

Caseworkers turned from psychoanalysis to education and resource linkage. The environment was a critical component of the problem assessment. The caseworker helped the client manipulate that environment and to use resources and what limited opportunities were available. The caseworker's goal was to help clients maintain themselves at an adequate level of functioning.

In 1935 Ellery Reed, director of the Research Department of the Cincinnati Community Chest, reflected this changed attitude toward the poor and unemployed. He expressed concern that "untrained" caseworkers would not understand what the client was suffering and would further the client's sense of defeat by patronizing sympathy or hard-boiled intolerance. Reed was concerned that thousands of persons without casework training were employed in community chest agencies. The most intolerant were those who had been recruited from the welfare rolls themselves.[13]

> Trained workers, although strongly in favor of work for clients when such can be found, at reasonable wages and under proper conditions, avoid using withdrawal of relief as a threat to club clients into accepting jobs which they sometimes resist as representing a further evidence of humiliation and failure . . . the psychology of defeat is often changed by understanding the social causes of their unemployment.[14]

1940s: An era of theory development

The 1940s brought a renewed emphasis on individual casework. The universities had become more involved in the education of caseworkers and new theories of human behavior and casework intervention were being developed. Leading theoreticians were adherents of the functional or diagnostic schools.

The diagnostic (or psycho-social) school of thought made a systematic effort to identify relevant psycho-social data, evaluate its significance, appraise the problem and the means of change for the client. Although it emanated from a Freudian base, this practice took into account both external and internal problems of the individual.

> Caseworkers at that time were admonished not to dabble in the psychoanalyst's domain of the unconscious and to refrain from dealing directly with the forces of transference, resistance, and repression. Although sensitive to the potency of these hidden motives, workers assumed guardianship of the more conscious and cognitive realms of their clients' lives, thereby entering into their clients' world of daily experiences of coping, planning, and thinking.[15]

The ideas of Florence Hollis are presented in *Casework, A Psycho-Social Therapy* published in 1964.

Florence Hollis, leading theorist of the diagnostic school, suggested that casework could operate on four different treatment levels: to modify the environment, to provide psychological support, to clarify (counseling), and to provide insight.[16] Adherents of the diagnostic school adapted the ego-psychology theories of Hartmann, Erikson, Horney, and Anna Freud to work with clients. Theorists like Hartmann gave greater emphasis to the ego's conscious ability to master cognitive tasks than to the force of intrapsychic drives. Hamilton and Hollis present casework as a "corrective experience" that involves the client's positive identification with the worker and the modification of the client's repetitive dysfunctional habits of living.[17]

The functional approach was based on Otto Rank's will psychology. Will referred to the individual's ability to mobilize himself toward a desired goal: "the deliberate use of time to arouse an awareness of motivation, the focus on the immediate present as the arena for mindful change, and the purposeful focus on the active processes occurring within the helping relationship."[18] Functional theory stressed the source of healing and helping power was part

Jessie Taft (1882–1960), a social work educator and an authority on Rank, translated many of his works into English.

Table 6–1
Contrast of Diagnostic and Functional Models of Casework

	Diagnostic	Functional
Theory	Freudian with an emphasis on the ego and its adaptive capacities.	Otto Rank's Will Psychology
Professional Role	Diagnostician and therapist. Scientific Objectivity	Helper
Client Role	Seen as ill and in need of treatment. May need protection from self or others.	Recipient of some specific service. Sets own goals.
Developed by	Gordon Hamilton	Virginia Robinson Jesse Taft
Method	Casework or group work. Treatment is a blend of processes directed toward modifying the person, his social or interpersonal environment, both person and environment, and the exchanges between them. The worker-client relationship is a major determinant of how much the client will be helped. In contrast to the specific social service of the functional school, the caseworker helps the client develop an understanding of the individual and his adaptive capacities. Relief of suffering can be obtained by the client's expressing fears, anxieties, and hostilities in the treatment interview.	Casework or group work. Casework is a method for engaging a client through a relationship process, essentially one-to-one, in the use of a social service toward the individual's and the general social welfare.

of the individual's innate power to grow and change. The "function" of the agency rather than the client's need became the pivotal problem in the helping process. Caseworkers were expected to know the helping process only as it related to the specific agency setting such as foster care, public welfare, or prisons. They were not expected to be knowledgeable about helping in situations unrelated to their own professional settings. Treatment consisted of support and stimulation to use all of the client's available capacities for decision and action, but the client, not the professional, determined the final outcome.

Virginia Robinson and Jessie Taft, lifelong companions, both taught at the Pennsylvania School of Social Work in the 1940s and 1950s.

Virginia Robinson and Jesse Taft were the primary theoreticians of the functional approach. In *A Changing Psychology in Social Casework* (1930), Robinson made the client the center of the process of helping, and made the client's choice of material from the past the caseworker's guide to what was important to the present.[19] It placed the dynamic of casework in the relationship between the client and the caseworker. Sharing with someone who had professional training made it possible for the client to see the problem more clearly and take hold of it with more courage and effectiveness.[20]

The 1940s were an important period for professional development as lively and sometimes heated debate took place between these different schools of thought. The intellectual stimulation generated by the debate was conducive to the growth of professional knowledge. Bertha Capen Reynolds, opposing the prevailing point of view, suggested that contributions made by the psychodynamic and functional schools were complementary, not contradictory.[21] The penetrating diagnoses and the dynamic relationships of each stressed something essential, and each, without the other, could be carried to an absurdity. "If diagnosis means *seeing into* or *seeing through,* that is not possible without a relationship with the client which releases him to be himself, to explore his trouble freely because a helping person is there."[22] Reynolds also felt professional relationships were enhanced by scientific training. Diagnosis effectively developed "weaves together the threads that both client and caseworker draw from life and work on together."[23] Subsequently Helen Harris Perlman's problem solving approach attempted to achieve a measure of rapport between the diagnostic and functional methods.[24]

Charlotte Towle (1896–1966) was influenced by both the functional and the diagnostic schools and tried to integrate the ideas in her writing and teaching at the University of Chicago.

1950s: The age of insecurity

The 1950s was an age of insecurity. An ever present possibility of war and an economic system undergoing major changes contributed to a sense of uncertainty. A nation-wide shift in the labor market occurred as increased specialization and routinization of work became the guiding principles of industry. With increased routinization, workers found less opportunity for creativity and less job satisfaction. Money became the single most important symbol of success and human relations were secondary. Political repressiveness also contributed to the lack of emphasis on poverty as a public issue. This was the heyday of McCarthyism and the witch-hunt—conformity was the byword. Working for

As an example, a classic social work text, *Common Human Needs,* was withdrawn by the Federal Security Agency who published it.

social change or even calling attention to flaws in American society was dangerous. Critics of American society were labeled communists and sometimes blacklisted or even imprisoned.[25]

Many people sought help for problems caused by financial pressures. But though these problems may have been caused by shifts in the labor market, they were treated as individual problems. Technique was stressed; a casework relationship that incorporated acceptance and self-determination was emphasized. Intake became a specialization. Emphasizing individual causes of poverty prompted some major methodological changes. Since individual problems engendered poverty, individual therapy was the supposed solution.

It was during the 1950s that caseworkers began to see behavior therapy as a valuable psychotherapeutic enterprise. Skinner, like Freud before him, provided a basis for believing that much of human behavior could be understood in terms of the individual.[26] Wolpe outlined techniques based on operant conditioning that were reportedly successful in dealing with neurotic behavior.[27] These techniques, assertiveness training, and systematic desensitization (as applied in the 50s), basically ignored environmental influences on individual behavior.

For a more contemporary look at behavior therapy as part of the social work knowledge base, see Chapter 11.

1960s: The elimination of poverty

The 1960s present a dramatic contrast between the different strains in the field of social work. Caseworkers, who were basically the powerholders in the profession, believed that with enough trained caseworkers poverty could be eliminated. Data from small pilot studies done in New York City supported their claims. Findings from these studies were reflected in the 1956 Social Security Amendments and became the rationale for the 1962 service amendments to the Social Security Act, which provided considerable federal money for training and hiring social workers. The profession accepted the premise that individual weakness caused poverty. If only the profession had adequate resources to train enough caseworkers, poverty would be eliminated. Since this analysis overlooked the social roots of poverty, casework became suspect because it could not deliver on its claim to "cure" poverty.

1970s: Human potential

New therapies introduced in the 1970s expanded the domain of therapists from dealing with problems to developing human potential. Some better known techniques included transactional analysis, gestalt therapy, EST, Rolfing, and sensitivity training. While these techniques were not used very extensively in dealing with the poor, they introduced a whole new middle-class market in which social workers could provide services. Ecological casework also gained prominence in the 70's; it differed from conservative or psychoanalytically-oriented casework primarily in the emphasis it placed on the individual's con-

Carel Germaine and Alex Gitterman describe the ecological perspective in *The Life Model of Social Work Practice* (1980).

tribution to the problem.[28] As would be expected, the ecological model stressed environmental causes of the problem.

Auerswald gives an example of what he sees as the difference between a specialist (psychiatric caseworker) and a social worker operating from an ecological perspective.[29] His example illustrates the differences in casework practice emanating from the differences between the philosophies of charity organization societies and the settlement houses. With the specialist orientation (similar to charity organization society), the person's problem is seen as belonging primarily to that person; the individual is sent to a specialist trained to deal with that certain kind of problem. The specialist, of course, sees the problem as an individual matter and does not look at how the person, the family, and the community relate; he is "often in the position of desperately trying to replace a fuse when the entire community power line has broken down."[30] In contrast Auerswald suggests that if the individual's problem is seen from a system's (ecological) perspective, it is much easier to determine in what life arenas the individual, the family, or the group need assistance to combat the anomie and dehumanizing character of our age. Pincus and Minahan reflect this idea when they suggest that the client and the target system may be very different individuals.[31]

Casework: Radical framework

Radical casework and therapy are recent social work phenomena with little history before the late 1960s. Traditional or psychoanalytic casework as generally practiced is politically conservative. Radical therapy, on the other hand, is more sensitive to the oppressive features of society. The goal of radical therapy is to help people recognize the injustices that may be causing or increasing their emotional distress. It raises the client's awareness that a competitive, consumption-oriented society shapes attitudes toward ourselves and those around us. Radical therapists encourage clients to understand how social institutions oppress them rather than delving into their past and blaming their parents. The desired outcome of radical therapy is client empowerment that leads the client to oppose the forces oppressing them. Radical therapists would suggest "therapy" is essential to dealing with internalized oppression and only someone with specific liberating therapeutic techniques can reintegrate a meaningful sense of self and the world. Misuse of therapy can lead to increased alienation rather than client empowerment.

Feminist therapy is one example of radical therapy. The literature on feminist therapy is vague about what a feminist therapist is and what he does. Walstedt defined a feminist psychotherapist as "someone who supports and understands the desire for female equality."[32] Silveira defined feminist therapy as "counseling which affirms women's liberation and proceeds without power differentials between the counselor and the counseled."[33] In an attempt to determine more specifically the nature and definition of feminist therapy,

Thomas surveyed 135 therapists and interviewed 19 in some depth. She found that feminist therapy does not fit the traditional theoretical model, i.e., a series of propositions and techniques, a model for problem assessment, and a training methodology, but instead is a part of a social movement or a belief system.[34]

Belief systems identified in Thomas's research were consistent in many ways. Some prevalent views may be enumerated.

Feminist social work practice as defined here is a good example of radical social work.

1. A rejection of the view that because of biological differences men and women serve different functions and engage in different social roles. Rather, a belief that different sex roles are the result of social conditioning and an institutionalized sexual class system.
2. Sex roles are oppressive to both men and women. There is particular emphasis on the psychological oppression of women, pointing to the damage suffered in regard to self-concept, identity formation, intellectual development and aspirations, and overall emotional well-being.
3. A strong emphasis on the potential of women and a belief that the woman knows what she wants and what is best for her.
4. A desire to free women of roles that prohibit them from realizing their goals.
5. A belief that the frame of reference for problem assessment must reach beyond traditional forms of assessment and address the psychological effects of the woman's social conditioning, sex roles, and secondary status.
6. An attempt to foster equality or mutuality in the relationship with the client. They view the traditional power imbalance between client and therapist as dysfunctional.
7. An emphasis on problem solving rather than emotive therapy.
8. A deliberate use of self—their values and experiences in conducting therapy.
9. A stress on increased independence. Therapy should not be a dependency producing interaction.
10. Therapy should include consciousness-raising.[35]

Thomas summarizes feminist therapy in a manner consistent with radical therapy. She suggests that unlike most therapy, feminist therapy does not merely alleviate stress but provides a way of life for the therapist and possibly the client as well.

Casework summary

Casework, that is, work with individuals, takes on goals based on the ideology adopted by the practitioner. Caseworkers facilitate individual adjustment, link resources, or empower clients based on their philosophy of people and society.

Psychiatric casework was first practiced by charity organization society workers and psychiatric caseworkers today tend to reflect assumptions similar to those underlying the charity organization movement. Ecological casework (under other names) was first practiced in the settlement houses; ecological (or systems-oriented) casework today operates on philosophical principles congruent with those of settlement workers. While radical casework has only developed over the last fifteen years, it is guided by principles consistent with radical social justice movements.

Group work

Group work—social work with more than one person—can also be practiced from a liberal, radical, or conservative perspective. The various forms of group work also spring from the philosophies inherent in the history of social work movements.

Conservative forms of group work

The theory and methods of the Charity Organization Society is presented in Chapter 5.

While the charity organization society movement is not usually seen as a source of group work practice, remedial group therapists tend to operate from assumptions common to conservative casework and the Charity Organization Society. Remedial group work emphasizes treating the behavior of the individual. The primary difference between psychiatric casework and remedial groupwork is the use of the group rather than the individual as a treatment tool. Remedial groupwork originally came into vogue with the child guidance movement. Psychiatrist Fritz Redl found that withdrawn or obstreperous children were not successful in the typical activity group. The social worker tried to develop the child's ability to relate to his peers and work cooperatively through specially designed therapy groups.

Robert Vinter, social work's leading remedial groupwork theoretician, wrote extensively on the process and knowledge necessary for group treatment. In Vinter's model the group leader was an eclectic therapist guided by social role theory, ego psychology, group dynamics, and more recently systems theory. Vinter outlined several principles for social work practice.

Principles summarizing a problem solving approach to group work are presented here.

1. Specific treatment goals must be established for each member of the client group.
2. The worker attempts to define group purposes so they are consistent with the several treatment goals established for the individual members.
3. The worker helps the group to develop the system of norms and values that is in accord with the worker's treatment goals.
4. The worker prestructures the content for group sessions based on the worker's knowledge of individuals expressed through his treatment goals as well as his knowledge of structural characteristics and processes that take place within the group.[36]

In this model the group leader uses a problem solving approach and is in a professional position of clinical authority. While the authority must be accepted by the group, it is not fundamentally established by the group. The therapist does for the client as well as with the client. There is no assumption of group autonomy.[37]

The client is someone suffering from social maladaptation or deficiency. The clinician helps the individual achieve a more desirable state of social functioning. Individual treatment goals supersede group goals and the group leader selects group members.

Group work as a treatment modality first gained popularity in the 1940s when a number of important theoretical advances were made. Guidelines were developed for diagnostic consideration of individual's functioning in the group. Criteria were developed for forming effective groups. The foundation was set for clinical team participation. Finally, there was diagnostic utilization of groups where other treatment modalities co-exist. Group therapy guided by individualistic conservative assumptions continues to be a prominent aspect of psychotherapy practice today.

Group work: Liberal perspective

While the settlement house movement furnished a more systems-oriented view to work with individuals, its major contribution was to the group work methodology. Vida Scudder summarized the methodology of the settlement movement.

The concepts underlying the settlement house movement are presented in Chapter 5.

> It aims to bring to bear on the seemingly hopeless misery of our great cities that spiritual help, that uplifting life which comes through the power of a broad and organized effort.[38]

Two types of group work—reciprocal and social goals models—have had their genesis in the settlement movement.

RECIPROCAL GROUP WORK

The reciprocal model aimed to help individuals by getting them more active in community decision making.[39] This individual move toward better citizenship benefited both the individual and society. Reciprocal group work seems to blend an ecological approach to casework with greater citizen participation in much the same way the settlement movement tried to train immigrants to citizenship and provide them the services they needed to meet their larger goal—to make the immigrants a force for progressive change. With effective services immigrants would join the ranks as reformers.[40]

Current reciprocal group work has been conceptualized by William Schwartz as a mediating model of group work. This view supposes the individual and the group to be interdependent with each other and with society. The

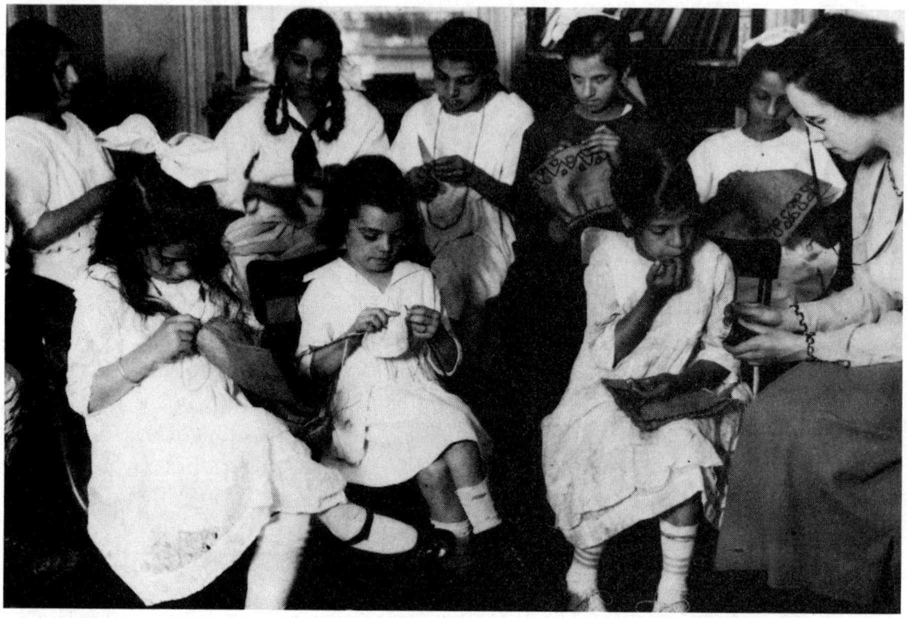

Some of the earliest forms of group work occured in the settlement houses. This group of young girls is learning to knit and sew. Photo courtesy of Social Welfare History Archives, University of Minnesota.

group leader is a mediator reaching out to help clients reach for what they need. The leader works with the client not only for the client; the leader himself has a deep investment in and emotional commitment to the process. The group's goals relate to self-fulfillment as individuals and as a group. The process serves both the individual and society.

This model presupposes an organic, systemic relationship between individual and society. The group nourishes and mediates individual and societal functioning. Breakdown in this interdependency can be insignificant or critical. There is no a priori prescription or desired outcome—the ideal state is mutual aid. Field and social systems are the underlying theoretical base with ideas from Adler, Fromm, and Sullivan carrying over into the assumptions that explain individual motivation and capacity for reaching out to collectives. Schwartz identified the tasks a reciprocal group worker must accomplish.

The primary tasks of the reciprocal group worker are presented here.

1. The task of searching out the common ground between the client's perception of his own need and the aspects of social demand with which he is faced.
2. The task of detecting and challenging the obstacles which obscure the common ground and frustrate the efforts of people to identify their own self-interest with that of their "significant others."
3. The task of contributing data—ideas, facts, and value-concepts—which are not available to the client and which may prove useful to him in atempting to cope

with that part of social reality which is involved in the problems on which he is working.

4. The task of "lending a vision" to the client in which the worker both reveals himself as one whose own hopes and aspirations are strongly invested in the interaction between people and society and projects a deep feeling for that which represents individual well-being and the social good.
5. The task of defining the requirements and the limits of the situation in which the client-worker system is set. These rules and boundaries establish the context for the "working contract" which binds the client and the agency to each other and which creates the conditions under which both client and worker assume their respective functions.[41]

Three primary principles guide this model of group work: the leader helps the group to strengthen its goals through consideration of what it has in common with what group members are seeking; the leader interprets his role and defines a clear contract; and the leader protects the focus of the work. The reciprocal model requires honesty and forthrightness with no withholding of information. Therapy includes intensive individualizing and social focusing. This model of group work stresses individual mental health, and it assumes a unity between community participation and psychological functioning. Basically it is designed to help the client help himself.

SOCIAL GOALS MODEL

The social goals model assumes that group work creates a broader base of knowledge and a skilled citizenry. The social worker is an "influence" person responsible for cultivating social consciousness in groups and also developing closer interpersonal relations. The leader is not to dictate a particular view but does seek to inculcate a value of social responsibility. Theoreticians that have influenced this model are economic and political democracy theorists such as Dewey, Kilpatrick, and Lindeman. Relevant theories include opportunity theory, conflict, deprivation, and inter-generational alienation. This model also assumes a unity between social action and individual mental health.

Groupwork: Radical framework

The radical group work framework can be compared to the radical casework perspective earlier in this chapter.

Radicals find group work methods particularly useful. Like radical caseworkers, group workers eliminate the authoritarian role of the therapist. While some individual therapy may be necessary, most radical therapy takes place in groups. Participants learn skills for helping one another. In addition to individual therapy, radicals involve clients in consciousness-raising groups, discussion groups, or classes which raise fundamental questions about the social system. In this setting the participant's power is maximized, and the authoritarian atmosphere is decreased.

Some radicals see group consciousness-raising a major means of liberation. Leonard typifies this group in the following statement.

> Working with people. . . in an action system to achieve change will, for the radical social worker, be a major method by which critical consciousness can develop. The group is central to such work, for conscientization cannot be undertaken by one individual on his own. Group support helps to carry the tensions and anxieties which a developing critical consciousness and the liberating action that must follow are bound to create. . . . By working in group situations, the radical social worker has available a range of strategies which he shares with the group. The strategies of campaigns, collaboration, and confrontation are to be used by the action system in relation to the target of intervention, according to a careful political assessment of concrete situation. . . [42]

While traditional reciprocal group work strives to help people adjust and become active citizens, radical reciprocal group work strives to empower clients and encourage them to bring about social change. The social goals model differs primarily in terms of the targets of change. The traditional social goals model assumes the present system is good and with citizen participation the government will be responsive to the poor and powerless in society. The radical social goals model suggests that inequality is inherent in the social system and that people must change the system. The change itself entails a redistribution of political and economic power.

Summary: Group work

This brief study of the history of group work methods provides further evidence for the argument that the problem solving process is consistent across models of social work practice. It has also been shown that the size of group one chooses to intervene in is not related to one's ideological perspective. Conservatives, liberals, and radicals have all found group methods conducive to their professional goals.

Community organization

The clearest ideological differences between traditional methods and radical methods is apparent in community organization. The earliest form of community organization dates back to the social planning techniques of the Charity Organization Society. Methods similar to locality development were widely adopted by the settlement workers. Social action methods were used by abolitionists (1840s) and unemployed worker councils (1920s) but did not become part of social work methodology until the 1960s.

Methods used by abolitionists and unemployed worker councils are discussed in Chapter 5.

This chapter will begin discussion of community organization methods with the earliest form of community organization—social planning. Locality development models will be briefly addressed as their history is similar to the social goals model of group work. Finally, social action community organization will be presented. Social action is the most frequently discussed and the least frequently used model of organizing.

Social planning

This approach to community organization dates back to the Charity Organization Society (COS) and is consistent with its ideology and methodology. A major goal of the COS was to bring rationality and control to relief giving. Administration as a specialization in social work has grown out of this approach to practice.

The social planning model is based on the premise that social change is a rational process. The community organizer or administrator identifies the social problem, its causes, and possible solutions. His professional roles may include data collector, analyst, program designer, implementor, and evaluator. The social planning model approaches community organization as a technical process to solve problems. The way to deal with social problems is through rational planning—deliberate, planned, and controlled change. Social planning requires expert planners with technical abilities.

The first community organizers to go through the educational system were groomed to manage organizations like Red Feather, Community Chest, and United Way. The assumptions underlying these programs has been that the social order is good and that deviations from this view are problematic. In the past and even today these organizations stress the desirability of private charity and giving only to the worthy poor. This ideological base is more consistent with the charity organization movement than either the settlement house or radical feminist ideology.

Community organization as a primary method of social work practice was not accepted by CSWE until 1962.

Rino Patti has summarized the history of administration in social work practice concisely.[43] His work illustrates the assumptions underlying administrative practice and its development in relationship to casework, the more prevalent social work method.

Patti suggests that social workers have been extensively involved in administration from the profession's beginnings. Since the first charity organization society was founded, social workers have been called upon to provide administrative leadership as well as policy planning and expertise for the social welfare sector. Some of our most luminous figures, Harry Hopkins, Julia Lathrop, and Grace Abbott, to name a few, have devoted much of their professional lives to developing and administering social programs. Patti identifies four periods (1900–1935, 1935–1960, 1960–1970, and 1970–1975) and analyzes developments in each period.

1900–1935

As social work entered the twentieth century, it comprised a loosely-knit network of volunteers, civic leaders, social reformers, labor organizers, paid workers, and agency administrators working in diverse settings and with diverse clientele. This network shared a commitment to improve the conditions of the poor and make the organization of charitable agencies more rational. There was no doubt within the profession that social casework was the preeminent methodology; administration received little attention. The consensus declared that administration was just an extension of the knowledge and skills of casework. The only training necessary for administration was training in social casework and experience as a caseworker.

Sophonisba Breckinridge (1866–1949) offered the first course in public welfare administration in 1921 at the University of Chicago.

Edith Abbott and Sophonisba Breckinridge, both of the Chicago School of Civics and Philanthropy, disagreed with this approach to administration. They argued that direct service practice was a necessary but insufficient preparation for administrative practice. They believed all caseworkers should prepare to eventually assume administrative and policy-making responsibilities. This debate reflects an ever present tension in social work—the tension between those who believe the profession's purpose is to discover and try to eliminate the causes of social problems, and those who argue that the profession's most important task is to treat the victims of social ills.[44]

While Abbott and Breckinridge believed sound administration required a specific base of knowledge, professionals in general assumed knowledge of and competence in social casework was the foundation of all professional practice. Having acquired this foundation, all the caseworker needed was experience and familiarity with an agency to become an administrator.

Few schools offered courses in administration and those that did failed to give them very much institutional support. Research and scholarship did not fare much better. The professional literature of that period suggests there was no national forum where the theory and practice of administration were discussed. A review of the literature suggests the only concern about administrators was that they serve an apprenticeship in direct services and adopt the norms and values of the profession. Some suggest this legacy continues to plague social work administration today.

While there was a need for more social work administrators, schools of social work were slow to respond to this demand.

1935–1960

The Depression had a tremendous effect on social work in general and social planning and administration in particular. Consistent with the COS philosophy that welfare should be under private auspices, what little administrative knowledge that had been developed addressed primarily the area of private voluntary services. The Social Security Act of 1935 stimulated an enormous demand for individuals to manage public social services. In spite of social work's lack of experience in public programs, government looked to it to help plan and administer the delivery of services. When federal grants were made available to train personnel to work in public agencies, schools reexamined their curricula to respond to the new demand. Rather than trying to develop new knowledge and skills necessary for effective administration, social work educators commonly tried to determine how existing casework and groupwork skills could be applied to supervisory responsibilities in public agencies.

Mary Parker Follett (1868–1933) articulated the psychological and philosophical foundations of administration.

Mary Parker Follett was an exception to this approach.[45] She wrote her first book on administration in 1924 but the field of management was too new to recognize her contributions; Follett was not fully appreciated until after her death in 1933. In 1940 many of her lectures were collected in a volume entitled *Dynamic Administraton.* Another volume of her works appeared in 1949.

The 1940s was actually the point when social work began to see administration as a special area of practice. In 1950 a major study of social work education criticized the profession for its failure to adequately prepare social workers for administrative positions.

1960S TO THE PRESENT

Administration is seen today as one of the primary social work methods in schools of social work.

The 1960s saw a tremendous expansion of the welfare bureaucracy but without a concurrent expansion in the number of students majoring in administration. Perhaps the generally negative view of social institutions at that time prompted students to see their role as fighting bureaucracies not running them. Fiscal scarcity in the 1970s had a profound effect on program managers too. While administrators in the sixties advocated program expansion, administrators in the seventies assumed new burdens of diminishing funds and increasing accountability. Social work was unprepared to provide professional managers to oversee either the expansion or the contraction of services. If this condition persists the profession risks losing not only status and jobs but also even more importantly the opportunity to espouse its traditional values and objectives.

There has been some response to this danger. As of 1982, at least forty schools had specialized administration programs; in 1976 the first social work journal devoted specificially to administration was founded. Still much remains to be done if social work is to continue to provide needed leadership in public and private agencies.

SUMMARY: SOCIAL PLANNING

The period from 1930 to 1960 saw the acceptance of administration as a bona fide method of social work practice, though some educators still insisted it was secondary to casework and actively resisted it. But in spite of this resistance, there was widespread incorporation of introductory administration content in social work education. The social planning practitioners of community organization had progressed from running charitable societies to running major governmental programs. The research and scholarship needed to prepare these practitioners lagged considerably behind the need. Early practitioners could draw upon their knowledge of casework and groupwork, but in the area they were required to practice (administration), they were limited to practical wisdom developed through trial and error. Social welfare administration is likely to be a growing area in social work practice for some time to come.

Locality development

Locality development is similar in both philosophy and technique to the social goals model of group work. Both methodologies flow from practices established in the settlement house movement. Since settlement workers were more concerned with pragmatic intervention than conceptualizing what they were doing, their methodology was not codified as early as casework's.

The roles that a social worker may use in locality development are presented in Chapter 3.

The goal of locality development is to improve social and economic conditions. Technological changes have produced an urban industrial society with social dislocation and alienation. In this model, dissatisfaction motivates change, and self-initiated change is believed to be more permanent than imposed change. This approach assumes that people want change and will work for change, and that pursuing change will lead to greater social integration. What the people of the community need is a facilitator who will give them confidence and know-how, increase their ability to solve problems, and help them achieve consensus and commitment. Involving the community in solving the problem is of paramount importance. The community knows best what it needs, and the change will be more permanent if the community works together to bring it about.

The community's capacity to change is related to the degree of integration and affected by apathy and prejudice as well as history and structure. The locality developer strives to overcome divisive and destructive tendencies among groups and to build common values and a consensus of community goals.

Specific examples of working with communities are given in Chapter 15.

The locality developer works primarily from a systems perspective. The community is essentially a social structural unit, a system in a system made of systems. As a social system the community tends toward stability—it tends to retain existing patterns of solving problems. Problems occur when established patterns become inadequate to deal with external change. The community organizer must assess three specific types of strain: faulty distribution of power, faulty patterns of energy or resource mobilization and use, and inadequate communication systems.

Given the community's conservative tendency, resistance tends to arise from four major sources: fear of the unknown or fear of ability to make the necessary change, reluctance to give up present conditions, existing patterns of relationships within systems and to other systems, and not knowing where to obtain assistance in making changes. The community organizer must address and overcome the client system's resistance to change and must overcome the divisive and destructive tendencies among groups to build common values and consensus.

SUMMARY: LOCALITY DEVELOPMENT

Locality development methods were practiced extensively in the settlement house movement. During the 1950s, locality development began to be taught in social work methods. The Community Action Programs sponsored by the War on Poverty adopted the assumptions of the locality development model (maximum feasible participation) and developed a considerable market for social workers with these skills. The 1980s has clearly experienced a move away from these organizing principles and a movement back toward technical social planning.

The major assumptions underlying locality development are summarized by Rothman.

1. Community change can best be pursued through broad participation of a wide spectrum of people.
2. Planning should be done at the community level with the community setting the goals.
3. The emphasis is on process not outcome.[46]

Social action

In stark contrast to the assumptions and tactics of social planning and locality development, lies the social action approach. Saul Alinksy, Frances Fox Piven, Richard Cloward, and George Wiley are the best known social action theorists. Consistent with radical principles, each of these theorists has been significantly involved in the practice of social action principles.

Piven and Cloward analyze both the conditions, potentials, and roles necessary for effective organizing.[47] First of all, they argue that leaders or organizers do not create social movements; rather social movements rise in response to momentous change in the social order. This analysis assumes the elite (or the ruling order) will not respond unless the lower-class threaten the social order.

Piven and Cloward suggest that many community organization theorists overlook the fact that protest and the shape it takes are determined by the institutional structure. We are so taken with the myth of political pluralism that we do not even realize our political strategies are not freely chosen. We do not see the constraints inherent in the social structure. Another failure Piven and Cloward see in traditional community organization strategy is the inability to understand who protests. They suggest that, contrary to popular belief, it is not the most alienated or oppressed who protest but rather those whose lives are rooted in the institutional context—people who are integrated into a social group. The people most capable of protesting are those drawn together by work or some other common base and with some type of common target to strike. The potential gains of protest are also structurally limited; these authors suggest that any concessions the protesters might gain are only those consistent with the interests of dominant economic groups.

Yet in spite of the many limitations Piven and Cloward see in organizing the poor, they set lofty goals for the radical organizer. Traditional community organization goals aim to reform; radical community organization goals aim to procure a bigger piece of the pie for the lower class. Organizers are limited but encouraged to enlarge the potential influence of the lower class however they can. In essence, then, the contributions of the radical community organizer are limited by social conditions, that is, community organizers cannot plan protests. They must wait for a protest to occur and then pursue strategies that escalate its momentum and impact.

Alinsky believed that in order for change to occur, conflict had to be generated.

Saul Alinsky, the father of radical methodology, would not disagree with the general principles developed by Piven and Cloward but would suggest that social action is possible and a redistribution of power and income can be attained through action at a community level. His strategies are outlined in *Rules for Radicals.*[48] He would assume that a disadvantaged group needs to be organized to receive its fair share from larger society, and redistributing power and resources is accomplished by making changes in the formal policies of organizations or communities. Alinsky would suggest that the effectiveness of these strategies is proven by programs like Model Cities and the Office on Economic Opportunity.

An explanation of private troubles and public issues is presented in Chapter 1.

Galper believes opportunities for radical community organizers abound in everyday practice.[49] He suggests their key task is to link immediate problems with longer-range agenda. (This is similar to the idea of linking "private troubles" and "public issues".) Each worker assignment will then be seen in terms of long-run movement building on structural changes. Every project or work assignment then offers numerous opportunities for linkage with the broader political process.

Summary: Community organization

Community organization, social work, or problem solving on a community level consists of a variety of techniques and goals. Just as casework and group work varied according to the practitioner's ideological perspective, so does community organization. The professional's view of the individual, the community, the state, and the economic system lead to diverse practical applications. Since the client system of the community organizer is by definition larger than that of casework or group work, it has the potential to make a greater impact on society. Community organization can either support the status quo or foster significant redistribution of resources.

Social work today

The debate over intrapsychic or environmental intervention continues today. While the profession articulates the poor as the primary target population and the interface of the individual and environment as the unique area of professional expertise, this does not seem to be reflected by present day social work students. Rubin and Johnson studied the interests and aspirations of 257 students entering direct practice program in 8 master of social work programs. They found most students saw the MSW as a route to becoming psychotherapists in private practice. These entering students claimed little commitment to social work's mission, dual focus, functions, or clientele.

> In particular, there is a pervasive impression that more and more of those entering the social work profession do so to work as psychotherapists in independent private practice—at the expense of those populations that need social workers in the public sector to help them obtain essential resources and acceptable living conditions.[50]

Social work educators have practical, theoretical, and philosophical concerns about the conservatism of today's MSW students. On a practical level, what becomes of a profession that concedes its unique domain and tries to compete with more established professions? Since practice is based on traditional social work roles and functions, which theory will guide this "new" profession? On a philosophical level, the concern is well stated by Rubin and Johnson.

> Social work's commitment to equity, social responsibility, relatedness, and sacrifice should be a source of pride for practitioners and should not be dismissed on the road to the practice of psychotherapy.[51]

The seriousness of this concern was underlined by an editorial that appeared in the *Journal of Education for Social Work* (Spring 1984, Vol. 20, No. 2). Hans Falck suggested that a paper by Rubin and Johnson

> . . . brings into focus a problem of which many of us have been intuitively aware for several years. That is, substantial numbers of students in schools of social work believe they are preparing for the private practice of psychotherapy.

Falck contended psychotherapy has little to do with social work or its societal mandate. He argued that social work's logic, tradition, and history are based on a commitment to help the poor. Falck rejected as rationalization the argument that the poor will not receive psychotherapy if it is not available through private agencies.

Until social workers reject public financing of their professional education, Falck believes social workers must serve society since their education "was made possible by those they elect to serve *and by those they do not.*"

Chapter summary

This chapter has traced the evolution of professional methodology. The early 1900s marks the onset of professionalization of "helpers." Mary Richmond,

Jane Addams, Grace Coyle, Vida Scudder, and the Abbott sisters are but a few of the individuals who contributed to professional practice by codifying its methods.

The prominence of the various methodologies has been closely linked with the prevailing ideology of the time. This remains true today as witnessed by the concern of social work educators that the conservative ideology of present MSW students will lead to a loss of the dual focus of practice. If the profession responds to the conservative ideology of the day and deserts traditional roles, functions, and clientele, will these be taken over by the newly emerging human service profession?

History suggests some interesting answers. Perhaps social work will continue on its conservative trend as long as the national temper is conservative but will reverse itself when the national temper changes again; clearly this is what has occurred historically. On the other hand social workers may not have a constitutency to return to if new professions claim the domain they are now deserting. Not only has there been an upsurge in the training of generic human service workers but the nursing profession too has taken an increasingly environmental approach to curing and preventing disease.

This review of history suggests both caution and optimism for the potential social worker. Historically the profession has accommodated liberal, conservative, and radical practitioners within its ranks. The danger is that the profession itself may be losing its focus and therefore its unique domain. The study of history provides a long-run perspective from which to view the pros and cons of these issues.

References

1. Louise C. Johnson, *Social Work Practice: A Generalist Approach* (Boston: Allyn and Bacon, 1981).
2. Herman Levin, "Conservatism of Social Work," *Social Service Review* 56, no. 4 (December 1982): 607.
3. Social Casework Generic and Specific: A Report of the Milford Conference (Reprint, Washington, D.C.,: National Association of Social Workers, 1974).
4. Helen Harris Perlman, *Social Casework: A Problem-solving Process* (Chicago: University of Chicago Press, 1957), 3.
5. Helen Northern, *Social Work with Groups* (New York: Columbia, 1969).
6. Murray Ross, *Community Organization: Theory, Principles, and Practice* (New York: Harper, 1955).
7. Allen Pincus and Anne Minahan, *Social Work Practice: Model and Method* (Itasca, Ill.: Peacock, 1973).
8. Betty Picard, *An Introduction to Social Work: A Primer,* revised ed., (Homewood, Ill.: Dorsey Press, 1979), 89.
9. Mary Richmond, *Social Diagnosis* (New York Russell Sage, 1917).
10. ———, *What Is Social Casework,* (New York: Russell Sage, 1922), 98–99.
11. Herman Borenzweig, "Social Work and Psychoanalytic Theory," *Social Work* 16, no. 1 (January 1971).

12. Levin, "Conservatism," 613.
13. Ellery Reed, "Efforts of Social Workers toward Social Reorganization," *Social Forces* xiv (1935), 88.
14. Ibid.
15. Howard Goldstein, "Cognitive Approaches to Direct Practice," *Social Service Review* 56, no. 4 (December 1982): 546.
16. Florence Hollis, *Casework: A Psychosocial Approach,* (New York: Random House, 1964).
17. Goldstein, "Cognitive Approaches," 546.
18. Ibid.
19. Virginia Robinson, *A Changing Psychology of Social Work,* Philadelphia: University of Philadelphia Press, 1930).
20. Bertha Capen Reynolds, *Social Work and Social Living* (New York: Citadel Press, 1951), 108.
21. Ibid.
22. Ibid.
23. Ibid.
24. Gordon Hamilton, *Theory and Practice of Social Casework* (New York: Columbia University Press, 1051).
25. Helen Ginsburg, *Poverty, Economics, and Society* (Washington, D.C.: University Press of America, 1981), 129.
26. B. F. Skinner, *Science and Human Behavior* (New York: Macmillan, 1953).
27. J. Wolpe, *Psychotherapy by Reciprocal Inhibition* (Stanford: Stanford University Press, 1958).
28. Carel Germain, "The Ecological Perspective in Casework Practice," *Social Casework* 54 (June 1973): 223–230.
29. Edgar Auerswald, "Interdisciplinary versus Ecological Approach," *Family Process* 7 (September 1968): 202–215.
30. Ibid.
31. Pincus and Minahan, *Social Work Practice.*
32. *Joyce Walstedt, The Anatomy of Oppression* (Pittsburgh: Know, 1971).
33. Jeanette Silveria, *The Effects of Sexism on Thought* (Pittsburgh: Know, 1971).
34. Susan A. Thomas, "Theory and Practice in Feminist Therapy," *Social Work* 13 (November 1977): 447–454.
35. Ibid.
36. Robert Vinter, *The Essential Components of Social Group Work Practice* (Ann Arbor, Michigan: University of Michigan School of Social Work, 1955).
37. Catherine Papell and Beulah Roberts Rothman, "Social Group Work Models: Possession and Heritage," *Journal of Education for Social Work* no. 2 (Fall 1966): 66.
38. Walter Trattner, *From Poor Law to The Welfare State* (New York: Free Press, 1974).
39. Vinter, *Essential Components.*
40. *Ralph Pumphrey and Muriel Pumphrey, The Heritage of American Social Work* (New York Columbia University Press, 1961).
41. William Schwartz, "The Social Worker in the Group," *Social Welfare Forum* (1961): 155.
42. Peter Leonard, "Towards a Paradigm for Radical Practice," in *Radical Social Work,* ed. Roy Bailey and Mike Brake (New York: Pantheon, 1976).
43. Rino Patti, *Social Welfare Administration* (Englewood Cliffs, N.J.: Prentice-Hall, 1983).
44. Stephen J. Diner, "Scholarship in the Quest for Social Welfare: A Fifty-Year History of the *Social Service Review,*" *Social Service Review* 51, no. 1 (March 1977).
45. Myron Weiner, *Human Services Management,* (Homewood, III.: Dorsey Press, 1982).
46. Fred Cox, John L. Erlich, Jack Rothman, and John E. Tropman, eds., *Strategies of Community Organization,* 3rd ed. (Itasca, III.: Peacock, 1979), 354–400.
47. Frances Fox Piven, and Richard Cloward, *Poor People's Movement* (New York: PANTHEON, 1977).
48. Saul Alinsky, *Rules for Radicals* (New York: Vintage, 1972).
49. Jeffry Galper, *Radical Social Work* (Englewood Cliffs, N.J.: Prentice-Hall, 1980).
50. Allen Rubin and Peter J. Johnson, "Direct Practice Interests of Entering MSW Students," *Journal of Education for Social Work* 20, no. 2 (Spring 1984): 5.
51. Ibid.

PART III

THE PROFESSION OF SOCIAL WORK

"It is important to remember that ethical decision making takes place within the context of professional values."[1]

A debate in many professions is the question of unionization. The Community and Social Agency Employees Union was an example of a social work union active in the 1950s. Photo courtesy of Social Welfare History Archives, University of Minnesota.

Throughout this text social work is viewed as it relates to the political, social, and economic environment. Part Three, however, examines the profession internally. Chapter Seven analyzes the attributes of a profession and also evaluates the degree to which each of these attributes is present in social work. Chapter Eight describes the organizations that govern and accredit the profession and identifies the levels of practice delineated by these organizations. The analysis then moves to a process approach that focuses on the interactions of groups within the profession, exchanges between professions and their external environment, and the movement of occupations toward professional status. In this context the external forces (political, social, or economic) are deemphasized and forces within the profession are given prominence.

Chapter Nine moves to a wider view of human service professions. Seemingly homogenous, professions are in fact loose amalgamations of groups that incorporate considerable diversity along with certain unifying characteristics. This chapter is designed to aid students in identifying that human service profession they would be most suited for and to develop realistic role expectations for other professionals with whom they will work.

on midterm

Attributes of Social Work

"No other profession is as self-examining and critically self-conscious as social work. There are many reasons for this phenomenon. In part, it relates to the profession's young history, to its ambiguous position in society, and to its multiple purposes and functions. . . In more elegant and "scientific" language social work activities consist of provision of resources, restoration of functioning and prevention of dysfunction and promotion of social well-being."[1]

This chapter summarizes the issues of professionalization as they relate to social work. What are the characteristics of a profession? To what degree does social work practice contain these characteristics? What are the functions and dysfunctions of increased professionalization for social work practice?

A debate about whether social work is a profession, a subprofession, or a paraprofession may seem irrelevant to an introductory social work class. However, the degree to which any occupational group possesses professional attributes has a significant effect on how that group operates in society. Professionalism and its role in social work has been a source of controversy among practitioners since the 1915 National Conference on Charities and Corrections.

Chapter 9 compares the components of several human service professions.

Today the National Association of Social Workers (NASW) strongly advocates licensure (the ultimate criterion of a profession), but when licensing legislation is introduced much of the opposition (in individual states) comes from social workers themselves. Since social workers tend to be their own worst enemy in the licensing battle, an early and thorough understanding of the debate is in order.

Currently over thirty-five states have some type of licensing regulations for social workers.

The reasons for resistance to licensing are varied. In some cases, licensing is perceived as a threat or a costly burden; in others resistance is based on the premise that including educational requirements in licensing discriminates against the educationally deprived, particularly racial minorities. To list all of the reasons why individual social workers oppose licensing would be time-consuming and probably not very enlightening. What is potentially more enlightening is an analysis of the philosophical debate that surrounds increased professionalism. A brief presentation of the arguments for and against licensing will be followed by a discussion of professional attributes.

There is some controversy over whether licensing is ultimately more beneficial to the client or to the social worker.

On the surface it seems natural that social workers would actively support increased professionalization. Benefits to the profession would include increased pay, prestige, community support, more money for research, and possibly a higher caliber of people entering the profession. The client should also receive increased protection and a higher quality of service. If social workers were licensed one of the most immediate benefits to the client would be the protection of confidential privilege; clients could confide in social workers without fear that the courts could require their social workers to testify against them. Licensing could also be expected to improve the quality control in the profession; without licensing there is no ready mechanism for sanctioning unethical or incompetent social workers. Many social workers also believe that licensing would increase the profession's power base; the public would be more likely to accept its advocacy of clients if social work were perceived as an "authority" that would lead to more effective advocacy for clients.

In contrast to this altruistic service-centered approach to professionalism, a conflicting perspective suggests professions are instruments of social control that protect and are guided by elite values and interests. Edelman reflects this view.

> The lay public by and large adopts the professional perspective; for its major concern is to believe that others can be trusted to handle the problem, which is potentially threatening to them but not a part of their every day lives. This public reaction is the politically crucial one, for it confers power upon professionals and legitimizes their norms for society generally. . . . . The special language of the helping professions extends and enlarges authority as well as defining and maintaining it. . . . The helping professions are the most effective contemporary agents of social conformity and isolation. In playing this political role they undergrid the entire political structure, yet are largely spared from self-criticism, from political criticism, and even from political observation through a special symbolic language.[2]

From this perspective professionalization is the process by which members of the working class are socialized to enforce the interests of the ruling class on their own class. Instead of protecting clients, licensing protects the professional. As professionalization increases so does the price of services; at the same time the access of the poor to those services decreases. Social workers who oppose licensing also question how effectively professionals can police themselves. To assess the validity of each of these positions requires familiarity with what is meant by a profession.

Attributes of a profession

Although social welfare activities have always existed, it is less than a century since the movement toward professionalism was set in motion. The debate continues as to whether social work is really a profession.

In 1957 Ernest Greenwood published the seminal article that identified five attributes of a profession: systematic theory, professional authority, community sanction, a code of ethics, and a professional culture.[3] Twenty years later, after analyzing the findings of twenty-four other investigators who had reported empirical studies during the intervening years, Greenwood suggested there are actually only three distinguishing attributes; all other characteristics are derivatives of these basic attributes. Other authors have identified as many as twelve attributes of a profession.[4] In fact, Greenwood recently commented that so much emphasis has been placed on what constitutes a profession that professional journals are filled with articles that could appropriately be entitled, "Model, Model on the Wall Are We a Profession After All?"[5]

As early as 1915 Abraham Flexner questioned whether or not social work was a profession.

Disagreement exists over the criteria on which to judge a profession.

The three basic attributes incorporating all of these more specific qualities are the cognitive (or intellectual) component, the collectivity orientation (or service) component, and the monopolistic component of professionalism.[6]

The National Conference on Social Welfare (NCSW), which began as the National Conference of Charities and Corrections in 1873, was the major annual forum for the discussion of national issues affecting social work. Photo courtesy of Social Welfare History Archives, University of Minnesota.

Cognitive or intellectual component

The knowledge base of cognitive component of social work is presented in Part IV

In Greenwood's model professional expertise must be grounded in a body of theory that is relatively abstract, systematic, and communicable, and that is being tested, clarified, and restructured constantly. Mastering this body of theory requires a college education that is carefully designed and intellectually demanding. Social workers must deal with three levels of theory in their professional education—a general theory of humanity, practice theory, and specific theories of practice.

A general theory of humanity includes an understanding of human behavior and the social environment that incorporates knowledge of human growth, development, and functioning and an understanding of the interrelationships between people. This theoretical body encompasses concepts of how human systems develop, change, and dysfunction, and how interrelationships between systems are formed and continue to operate or dysfunction.[7] This knowledge base includes the understanding of general political, social, and economic systems in addition to unique systems.

Practice theory is a statement of the nature of the principles and processes of the profession and of the responsibilities assumed by the practitioner. This incorporates professional norms and values. In other words, social workers must learn to use their theoretical knowledge in a manner consistent with the methods and values of the profession.

Finally, social workers seek mastery of theories of practice—the specific operational procedures and skills of the social work profession.[8] Some currently popular theories of practice include the generalist model,[9] life model,[10] and task-centered model,[11] as well as the traditional casework, groupwork, and community organization models.

GENERAL BODY OF THEORY

These disciplines are compared in Chapter 9.

An example of a "knowledge statement" is "one out of every four girls experiences sexual abuse." A "value statement" is "sexual abuse of chldren is wrong."

The body of theory applicable to social work emanates from sociology, psychology, economics, political science, and related disciplines. Little of that theory has been thoroughly tested, however; practitioners are largely dependent upon assumptive knowledge that has not actually been tested but is conducive to empirical investigation. Bartlett suggests social workers have knowledge propositions which are verifiable and appear in the form of rigorous objective statements.[12] Knowledge statements describe what can be confirmed; value statements describe what is preferred. Both are important, but they are not equivalent.

Choice of a theory may also be dictated by the agency and its commitment to a particular theory.

Garvin agrees that while values and theories are not interchangeable, they are interrelated.[13] Values have a substantive effect on which theory a social worker will employ. Garvin suggests that the role of the social worker in each setting also determines the theory she will adopt. To what degree is the social worker responsible for bringing about change in the situation? How serious is the problem behavior? What control does the social worker seek to exert?

This relationship can be seen in the historical debate between the functionalist and diagnostic schools of thought discussed in Chapter Six. Gordon Hamilton and adherents of the diagnostic school saw the social work process as "study, diagnosis, and treatment." Hamilton's theoretical framework was psychoanalytic and this influenced her view of personality and practice. Clients were viewed as the locus of their problems; they needed professional help to be cured. Jesse Taft and the functionalists did not see the client as sick or deviant but as a person requesting a specific service. Their practice was based on theory developed by Otto Rank that stressed the strength of the ego.

The debate between the "diagnostic" and "functionalist" perspectives was strongest in the 1930s and 1940s.

Each of these theories has had a substantial impact on how social work practice has developed but certainly neither of these theories constitute *the* theoretical base of social work practice. In the 1940s the theoretical debate centered on Psychoanalysis vs. Ego Psychology. In the 1970s the debate centered on systems and learning theory. In the 1980s ego psychology has regained prominence. Throughout history there have also been radical theoreticians (such as Reynolds, Van Kleeck, Fischer, Piven and Cloward, Gil, and Galper) who have insisted that social work needs to address power and conflict theory as it relates to the profession and to clients. If being a profession requires consensus on what constitutes *the* body of theory, then social work does not meet this criterion. All social workers agree that practice must be guided by theory; but the question of which theory has not been answered.

THEORY BASE IN THE NASW CODE OF ETHICS

The profession's strong commitment to theory-based practice is reflected in the NASW Code of Ethics, which guides the social worker to become and remain proficient in professional practice and the performance of professional functions. It requires that the social worker accept responsibility for employment only on the basis of existing competence or the intention to acquire the necessary competence. It prohibits the social worker from misrepresenting professional qualifications, education, experience, or affiliations.

The original Code of Ethics was adopted in 1960. The most recent version appears at the end of this chapter.

The code also encourages social workers to engage in scholarship and research to expand the knowledge base while at the same time protecting participants from unwarranted physical or mental discomfort, distress, harm, danger, or deprivation. Social workers who evaluate services or cases should discuss them only for professional purposes and only with persons directly and professionally concerned with them. Information obtained about participants in research must also be treated as confidential.

Social work as a profession has a firm commitment to theory development and theory-based practice, but most social workers would agree that the complexity of problems they deal with are not amenable to explanation by a single body of theory; in spite of the lack of consensus on which theory is most useful, the profession has developed a considerable body of knowledge to guide practitioners; and finally, the profession is better served by avoiding premature closure on what one theory should guide practice.

The mandate for service

A commitment to service directs the social worker to provide the best possible service to every client regardless of the client's problem or social status and to put the client's needs ahead of the worker's should there be a conflict. Social work has traditionally been the primary profession serving the most socially and financially oppressed groups in our society. Private practitioners who serve clients for a fee are the exception, although some evidence suggests they may be less exceptional by the end of the 1980s.

Pearson has studied the motivations of students entering the social work profession and suggests that the choice of a social work job represents an often "barely articulated form of commitment to certain standards of human values, and a curiosity and a compassion towards some aspects of the man-made world."[14] Some of the social work students in Pearson's study reported a fear of boredom, commercialism, and the rat-race; they thought the world of business would turn them into narrow-minded and prejudiced men and women. They felt social work would allow them to provide service to others which they preferred to the individualistic competitiveness of the business world.

The Code of Ethics requires that social workers have a commitment to serve society.

The NASW Social Work Code of Ethics strongly reflects the profession's commitment to society and to service: "The social worker should regard as primary the service obligation of the social work profession." In practice this suggests that social workers retain ultimate responsibility for the quality and extent of the service they provide as well as for preventing inhumane or discriminatory practices.

A client has a right to know if what is said to the worker will be held in confidence. A social worker is obligated by law to report any abuse of children that is disclosed by a client.

The profession's commitment to the general welfare requires that social workers act in accordance with the highest standards of professional integrity and impartiality. The code warns the social worker to "be alert to and resist the influences and pressures that interfere with the exercise of professional discretion and impartial judgment required for the performance of professional functions." Social workers are not allowed to use professional relationships for personal gain. Primacy of the client's interest is also reflected in the code's mandates to service clients with devotion, loyalty, determination, and the maximum application of professional skill and competence. To do this the social worker must avoid relationships or commitments that conflict with the interest of clients. Clients must be apprised of the risks, rights, opportunities, and obligations associated with social service to them. To provide the best quality of service possible, the social worker is to seek advice and counsel of colleagues and supervisors whenever such consultation is in the best interest of the clients. In addition, social workers are to terminate service to clients when such services are no longer required. In withdrawing services the social worker takes care to minimize possible adverse effects. The client's best interest requires that the social worker make every effort to foster the client's maximum self-determination. When the social worker must act on behalf of a client, she is obliged to safeguard the client's interests and rights; if another individual has been legally authorized to act in the client's behalf, the social worker should deal with that person always with the client's best interest in mind.

Finally, the NASW Code charges social workers with promoting the general welfare of society as well as the individual good. Social workers act to prevent and eliminate discrimination against any person or group on the basis of race, color, sex, sexual orientation, age, religion, national origin, marital status, political belief, mental or physical handicap, or any other preference or personal characteristic, condition, or status. Social workers act to ensure that all persons have access to the resources, services, and opportunities they require.

Social workers strive to expand choice and opportunity for all persons, with special regard for disadvantaged or oppressed groups and persons and to promote conditions that encourage respect for the diversity of cultures that constitute American society. This may require the social worker to advocate policy change and legislation to improve social conditions and to promote social justice. Social workers encourage and facilitate informed participation by the public in shaping social policies and institutions.

Chapter 18 presents more information about ethnic-sensitive social work practice.

Portions of the code of ethics convey social work's dual mandate to cure specific problems (solve private troubles) and to advance the whole society (address public issues). This mandate reflects the collectivity orientation in the broadest sense.

Monopolistic component of professionalism

When a profession attains a monopoly, it provides services no other profession is allowed to provide, controls the mechanisms for recruitment and education, accredits professional schools, sets requirements for licensing and regulation, and evaluates and sometimes censures unprofessional behavior.

Privileges of a profession can be controlled by licensing, registration, certification, and administrative requirements.

Licensing is the ultimate sanction of the monopoly by the community. By 1983 thirty-three states had some form of social work licensing.[15] Other forms of regulation are less powerful in protecting professionals. The least protective would be a registration system; certification is only slightly more protective. The highest degree of "turf protection" comes through the power of licensure. A more in-depth scrutiny of regulation equips us to evaluate the potential functions and dysfunctions of increased professionalization.

REGISTRATION

Registration is a self-identified listing of social workers. A state may require certain credentials to place one's name on the registry, but no law prohibits a potential employer or client from hiring a nonregistered social worker. The National Association of Human Service Workers, for example, is presently conducting a national registration drive; it publishes a list of all registered human service workers. The only requirement for registration is work experience in the human services. There is no specific educational requirement.

Twenty states have some type of registration or a combination of licensing and registration for social workers.

CERTIFICATION

Certification goes a step beyond registration since applicants must meet specific requirements/conditions to obtain certification; these prerequisites may be related to education and/or experience. Certification implies some degree of competence in the field. States that require social workers to be certified may require education, supervised experience, and an acceptable score on a written or oral examination. Certification does not keep individuals who have not met the qualifications from practicing social work, but it does prohibit them from using the title "certified" social worker.

LICENSING

Licensing is the strongest form of legal regulation. Its purpose is to ensure that individual practitioners have achieved the required educational status and are capable of practicing with at least a minimum level of competence. Applicants must pay a fee for a license; they face legal action if they practice unethically or without a license. Licensing protects both the job title and the professional activities. For example, barbers are licensed; unless they fulfill stated requirements and receive a license they cannot advertise as barbers or make money cutting hair. Although barbers have a more limited knowledge base and social responsibility than social workers, they have more job protection, and society has more protection against unqualified barbers than it has against unqualified social workers.

It may be useful to review the comparison of human service professions in Chapter 9.

In states that have passed social work licensing, it has not been problematic to grant exclusiveness of title; instead problems emerge as states try to determine what activities should be limited to those individuals holding a social work license. Social workers are trained to do many tasks that are beneficial to society; few would want to limit others from performing these socially constructive tasks. States that have licensing tend to grant a monopoly on the use of title, enforce credential requirements, require examination of knowledge and skills upon entry into the profession, and require some kind of continuing education requirement. These states assume that granting licensure privileges to the social work profession is important for the protection of clients. No state would allow licensure merely to protect a professional monopoly.

ADMINISTRATIVE REQUIREMENTS

A less frequently discussed but potentially more powerful means of protecting a monopoly on welfare or social services is to have certain conditions attached to receiving public funds. An example of this would be the requirements in the Title XIX (Medicaid) amendments that state any nursing home receiving Medicaid funds must have a social worker involved in admitting, caring, and planning for patients. This legislation specifically requires that the social worker receive a degree from an accredited undergraduate program or be receiving supervision from a person with a master's degree in social work.

This is just one example of a policy requiring a specific kind of social work education. The economic incentive in these policies to hire professionals with the required qualifications has as much effect as a regulatory system.

The domain of social work practice

A variety of definitions about the domain of social work practice are given in Chapter 1.

One primary obstacle to social work receiving licensure (a monopoly on services) is inability to define an exclusive domain or mission. The September 1977 issue of *Social Work* provides a number of different views of what constitutes the unique domain of social work practice. Shirley Cooper suggests that social work's unique contribution is being the "conscience of the community." She argues that society needs a mechanism that continually presses for humanistic changes. To her, social work is this mechanism.[16] Robert Morris, however, suggests a different unique niche for social work:

> There is one essential social function that these other professions are neither competent nor have the authority to perform: taking care of people who must be cared for. This could be the exclusive domain of social work.[17]

Neil Gilbert's approach to the unique mission is similar to Morris's but he takes a more institutional approach. He suggests that it is "social work's connection to the institution of social welfare and the functions this institution performs in society."[18] He points out that even though the other professionals may be involved in certain welfare programs, social workers clearly predominate the broad range of social programs including corrections, child welfare, public welfare, and institutional care.

The summary report from the 1977 Conference in Madison, Wisconsin, contains the most widely accepted description of the unique domain of social work practice.

> What social work brings that is different is the ability to assess both the individual and the social context and to include immediate, intermediate, and long-range planning in terms of mobilizing both the inner resources of clients, their support systems, and the environment. In the process, social workers also have the responsibility for identifying those gaps in the social system.[19]

While the majority of social workers would suggest this is an accurate description of practice from a social work perspective, few would support any action that would limit other professions from adopting this perspective. In fact, most feel that all professional practice could be enhanced by including what they see as the "social work perspective." Social workers face a dilemma when they try to define and protect the unique qualities and functions of their profession. If they are effective, other professionals will increasingly respond to the importance of the social environment in individual functioning, and the social work perspective will no longer be unique to the profession. As teams of professionals become more effective, they naturally become more knowledgeable about related disciplines.

Code of ethics Throughout this chapter portions of the NASW Code of Ethics have been used to illustrate professional attributes. Of course some subgroups within the profession do not feel that the code adequately reflects their professional views. The National Association of Christian Social Workers (NACSW), certain radical social workers, and the Association of Black Social Workers (ABSW), for example, have either taken issue with or expanded on the professional code. The NASW Code is presented here in its entirety. In addition, students may examine some of the points Jeffrey Galper makes in his radical code of ethics, and the unique perspective of the NACSW. The special concerns of the ABSW are outlined briefly in Chapter 8.

The NASW Code of Ethics*

This code is intended to serve as a guide to the everyday conduct of members of the social work profession and as a basis for the adjudication of issues in ethics when the conduct of social workers is alleged to deviate from the standards expressed or implied in this code. It represents standards of ethical behavior for social workers in professional relationships with those served, with colleagues, with employers, with other individuals and professions, and with the community and society as a whole. It also embodies standards of ethical behavior governing individual conduct to the extent that such conduct is associated with an individual's status and identity as a social worker.

This code is based on the fundamental values of the social work profession that include the worth, dignity, and uniqueness of all persons as well as their rights and opportunities. It is also based on the nature of social work, which fosters conditions that promote these values.

In subscribing to and abiding by this code, the social worker is expected to view ethical responsibility in as inclusive a context as each situation demands and within which ethical judgement is required. The social worker is expected to take into consideration all the principles in this code that have a bearing upon any situation in which ethical judgement is to be exercised and professional intervention or conduct is planned. The course of action that the social worker chooses is expected to be consistent with the spirit as well as the letter of this code.

In itself, this code does not represent a set of rules that will prescribe all the behaviors of social workers in all the complexities of professional life. Rather, it offers general principles to guide conduct, and the judicious appraisal of conduct, in situations that have ethical implications. It provides the basis for making judgements about ethical actions before and after they occur. Frequently, the particular situation determines the ethical principles that apply and the manner of their application. In such cases, not only the particular ethical principles are taken into immediate consideration, but also the entire code and its spirit. Specific applications of ethical principles must be judged within the context in which they are being considered. Ethical behavior in a given situation must satisfy not only the judgement of the individual social worker, but also the judgement of an unbiased jury of professional peers.

This code should not be used as an instrument to deprive any social worker, of the opportunity or freedom to practice with complete professional integrity; nor should any disciplinary action be taken on the basis of this code without maximum provision for safeguarding the rights of the social worker affected.

The ethical behavior of social workers results not from edict, but from a personal commitment of the individual. This code is offered to affirm the will and zeal of all social workers to be ethical and to act ethically in all that they do as social workers.

The following codified ethical principles should guide social workers in the various levels of responsibility in which they function professionally. These principles also serve as a basis for the adjudication by the National Association of Social Workers of issues in ethics.

In subscribing to this code, social workers are required to cooperate in its implementation and abide by any disciplinary rulings based on it. They should also take adequate measures to discourage, prevent, expose, and correct the unethical conduct of colleagues. Finally, social workers should be equally ready to defend and assist colleagues unjustly charged with unethical conduct.

I. The Social Worker's Conduct and Comportment as a Social Worker
- A. Propriety—The social worker should maintain high standards of personal conduct in the capacity or identity as social worker.
  1. The private conduct of the social worker is a personal matter to the same degree as is any other person's, except when such conduct compromises the fulfillment of professional responsibilities.
  2. The social worker should not participate in, condone, or be associated with dishonesty, fraud, deceit, or misrepresentation.
  3. The social worker should distinguish clearly between statements and actions made as a private individual and as a representative of the social work profession or an organization or group.
- B. Competence and Professional Development—The social worker should strive to become and remain proficient in professional practice and the performance of professional functions.
  1. The social worker should accept responsibility or employment only on the basis of existing competence or the intention to acquire the necessary competence.
  2. The social worker should not misrepresent professional qualifications, education, experience, or affiliations.
- C. Service—The social worker should regard as primary the service obligation of the social work profession.
  1. The social worker should retain ultimate responsibility for the quality and extent of the service that individual assumes, assigns, or performes.
  2. The social worker should act to prevent practices that are inhumane or discriminatory against any person or group of persons.
- D. Integrity—The social worker should act in accordance with the highest standards of professional integrity and impartiality.
  1. The social worker should be alert to and resist the influences and pressures that interfere with the exercise of professional discretion and impartial judgement required for the performance of professional functions.
  2. The social worker should not exploit professional relationships for personal gain.
- E. Scholarship and Research—The social worker engaged in study and research should be guided by the conventions of scholarly inquiry.
  1. The social worker engaged in research should consider carefully its possible consequences for human beings.
  2. The social worker engaged in research should ascertain that the consent of participants in the research is voluntary and informed, without any implied deprivation or penalty for refusal to participate, and with due regard for participants' privacy and dignity.
  3. The social worker engaged in research should protect participants from unwarranted physical or mental discomfort, distress, harm, danger, or deprivation.

4. The social worker who engages in the evaluation of services or cases should discuss them only for professional purposes and only with persons directly and professionally concerned with them.
5. Information obtained about participants in research should be treated as confidential.
6. The social worker should take credit only for work actually done in connection with scholarly and research endeavors and credit contributions made by others.

II. The Social Worker's Ethical Responsibility to Clients

F. Primacy of Clients' Interests—The social worker's primary responsibility is to clients.

1. The social worker should serve clients with devotion, loyalty, determination, and the maximum application of professional skill and competence.
2. The social worker should not exploit relationships with clients for personal advantage, or solicit the clients of one's agency for private practice.
3. The social worker should not practice, condone, facilitate or collaborate with any form of discrimination on the basis of race, color, sex, sexual orientation, age, religion, national origin, marital status, political belief, mental or physical handicap, or any other preference or personal characteristic, condition or status.
4. The social worker should avoid relationships or commitments that conflict with the interest of clients.
5. The social worker should under no circumstances engage in sexual activities with clients.
6. The social worker should provide clients with accurate and complete information regarding the extent and nature of the services available to them.
7. The social worker should apprise clients of their risks, rights, opportunities, and obligations associated with social service to them.
8. The social worker should seek advice and counsel of colleagues and supervisors whenever such consultation is in the best interest of clients.
9. The social worker should terminate service to clients, and professional relationships with them, when such service and relationships are no longer required or no longer serve the clients' needs or interests.
10. The social worker should withdraw services precipitously only under unusual circumstances, giving careful consideration to all factors in the situation and taking care to minimize possible adverse effects.
11. The social worker who anticipates the termination or interruption of service to clients should notify clients promptly and seek the transfer, referral, or continuation of service in relation to the clients' needs and preferences.

G. Rights and Prerogatives of Clients—The social worker should make every effort to foster maximum self-determination on the part of clients.

1. When the social worker must act on behalf of a client who has been adjudged legally incompetent, the social worker should safeguard the interests and rights of that client.
2. When another individual has been legally authorized to act in behalf of a client, the social worker should deal with that person always with the client's best interest in mind.
3. The social worker should not engage in any action that violates or diminishes the civil or legal rights of clients.

H. Confidentiality and Privacy—The social worker should respect the privacy of clients and hold in confidence all information obtained in the course of professional service.

1. The social worker should share with others confidences revealed by clients, without their consent, only for compelling professional reasons.
2. The social worker should inform clients fully about the limits of confidentiality in a given situation, the purposes for which information is obtained, and how it may be used.
3. The social worker should afford clients reasonable access to any official social work records concerning them.

4. When providing clients with access to records, the social worker should due care to protect the confidences of others contained in those records.
5. The social worker should obtain informed consent of clients before taping, recording, or permitting third party observation of their activities.

I. Fees—When setting fees, the social worker should ensure that they are fair, reasonable, considerate and commensurate with the service performed and with due regard of the clients' ability to pay.

1. The social worker should not divide a fee or accept or give anything of value for receiving or making a referral.

III. The Social Worker's Ethical Responsibility to Colleagues

J. Respect, Fairness, and Courtesy—The social worker should treat colleagues with respect, courtesy, fairness, and good faith.

1. The social worker should cooperate with colleagues to promote professional interests and concerns.
2. The social worker should respect confidences shared by colleagues in the course of their professional relationships and transactions.
3. The social worker should create and maintain conditions of practice that facilitate ethical and competent professional performance by colleagues.
4. The social worker should treat with respect, and represent accurately and fairly, the qualifications, views, and findings of colleagues and use appropriate channels to express judgements on these matters.
5. The social worker who replaces or is replaced by a colleague in professional practice should act with consideration for the interest, character, and reputation of that colleague.
6. The social worker should not exploit a dispute between a colleague and employers to obtain a position or otherwise advance the social worker's interest.
7. The social worker should seek arbitration or mediation when conflicts with colleagues require resolution for compelling professional reasons.
8. The social worker should extend to colleagues of other professions the same respect and cooperation that is extended to social work colleagues.
9. The social worker who serves as an employer, supervisor, or mentor to colleagues should make orderly and explicit arrangements regarding the conditions of their continuing professional relationship.
10. The social worker who has the responsibility for employing and evaluating the performance of other staff members, should fulfill such responsibility in a fair, considerate, and equitable manner, on the basis of clearly enunciated criteria.
11. The social worker who has the responsibility for evaluating the performance of employees, supervisees, or students should share evaluations with them.

K. Dealing with Colleagues' Clients—The social worker has the responsibility to relate to the clients of colleagues with full professional consideration.

1. The social worker should not solicit the clients of colleagues.
2. The social worker should not assume professional responsibility for the clients of another agency or a collegue without appropriate communication with that agency or colleague.
3. The social worker who serves the clients of colleagues, during a temporary absence or emergency, should serve those clients with the same consideration as that afforded any client.

IV. The Social Worker's Ethical Responsibility to Employers and Employing Organizations.

L. Commitment to Employing Organization—The social worker should adhere to commitments made to the employing organization.

1. The social worker should work to improve the employing agency's policies and procedures, and the efficiency and effectiveness of its services.
2. The social worker should not accept employment or arrange student field placements in an organi-

zation which is currently under public sanction by NASW for violating personnel standards or imposing limitations on or penalties for professional actions on behalf of clients.

3. The social worker should act to prevent and eliminate discrimination in the employing organization's work assignments and in its employment policies and practices.
4. The social worker should use with scrupulous regard, and only for the purpose for which they are intended, the resources of the employing organization.

V. The Social Worker's Ethical Responsibility to the Social Work Profession

M. Maintaining the Integrity of the Profession—The social worker should uphold and advance the values, ethics, knowledge, and mission of the profession.

1. The social worker should protect and enhance the dignity and integrity of the profession and should be responsible and vigorous in discussion and criticism of the profession.
2. The social worker should take action through appropriate channels against unethical conduct by any other member of the profession.
3. The social worker should act to prevent the unauthorized and unqualified practice of social work.
4. The social worker should make no misrepresentation in advertising as to qualifications, competence, service, or results to be achieved.

N. Community Service—The social worker should assist the profession in making social services available to the general public.

1. The social worker should contribute time and professional expertise to activities that promote respect for the utility, the integrity, and the competence of the social work profession.
2. The social worker should support the formulation, development, enactment and implementation of social policies of concern to the profession.

O. Development of Knowledge—The social worker should take responsibility for identifying, developing, and fully utilizing knowledge for professional practice.

1. The social worker should base practice upon recognized knowledge relevant to social work.
2. The social worker should critically examine, and keep current with, emerging knowledge relevant to social work.
3. The social worker should contribute to the knowledge base of social work and share research knowledge and practice wisdom with colleagues.

VI. The Social Worker's Ethical Responsibility to Society

P. Promoting the General Welfare—The social worker should promote the general welfare of society.

1. The social worker should act to prevent and eliminate discrimination against any person or group on the basis of race, color, sex, sexual orientation, age, religion, national origin, marital status, political belief, mental or physical handicap, or any other preference or personal characteristic, condition, or status.
2. The social worker should act to ensure that all persons have access to the resources, services, and opportunities which they require.
3. The social worker should act to expand choice and opportunity for all persons, with special regard for disadvantaged or oppressed groups and persons.
4. The social worker should promote conditions that encourage respect for the diversity of cultures which constitute American society.
5. The social worker should provide appropriate professional services in public emergencies.
6. The social worker should advocate changes in policy and legislation to improve social conditions and to promote social justice.
7. The social worker should encourage informed participation by the public in shaping social policies and institutions.

SUMMARY OF MAJOR PRINCIPLES

I. The Social Worker's Conduct and Comportment as a Social Worker
   A. Propriety. The social worker should maintain high standards of personal conduct in the capacity or identity as social worker.
   B. Competence and Professional Development. The social worker should strive to become and remain proficient in professional practice and the performance of professional functions.
   C. Service. The social worker should regard as primary the service obligation of the social work profession.
   D. Integrity. The social worker should act in accordance with the highest standards of professional integrity.
   E. Scholarship and Research. The social worker engaged in study and research should be guided by the conventions of scholarly inquiry.

II. The Social Worker's Ethical Responsibility to Clients
   F. Primacy of Clients' Interests. The social worker's primary responsibility is to clients.
   G. Rights and Prerogatives of Clients. The social worker should make every effort to foster maximum self-determination on the part of clients.
   H. Confidentiality and Privacy. The social worker should respect the privacy of clients and hold in confidence all information obtained in the course of professional service.
   I. Fees. When setting fees, the social worker should ensure that they are fair, reasonable, considerate, and commensurate with the service performed and with due regard for the clients' ability to pay.

III. The Social Worker's Ethical Responsibility to Colleagues
   J. Respect, Fairness, and Courtesy. The social worker should treat colleagues with respect, courtesy, fairness, and good faith.
   K. Dealing with Colleagues' Clients. The social worker has the responsibility to relate to the clients of colleagues with full professional consideration.

IV. The Social Worker's Ethical Responsibility to Employers and Employing Organizations
   L. Commitments to Employing Organizations. The social worker should adhere to commitments made to the employing organizations.

V. The Social Worker's Ethical Responsibility to the Social Work Profession
   M. Maintaining the Integrity of the Profession. The social worker should uphold and advance the values, ethics, knowledge, and mission of the profession.
   N. Community Service. The social worker should assist the profession in making social services available to the general public.
   O. Development of Knowledge. The social worker should take responsibility for identifying, developing, and fully utilizing knowledge for professional practice.

VI. The Social Worker's Ethical Responsibility to Society
   P. Promoting the General Welfare. The social worker should promote the general welfare of society.

A Code of Ethics for Radical Social Service Workers*

JEFFREY GALPER

As an effort to contribute to the development of a radical ideology and commitment capable of informing radical practice, we close by returning to the Code of Ethics of the professional social work association, the National Association of Social Workers. In an earlier chapter we argued, point by point, that this Code contains a conservative bias that serves the best interests of neither client, worker, nor social well-being in general. We will consider each item of this Code, therefore, and suggest how it might be revised were it organized in service of the development of the kind of society we hope to build. In a sense, the following point-by-point comparison summarizes this book. As the existing Code encapsulates the analysis and goals of conventional practice, so our modifications encapsulate the analysis and goals of the radical social service worker. Our Code will have fourteen planks.

1. I regard as my primary obligation the welfare of all human kind.

The existing Code suggests that the social welfare worker regards as a primary obligation the welfare of the individual or group served. The limiting and destructive nature of the individualistic and pluralistic strategies that follow from this obligation have been documented numerous times in this book. The well-being of any one of us is inseparable from the well-being of all of us, and this awareness must be reflected in radical practice.

2. I will work toward the development of a society that is committed to the dictum, "From each according to his or her ability, to each according to his or her need."

The existing Code is concerned with nondiscrimination, in the civil libertarian sense, and commits the worker to serving all persons without bias. We have described the limitations inherent in the notion of equality of opportunity, which this plank reflects, and have suggested that our focus must be on outcomes as well as processes.

3. I will struggle for the realization of a society in which my personal interests and my personal actions are consistent with my interests and actions as a worker.

At present, the Code suggests that personal interests be subordinated to professional responsibility and that statements and actions as a professional be kept apart from statements and actions as a private person. The personal fragmentation and politically conservative implications of this arrangement received attention elsewhere in this book. Our work and our lives must become increasingly integrated.

4. I will consider my self accountable to all who join in the struggle for social change and will consider them accountable to me for the quality and extent of the work we perform and the society we create.

The current Code commits the worker to be responsible to himself or herself for this work. The need for collective accountability and struggle, however, is paramount. While personal standards are always desirable, we must add to them the critical collective concern.

5. I will work to achieve the kind of world in which all people can be free and open with one another in all matters.

The existing Code's commitment is to respect the privacy of all persons served. Without suggesting that one violate the trust of others, the emphasis on privacy must be counteracted inasmuch as our society is adept at using privacy to control us by keeping us apart. Openness is critical to the devel-

*Jeffrey Galper, *The Politics of Social Service,* © 1975, pp. 224–227. Reprinted by permission of Prentice-Hall, Inc., Englewood Cliffs, New Jersey.

opment of a society organized around positive mutual commitments.

6. I will use information gained from my work to facilitate humanistic, revolutionary change in the society.

The Code's commitment to the responsible use of information gained in professional work on the one hand implies a desirable concern for integrity. On the other hand, it suggests commitment to professional practice above a commitment to radical social change. This is not acceptable in radical practice.

7. I will treat the findings, views, and actions of colleagues with the respect due them. This respect is conditioned by their demonstrated concern for revolutionary values and radical social change.

This plank in the old Code argues for respect of colleagues per se. No commitment can be made to professional colleagues that is not in the context of a commitment to larger social values. Inasmuch as they do not have such a commitment, their findings, views, and actions must be rejected and challenged, though their humanity must always be acknowledged.

8. I will use all the knowledge and skill available to me in bringing about a radically transformed society.

The old Code's concern is that practice be conducted within the recognized knowledge and competence of the profession. This does not facilitate the kind of total engagement and total use of all resources which is required in the struggle for radical change.

9. I recognize my responsibility to add my ideas and findings to our society's knowledge and practice.

The existing code's concern for adding such ideas and findings to social welfare knowledge and practice is worthy but limiting. Social work is a vehicle and servant. It is neither the temple nor the master.

10. I accept my responsbility to help protect the community against unethical practice by any individuals or organizations in the society.

The present Code asks for protection against such practices in the social welfare field. This is not enough. Our commitment is to struggle against the destructive elements of the whole.

11. I commit myself to use myself fully in the struggle for revolutionary change.

The existing Code urges readiness to provide services in public emergencies. Our society, at this time, is experiencing an emergency in an ongoing way. There is no more appropriate time for us to engage. Earthquakes, floods, and fires are minor happenings compared to the daily destruction wreaked by our institutions in the normal course of events.

12. I support the principle that all persons can and must contribute to the realization of a humanized society.

The old Code stresses the need for professional education for professional practice. Inasmuch as radical work is concerned with the fundamental reorganization of our society, all persons are potentially equally qualified and engaged students and participants.

13. I accept responsibility for working toward the creation and maintenance of conditions in sociey that enable all people to live by this Code.

The present Code's stress on enabling social workers in agencies to live by that code is isolating and limiting in view of the tasks before us.

14. I contribute my knowledge, skills, and support to the accomplishment of a humanistic, democratic, communal socialist society.

The Code's suggestion that we contribute knowledge, skills, and support to programs of human welfare is desirable but limited. We must be clear about our goals and courageous in putting the notion of a radically altered society on the agenda.

It seems likely that, for any one of us, if there is a will, there is not necessarily a way. Acting collectively, however, the possibilities of what we can create are very exciting. While radicals are more given to manifestos than Codes of Ethics, we need to find ways to think together about how we can proceed. If this Code, and this book, serve any useful political purpose, it will be to facilitate that thinking.

NACSW Statement of Objectives and Faith

I. Objectives of NACSW
   A. To provide Christians in social work with opportunities for fellowship, personal growth, educationach, and a corporate witness to, and influence on, the world.
   B. To promote a Christian world view in social work and social welfare expressed through social agencies, local churches, educational institutions, and national organizations.
   C. To encourage awareness within the Christian community of contemporary human need and of the social work profession as an avenue for ministering to this need.

II. Statement of Christian Faith
   A. We believe that the Bible is the inspired and infallible Word of God, and that it is the authoritative basis for what we believe and how we live.
   B. We believe that there is one God, eternally existent in three persons: Father, Son, and Holy Spirit.
   C. We believe in the deity of our Lord Jesus Christ; His virgin birth; His fully human but sinless life; His ministry of reconciliation, and forgiveness; His vicarious and atoning death; His bodily resurrection; and His ascension to the Father.
   D. We believe that for the Salvation of lost and sinful humanity, regeneration by the Holy Spirit is essential.
   E. We believe in the present ministry of the Holy Spirit by whose indwelling Christians are enabled to live godly lives individually and corporately.
   F. We believe in the spiritual unity of all believers in our Lord Jesus Christ, who together provide a caring community and a corporate witness to faith in Him.
   G. We believe in the interdependence of all humanity and the necessity of commitment to the total well-being of all people.
   H. We believe in Christ's present Lordship over all areas of our lives including, but not limited to, our involvement in social, economic, and political systems.
   I. We believe in the personal return of our Lord Jesus Christ to the earth, in power and judgement.

III. Statement of Social Work Practice
   A. We recognize a dynamic relationship between our life in Christ and our professional activities.
   B. We are committed to working toward actualizing each person's total well-being and to eliminating oppression and violence.
   C. We acknowledge that we are not to be motivated by earthly power, wealth, or security.
   D. We encourage and support the highest standards of social work education, practice, and ethics for individuals and agencies.

Summary

Professionalization of social work has had a shifting course over the last fifteen years. During the Nixon administration the government launched a direct atack on the profession. John Ehrlichman, infamous for his contributions to the Watergate scandal, openly asserted that it was time for social workers to find "honest" work. Social work was caught in the crossfire between the Left, which criticized its conservatism, and the Nixon administration, which branded it as radical. In the 1980s Reagan's advisers in *Mandate for Leadership* called for more training for professional social workers because the liberal arts majors who supposedly dominated the profession were too radical. In a nutshell these contradictory responses reflect the conflicting assumptions about the social work profession. One conservative president (Nixon) saw increased professionalization as a radical threat; another conservative president (Reagan) sees increased professionalization as a conservative influence.

The debate about the desirability of social work becoming more professionalized is complex. If social workers pursue increased professionalization, it is certain that educational requirements will become more demanding, regulation will be more strictly enforced, money for research will be more readily available, salaries will increase, and more prestige will attach to the field. Should the profession move toward deprofessionalization educational requirements will be relaxed, less money will be spent on licensing, and workers already employed in related fields will have greater access to the profession; the profession's consequent growth will enhance the political influence of social workers as a group.

This chapter has presented the general attributes of social work as a profession, the cognitive, collective, and monopolistic components. The cognitive component includes three kinds of theory: general theory, practice theory, and theories of practice. The social work mandate for service (collective component) includes service to individuals, society, and the profession. The monopolistic component addresses the regulatory mechanisms as well as the domain protection afforded to a societally recognized profession. These characteristics are consistent with the NASW's Code of Ethics.

References

1. Lydia Rapoport, "In Defense of Social Work," *Social Service Review* 34, no. 1 (March 1960): 62–74.
2. Murray Edelman, "The Political Language of the Helping Professions," *Politics and Society* 4, no. 3 (1974): 295–310.
3. Ernest Greenwood, "Attributes of a Profession," *Social Work* 2, no. 3 (July 1957): 45–55.
4. Ernest Greenwood, "Attributes of a Profession Revisited," in *The Emergence of Social Welfare and Social Work,* 2nd ed., ed. N. Gilbert and H. Specht (Itasca, Ill.: Peacock, 1981).
5. Ibid.
6. Ibid.
7. Beulah Compton and Burt Galaway, *Social Work Processes* (Homewood, Ill.: Dorsey Press, 1979), 49.
8. Ibid., 41.
9. Allen Pincus and Anne Minahan, *Social Work Practice: Model and Method* (Itasca, Ill.: Peacock, 1973).
10. Carel Germain, "The Ecological Perspective in Casework Practice," *Social Casework* 54, no. 6 (June 1973): 223–230.

11. Wm. J. Reid and Laura Epstein, *Task-Centered Practice* (New York: Columbia University Press, 1977).
12. Harriet Bartlett, "Social Work Practice," *Encyclopedia of Social Work* vol 16 (New York: NASW, 1970): 1479.
13. Charles Garvin. "The Selection of Theory for Social Work Practice with Individuals," Mimeographed paper (Ann Arbor, Mich: Univ of Michigan, 1972).
14. Geoffrey Pearson, "Making Social Workers: Bad Promises and Good Omens," in *Radical Social Work,* ed. Roy Bailey and Mike Brake (New York: Pantheon, 1975), 13–45.
15. Myles Johnson, "State Comparison of Laws Regulating Social Work," (Silver Spring, Md.: NASW, 1983).
16. Shirley Cooper, "Social Work: A Dissenting Profession," *Social Work* 22, no. 5, (September 1977): 360–368.
17. Robert Morris, "Caring for vs. Caring About People," *Social Work* 22, no. 5 (September 1977): 347–352.
18. Neil Gilbert, "The Search for Professional Identity," *Social Work* 22, no. 5 (September 1977): 401–406.
19. "Excerpts from the Discussion," *Social Work* 22, no. 5, (September 1977): 382–386.

CHAPTER EIGHT

Professional Associations

"For all its weaknesses and ambiguities, the profession of social work is strong, growing, and a fundamental part of contemporary society."[1]

The National Conference on Charities and Corrections was first convened in 1874 by the leaders of the State Boards of Charity. Leaders of the private welfare sector were invited and soon took control of the conference. Early conferences chronicle the debate between indoor and outdoor relief and public versus private welfare.[2] The twentieth century ushered in specialization among social workers and this is reflected in the development of professional organizations.

The National Conference was the only national organization for employees of social agencies.

1918	American Association of Medical Social Workers
1919	National Association of School Social Workers
1921	Family and Child Welfare Association
1921	American Association of Social Workers
1926	American Association of Psychiatric Social Workers
1946	American Association of Group Workers
1946	Association for Study of Community Organization
1949	Social Work Research Group

The National Association of Social Workers

In 1952 a temporary Inter-Association Council of Social Work Membership met to consider the possibility of merger between the various associations. This led to the establishment of the National Association of Social Workers (NASW) in 1955.[3] Today the NASW is the professional organization that sanctions and regulates social workers in a variety of settings. NASW's primary functions include promoting professional development, establishing professional standards of social work practice, advancing sound social policies, and extending membership. Because social workers work in so many settings and deal with so many kinds of problems, the NASW Code is general and unexceptional. The NASW has little power to enforce its code; instead the code embodies the values accepted by most social workers.

In addition to the Code of Ethics NASW has developed Standards for Social Work Personnel Practices, Standards for the Classification of Social Work Practice, Standards for the Regulation of Social Work Practice, and Standards for Continuing Professional Education. Practice standards set by NASW include Standards for Social Work in Health Care Settings, Social Work Services in School, Social Work Practice in Child Protection, and Social Work Services in Long Term Care Facilities. NASW also provides leadership by organizing professional conferences, publishing professional journals, and lobbying for professional and client interests.

For the 1980s NASW has established major priorities in five crucial areas: securing adequate public and private financing for human services, gaining

The American Association of Social Workers (AASW), the National Association of School Social Workers (NASSW), and the American Association of Schools of Social Work (AASSW) are all examples of specialized professional organizations in social work. In the 1950s they set up booths at the National Conference on Social Welfare to inform social workers about the different organizations. Photo courtesy of Social Welfare History Archives, University of Minnesota.

public recognition and legal regulation for the social work profession, combating discrimination, promoting political and legislative activity, and encouraging continuing professional education.

NASW is the largest organization of professional social workers in the world. Its 90,000 members are drawn from 55 chapters throughout the United States, the Virgin Islands, Puerto Rico, and Europe.[5]

Council on Social Work Education

The AASSW began reviewing and accrediting schools of social work in 1932.

Since 1940 professional educators have been debating the appropriate level of education for beginning professional practice. Early graduate programs in social work tended to be in urban endowed universities. State universities, rural welfare administrators, and social workers in general were concerned about the failure of the American Association of Schools of Social Work (AASSW) to meet public welfare training needs on a broad scale. The AASSW held strongly to the view that professional education was graduate education.

In spite of the protestations of professional accrediting bodies, however, undergraduate programs were continuing to develop, often in sociology departments. This group formally challenged AASSW by forming the National Association of Schools of Social Administration (NASSA) and their stated reasons for forming an independent organization were: The AASSW program was not practical in any but the largest educational institutions; the Association reflected the goals and structure of privately endowed schools; the Association ignored the needs of rural populations and publicly funded social service positions; AASSW was charged with being an autocratic organization dominated by the thinking of two or three schools.[6]

The conflict between AASSW and NASSA was basically a conflict between advocates of undergraduate social work education and educators who held out for the graduate degree as the professional degree. A study sponsored by the Carnegie Foundation looked at the entire field of social work education, and after extensive negotiations that recognized the limitations of separate associations NASSA and AASSW agreed in 1952 to renounce their separate identities and merge into a new organization, the Council on Social Work Education. But even though the profession now has one accrediting body, the debate on undergraduate education continues.

Through its control over accreditation and curriculum policy the CSWE attempts to influence educational standards. CSWE's most ambitious curriculum program was its thirteen volume study published in 1959.[7] More recently it has attempted to differentiate between master and bachelor degree programs in social work. This new concern has led to the formation of subgroups within the council committed to promoting and protecting each curriculum policy area. Whether or not this debate has been constructive or destructive is unclear; it has certainly consumed a large amount of energy and resources.

Black professional organizations

The Black Social Workers Association developed thirteen years after the formation of NASW.

The 1968 National Conference on Social Welfare in San Francisco was the beginning of the Black Social Workers Association. Although many reasons prompted its formation, the growing importance of the black power movement was a principal cause of its establishment. The failure of integration, an increased emphasis on black organizations, and a growing sense of racial solidarity were also important. Black social workers believed there was a need for more direct action to bring about meaningful change.[8]

The charter of the Black Social Workers Association stressed key issues.

1. The ethnic composition of the NASW board and its planning, executive, and nominating committees was disproportionate to that of the conference.
2. White racism was the major mental health problem facing the nation.
3. The BSWA should lend its full support to the National Welfare Rights Organization.
4. The BSWA should commit itself to reconstructing systems relevant to the needs of blacks through whatever means necessary.[9]

A similar group formed at the 1968 National Association of Social Workers conference called themselves the Association of Black Catalysts. Subsequently the Philadelphia Alliance of Black Social Workers held the first annual National Conference of the Association of Black Social Workers (ABSW) in 1969; the ABSW currently has over twenty chapters in the U. S. and is established as a national nonprofit organization.[10]

Since its formation the ABSW has initiated and participated in many activities to help bring a better understanding of the black community to the profession. It has helped develop the Black Coalition for Welfare Rights and given technical assistance toward the organizing of several other black groups and organizations. The ABSW has also helped improve the image of the social worker in the black community. Finally, the ABSW has stimulated black and white social workers to examine their sensitivity to the black experience and how it relates to the field of social welfare.

The ABSW has not supported licensing efforts for social workers.

So rather than allow themselves to be absorbed into the mainstream of the social work profession, many blacks have decided to form subgroups of their own to have their voices heard more clearly. "Once again it shows that traditional Social Work methods were not meeting the needs or desires of its Black clients nor its Black membership and the alternative left to the Blacks was to help themselves and that is what they have begun to do."[11]

National Association of Christian Social Workers

The National Association of Christians in Social Work began at a series of annual conferences at Wheaton College in the 1950s. Originally incorporated as the Evangelical Social Work Conference and later renamed, the NACSW has expressed concern that:

> . . . our social structure has tended to place increasing responsibility for the general welfare in the hands of government. Social work concern and activity, in spite of its firm roots in a Christian world view, has become displaced from its foundation, and reflects a humanistic value system and understanding of humanity. This creates areas of tension for Christians who desire to act on the social concern by entering the social work profession.[12]

See the inset on the objectives of the NACSW in Chapter 7.

Membership in this association is open to persons who support its objectives, accept its Statement of Christian Faith, identify with its State of Social Work Practice, and pay the annual dues. The NACSW has identified specific organizational objectives, and adopted a statement of Christian faith and social work practice.

Summary of professional associations

The National Association of Social Workers (NASW) is the primary professional organization of social workers and the Council on Social Work Education (CSWE) is the accrediting body of the social work profession. In addition subgroups exemplified by the associations for black and Christian social workers serve to express concerns of special clientele or to voice unique philosophical perspectives. Numerous other subgroups (such as Rural Social Workers or Psychiatric Social Workers, to name a few) suggest the continuing diversity within the profession. Christian and black social work groups clearly illustrate the paradox of social work practice. The NASW is attacked on the one hand for being too concerned with materialistic matters and on the other for not adequately addressing the political and economic needs of other groups.

Levels of practice

One task of the NASW is to define the professional domain and the parameters of social work practice. In 1979 the NASW set up a task force to classify levels of practice; it examined four areas to differentiate requirements at the four practice levels: knowledge required by the position, degree of autonomy in practice, type and complexity of skill required, and complexity of problems faced by clientele.

Table 8–1
LEVELS OF SOCIAL WORK PRACTICE

Practice Level	Description of Level	Preparation for Practice
1. Basic Professional	Practice requiring professional practice skills, theoretical knowledge, and values that are not normally obtainable in day to day experience but that are obtainable through formal professional social work education. Formal social work education is distinguished from experiential learning by being based on conceptual and theoretical knowledge of personal and social interaction and by training in the disciplined use of self in relationship with clients.	Requires a baccalaureate degree (BSW) from a social work program accredited by the Council on Social Work Education (CSWE).
2. Specialized Professional	Practice requiring the specific and demonstrated mastery of therapeutic technique in at least one knowledge and skill method, as well as a general knowledge of human personality as influenced by social factors, and the disciplined use of self in treatment relationships with individuals or groups, or a broad conceptual knowledge of research, administration, or planning methods and social problems.	Requires a master's degree (MSW) from a social work program accredited by the CSWE.

*Source: Copyright 1981, National Association of Social Workers, Inc. Reprinted with permission from *NASW Standards for the Classification of Social Work Practice* (Washington, D.C.: The Association, September 1981), p. 9.

It is clear from these standards that associate degrees or years of experience do not qualify one for membership in the professional organization. In reality these standards represent a desired professional norm rather than an accurate description of who is practicing social work.

A person with an Associate of Arts degree is not considered to be a professional social worker.

Entry level: non-degreed

For most of our professional history, the majority of workers in public welfare agencies who were identified as social workers or caseworkers had little or no professional education in preparation for their position. Most of these people

Table 8–1
LEVELS OF SOCIAL WORK PRACTICE

Practice Level	Description of Level	Preparation for Practice
3. Independent Professional	Achievement of practice based on the appropriate special training, developed and demonstrated under professional supervision, which is sufficient to ensure the dependable, regular use of professional skills in independent or autonomous practice. A minimum of two years is required for this experiential learning and demonstration period following the master of social work program. This level applies both to solo or autonomous practice as an independent practitioner or consultant and to practice within an organization where the social worker has primary responsibility for representing the profession or for the training or administration of professional staff.	Requires an accredited MSW and at least two years of post-master's experience under appropriate professional supervision.
4. Advanced Professional	Practice that carries major social and organizational responsibility for professional development, analysis, research, or policy implementation, or is achieved by personal professional growth demonstrated through advanced conceptual contributions to professional knowledge.	Requires proficiency in special theoretical, practice, administration, or policy or the ability to conduct advanced research studies in social welfare; usually demonstrated through a doctoral degree in social work or a closely related social science discipline.

held the title of social worker but were ineligible for membership in the professional association.

The 1960s saw considerable development of human service careers sponsored by programs such as the Manpower Development Training Act. This legislation encouraged hiring of indigenous workers. Technical schools have responded by developing Associate Degrees for human service workers. The NASW, however, does not recognize this as a professional degree and assumes that limiting oneself to this level of education will seriously curtail professional career advancement.

States differ on entry level requirements. While the normal route to social work positions may increasingly come through a professional school, many people are still entering social work without a degree. As of 1976 only 78,000 of 330,000 social work positions were held by people with professional training prior to employment.[13] By 1982, 88,000 social workers were members of NASW, which requires professional education as a prerequisite for membership; in the same year 384,000 social workers were employed in the United States.[14] Social service aides may hold an associate degree in social welfare or human services or have even less formal education. A person with a BA in a field other than social work who is employed in a social work position is also called a social service aide.[15]

Bachelor of Social Work degree

The first level of professional social work practice has been at the bachelor's level since 1970.

Before 1970 the NASW admitted only MSWs to full membership in the professional organization. In 1970 they admitted to full membership persons with a BA or BSW from a CSWE accredited school. This move clearly made the association more representative of the reality of the profession; it also provided increased impetus for undergraduate education. Before 1970 students assumed no immediate benefit by pursuing a social work degree instead of another social science degree even if they planned to pursue a career in social work. By admitting BSWs to membership and increasing undergraduate professional requirements the profession moved toward deprofessionalization. The CSWE now requires BSW programs to provide a liberal arts education along with approved courses in social welfare institutions and policies, human behavior and the social environment, practice, research and field experience.

Task differentiation among social service aides, BSWs and MSWs is unsettled. Who may do what is ambiguous and not legally defined. The social service classification plan developed by NASW in 1973 outlined appropriate tasks for social workers with bachelor's degrees. They are qualified to

Provide supportive casework services,
Conduct workshops to promote and interpret programs or services,
Organize local community groups and coordinate combined efforts of groups regarding social problems,
Consult with other agencies on problems of cases served in common; coordinate services between agencies in helping multi-problem families,
Conduct basic data-gathering or statistical analysis of data on social problems,
Develop information to assist legislators and other decisions-makers to understand problems and community needs,
Serve as an advocate of clients whose needs are not being met by available programs or by a specific agency,
Work with groups to assist them in defining needs or interests and in deciding upon a course of action, and
Administer units of program within an overall structure.[16]

Illustrative Practice Competencies for the Basic Professional Social Worker (BSW)*

KNOWLEDGE

Basic and general knowledge of human behavior, social systems and social institutions.

Awareness of social problem areas—their cause and impact on individuals, families, and communities, and the appropriate resources and methods involved in dealing with them.

Knowledge of basic theories and methods of case work or group work.

Working knowledge of at least one specific method of intervention or treatment.

Working knowledge of basic research techniques and sources of specialized, professional knowledge.

Specific knowledge of social planning and community organization methods.

RESPONSIBILITY

Functions under direct and regularly provided professional supervision.

Is instructed in specific details of tasks, assuming a general knowledge of professional methods, functions, and objectives.

Casework or other professional judgments must be renewed to confirm decisions that affect clients in complex situations.

Acts professionally on one's judgment within an assigned scope of practice.

Determines client's or community's needs for service within one's practice area. Initiate or terminate one's own or another's services.

Supervises others in services they are qualified to provide.

Is advised of administrative or consultative supervision. Requires regular direct supervision. Requires regular direct supervision for learning specialized practice.

SKILL

Ability to relate in positive or appropriate relationships under adverse conditions.

Ability to recognize primary behavioral dysfunction of individuals and groups.

Ability to make a basic social assessment and service plan.

Awareness of community resources relevant to identified needs.

Ability to relate as a professional participant in an agency program.

Ability to carry out basic techniques of social research.

Ability to conduct or participate in methods of community organization and planning.

Ability to conduct a comprehensive social study or treatment plan within a given service.

Ability to initiate and develop community-group programs within given standards.

SITUATIONAL COMPLEXITY

Routine service or tasks whose goal is easily achievable.

Single function of limited difficulty.

Clear expectation of clients.

Clients with noncompetitive interests when resources are available.

Temporary, uninvolved helping relationship.

Identified emotional and social needs with only limited or potential resources.

*National Association of Social Workers, 1981. Reprinted with permission from *NASW Standards for the Classification of Social Work Practice* (Washington, D.C.: The Association, September 1981), 20–21.

Some degree of unconscious motivation.
Service goals are achievable.

SOCIAL CONSEQUENCES

Minor potential effect, the impact being limited to one or a small number of clients.
Potential errors or shortcomings limited in scope.
Benefits significant, but not essential to health or life.
Service or program involves a significant social problem.

CLIENT VULNERABILITY

Minimal risk to persons or groups.
Potential risks temporary or correctable.
Client or groups with a clear and valid expectation of service.
Actions closely or regularly supervised or evaluated.
Actions or decisions governing a client's situation subject to prior approval.
Actions or activities have no significant impact on costs.
Significant health or emotional need or risk of injury involved.
Service or treatment errors not readily corrected or ameliorated.
Clear identifiable impact on the client or community.
Administration and planning of a program have a minor impact on costs.

SOCIAL FUNCTION

To provide information on rights, benefits, and services.
To obtain social and personal information or data within specified limits of ethics and confidentiality.
To advise the public or clients of social expectations and requirements in a constructive, helping relationship.
To develop data or other research information for the analysis or study of social problems.
To deal with negative or mildly hostile persons or groups on behalf of society.
To enable clients or persons seeking aid to understand, accept, or use help in relation to a social problem.
To interpret and build trust among resident individuals or groups in services designed to provide help.
To enable individuals or groups to involve themselves in socially constructive activities or changes in conduct.
To work with hostile persons or groups to achieve or improve understanding or cooperation.

Master of Social Work

The MSW is the premier degree of social work practice. From 1940 until 1970, and in spite of resistance from undergraduate programs, it was the only recognized level of professional practice. Since the 1970 decision to recognize BSWs as professionals, debate and confusion over how to differentiate the degrees has reigned. At one point it seemed the difference between BSWs and MSWs would be the difference between the emphasis of generalist and specialist. In 1976 the House of Delegates of CSWE approved a policy stating: "Graduate degree programs in social work shall consist of advanced specialized education that requires and is built upon the core of social work knowledge, skills, and attitudes, and content in basic supporting disciplines."[17] NASW Standards (1973) suggested that MSWs should be prepared to

> provide therapeutic intervention under supervision,
> organize a community coalition to work on broad-scale problems,
> provide a social work component within a multi-disciplinary setting,
> conduct group therapy sessions within a clinic setting,
> develop and conduct research involving basic statistical techniques,
> work on program planning for a major public agency providing social services,
> teach on a social work faculty,
> administer a social service program,
> serve as a team leader in a service unit, and
> work in a program planning section of a social service agency.[18]

The tasks identified for MSWs and BSWs are similar. In addition no task on the MSW roster other than teaching on a social work faculty is not done regularly by BSWs or in some cases by social service aides. This debate over differentiation of practice levels will no doubt continue for some time. Instead of clarifying differences between the BSW and MSW, the report of the 1979 task force was less specific.

Illustrative Practice Competencies for the Specialized Professional Social Workers (MSW)*

KNOWLEDGE

Knowledge of personality theory, interpersonal communications, social group relations, or community organization theory.
A working knowledge of several methods of interpersonal helping or treatment. Knowledge of at least one psychotherapeutic technique.
A broad and beginning specialized knowledge of at least one such knowledge area.
Knowledge of the theory and techniques of professional and personnel supervision and organizational administration.
Basic knowledge of the administration of social programs.
Knowledge of the appropriate techniques and methods of research or planning.

RESPONSIBILITY

Normally functions under periodic or consultative supervision. Requires learning for specialized practice.
Is advised of administrative requirements and expected to adhere to them adequately.
Requires instruction only in highly complex, specialized, or new methods or procedures.

*National Association of Social Workers, 1981. Reprinted with permission from *NASW Standards for the Classification of Social Work Practice* (Washington, D.C.: The Association, September 1981), 22.

Directs or administers a program staffed by professional social workers and other personnel.
Reviews work of subordinate professional workers. Assigns and evaluates social work activities.

SKILL

Ability to establish constructive relationships with resistant clients by overcoming strong initial resistance or dealing with conflict-laden or complex situations.
Ability to design and conduct research.
Ability to provide psychotherapeutic treatment under supervision.
Ability to administer a social service program of limited scope within a larger setting.
Ability to determine differential treatment needs.
Ability to provide professional social work training or supervision.
Ability to represent the discipline of professional social work within an interdisciplinary program.
Ability to develop and conduct a treatment-therapy program or service without direct supervision.
Ability to provide a specialized treatment or method of service.

SITUATIONAL COMPLEXITY

Involves two or more clients with divergent interests.
Multiple service functions with responsibility for coordination of services or personnel.
Goals present major difficulties.
Clients who are emotionally confused or have conflicting social needs.
Resources not readily available.

SOCIAL CONSEQUENCES

Activity requires interdisciplinary coordination.
Actions have a serious but temporary impact and involve more than one client.
Service or program involves a significant social problem.

CLIENT VULNERABILITY

Actions involve the potential for a long-lasting but not life-threatening condition or a risk to mental stability.
Ability of client or groups to identify needs is severely limited.

SOCIAL FUNCTION

To overcome strong resistance to participation or use of socially required assistance or conduct involving the protection of others.
To achieve socially desirable changes in conduct involving significant emotional and mental growth and change.
To achieve long-lasting or broad-scale change toward socially desired objectives.

Academy of certified social workers

MSWs and PhDs may also become members of the Academy of Certified Social Workers by completing two years of employment supervised by an academy certified social worker, completing an exam, submitting professional references, an oral interview, and paying required dues. The goal of the Academy is to protect clients from abuse and incompetence of inadequately prepared practitioners. It is unclear how effective the Academy has been in achieving its goal. Some agencies reflect considerable faith in ACSW standards and require potential employees to show certification; schools of social work also frequently require certification of faculty members not holding the Ph.D. As doctoral programs increase the role of the Academy may diminish.

Illustrative Practice Competencies for the Independent Professional Social Worker (MSW plus experience)*

KNOWLEDGE

Sufficient expert knowledge to teach or communicate social work practice and theory to professionals in other disciplines or in an interdisciplinary service.

A thorough knowledge of at least one method of professional practice and specialized knowledge of others.

RESPONSIBILITY

Acts professionally on his or her judgment.

Determines clients' or the community's need for service within one's own practice area. Initiates or terminates one's own or another's services.

Requires instruction only in highly complex, new or specialized methods or procedures of treatment, research, planning, or other mode of work.

Obtains professional supervision on a consultative basis, as needed.

SKILL

Ability to conduct a psychotherapy of a highly complex or demanding nature.

Ability to conduct differential diagnoses of individuals or groups, involving complex and unconscious factors.

Ability to administer an autonomous social work, health or mental health program of limited scope or one of major scope within a larger organization.

Ability to take full professional responsibility in a multidisciplinary setting or for general community development or services.

SITUATIONAL COMPLEXITY

Severe conflicts between persons or groups served.

Multiple causative factors—major lack of resources.

Clear evidence of unconscious needs that restrict the ability of a client to change.

Highly complex emotional and social goals of service.

SOCIAL CONSEQUENCES

Actions with the potential for a major or long-lasting impact.

Activities that provide the basis for reviewing, studying, or developing a policy.

*National Association of Social Workers, 1981 Reprinted with permission from *NASW Standards for the Classification of Social Work Practice* (Washington, D.C.: The Association, September 1981), 23.

VULNERABILITY

Administration, planning, or research involve moderate costs or risks.

Actions involve the potential for a risk to mental stability.

Inability of clients or groups to identify their own needs.

SOCIAL FUNCTION

To negotiate and mediate among deeply opposed persons or groups to achieve socially sanctioned objective.

To conduct broad-scale research studies that deal with specific social or community issues.

To provide treatment to overcome major problems involving social dysfunctions, behavior, or severe risk to others.

Doctorates

Some professional schools offer a D.S.W. (doctorate in social work) while others offer a Ph.D. in Social Work or Social Welfare.

Doctoral education in social work officially began at Bryn Mawr College in 1920. By 1976, 1507 social work doctorates had been awarded. Doctoral programs continue to grow. In 1975, 155 doctorates were granted, and in 1980, 213 doctorates were granted.[19] The purpose of doctoral education has been consistent throughout its sixty year history. The core objectives were outlined by the Advisory Committee on Advanced Education (CSWE) in 1964.

> Core objectives for all doctoral programs are to equip the student for continuing scholarship and to prepare him for leadership in advancing the profession and its practice. Specifically, the doctoral program is designed to enable the student to extract, organize, extend, test, communicate or apply knowledge to achieve the purpose of social work in society.[20]

As the CSWE report suggests, doctoral education is geared primarily to preparing educators and researchers; current programs put little emphasis on training administrators. There is some sentiment in NASW that there should also be a practice doctorate; some people feel this could be a D.S.W. rather than the Ph.D. While this may become the practice in the future, some people argue that at the present time there is little difference between the DSW and the Ph.D.

Illustrative Practice Competencies for the Advanced Professional Social Worker*

KNOWLEDGE

Advanced and expert knowledge in practice, research, administration, planning or teaching.

Highly specialized and expert knowledge in a social work content area.

A thorough knowledge of several types of vulnerable populations, corresponding service delivery systems, methods for assessing needs and planning to relate the service delivery systems to human needs that are high priorities.

RESPONSIBILITY

Directs major research study involving design, staffing, management, technical responsibility, writing and budget.

Has chief administrative responsiblity for major social service or multiservice department or organization.

Has responsibility for a major planning or policy-setting function.

SKILL

Ability to design and conduct complex or extended research or planning studies involving multiple or discordant factors.

Highly specialized expertise in at least one social work method.

Ability to administer a major social work, social welfare, mental health, or health program or department with broad management and budgetary responsibilities.

SITUATIONAL COMPLEXITY

Multiple, complex technical operations.

Broad-ranging organizational and administrative requirements and policies.

Long-range planning for the development of resources.

SOCIAL CONSEQUENCES

Actions that have major public or social consequences.

CLIENT VULNERABILITY

Administration, planning, and research involve long-lasting or major public costs risks.

SOCIAL FUNCTION

To develop techniques or policies designed to further social objectives.

To conduct, write and present social research studies of major scope.

*National Association of Social Workers, 1981. Reprinted with permission from *NASW Standards for the Classification of Social Work Practice* (Washington, D.C.: The Association, September 1981), 24.

Summary: levels of practice

Identifying distinguishing characteristics of each level of practice continues to present difficulties for the profession. Throughout its history the NASW has had task forces working on this problem. While the classifications are not by any means fully developed or mutually exclusive, the most recent (1981) differentiation by competencies have been presented; these classifications illustrate both the diversity and the potential of social work practice.

References

1. Ralph Dolgoff and Donald Feldstein, *Understanding Social Welfare* (San Francisco: Harper and Row, 1980).
2. June Axinn and Herman Levin, *Social Welfare,* 2nd ed. (New York: Harper and Row, 1982).
3. Roy Lubove, *The Professional Altruist* (New York: Athenium, 1971).
4. Betty Picard, *An Introduciton to Social Work,* (Homewood, Ill.: Dorsey Press, 1983).
5. NASW, *Code of Ethics of the National Association of Social Workers* (Silver Spring, Md.: NASW, 1980).
6. Leslie Leighninger, "Graduate and Undergraduate Social Work Education: Roots of Conflict," *Journal of Education for Social Work* (Fall 1984): 66–77.
7. Lubove, *The Professional Altruist.*
8. Charles Sanders, "Growth of the Association of Black Social Workers," *Social Casework* 52, no. 5 (May 1970): 278–279.
9. Ibid., 279.
10. Ibid.
11. Toby Ferrell, "Why Not Us?: Blacks in Social Work" (Unpublished monograph, 15 September 1981).
12. Pamphlet published by the National Associaiton of Christian Social Workers.
13. Dolgoff and Feldstein, *Understanding Social Welfare.*
14. Ibid.
15. Ibid.
16. *Standards for Social Service Manpower* (NASW, 1973).
17. Policy Statement on Social Work Practice and Education and Structure and Quality in Social Work Education. Adopted by the CSWE House of Delegates, March 1976.
18. *Standards for Social Service Manpower.*
19. Allen Rubin, ed., *Statistics on Social Work Education in the United States, 1980.* (New York: Council on Social Work Education, 1981), 11–12.
20. Jeanette Regensburg, *Some Educational Patterns in Doctoral Programs in Schools of Social Work* (CSWE, 1966).

CHAPTER NINE

Human Service Professions: A Comparative Analysis

"More than any other "helping professional" the social worker is expected to understand the influence of the environment—both the broad societal context and the more immediate environment as they contribute to individual situations."[1]

Economic and scientific development in the industrialized world has created a paradox. As society's ability to provide for physical needs increases, the individual's ability to achieve personal fulfillment and satisfying relationships tends to decrease. In response to these perceived human and social problems, we have attempted to find solutions guided by the social or life sciences; sociology, anthropology, psychology, political science, and economics are just some of the disciplines that have attempted to study the human condition with the goal of increasing life satisfaction. Along with this commitment of scientific resources to studying human problems, a considerable cadre of human service professions has emerged that attempts to intervene in human problems guided by knowledge of the social sciences.

Given the complexity of human behavior, it is not surprising that these disciplines often overlap. As our understanding of human behavior increases so does the overlap in the tasks, roles, and functions of human service professionals. Many students enter social work programs knowing they want to help people but not understanding how their choice of a profession will make a difference. This chapter provides a basic survey of differences between the many human service professions. While not denying the considerable overlap among the human service professions, the range of services they provide and the specific training and education they require is tremendous. It varies from doctoral level and medical school training of psychiatrists to the "learning by doing" training of the indigenous workers. Not only do these professions demand different kinds of education and training, but they also reflect different guiding theories and frames of reference and require different kinds of regulation. But more importantly each profession has a specific expertise that the others may or may not have but is basic to the given profession. For example, community psychiatrists may adopt the person in environment emphasis of social work, but not all psychiatrists adopt a community based approach. On the other hand, just as we expect psychiatrists to be knowledgeable about drug therapy, we expect social workers to be knowledgeable about community resources. And like the community psychiatrists who draw heavily on the expertise developed in the social work profession, psychiatric social workers tend to be knowledgeable about drug therapy, although social workers in general are not.

Although specific aspects of these comparisons may raise debate, they can provide a general overview of the differences between the human service professions and delineate social work's unique niche by comparing it with other human service professions. The comparison should help students understand each of the professions, discover which profession is most compatible with their attitudes, values, and skills, and gain some insight into the expectations that will be made of them in the profession they choose. This discussion is limited to a comparison with sociologists, psychologists, psychiatrists, counselors, and attorneys, since these are the professionals with whom social workers are most likely to work. New human service professions continue to develop but have not identified unique characteristics necessary to be included in this comparison; sociologists are not included in the table since few sociologists are involved in direct practice.

Social workers

The distinguishing characteristics of social work will be presented first to facilitate comparison.

1. Social work focuses on the totality of the problem situation. Social workers assess problems from psychological, sociological, political, and economic perspectives.
2. Social workers see the individual or group experiencing the problem as part of a larger social system. Primary support systems such as family, church, community, and neighborhood are important components of this system. More formal components of the system may be schools or places of employment, for example.
3. Social workers must have a comprehensive knowledge of community resources, how to use appropriate resources, and how to develop them if they do not exist.

Chapter 3 describes the generalist model of social work practice based on systems theory.

Table 9-1

A COMPARATIVE VIEW OF PROFESSIONS

	Social Worker	Attorney	Psychiatrist	Psychologist	Counselors
Emphasis	Totality of problem	Legal defense	Internal functioning	Psychological adjustment	Education or employment
Unique Expertise	Social environment Resource development	Law Legal representation	Electroshock therapy Drug therapy	Psychological testing	Aptitude testing
Frame of Reference	Psycho-social Political-economic	Statutes-Constitution	Medical model	Psychological theory	Educational psychology
Regulation	Basically (33 states) regulated by profession Not law	Licensed	Licensed	Licensed	Unregulated
Education	BSW MSW PhD.	Doctor of Jurisprudence J.D.	Doctor of medicine-M.D. and residency	Primarily Ph.D.	BS or BA in various disciplines
Sanction	Salaried public employees (approximately 90 percent)	Primarily private practice (fee for service)	Primarily private practice (fee for service)	Either private practice or salaried public employee	Salaried public employee
Professional Goal	Client empowerment	Legal protection	Cure of (mental) disease	Coping with adjustment	Self support
Role	Enabler Counselor Advocate Broker Resource linkage	Pure advocate	Healer	Therapist	Advice giver
Client Role	Client—limited power or choice	Consumer—considerable power & choice	Patient—limited power	Patient—limited power	Advice seeker

4. Social work emphasizes social interaction and resultant social functioning and malfunctioning. Social workers must have considerable knowledge of interpersonal relationships, conflict resolution, and group facilitation.
5. Social work recognizes that many individual problems are social. To understand individual problems, social workers must understand how those problems are rooted in societal institutions. Although social workers may disagree about what needs to change (the individual or society), all social workers must recognize the need to address both individual and institutional problems.
6. The basic goal of social work is client empowerment. The social worker helps the individual or the group function effectively. While the sociologist generally spends time ferreting out the facts, the social worker spends time understanding the client or the community, making appropriate diagnosis, and proceeding with an intervention; she hopes this intervention will lead to problem resolution and change.[2]

For a review of social work change efforts, see Chapter 6.

Sociology is the primary discipline involved in the study of the social environment, and sociological theory has made significant contributions to the knowledge base of social work. To succintly describe the differences between a sociologist and a social worker it could be said that a sociologist's primary goal is to develop and test theories about social phenomena, and a social worker's primary goal is to solve human problems.

The educational preparation of each reflects these different goals. Sociology students spend their time studying theory and research methods. Social work students spend a greater portion of their education applying those theories in practicums or field experiences. The doctorate is the terminal degree in sociology; the master's degree is generally the terminal degree in social work. Most sociologists work at universities or in other research settings and deal with ideas. Social workers generally work in public or private social welfare agencies and deal with clients.

Psychiatry and social work

One text summarized the difference between psychiatry and social work in this way.

> Psychiatry tends to focus on pathology and healing of illness; social work concentrates on strengths and the development of potential. The psychiatrist is particularly interested in the internal dynamics of individual and group behavior. The social worker is especially concerned about social functioning involving community factors and interactions.[3]

The way in which social workers and psychiatrists work together on a mental health team is presented in Chapter 17.

Psychiatrists and social workers frequently find themselves working together. Some of the roles they play (consultant, therapist, group facilitator) may even overlap. Due to the status differential between social workers and physicians, it is important that social workers be cognizant of their unique contributions and not become a mere nonmedical extension of the physician.

A psychiatrist is trained in medicine. Having completed all the requirements of medical school and an internship, a physician can then serve a residency to qualify as a psychiatrist. Psychiatrists are trained to understand the dynamics of family life, personality development, and human functioning, but her treatment focuses on illness and is based on the medical model. Psychiatrists are also the only mental health professionals who can prescribe medication or administer electro-shock therapy; though of course, not all psychiatrists use these therapies to treat their patients.

Social workers working with clinically depressed or schizophrenic patients might use more socially oriented types of treatment and would tend to assess their problems differently. The social worker would focus on problems and strengths in human relationships, analyze how the social environment is contributing to the mental illness, and attempt to determine how it could be altered to support healthy behavior. The social worker could also be expected to have a more comprehensive knowledge of community resources. The psychiatrist usually concentrates on the identified patient; the social worker interacts with the client's larger social network. The psychiatrist is more likely to deal with unconscious motivation; the social worker is more likely to operate on a behavioral level. The physician's role might be seen as healer; the social worker's role is likely to be enabler, resource developer, or even advocate. All states protect the physician and the patient by licensing. Only thirty-three states register or license the social worker; regulation within social work flows primarily from the NASW and professional values, norms, and the NASW Code of Ethics. And although some states do require licensing, and other states have licensing bills under consideration, social work licensing legislation achieves the same level of regulation that guides physicians.

The psychiatrist is likely to be paid on a fee for service basis. The social worker is more likely to be on a salary. Most psychiatrists are employed in private practice; social workers are usually employed in agencies. The client's role sometimes varies too. Because of psychiatry's association with medicine both psychiatrist and the person being treated may view their relationship as a doctor-patient relationship. Social workers tend to see individuals as clients; their perception implies more power and choice for the person receiving their service.

Psychologists and social workers

The clinical psychologist may engage in some of the same tasks as a psychiatrist or a social worker. All engage in some form of psychotherapy, but each profession has a different emphasis. The psychologist draws on psychological theories of human behavior rather than the medical model of the psychiatrist. Both psychiatrists and psychologists concentrate on understanding the individ-

Chapter 11 outlines the psychological foundations of social work practice.

ual psyche. Clinical psychologists use the individual psyche as their frame of reference for therapy; experimental psychologists are engaged in research to increase our understanding of the human psyche. The field of psychology has developed a considerable array of psychological tests to help understand and predict human behavior, and psychologists in general are likely to have expertise in psychological testing. Because the profession places considerable credence in the potential contributions of psychological testing, psychologists are usually trained to administer and interpret such tests. Psychological testing is also an integral part of insurance (public and private) reimbursement requirements.

Psychologists are more likely to be licensed than social workers.

Psychologists are required to be licensed although the monopolistic components are not developed to the same degree as the medical profession. Psychologists work in both private practice and public agencies. Psychologists in private practice tend to have doctorates; psychologists with less academic preparation usually work under the supervision of a doctorally trained psychologist. Psychologists in the school systems and state agencies, for instance, are not required to complete the doctorate or be licensed. Psychologists ordinarily assume the role of therapist, and their view of the patient's role tends to parallel the psychiatrist's more closely than the social worker's. However, depending upon which type of psychotherapy is chosen the patient's role may change. Chapter Ten presents some of the theories that guide psychotherapy.

Counselors and social workers

Counselors also have areas of overlap with psychologists, psychiatrists, and social workers. Like social workers, most counselors are not licensed by the state. Both psychologists and psychiatrists have their professions regulated by licensure. One advantage (from an academic perspective) of licensing is that it helps define the boundaries of the profession; psychiatrists and psychologists have not only professional but also legal guidelines that determine the appropriate domain of practice.

Counselors may have very specific roles depending upon the agencies they serve.

There are many types of counselors. The most common types are marriage and family, employment, school, and rehabilitation counselors; social workers too have been involved in each of these areas. Marriage and family counseling, for example, is not a separate profession but instead a specialization pursued by psychiatrists, psychologists, and social workers. Few graduate programs prepare marriage counselors who do not have a degree in one of the other professional fields. The American Association of Family and Marriage Counselors has members from all of these disciplines.

Social workers are often confused with school counselors. Ordinarily the school counselor has an undergraduate degree in education, at least some teaching experience, and a graduate degree in counseling. More affluent schools often require students to see a counselor who helps them plan their course schedules and careers. These are usually brief encounters, and it is not unusual for students to visit various school counselors interchangeably. In contrast, students who see a school social worker have usually been sent to her because their behavior (in the classroom or in the community) has been defined as problematic. The relationship between social worker and student tends to be more extensive and change oriented. A student approaches a counselor for information; a student is usually required to see a social worker based on something she has done or failed to do.

Employment and rehabilitation counselors ordinarily have at least some training in common. They are qualified to administer and interpret certain aptitude tests; they know what employment suits the individual's capabilities. The rehabilitation counselor usually has additional training in the special needs and abilities of handicapped people. Both employment and rehabilitation counselors have specific training the social worker is unlikely to have, and the social worker frequently works with these professionals to determine a client's academic or employment potential. The social worker then helps activate the resources necessary to allow the client to meet her potential. For example, a social worker may have to work with a client's family to help them get the necessary resources or adjust to allowing their child to risk herself in the educational or occupational world outside the home.

One of the social worker's roles is to work cooperatively with other human service professionals to best meet the needs of the client. Photo courtesy of Student Support Services Publication Center, University of Minnesota.

Attorneys and social workers

Attorneys and social workers frequently work with the same clients, either as members of the same team or as adversaries. The attorney's role in the legal setting is clear; she acts as an advocate for the client's legal defense. She is obliged to advise the client what she feels is in the client's best interest, but the client makes her own decisions in the end. Legal clients, in theory, have more power in the professional-client relationship than clients of other human service professionals.

Legal practice, like social work practice, is undergoing changes. Attorneys have traditionally been involved in private practice, but more and more are now finding employment in public programs where they almost always receive a salary rather than a fee for service. Clients of attorneys in private practice usually assume the role of consumer; placing attorneys in public settings changes that role. Individuals who hire an attorney have considerable choice (assuming they have the ability to pay). In public programs clients are more likely to be assigned an attorney. Nonetheless attorneys in either setting have the same obligation to their clients.

Attorneys must be licensed. Most states require practicing attorneys to complete law school and pass a state bar exam. Many states also require continuing education credits to retain the license to practice.

Attorneys and social workers may both serve as partisan advocates for clients.

Both attorneys and social workers may work as advocates, but how each profession defines advocacy points up some important differences. The mandate to a legal advocate is clear—an attorney must use every means within the legal system to promote and defend her client's position. The responsibility of the social work advocate has traditionally been ambiguous. Historically, it was assumed that the social work advocate was limited by her responsibility to balance the best interests of society and the client. However, Charles Grosser represents a different view of the advocacy role for social workers. He suggests

> the impartiality of the enabler and the functionalism of the broker are absent. Nor is the worker expert, consultant, guide or social therapist. He is, in fact, a partisan in social conflict. His expertise is available exclusively to serve client interests, since other actors in this social conflict may be using their expertise and resources against the client.[4]

While Grosser was not specifically addressing the legal setting, such a definition of an advocate implies the expertise and ethics of the professional practitioner are not compromised in social and legal conflicts. By acting as legal advocates social workers are providing clients the benefits of favorable professional assessments that are always available to the wealthy. Clearly the inconsistency in interpreting the role of social work in the legal setting makes the comparison of attorney and social worker somewhat controversial. It is to be hoped that the NASW will develop some leadership in defining the social worker's role in the legal setting.

Summary

A general comparison of the similarities and differences among psychologists, psychiatrists, social workers, counselors, and attorneys has been presented. While there is frequently more similarity than difference between human service professions, it is useful for individuals deciding on a human service career to address potential differences. This chapter has focused on differences among those professions in emphasis, unique expertise, frame of reference, regulation, amount and type of required education source of sanction, professional goals, and finally professional and client roles.

References

1. Donald Brieland, Lela Costin, and Charles Atherton, *Contemporary Social Work,* 2nd ed. (New York: McGraw-Hill, 1980), 13.
2. Rex Skidmore and M.G. Thackeray, *Introduction to Social Work,* 3rd ed. (Englewood Cliffs, N.J.: Prentice-Hall, 1982), 14.
3. Ibid., 16.
4. Charles Grosser, "Community Development Programs Serving the Urban Poor," *Social Work* 10, no. 3 (July 1965): 18–21.

PART
IV

THE KNOWLEDGE BASE: GENERAL THEORY

"Without theory, practice becomes chaotic. . . . Theory gives meaning and clarity to what would otherwise be specific and isolated cases. On the other hand, without practice, theory becomes mere speculation. The realities of practice provide a check upon pure speculation . . . also, practice provides the problems which must be dealt with by any comprehensive theory."[1]

Every organization uses some kind of technology to accomplish its goals. At the Ford Motor Company the technology is tangible because the process of assembling the elements results in a concrete product, an automobile. Automaking is characterized by a high degree of routinization; once the operational system is in place, the tasks become clear, the cause and effect relationships are clear, the process is repetitive, and the product is standardized. Technicians can be trained to know exactly what to do since there is little or no variation in the problems they face accomplishing their task.

Part IV discusses the knowledge base of the profession including sociological and psychological theories.

Professionals face a different kind of task. The professional's theoretical knowledge explains the technical knowledge and guides its application under different circumstances. Technicians apply technical knowledge repeatedly in identical or similar situations. Professionals do not simply apply rules; instead they learn to think in a particular way and to exercise judgment in specific situations guided by their general knowledge base. Not only must they master a knowledge base, but they must also use their intelligence and judgment—the hallmark of a profession. Rigid rules and details impede good professional practice. The professional person who masters technical information and knows concepts and theories but cannot make sound applications or good judgments is not effective.[2]

Practice theories are presented in Chapter 3 and specific social work methods are reviewed in Chapter 6.

The knowledge base of social work practice contains three different levels of theory: general theory drawn from the related disciplines like psychology, sociology, anthropology, political science, and economics; practice theory (including knowledge of policy, services, programs, institutions, and the social worker's role in relationship to each of them[3]) that explains some of the ways social workers use knowledge in their day to day work; and specific social work methods, that is, theories of practice.

Louise Johnson describes the social work knowledge base as "eclectic, interdisciplinary, tentative at best, complex and often subjective."[4] Since the disciplines from which it draws its theoretical underpinnings have conflicting theories, the social work knowledge base is understandably tentative. Social work can not develop an integrated theory base as long as it builds upon disciplines that offer contrasting models of human behavior.

Social work practice is filled with controversy regarding the relationship of theory and practice. Social work educators are committed to either theory-based or knowledge-guided practice. In core introductory courses a student is often impressed with the importance of theory to practice. It is not unusual, however, to have the student's practicum guided by a social worker who suggests she forget all the theory she learned in the classroom because it does not apply in practice. These practitioners suggest that the complexity and incongruity of theories are evidence of theory's irrelevance to practice since it cannot determine what the best course of action may be. It is true that while social work educators believe in the superiority of theoretically informed practice, they cannot always identify what this actually involves and how it might be achieved, let alone its practical outcome.[5]

This inability to articulate social work knowledge has been at least partially responsible for the anti-intellectual stance of many practitioners. Since social work is a purposeful activity, practitioners have to select, integrate, and use knowledge in the light of their functions, tasks, and the people and problems with whom they work. In many cases practice has been forced to move beyond what has been articulated in theory; and practitioners have not been prone to create theory by clear and explicit articulation of what it is they do and why they do it. However, to argue that practice is and should be atheoretical is problematic. While knowledge is no guarantee of certainty, it does increase the frequency with which socially appropriate decisions will be made. No one can operate with a totally objective view. Everyone holds assumptions and beliefs about individuals; these assumptions and beliefs have practical consequences.

Scott Briar and Henry Miller contend that the choice for practitioners is not whether or not to have a theory, but what theoretical assumptions to hold. The atheoretical position amounts to a preference for implicit and hidden rather than explicit and self-conscious knowledge in social work. This preference protects practitioners from having practice evaluated on either political, ethical, or intellectual grounds. Since theories have implications for problem assessments and intervention decisions, an important step in improving practice is to understand how knowledge is used.[6]

Part of the demystification process in social work is related to the recognition of the different functions of knowledge to the profession. Knowledge in the liberal tradition is seen as a source of enlightenment; conscious calculation is believed to be superior to blind assumptions. This is the major traditional assumption about the contribution of social science knowledge to practice. Unfortunately that assumption has not always had fruitful consequences, since most of what has been taught and written has been relatively unhelpful for direct practice. If social science is to be useful to direct practice, it has the important mapping function of codifying, conceptualizing, and documenting the process and content of practice activity; it must make the implicit explicit.[7]

So far it has been suggested that social workers must take action on the basis of knowledge. But since social workers cannot conquer the total social science arena, what kind of knowledge is needed to support practice? Social workers need to understand developmental, cognitive, affective, and interpersonal processes; they must also know how personality functions and evolves in various situations. In addition, to practice effectively, social workers must have more than a nodding acquaintance with socioeconomic and demographic theories, fields of social policy, systems theory, and institutional organizations.[8] Social workers must have a theory base that makes them aware that the structure of society and transactions with others are reflected in the self and the life structure of each individual. Each human being has her own particular world that presents her with opportunity, meaning, feeling, identity, and myths she uses and internalizes selectively.[9]

While the complexity and size of the social work knowledge base prohibits its thorough analysis in this text, the beginning student may profit by a discussion of a few areas of knowledge and how these areas relate to practice. This section provides a survey of specific psychological, sociological, and political science theory that is identified as part of the general social work knowledge base, some exposure to practice theory, and examples of methods or theories of practice.

The first two chapters in this section are designed to further an understanding of human behavior from a sociological and psychological perspective. The sociological material presents an analysis of the social functioning of individuals and groups and social work's role in maintaining society. Social work and the social welfare institution are vital components in maintenance of society.

The psychology section introduces the study of personality theory and presents the three most widely held theories—psychoanalysis, behaviorism, and self theory. We present each with an example to reveal how theory can be applied in practice.

In addition to an understanding of human behavior and social functioning, social work practice is enhanced by understanding the context in which practice takes place. Practice reflects the political, social, economic, and cultural environment, and societal values are codified in social welfare policy. The organizational structure in which services are provided are also important to effective practice.

Social policy sets the limits and potential for what social workers can accomplish. Understanding the nature of policies and becoming involved in making decisions are potential sources of power for both the social worker and the client. Social welfare policy determines how social workers will be involved either in making decisions or in implementing policies. Specific policies are not addressed except to illustrate some of the policy concepts covered; instead this section is limited to a discussion of the social worker's role, the policy making process, and the dimensions of choice. It touches only lightly upon the vast store of political science knowledge that students may want to pursue further.

The social policy and sociology sections each contributes to the understanding of forces shaping society and social policy. Knowledge of problems, policies, and programs are an inherent part of a knowledge base that social workers use daily.

Finally since most social workers work in agencies and are required to coordinate services with other agencies, a discussion of organizational theory can greatly enhance practice. Social work programs usually offer no more than a sampling of this subject in the human behavior sequence; organizational theory tends to take second place to theories of personality as most instructors are more knowledgeable in those areas. But an understanding of interagency coordination and cooperation is useful to social workers at any level of practice. If indeed not enough social workers are trained in administration, perhaps it is because students are not exposed to the subject. This chapter will not prepare students to be administrators, but it may help them become more effective organizational members. It may also entice them into specializing in administration.

References

1. Ralph Tyler, "Distinctive Attributes of Education for the Professions," *Social Work,* no. 33 (April 1952): 61.
2. James Gustafson, "Professions as'Callings'," *Social Service Review* 56, no. 4 (Dec. 1982): 501–515.
3. Pauline Hardiker and Mary Barker, *Theories of Practice in Social Work* (San Francisco: Academic Press, 1981), 1.
4. Louise Johnson, *Social Work Practice: A Generalist Approach* (Boston: Allyn and Bacon, 1983), 49–50.
5. J. Bailey, *Ideas and Intervention: Social Theory for Practice* (London: Rutledge and Kegan Paul, 1980).
6. Scott Briar and Henry Miller, *Problems and Issues in Social Casework* (New York: Columbia University Press, 1971), 180.
7. Hardiker, *Theories of Practice,* 4.
8. Shirley Cooper, "Social Work: A Dissenting Profession," *Social Work* 22, no. 5 (Sept. 1977): 363.
9. D. J. Levinson, *The Seasons of a Man's Life* (New York: Knopf, 1978), 1.

CHAPTER TEN

Understanding Social Functioning: The Conflict Order Debate

"Life in society is organized around complex systems in which, and by which, man tries to bring some semblance of order to his universe. Life is organized around institutions of all sorts: some are man-made, others have developed, it seems without concrete design."[1]

People have always strived to organize their existence. Every society needs to establish social order. Sociological analysis examines how social work fits into the broader social structure. It attempts to explain why a society so strongly committed to individualism and private acquisition of wealth supports a profession committed to the redistribution of resources. Sociology addresses this question by looking at the social structure of our society.

Social order

Social order refers to the regularity or patterns seen in human behavior. Many aspects of social order are so internalized that people do not recognize how it affects the way they do things and how they perceive reality. Social order comprises an unwritten code of behavior governing such mundane matters as showing common courtesy and respect for others to such complicated political processes as presidential elections. Social order is not a matter of people doing what they are told to do but rather a generally accepted understanding of "this is the way things are done."

In fact, society is threatened when things are not done a certain way. For example, only 53 percent of the potential electorate voted in the 1984 presidential election; almost half of the eligible public chose not to vote, a problem in a democracy. Some people feel it reflects the alienation of the populace; others see it as an indication of apathy and lack of responsibility of citizens. Whether one believes society or the individual is at fault, democratic principles important to our society are at risk when citizens choose not to vote.

Earl Babbie illustrates the strength of social order on a personal behavior level. His illustration conveys how social order sometimes goes against what is verbalized as socially desirable. Babbie was interested in the nature of responsibility for public matters: specifically, who is responsible for keeping public places clean? On the one hand government workers are hired to maintain public places and are blamed when those facilities are not clean. What fascinated Babbie was how this assignment of responsibility to one group not only relieved the average citizen of the responsibility but actually prohibited him from taking responsibility. When an unauthorized person took responsibility for picking up litter in a public park, for example, instead of receiving approval, he was subjected to negative sanctions. The formal norms of society would suggest that voluntarily picking up litter is a sign of good citizenship, but in reality strong informal agreements about taking responsibility for public things supersede the formal norms.[2]

Many important components of social order, then, are not rules or laws at all but unwritten guides to behavior. Social order is dynamic; people are born into it. Nearly everyone accepts the premise that social order exists because individuals are morally or psychologically dependent on society. Every individual needs the cooperation of other human beings, and in any group there must be order.

To maintain that order certain social functions must be met—producing and distributing food and other goods, for example, dividing labor, or allocating authority. As a society becomes more complex, the institutions designed to fill these social functions become more formalized. Sociologists study how society meets each of the essential social functions, what kinds of institutions have been developed to provide these functions, and how social work and the social welfare institution fit into the social structure.

One view of society and institutions, combining elements common to the conservative and liberal views (as explained in chapter 4), is called the order perspective. It suggests that societal systems operate to maintain order and the status quo. In contrast the radical perspective argues that social systems exploit the working class and protect the ruling class. Both views provide a functional analysis of the social work profession.

The liberal, radical and conservative perspectives can be reviewed in Chapter 2.

Social structure

To survive a society must perform certain essential functions that have been categorized as production, consumption, and distribution; socialization; social control; social integration; and mutual support.[3] To accomplish these functions, societies develop institutions, defined by Neil Gilbert and Harry Specht as "networks of relationships" that are generally accepted as the way to carry out essential social functions.[4] Institutions are probably the most significant structured element in any society; the economic, political, religious, social welfare, and educational institutions, along with the family are among the most visible and powerful. Within each of these institutions there is a recurrent and consistent pattern of social relationships. Each is expected to fulfill certain of the essential social functions. The economic institution has primary responsibility for the production, consumption, and distribution function. The political institution has primary responsibility for social control. The family, the church, and the schools are responsible for socialization and social integration. The social welfare institution too is designed to fulfill essential social functions, but no consensus defines those functions or even its structure. Most texts suggest that the social welfare institution is a backup that takes over when the primary institutions (the family or the economic system, for example) fail. Others argue that the social welfare institution has a primary function of providing for the well-being of people in the society and its services are not and should not be dependent on the breakdown of the family or the market system. Wilensky and Lebeaux refer to the first view as a residual conception of social welfare and the second view as the institutional conception of social welfare.[5] Sociologists have expanded on these ideas and have provided considerable insight on the functions and dysfunctions of the social welfare institution and its relationship to the other major institutions. This chapter draws upon this knowledge to illustrate the complexity of the relationship between social welfare and other institutions. While it does not provide any definitive answers about the "proper" role of any of the institutions, it does provide a framework for determining that role and understanding how welfare programs serve the interest of society as well as clients.

The concepts of residual and institutional social services were introduced in Chapter 2.

Production, consumption, distribution

The production, consumption, and distribution of goods and services is the primary domain of the economic system. The complexity of society today precludes individuals or even families from producing everything they need. Instead people specialize by producing more than what they need of one commodity and exchanging either that one commodity or their labor (wages) to get the things they need. The way a society organizes to allow this exchange is referred to as the economic system. In pre-industrial times most exchanges could be made on an informal community basis. With the advent of industrialization societal structures have developed to deal with this exchange in a more formal and predictable manner.

The economic institution is of such critical importance that societies are frequently classified by the types of economies they possess—capitalistic, communistic, or socialistic. Such oversimplification of economic systems fosters a naive perception of their relationship to other societal institutions. Social workers are particularly interested in the economic system as it relates to the social welfare system. Does the economic system support the welfare system? Or, does the welfare system support the economic system? Who benefits from the present economic arrangements? Who benefits from the present social welfare programs? Conflict and order theorists provide different assessments of how the economic and social welfare institution interface.

ORDER PERSPECTIVE

From the functionalist perspective, all parts of every system are either functional or dysfunctional. The functional parts help maintain the system in a balanced state and reinforce the status quo; dysfunctional components have either no effect or a negative effect. In a capitalistic society acquisitiveness and competitiveness are functional to both the social and economic system. The economic system is inherently good because it produces large scale affluence. Workers not producing for a wage are viewed as dysfunctional.[6] In theory they decrease the standard of living for everyone.

This value system can be seen in societal attitudes toward the elderly, the disabled, and mothers on welfare. Since the elderly and the disabled tend to be out of the paid work force, they are less valued. In 1978 a successful gubernatorial candidate suggested society had to prevent the elderly from becoming a "millstone around the neck of their children." In 1984 another governor implied that the elderly should be willing to die and make place for the young; he was concerned that precious resources not be spent on health care for the elderly. Although he later said he was misquoted, in reality he put into words the concern of many Americans that we are spending too much money on the care of "non-productive" people. Some societies stress what the elderly have accomplished and what they know: the younger generation feels indebted to the elderly. The functional perspective of a capitalistic society limits its analysis to production and usefulness. Functional analysis provides a rationale for evaluating and criticizing particular policies and structures within a consensual society whose basic values and structures are not disputed. Instead, we question individuals or institutions that do not fit into the social order.

CONFLICT PERSPECTIVE

Conflict theorists suggest the economic institution itself is responsible for social problems, and the role of the social welfare institution has been to pre-

Some societies value the elderly for their knowledge and experience. What is their place in the American system? Photo by David S. Strickler.

serve and protect the economic system rather than to promote the welfare of society. Ray Bailey and Mike Brake suggest that society needs a healthy, docile, and expendable labor force, and the welfare state only mitigates the most disastrous effects of poverty and exploitation that would occur if the capitalistic system were to operate freely. They suggest that even though welfare, on the surface, has evolved from long political battles and is executed by an administration separate from the interests of business, "it is still used to subsidize business and industry."[7]

From the conflict perspective unemployment is the social problem most clearly connected to the economic system. David Gordon, for example, defines two stages in the determination and distribution of income. First, a complex set of social, economic, and technical forces determine a given worker's total productivity depending on his skill and position. Then, the relative power of employer and employee determines the proportion of profit the worker receives in wages. The wages workers actually receive are not based only on their skills and productivity (over which they have some control) but also on the relative power of the group with which they are identified. For example, union members receive higher wages than non-union members. Grade school teachers, who supposedly perform one of the most important roles in society, continue to receive very low pay; only through unionization have they been able to increase their pay.

Conflict theorists see the social welfare institution as one of the important tools for protecting the owners of production from having to pay a fair share of profits to workers. They suggest the present relief programs assure a ready pool of labor—the unemployed who receive welfare benefits only as long as they are willing to accept whatever work is available.

As a society we believe that every member of society should work; radicals suggest the work-relief relationship is not a simple matter. They suggest there are two major choices. Relief programs can be designed to force workers to take employment at inadequate wages or lose their benefits; or they can be designed to require employers to provide an adequate wage to attract workers. The Aid to Families with Dependent Children (AFDC) is criticized by conflict theorists for subsidizing substandard wages for women. Work requirements force AFDC recipients to accept work at minimum wage if their children have reached six years of age. Some have even suggested that welfare recipients take jobs paying less than minimum wage. The poor have some protection in this area, since labor unions feel such a move would erode their bargaining power. Robert Lekachman summarizes the industry-welfare relationship.

The radical view of social welfare systems is explained in Chapter 2.

> In this exceedingly conservative country, it is more politically popular to blame victims than villains—welfare clients and laid-off workers rather than the heads of mismanaged corporations and the compliant politicians who serve their interests. Recent public policy focuses tax rewards upon the mismanagers of the private sector and benefit reductions and unemployment upon the casualties of their blunders.[9]

The relationship between the social welfare institution and the economic system is extensive. What is not clear is which segment of society is the primary beneficiary of the system. Is it more accurate to say the economic system makes possible the broad array of services designed to benefit the poor, or does the social welfare system operate in a manner that ultimately benefits the present economic arrangement (the wealthy) even at great cost to the poor. Who does the welfare system serve? Are the poor victims of, or recipients of, our welfare services?

Socialization

Socialization is the process through which individuals acquire the knowledge, skills, and values that enable them to participate effectively in society. Historically the family and the church were the primary institutions that fulfilled the socialization function. As society developed and more complex skills and knowledge were required, new institutions developed or expanded to meet that function. Today educational and social welfare institutions such as schools, colleges, and daycare centers are essential to the socialization function. Just as there were differing views on who benefits from the way the economic system organizes to meet the production, consumption, and distribution function, there are differing views on how socialization is achieved. Since education is a primary agent of socialization, a discussion of how education influences socialization will exemplify opposing views.

ORDER PERSPECTIVE

The most widely accepted view of the educational system is that it has evolved to meet the needs of the economic system while providing opportunity and social mobility to the disadvantaged. The great equalizer in our society, education has been the vehicle for disadvantaged groups to achieve social mobility. Education provides equality of opportunity too. If other social and economic structures foster inequality, schools should counter this influence by showing the way for disadvantaged groups.

As an example, education can be considered from the order perspective and the conflict perspective.

In the order perspective, then, the educational system is the means by which the underclass can achieve equality and social mobility. The purpose of the schools is to improve the productivity of the unskilled and the poor. Schools accomplish this by instilling values and teaching skills consistent with the needs of the economic system. If young people stay in school, study hard, and develop skills, they will be able to improve their social position. Poverty would not exist if the poor were properly educated. This view has led to social policies such as Title I, which provides money for education in areas with a high concentration of poor people. The assumptions of the order perspective derive from common views of the functioning of the marketplace.

1. Increased education will lead to increased economic productivity.
2. Testing done in the school system is a measure of the skills necessary for increased production.
3. The role of education is to decrease inequality.
4. Education is the key to social mobility.

Gordon summarizes this perspective.

> Together these four principal assumptions about education produced a single coherent perspective on educational objectives: that to improve the productivity of the low-skilled and the poor—in order to equalize their economic opportunities—we must improve their education; that to improve their education in that sense, we must raise their level of cognitive achievement by improving their abilities to read and reason; that the schools can effect this increasing equality of opportunity because they have played that role historically; and that, in general, it is becoming easier for the schools to fulfill this equalizing function because our society is continuing to become more educationally mobile (and simultaneously more meritocratic) over time.[10]

CONFLICT PERSPECTIVE

In contrast to the view of education as the great equalizer, some view education as the stabilizer of the present class system. Ryan suggests that what schools are really about is not helping people rise in the social structure but keeping them in their places, and training young people to take their allotted positions in the inequality structure without making "a stink" about it.[11] Bowles reflects the radical view of how our educational system prepares the working class to take its place in the structure of inequality:

> . . . socialization patterns in schools attended by students of different social classes do not arise by accident. Rather, they stem from the fact that the educational objectives and expectations of both parents and teachers, and the responsiveness of students to various patterns of teaching and control, differ for students of different social classes. . . . class inequalities in school socialization patterns are reinforced by the inequalities in financial resources. . . . The paucity of financial support for the education of children from working-class families not only leaves more resources to be devoted to the children of those with commanding roles in the economy; it forces upon the teachers and school administrators in the working-class schools a type of social relations which fairly closely mirrors that of the factory. Thus, financial considerations in poorly supported working-class schools militate against small intimate classes, against a multiplicity of elective courses and specialized teachers (except disciplinary personnel), and preclude the amounts of free time for the teachers and free space required for a more open, flexible educational environment. The lack of financial support all but requires that students be treated as raw materials . . . ; it places a high premium on obedience and punctuality; there are few opportunities for independent, creative work of individualized attention by teachers. . . . well-financed schools . . . can offer much greater opportunities for the development of the capacity for sustained independent work and the other characteristics required for adequate job performance in the upper levels of the occupational hierarchy.[12]

SUMMARY

The educational system is critical to the smooth functioning of society. It is a primary tool of socialization; it does impart knowledge, values, and skills. From the order perspective, it appears the schools socialize students to strive for achievement and to make contributions to the society while they attempt to improve their own social status. The conflict perspective contends the schools socialize students to take their predetermined place in the structure of inequality and to be satisfied with what they have.

Whether schools socialize for conformity or creativity and productivity, their impact is felt by all of society. Social workers tend to deal with people who have not been adequately socialized, who for various reasons, have not accepted societal values or have failed to gain the knowledge and skill necessary for productive citizenry. A systems approach to practice suggests the social worker needs to look at the system as well as the individual to see why this socialization has not occurred.

The socialization process is of course much too complex to be attributed only to the schools. The values held by the people of a community (political and religious), the kinds of social structures available, the legal system, and the police are just some of the means society has at its disposal to channel people into the roles it finds necessary for its maintenance.[13]

Social control

Every society requires a means of assuring that citizens conform to societal norms. The political institution, particularly through its law-making and law enforcement function, is the primary institution of social control. If members of a group (society) are willing to restrict their own activities, or if their activities are inconsequential, laws are unnecessary. Further, the more effective the socialization, integration, and mutual support functions are, the less visible and important the social control mechanisms become.

The role of social worker as an agent of social control is debated in Chapter 17.

Two well-known sociologists, Hage and Parsons, have noted that social control over individuals can be accomplished by either socialization or sanctions.[14 15] The concept of controlling with sanctions can best be illustrated with our political institution. Certain laws and rules must be followed; if individuals do not abide by them, they will be punished. If the rules or laws are clear and fair, it is not necessary to punish very often. A society that sets rules but does not have the ability to enforce those rules will not have control. The more frequently a society must impose sanctions, the less harmonious it is likely to be. There is considerable debate in the criminal justice area around what kind of sanctions are most effective in maintaining social control. Some theorists argue that imposing longer sentences on offenders would deter crime. Others argue that more certain but less severe punishment would decrease crime. Proponents of longer sentences see deviance being controlled strictly through punishment; the harsher the punishment the less likely the individual is to commit a crime. Proponents of shorter but more certain sentences attempt to combine punishment with socialization; they feel the certainty of even a moderate punishment will always make a stronger impression than the fear of a more severe penalty combined with the hope for impunity. Positive sanctions also have a place in this analysis. People who look forward to rewards for following the rules are unlikely to break the rules. This may mean merely that they see themselves as filling their own roles appropriately and that they are receiving appropriate benefits for their efforts.

An historical example of the socialization of women is found in Chapter 5 in the discussion of social feminism.

Socialization assumes the presence in a society of consistent and controlling messages about what the proper behavior is for the individual. Jo Freeman suggests that socialization is one of the less visible but most powerful means of social control. In her examination of how society limits or controls women she found that society does not control the alternatives for women, but through socialization it controls her motivation to choose any but traditional alternatives: Women have so thoroughly internalized the social definition of their role as servants to men as wives, and caretakers of the next generation of men that no laws are necessary to enforce this choice. "Women reach this condition, the acceptance of their secondary roles as right and just, through the most insidious mechanism of social control yet devised—the socialization process."[16]

Any discussion of societal mechanisms to achieve social control must address the issue of professionals as social control agents. Radicals suggest that professionals, doctors, lawyers, social workers, and teachers are primarily agents of social control. Many social workers find the notion of being agents of social control a troubling one. Peter Day's book, *Social Work and Social Control* defended the thesis that social control functions are complementary to the social worker's caring and rehabilitative functions. He further implied that particular forms of social control are themselves prerequisites to helping clients work on their problems. The data collected for this study were drawn from clients of probation and parole officers. These clients agreed that the social control aspects were functional to their treatment.[17] But in spite of Day's findings or similar studies that delineate the positive contributions of the social control role, it still remains a problematic one for some social workers who see it in conflict with the principles of client self-determination and non-directiveness.

Social workers frequently operate as agents of social control. In fact, it is reasonable to question whether social work would exist if other social control mechanisms were really effective. Social workers most obviously perform social control functions in prisons, welfare offices, and probation and parole offices. They serve the same function, however, in less obvious settings—therapy sessions, hospitals, and nursing homes, for example. The social worker is an agent of control whenever he intervenes to get the client to cooperate or adjust to institutional needs rather than continue to engage in behavior that may be personally satisfying but is disruptive to those around him. Whether the patient behaves because a social worker convinces him it is in his best interest or whether he behaves to avoid punishment, it is still social control.

Social integration

Social integration is the process by which individuals come to value their membership in a society and to feel responsible for abiding by its rules. Emile Durkheim studied the role of social integration over one hundred years ago.[18] He saw lack of integration into the social structure as being a cause of suicide. He hypothesized that in any society the stronger the forces throwing the individual onto his own resources and the fewer the social supports, the greater the suicide rate. Social integration is essential to both society and the individual. His studies looked at religion as one of the major integrating institutions; the more integral religion is to one's life the less likely one is to commit suicide. Religion gives one a sense of being part of larger society. Without some kind of integrating mechanism the individual becomes alienated from the society in which he lives.

Peter Blau describes a person as integrated if other members find him sufficiently attractive to freely associate with and accept him into their midst as one of them.[19] Piven and Cloward describe this phenomenon on a societal basis as a superstructure which includes an elaborate group of beliefs or ritual behaviors which define for people what is right and what is wrong and why; what is possible and impossible; and the appropriate behaviors that follow from these beliefs.[20] They also see the social integration function of a capitalistic society inherently related to its economic system. Piven and Cloward contend that the regulation of civil behavior in all societies is intimately dependent on stable occupational arrangements. As long as people are fixed in their work roles, their activities and their future also seem fixed; they do what they think is right. These behaviors are shaped and reinforced by receiving a paycheck—their livelihood. When mass unemployment breaks that bond, people are cut off from the main institution by which they are regulated and controlled.

Lawrence Mead contends that the main goal of the welfare state has always been to integrate the disadvantaged into the mainstream of society.[21] His view of the importance of work for social integration is as strong as that of Piven and Cloward and yet he arrives at very different assessments of the solution to this problem. Mead contends that merely raising the income of the lower class does not guarantee they will acquire the skills and attitudes necessary to participate freely in American life. The disadvantaged do not need further economic resources but a more secure sense of order in themselves and the neighborhoods around them; their problem is more moral than economic. He further suggests that the troubling behavior and condition of this disadvantaged group may be due to the social programs on which so many have become dependent: the same concern that charity organization societies expressed in the 1880s. According to Mead these programs govern the lives of many poor and disadvantaged more directly than overt discrimination in the past ever did. The drawback of social welfare programs is that they give things to recipients and expect nothing in return. Mead contends that the welfare state is a "hole in the polity" through which millions have dropped out of active involvement in American life. To maintain these programs and socially integrate the disadvantaged, he believes society must obligate the disadvantaged to function as other people do. They can only be equals if society is willing to require them to contribute.[22]

It appears then that Mead, a conservative, and Piven and Cloward, radicals, all agree on the importance of work to society and the individual but disagree on whether our present economic system should be willing or even able to provide that work. They also disagree on basic questions about forced work and the responsibility for providing a living wage or a decent standard of living. The question is not whether work should be required, but under what conditions does the work requirement lead to alienation. The social problems created by widespread alienation can be more costly than relief programs. How can a society provide work opportunities for everyone under conditions that increase societal integration? No clear consensus on that question has yet emerged.

SUMMARY

Social integration is primarily a function of families, religion, the schools, and the market system. Since our society values individuals according to their contributions to the work force, employment is crucial for social integration. However, if or when the market system cannot use the labor force profitably, the social welfare system steps in to provide unemployment benefits, minimal welfare payments if necessary, and social services to help the unemployed readjust their assumptions about society. The question some, such as Mead, would raise is whether this aid increases or decreases the social integration.

Mutual aid

Mutual aid is as old as society itself. In a study of animals and humans, Peter Kropotkin concluded that the species that survive are not necessarily the most powerful, but rather those species most able to cooperate with one another.[23] It is impossible for individuals to grow, develop, and make the most of their potential without support from other people. Other people provide affection, approval, food, shelter, and clothing. Individuals and societies require exchanges of support and services.

Black self-help groups use mutual aid because they are often denied access to traditional services. See Chapter 5.

This reality contradicts individualism, a value cherished by most Americans. Not only does society subscribe to the self-sufficient ideal, but it has even glorified the supposed self-sufficiency of our ancestors. If one were to believe a typical history text, he would be led to the certain conclusion that we have all descended from rugged pioneers who were totally self-sufficient. The reality of social and economic development in America is very different from what that myth suggests. Life on the frontier was difficult; a community spirit was required for mere survival. In pioneer days communities banded together to hire a community doctor (an early form of socialized medicine), to build homes, to gather crops, and to survive the hardships of bitterly cold winters.

As our society became increasingly complex, we have become increasingly interdependent. With each passing day and with each technological advance, the proportion of essential survival functions an individual can accomplish single-handedly decreases. Even so, society continues to idealize the rugged individualist to the detriment of the social welfare system. Ralph Dolgoff and Donald Feldstein summarize the major assumptions of the American myth upon which our welfare programs are based.[24]

It may be helpful to compare and contrast these values with the social work values toward clients found in the NASW Code of Ethics. (See Chapter 7.)

1. The "best" people are those who are physically strong, psychologically independent, and able to flourish without help.
2. "Making it" is what counts. We are even willing to overlook the means by which people achieve their financial success.

3. Everything is possible. If you only try hard enough you can accomplish anything.
4. Humans strive for material goods. Money is the prime human motivator. Seeing self-fulfillment as an end in itself is unreal or idealistic.
5. The corollary of these first four points is that those who fail to "make it" are at the least incompetent and more likely lazy or immoral. Somehow, if things do not go well, there is no one to blame but one's self. This has been referred to by Ryan as "blaming the victim."[25]

Even though many cultures value achievement, the United States is unusual in its victimization of "underachievers." We blame the victim who loses his sense of worth and strength. We then develop a profession such as social work to reintegrate the individual and rebuild the individual's sense of worth. An article by Roger Simon illustrated how the lack of societal support for vic-

The Amish survive as a group through community spirit. Photo by the Columbus Dispatch.

tims leads to the individual's disempowerment (*Milwaukee Sentinel,* June 21, 1983). A woman who found herself being molested on a crowded subway did not shout or even complain—even when she squirmed around to face her smiling molester. "I knew I should have, but, well, to scream on a train. I was embarrassed. I just tried to squirm away. I didn't want to make a fuss."

Though Simon's example relates to sexual harrassment, victims of the economic system or other social problems often suffer a loss of confidence and self-concept. If victims of the downturn in the economic cycle had the courage to reject the blame, to fight for their economic security, and to scream when threatened, government would more likely respond humanely to their problems. Since a society accepts individual human failure as the cause of poverty, the extent to which the social welfare system will be designed to aid in the mutual support function is very limited. Historical, political, economic, and social factors have conspired to influence the societal approach to providing mutual aid. Our emphasis on individualism has led to a residual conception of social welfare: mutual aid activities should come into play only when human needs are not being met by the family, the political, religious, or the market system. Mutual aid is a short term intervention designed to let other institutions take over as soon as possible. Benefits should be minimal and a privilege rather than a right. Many social work programs are designed with these guiding assumptions and are clearly related to the myth of the rugged individual.

Another view of the social welfare institution takes a much broader approach. The mutual aid function is appropriate to all private and public organizations that have a primary concern for both the well-being of the individual and society as a whole. Everyone's daily life is directly or indirectly dependent on and subsidized by government; everyone benefits from the support of governmental and nongovernmental social welfare.[26] This approach to social welfare forces us to take a much broader look at the relationship between our tax system and the benefit system. In fact it requires seeing the total governmental structure as being of benefit to all citizens and necessary to maintain social order. The federal structure is a necessity for the survival of democracy. Since everyone benefits from having this structure, everyone must share the responsibility for supporting the structure.

Senator Fritz Hollings, a contender for the Democratic presidential nomination in 1984, gave an example of how much people benefit from government and how easily they forget the source of the benefit.

> A veteran returning from Korea went to college on the GI Bill; bought his house with an FHA loan; saw his kids born in a VA hospital; started a business with a SBA loan, got electricity from TVA and, later, water from an EPA project. His parents retired to a farm on social security, got electricity from REA and soil testing from USDA. When the father became ill, the family was saved from financial ruin by Medicare and a life was saved with a drug developed through NIH.

> His kids participated in the school-lunch program, learned physics from teachers trained in an NSF program and went to college with guaranteed student loans. He drove to work on the interstate and moored his boat in a channel dredged by Army engineers. When floods hit, he took Amtrak to Washington to apply for disaster relief, and spent some time in the Smithsonian museums. Then one day he wrote his congressman an angry letter asking the government to get off his back and complaining about paying taxes for all those programs created for ungrateful people.[27]

One should consider several policy questions: Who should pay into the system? In what proportion should one pay into the system? Who should benefit and how much from the system? Adam Smith, the father of conservatism, contended that the rich should pay the most taxes because they receive the most from government.[28] Most people do not really recognize the tremendous benefits the government confers. Without taxes there would be few schools, no roads, no garbage pick-up, etc. David Gordon argues that the mutual support function of the social welfare institution is clearly not designed with the poor as the primary beneficiaries. He argues that the distribution, allocative, and stabilizing function of the state are inextricably intertwined and that the primary beneficiary of the social welfare institution is the ruling class.[29] Mead, whose approach to welfare is considerably more conservative, would agree that the social welfare institution responds not only to the poor; the welfare state refers to something much larger than just social programs for the poor.[30] Today all Americans are "on welfare" in the sense that they claim (from government programs) benefits they have not direcftly earned. Since programs that benefit the general population (social security, for example, or Medicare) are principally responsible for the government's fiscal problems, it seems reasonable to say that welfare programs for the lower class have not created the welfare state and our present financial crisis.

Chapter summary

At the outset we suggested that every society must meet the essential social functions of production, consumption, distribution; social control; socialization; social integration; and mutual support to maintain social order. The political, economic, religious, educational and familial institutions have a relatively clear relationship to each of the essential social functions; the social welfare institution on the other hand does not foster the same consensus about its appropriate functions, although most would agree that it does impinge on the other institutions. Diverse views of what the social welfare institution actually does and what it "should" do, and correspondingly diverse views of the state are related to diverse assumptions about people, their rights and their responsibilities. The complexity of social work's relationship to the broader social structure suggests some reasons social work does not always receive support equivalent to the importance of the problems it must address.

Analyzing social welfare's fucntion is just one of the ways sociology contributes to the knowledge base of social work practice. It moves problem analysis and interventions from an individual (private trouble) to a societal (public issue) basis. Sociological analysis provides the tools to assess social work practice from a structural as well as an individualistic view. Understanding social structure helps the social worker understand how individuals and society function. It suggests social welfare programs operate in the best interest of society and help meet the essential social functions of integration, socialization, mutual support, and social control. Considerable evidence suggests that social welfare is functional to the operation of the economic system. While direct payments or services may go to the poorest in our society, indirect benefits go to the total society.

References

1. John P. Van Gigch, *Applied General Systems Theory,* 2nd ed. (New York: Harper, 1978), 1.
2. Earl Babbie, *The Practice of Social Research,* 2nd ed. (Belmont, Calif.: Wadsworth, 1979), 208.
3. Neil Gilbert and Harry Specht, *Dimensions of Social Welfare Policy* (Engelwood Cliffs, N.J.: Prentice-Hall, 1974), 5.
4. Ibid., 5.
5. W.L. Wilensky and C.N. Lebeaux, *Industrial Society and Social Welfare* (New York: Free Press, 1958), 138.
6. F.J. Pierce, "A Functional Perspective of Social Welfare," *Social Work Education Reporter* 18, no. 1 (March 1970), 48–50.
7. Roy Bailey and Mike Brake, eds., *Radical Social Work* (New York: Pantheon Books, 1975), 3.
8. David Gordon, *Problems in the Political Economy* (Lexington, Mass; Heath, 1977), 24–25.
9. Robert Lekachman, Guest editorial in *American Spectator* 15, no. 12 (December 1982): 1.
10. Gordon, *Problems,* 210.
11. William Ryan, *Equality* (New York: Pantehon, 1981), 122.
12. Samuel Bowles, "Unequal Education and the Social Division of Labor," *The Review of Radical Political Economics* Vol. 3, no 4 (Fall-Winter 1971) 38–66.
13. Ryan, *Equality,* 170–171.
14. Jerald Hage, *Communication and Organization Control* (New York: Wiley, 1974), 5.
15. Talcott Parsons, *The Theory of Social and Economic Organization,* ed. and trans. by A.M. Henderson and T. Parsons (New York: Macmillan, 1975).
16 Jo Freeman, "The Building of the Gilded Cage," *The Second Wave: A Magazine of the New Feminism* 1, no. 1 (Spring, 1971); Reprinted in *Crisis in American Institutions,* ed. Jerome Sholnich & Ellito Currie (Boston: Little, Brown, and Co., 1979), 209.
17. Peter Day, *Social Work and Social Control* (London: Tavistock, 1981), 29.
18. Emile Durkheim, *Suicide* (New York: Free Press, 1951), 3.
19. Peter Blau, "A Theory of Social Integration," *American Journal of Sociology* 65 (May 1960).
20. Frances Fox Piven and Richard Cloward, *Regulating the Poor* (New York: Pantheon, 1971), 341–348.
21. Lawrence Mead, "Social Programs and Social Obligations," *The Public Interest* no 69 (Fall 1982).
22. Ibid.
23. Peter Kropotkin, *Mutual Aid: A Factor of Evolution* (New York: Knopf, 1925), 293.

24. Ralph Dolgoff and Donald Feldstein, 2nd ed., *Understanding Social Welfare* (New York: Harper, 1984), 5–6.
25. William Ryan, *Blaming the Victim* (New York: Vintage, 1976).
26. Beulah Compton, *Introduction to Social Welfare and Social Work* (Homewood, Ill.: Dorsey Press, 1980), 14.
27. Hollings as quoted by George F. Wills in *Newsweek* (20 December 1982), 92.
28. Adam Smith, *The Wealth of Nations* (1776; reprint, New York: Penquin Books, 1978), 23–24.
29. Gordon, *Problems,* 210–211.
30. Mead, "Social Problems."

CHAPTER ELEVEN

Understanding Human Behavior: A Psychological Perspective

"That's what sets true professionals apart: they draw upon their knowledge of science, using their skills to objectively evaluate what is needed, and they then choose a course of action. It's rarely very clear precisely what that should be; sometimes several treatment alternatives would be appropriate. One simply has to make a choice and, if things don't work out, be prepared to switch to another approach."[1]

Social workers deal with people. Some clients have difficulty adjusting to job or domestic problems. Others may have difficulty relating to their friends or their communities. Still others are experiencing internal problems; they feel tense, unhappy, angry, suspicious, and untrusting without understanding why. Psychology provides the social worker with the knowledge to increase her understanding of these personal problems.

What makes one person respond to a new problem or situation one way and another person respond in a totally different manner? Individual differences are the central issue of psychology but are also vital to effective social work practice. Recognizing the unique qualities of each person, psychology attempts to devise a system that ties together the various components of personality. Depending upon the system that guides the study of personality, those components have greater or lesser significance. This chapter focuses on the work of Sigmund Freud, Carl Rogers, and various behavioral theorists since their work has been widely applied in social work practice. None of them provide a verifiable or complete theory of personality, but many of their concepts help the social worker analyze and understand how individual personality contributes to the presenting situation. Historically, social work has been profoundly affected by the dominant psychological theory of the day.

A comparison of psychologists, psychiatrists, and social workers is made in Chapter 9.

Freud: Psychoanalytic theory

The history of the social work profession is inextricably linked with the development of Freudianism. Herman Borenzweig suggests that psychoanalytic theory has been "both a stimulus and an impediment to the development of the social work profession."[2] While the effects of Freudianism are numerous, this chapter will address just two of its important ramifications: its present contribution to the social work knowledge base and the relationship between its history and social work.

Psychic determinism is a key principle of Freudian theory and suggests that every thing human is meaningful. Nothing a person says or does is accidental; no matter what a person does, her reason for doing it can be traced to internal causes. Dreams are not insignificant but important clues to understanding human functioning. A slip of the tongue (a "Freudian slip") has its cause in one's psyche. An individual is driven by her unconscious. To be healthy she must bring these unconscious forces to consciousness and under control.

Freud distinguished between the unconscious and the preconscious. The preconscious is that part of the mind an individual can call to mind when necessary. The unconscious, on the other hand, cannot be called to consciousness under ordinary circumstances but only through interaction with another properly trained person. Freud's theory suggests that unconscious desires motivate people to do things they cannot rationally explain.

Transference may occur in the relationship between a social worker and a client.

Therapists particularly deal with what Freud calls the dynamic unconscious—those parts of the unconscious repressed because of anxiety. Neurosis is a fixation on or a regression to some phase of infantile sexuality. The earlier the fixation, the greater the psychopathology. This psychopathology is dealt with through the transference-resistance phenomenon in psychotherapy. In transference the analyst utilizes the therapist-patient relationship for therapeutic purposes. In transference the patient comes to identify with the analyst, and the analyst with persons who have been important figures in the patient's childhood or fantasies. As the patient transfers the feeling (psychic energy) from the former figures to the analyst, the analyst becomes a catalytic agent releasing the energy attached to old fixations and repressions and attaching it to the reality of the environment. Resistance encompasses all the forces that oppose conscious recognition of something in the individual's deeper mental life.[3] Freud described psychoanalysis.

> It may thus be said that the theory of psychoanalysis is an attempt to account for two striking and unexpected facts of observation which emerge whenever an attempt is made to trace the symptoms of a neurotic back to their sources in his past life; the facts of transference and of resistance. Any line of investigation which recognizes these two facts and takes them as the starting point of its work may call itself psychoanalysis, though it arrives at results other than my own.[4]

Basically, psychoanalysis suggests that human beings are naturally unhappy because of inadequate or traumatic experiences in early childhood. Unhappiness grows out of inherent conflict between basic instinctual drives and the requirements of the social structure. Freud suggests that individual well-being or mental health is dependent upon a harmonious relationship between the various parts of the mind, and between the person and the real world she lives in.

The id, ego, and super-ego can be seen as a system. Systems theory is discussed in Chapter 1.

Freud conceived personality to have three parts: the id, the ego, and the super-ego. The id, an important part of the unconscious, consists of all organic cravings or tensions; it contains primitive instinctual impulses and is a reservoir of psychic force. The ego is the conscious self that deals with thought, feeling, and acts; one of its most important functions is testing reality. A newborn child's personality is largely id. As the child becomes part of the social environment her personality must undergo modification. The ego acts as an adjusting agent between environmental requirements and instinctual wishes. Intrapsychic conflict develops when a satisfactory adjustment cannot be made between the inner and outer demands. The id is governed by the pleasure priniciple, the ego by the reality principle. The third element in the psyche is the super-ego; it plays the role of repressor and judge. The super-ego incorporates cultural ideals and requirements within the personality. It censors and judges according to social demands. In addition to this unconscious censor, the super-ego contains a conscious part, the ego-ideal or conscience, representing the pattern to which the ego consciously tries to adapt. If the unconscious super-ego dominates, the individual feels guilt and inferiority. Therapy attempts to harmonize the conscious and unconscious elements of the id.[5]

The goal of psychoanalysis is to provide a harmonious relationship between the ego, the id, and the super-ego, and between the individual and the world in which she lives. Freud believed that patients could be helped by bringing to consciousness the traumatic experience that initially caused the conflict. He encouraged patients to talk freely and without inhibition hoping he could interpret the unconscious force behind what they said. His method of free-association was to encourage people to say whatever came to their mind no matter how absurd. When the patient could no longer respond, Freud saw this as "resistance" and an indication that he was getting close to the correct interpretation of the repressed complex. Cure depended on bringing this repressed material back into conscious.[6]

Successful psychoanalysis provides self-knowledge and understanding. The "cured" patient can use this knowledge in various ways: she may replace the unhealthy repression of instincts by rational, conscious control of them (suppression rather than repression), divert them into alternative acceptable channels (sublimation), or decide to satisfy those instincts. Freud did not believe there was any danger that psychoanalysis would unleash uncontrollable primitive instincts. Self-knowledge would increase the individual's ability to control her unconscious.[7]

The impact of psychoanalysis on social work

Sigmund Freud resided in Vienna for the greatest share of his working life, but his work received its initial and most widespread acceptance in the United States. European physicians tended to be more scientifically-oriented, and some evidence suggests Freud's Jewish heritage made him less acceptable in the medical community. Freud's first appearance in the United States was arranged by G. Stanley Hall, President of Clark University and a renowned child psychologist. The time was September 1909, and the occasion was the twentieth anniversary of Clark University.

One reason caseworkers were enthusiastic about psychoanalytic theory was that they wanted to define and perfect professional techniques and theory. In 1915 Dr. Abraham Flexner, America's foremost authority on graduate professional education, read a paper at the National Conference on Charity and Correction entitled "Is Social Work a Profession?" To his audience's dismay, Flexner determined social work was not a profession because it did not have a unique method or theory base. His paper had a profound effect on social workers. Mary Richmond's book *Social Diagnosis* (1917) responded to the criticism of unique methodology, and Freudian theory provided a theoretical base compatible with casework methodology and professional values.

This argument is reviewed in Chapter 7.

Dr. James F. Putnam, Chief of Neurological Services at Massachusetts General Hospital, was an early enthusiast of the Freudian approach. He suggested "service was to be founded upon understanding, and understanding upon service, and psychoanalysis was the scientific method by which to understand personality and therefore a person." Social work could no longer deal with narrow problems of economic dependency and relief but with universal problems of mental health and emotional adjustment. In identifying with the higher status profession of psychiatry and the clinical team, the social worker sought to overcome the stigma of charity and unprofessionalization attached to past efforts.[8]

While social work in the 1920s was striving for increased status and professionalization that led to the desire for a theoretical base, the country's needs in facing World War I also fit in neatly with Freudian casework. Physicians and psychiatrists examining men for service were faced with large numbers of men whom they rejected for emotional reasons. Psychoanalytically oriented caseworkers were especially well-qualified to help these people deal with problems of social adjustment. In addition there was increased demand for psychiatric social workers to deal with victims of shell-shock, individuals facing problems rooted not in the present social environment but in their emotional and intellectual perception of that environment. Veterans suffered from problems that social workers felt were much better explained by emotional and unconscious factors.

The diagnostic or Freudian school of thought was most prominent during the 1930s and 1940s.

Freud's influence is most apparent in the techniques of psychiatric caseworkers, but his most profound effect was the acceptance by social workers that insight into emotions and psychic life was a key element in all social work.[9] Freudian explanations of the unconscious were welcome additions to the rational model of social diagnosis outlined by Mary Richmond. Psychoanalysis helped to explain the irrationality these workers observed in their practice.

Summary

No consensus exists within social work about the impact of Freudian thought. It has been blamed for moving social work out of the reform movement into an individualistic view of social problems. It has even been accused of fostering a "blame the victim" stance. On the other hand, it has provided important psychological insights that have greatly enhanced the effectiveness of social work techniques. Reuben Fine describes psychoanalysis as the "greatest intellectual revolution of the twentieth century" in the social sciences. He suggests that it has provided an important research tool through the concept of the unconscious and related ideas; psychoanalysis has provided a "solid basis for the investigation of man in all his psychological and social functioning."[10] Alfred Baldwin reflects a similar view.

> As a result of the specificity and generality of psychoanalytic theory it seems fair to say that at the present time no theory of human behavior comes closer to accomplishing the full purpose of behavioral theory; no other theory accounts for all the data of human behavior, its development and its pathological deviations in terms of a basic set of postulates and deviations."[11]

Whether one sees the effect of Freudianism as negative or positive, it has indisputably affected the direction of social casework. Freudian theory contains two assumptions that have become basic principles of social casework: human behavior is purposeful and determined, and some determinants of behavior are unconscious. Social casework is no longer a method only for the poor. Early childhood experiences and memories join external and social forces as important components of social histories and diagnoses.[12]

Carl Rogers: Self theory

Carl Rogers' impact on social work has been significant enough to warrant mention in almost every social work text. Recent analysis of Roger's work suggests it may be especially relevant for radical social workers committed to human liberation. Though client-centered therapy has traditionally been considered conservative and apolitical, recent analysts have suggested its basic tenet, client empowerment, is fundamental to radicalism. Rogers himself concluded in 1974 that he had been practicing and teaching politics all of his life but did not realize it.[13]

Bernard Davies compared Roger's approach to education with that of Paulo Freire whose clear intention was to use learning for revolutionary ends.

For both Rogers and Freire learning is by definition a personal experience. The teacher cannot bestow knowledge on passive and docile students. Rather, education requires that the learner changes both emotionally and intellectually.[14] For meaningful learning to occur, Rogers suggests that the learner must analyze the rigid way she has construed the meaning of experience. The learner must realize that many facts are only facts because she regards them as such. Real learning requires discovering previously unrecognized feelings.[15]

Rogers also contends the most significant learning occurs in situations perceived as problems. He asserts that

> placing the students in direct experiential confrontation with practical problems, social problems, ethical and philosophical problems, personal issues and research problems is one of the most effective modes of promoting learning.[16]

Rogers also recognizes however, that this type of learning has consequences for society at large; he questions whether or not our social order allows students to come into contact with real issues.

> Our whole culture—through custom, through the law, through the efforts of labor unions and management, through the attitudes of parents and teachers—is deeply committed to keeping young people away from any touch with real problems.[17]

Rogers' view of what education could and should be clearly shifts power and responsibility toward the learner. In fact Rogers has a strong commitment to student power. He suggests that when the learner chooses the direction, discovers the learning resources, formulates the problems, decides the course of action, and lives with the consequences of those choices—then significant learning is maximized.[18] While many educators believe as John Dewey and William Kilpatrick did that skillfully guided discussion should lead the student to the "right" conclusion, Rogers believes that good discussion might lead a student to a conclusion completely at odds with the instructor's.

Rogers' view of the educational process is pertinent for students. The role of the teacher, as he perceives it, is important to social workers since so much of what they do involves educating clients and the public. Client-centered therapy and student-centered learning stem from the same assumptions about inherent qualities and potentials of human beings. To develop a better understanding of how Rogerian theory has influenced social work practice it is useful to outline the development of Rogerian theory in historical context, address how this theory explains human development, and how the theoretical assumptions translate into therapeutic techniques.

Historical context

Carl Rogers published his first book *The Clinical Treatment of the Problem Child* in 1937.[19] In 1942 he published *Counseling and Psychotherapy*, which reflected the crystallization of client-centered therapy. Rogers' writings appeared at a time when the two primary schools of thought in social work were the functional and the diagnostic schools.

The diagnostic school was based primarily on psychoanalytic theory. Basic to this school was the idea that the therapist was the expert who diagnosed the client and, on the basis of this diagnosis, determined what direction the client should take. Adherents of this school diagnosed, categorized, and prescribed with little concern about what the patient thought.

A comparison of the diagnostic and functional approaches can be found in Chapter 6.

In contrast the functional school adopted the theory of Otto Rank. Rank believed the individual has self-directing capacities that emerge through therapy. Rank identified three critical factors in psychotherapy: the individual, the therapist, and the relationship between them. The client contains constructive forces within her that constitute a will to health. The therapist facilitates the client's self-understanding and self-acceptance. The therapist as a person is the curative agent, not her technical skill. The spontaneity and uniqueness of therapy lived in the present propel the patient toward health.[21] Rogers became acquainted with Rank's ideas through social workers in his agency who had been trained in the Rankian method.[22] It is not clear whether Rank's ideas influenced Rogers or whether Rank and Rogers simultaneously adopted similar views of clients and therapy; Rogers does refer to Rank's "passive therapy" in his first book. For social workers of the functional school client-centered therapy was compatible. The central hypothesis of client-centered therapy is that if genuineness, empathy, and positive regard are present in the attitude of the therapist positive personality change will occur in the client.[23]

Developmental aspects of theory

While Freudian theory is based on a genetic theory, client-centered theory centers on immediate relationships. From birth the world of the infant is the world it experiences. Within its world the infant has one basic drive, the tendency toward self-actualization—

> [the] inherent tendency of the organism to develop all its capacities in ways which serve to maintain or enhance the organism.[24]

The infant also has the inherent ability to value experiences that enhance its organism. This "organismic" valuing process directs the infant's behavior toward self-actualization.[25]

As the infant grows, it acquires a sense of self (the "self concept") derived from its own being and function within the environment. The development of self concept is strongly dependent on the individual's perception of her experiences and environment, and her perception is influenced by her need for positive regard, a pervasive and persistent human need. The individual's need for positive regard can only be satisfied by others and the effect of significant others is particularly potent. The total of these experiences produces a sense of self-regard, a learned sense of self based on the individual's perception of how others regard her. The sense of self-regard becomes a pervasive influence on her behavior.

Experiences not consistent with the individual's concept of self are perceived as a threat. Such experiences create anxiety and arouse defense mechanisms that either distort or deny those experiences. Because of the individual's need to deny accurate perceptions of conditions contrary to her sense of worth, she often develops a rigid perception of her experiences. In a relationship (therapy) in which the individual receives unconditional positive regard, it is safe to allow into awareness previously distorted or denied experiences. Ideally therapy is a process in which the individual exchanges conditions of worth for a trust and valuing of the wisdom of his developing organism in its entirety.[26]

Therapeutic process

The process of therapy is described by Rogers as being

> "synonymous with the experiential relationship between client and therapist. Therapy consists in experiencing the self in a wide range of ways in an emotionally meaningful relationship with the therapist. The words—of either client or counselor are seen as having minimal importance compared with the present emotional relationship which exists between the two."[27]

Rogerian theory stresses empathy, positive regard, and genuineness, not technical skills or knowledge. The therapist must be able to convey a sincere acceptance of and interest in the client. The attitudes Rogers considers requisite to effective therapy are clearly consistent with social work values.

EMPATHY

The ideal social work relationship with a client draws heavily on Rogers' ideas. See Chapter 3.

Rogers defined empathy as understanding the client's world as the client sees it. Empathy requires more than understanding the client's words. The therapist must immerse herself in the feeling as well as the words of the client; the therapist must understand things the client may not have allowed into consciousness. Lawrence Shulman has delineated empathy into three skills: reaching for feelings, developing understanding of the client's feelings, and putting the client's feelings into words.[28] Reaching for feelings is the skill of asking the client to share the affective portion of the spoken message; empathy involves summoning an affective response that comes as close as possible to the experience of the other.

Understanding a client's feelings involves displaying comprehension through words, gestures, expression, physical posture, or touch. The key component of this skill is to convey understanding not reassurance. The important work that needs to be done can only proceed after the client knows the worker understands. Workers who attempt to move clients without first having experienced the affect will be perceived as "not understood."

Occasionally it will be useful for the worker to put the client's feelings

A Rogerian approach to counseling includes an emotionally meaningful relationship based on empathy, genuineness and positive regard. Photo courtesy of Student Support Services Publication Center, University of Minnesota.

into words. Sometimes the client does not fully understand her feeling or cannot articulate it. By articulating unspoken emotions (being one-half step ahead of the client) the worker gives the client permission to discuss feelings she may have been repressing or hiding.

POSITIVE REGARD

Positive regard is an important idea in social work literature. Authors such as Beulah Compton and Burt Galaway refer to it as "concern for the other."[29] Basically positive regard is an unconditional affirmation of the individual's life and needs. The therapist genuinely cares for the client and remains nonjudgmental in words and actions. The therapist does not express approval or disapproval but instead trusts the client's ability to discover what is best for herself. The therapeutic effect of unconditional positive regard is that the client allows into awareness those portions of inner experience inconsistent with the self-concept. The patient receives confirmation of genuine understanding from another person and positive acceptance of the changing, new self.[30]

GENUINENESS

Rogers suggests that genuineness requires the therapist to rely on moment to moment felt experiencing in the therapist-client relationship. The understanding arising from the therapeutic relationship is not only intellectual but also organismic. Genuineness and empathy combine as the therapist experiences what the patient is feeling.[31]

Compton and Galaway expand on this concept and relate it to social work practice. They delineate three conditions necessary for a social worker to be congruent and genuine: an honest knowledge of herself, a clear knowledge of agency procedures and policies and the professional role (as it relates to both worker and client), and an internalization of the first two and our concern for the other, acceptance of clients, commitment to their welfare and to the authority aspects of the worker's role and position. These qualities need to become so natural that the worker can turn full attention to the client and her situation. Compton and Galaway summarize these points by suggesting that people who are genuine and congruent in a helping relationship are people who know themselves and are unafraid of what they see in themselves and others.[32]

Students who feel most comfortable with clearly delineated skills and techniques will have difficulty relating to the therapeutic process of Rogerian or client-centered therapy. Rogers contends attitudes, not techniques, lead to constructive change.

> The more the therapist is perceived by the client as being genuine, as having empathic understanding, and unconditional regard for him, the greater will be the degree of constructive personality change in the client.[33]

Impact on social work

Virginia Robinson, a functionalist, wrote extensively about the importance of a professional relationship.

It is difficult to separate the impact of Rogers and Rank. The functionalists clearly recognized the importance of client strength in the therapeutic relationship, and were keenly aware of the importance of the relationship itself. Perhaps Rogers's contribution was the degree to which he developed many of the concepts with which the functionalist school was concerned. Rogers is a prolific writer who has clearly addressed the importance of the client-professional relationship. His work is particularly applicable to the enabler and teacher roles that social workers perform.

In addition to the contribution he has made to the client-professional relationship Rogers has applied his theoretical constructs to the educational process. This aspect of his work has not had wide effect, but it may hold a great deal of promise for educating future social workers. Particularly in professional education we assume students change both emotionally and intellectually. Perhaps this process of change could become more effective if social work educators applied Rogers's ideas of student empowerment. But Rogers would suggest that whether or not educators apply these concepts, students should enhance their learning experiences by increasing their participation in defining the learning process.

Learning theory: Behavior therapy

Behavior therapy is the systematic application of the principles of learning theory for the purpose of therapeutic behavior change.[34] Learning theory, particularly stimulus-response theory, dates back to the work done by Ivan Pavlov (1849–1936) with his dogs. Pavlov demonstrated that by simultaneously presenting an unconditional stimulus (meat) and a conditioned stimulus (sound of tuning fork), the conditioned stimulus would come to elicit the response (salivation) originally elicited only by the unconditional stimulus. The salivation response to the sound of the tuning fork was referred to as a conditioned response. These experiments were the beginning of what every student who has passed introductory psychology knows as operant or respondent conditioning. J.B. Watson adopted Pavlov's principles of conditioning, combined them with his own ideas of personality development, and called his theory "behaviorism."[35] He conducted experiments applying Pavlovian principles to psychological disorders in human beings.[36] Edward Thorndike was simultaneously developing the principles of operant conditioning. He demonstrated the importance of reward and punishment in the learning process; his "law of effect" has become a cornerstone of modern learning theory.[37]

But in spite of the considerable behavioral research being done in the early 1900s social workers did not incorporate these principles into practice. In the first place social workers identified with and emulated psychiatry. As social workers sought professional status they turned to psychiatry rather than psychology to increase their understanding of and ability to deal with human behavior. Psychiatric training was largely grounded in psychoanalytic theory with little emphasis on experimentally based psychological principles. Then too, psychologists involved in therapy were relatively rare until the late 1940s.

The first extensive effort to integrate therapy and behaviorism was little more than an attempt to translate Freudian concepts into behavioral language. John Dollard and Neal E. Miller developed a well known prototype of this approach. They combined knowledge not only from psychoanalytic theory and stimulus-response theory but also from social anthropology. They attempted to take a small number of concepts and apply them to phenomena that concerned psychoanalytic therapists: regression, displacement, and conflict. These authors attempted to derive from psychoanalytic theory and clinical observation knowledge about behavior which in turn they incorporated with stimulus-response concepts. Dollard and Miller expanded on stimulus-response theory in an attempt to make predictions concerning unobserved empirical events.[38]

Dollard and Miller describe learning theory as the "study of circumstances under which a response and cue are connected." While they agree with "pure" behaviorists that learning takes place according to definite psychological principles, they interject that only certain conditions allow the response to become strengthened. Practice does not make perfect. These necessary conditions are "drive, cue, response, reward."[39] While some behaviorists reject dealing with unobservable factors such as drive, Dollard and Miller's reinforcement theory is closer to the behavioral principles incorporated in social work practice today.

Two additional names important to the development of behavior therapy and to social work in general are Joseph Wolpe and B.F. Skinner. Their books—*Science and Human Behavior*[40] and *Psychotherapy by Reciprocal Inhibition*[41]—established the foundation of behavioral therapy. Wolpe conceptualized human neurosis in terms of Pavlovian learning principles and outlined specific therapeutic techniques for dealing with neurotic behaviors. Wolpe amassed considerable case history data to support the value of his therapeutic techniques. Though few students may be familiar with Wolpe, most will at least have heard of his therapeutic techniques—systematic desensitization and assertiveness training. While Andrew Salter's *Conditioned Reflex Therapy* predates Wolpe's publications on assertiveness training, Wolpe's work had considerably greater impact than Salter's.[42] Social workers today are involved in assertiveness training in many different settings. While systematic desensitization is a less widely applied technique for social workers, many clinical social workers use this technique.

Social workers have used assertiveness training with the elderly, women who have low self-esteem and the chronically unemployed.

Most students will have at least heard reference to Skinner's utopian novel *Walden Two*,[43] which became synonymous for many with behavioral engineering and social control by government. *Walden Two* is essentially a proposal to apply behavioral technology to the construction of a workable, effective, and productive pattern of government. Skinner believes most human behavior can be understood in terms of operant conditioning. The implications of this belief go well beyond individual behavior. It suggests, for example, not that we preserve freedom, but rather that we address what kinds of control we use and to what end. The dangers inherent in control of human behavior are real, but increased knowledge of human behavior can also mean a new and exciting phase of human life. The key to the future is intelligent and humane analysis of control.[44]

Theory

Discussing nuances introduced by the various theorists conveys the complexity of learning theory. This summary addresses general principles of behavior theory that can be helpful in understanding human behavior.

Consideration of the person within the environment is a key concept of social work practice. **See Chapter 1.**

Basically, behavior theory sees human behavior as determined by the environment. Behavior is learned from situational factors, not from within the organism. Since behavior is learned, it can be unlearned. Difficulties occur when learned maladaptive behavior results in anxiety; the anxiety is learned as a contingency (conditional response) of the learned maladaptive behavior. Behavior theory assumes the individual has no inner control of her behavior, no self-determinism. Values, feelings, and thoughts are ignored and only concrete observable behaviors are considered.[45] David Rimm and John Masters outline seven assumptions basic to behavior therapy.[46]

1. Behavior therapy concentrates on the maladaptive behavior itself rather than on underlying causes.

This assumption is most clearly contrasted with the medical model that sees maladaptive behavior as a function of some relatively autonomous, highly inaccessible state of mental disease. Rimm illustrates the difference with an example of a hospitalized patient who inappropriately fondles a ward nurse. Operating from a medical model, the staff decided to ignore the behavior because it could be expected from someone who was mentally ill. In contrast a behaviorist would have communicated the inappropriateness of the behavior and changed circumstances to reinforce desired behavior so that the patient would be discouraged from repeating undesirable behavior.

2. Maladaptive behaviors are acquired through learning.

Behavior theorists believe that human beings are products of their environment. Behavior therapy specifies rather precisely how the environment influences people. Learning principles include classical and operant conditioning and modeling. Both adaptive and maladaptive behaviors are responses to the individual's learning history and follow the same general principles of learning. The difference is in the impact they have on people around them.

3. Learning principles can be extremely effective in modifying maladaptive behavior.

The degree to which a response was learned will affect the ease with which it can be modified. The authors suggest that persons labeled as autistic, schizophrenic, or even epileptic are frequently victimized by significant others who underestimate their ability to learn. These people then experience a major learning deficit and a misguided prophecy is fulfilled. By understanding both the increased attention necessary to teach these children and the potential effectiveness of applying learning principles, teachers and caretakers can have a major impact on their charges.

4. Behavior therapy involves setting specific clearly defined goals.

The importance of clearly defined goals and contracting is a part of the social work process. Refer to Chapter 3.

This particular aspect of behavior therapy has affected social work practice. Traditionally social work has been a goal-oriented change process; increasingly social workers make contracts with their clients based on outcomes that are specific, observable, and measurable.

In therapy behaviorists help alleviate a specific problem that is interfering with the client's life. A behaviorist's goal is not to restructure the client's personality. If a person is unhappy, a behaviorist will work to determine the specific events that lead to her unhappiness rather than deal with a general state of unhappiness.

5. The therapist adapts the method of treatment to the client's problem.

Behaviorists tend to take more responsibility for the outcome of therapy. While many therapies suggest the therapy is only as successful as the client's motivation, behavior therapists see premature dropout from therapy as a therapist error. In the words of one behavioral therapist:

> To blame the patient through rationalizations such as the patient's not being sufficiently motivated or not having enough ego strength to withstand the pressures of therapy is an inexcusable exercise. Therapy is the therapist's responsibility. It is the therapist who at the very least implicitly establishes himself as the expert and any failure is the therapist's failure.[47]

6. Behavior therapy concentrates on the here and now.

Behavior therapy rejects the idea that gaining insight is curative. While a certain amount of biographical information is usually helpful, detailed explorations of the client's childhood is not productive.

7. Any techniques labelled as behavior therapy techniques have been empirically tested and found to be relatively effective.

Behavior therapy more than any other has been concerned with scientific validation of its techniques. Since behavior therapy stresses observable and measurable outcomes, behaviorists are in a better position to document their findings than therapists dealing with "conscious states." But behavior therapies are still limited primarily to case studies and short-term outcomes. Laudable efforts have been made to test effectiveness, but behavior therapy cannot yet make definite cause and effect statements.

Application to social work practice

Behavior modification is a controversial area of practice. It has been heralded for its effectiveness in dealing with retarded and disturbed individuals, especially children; it has also been damned as manipulative, unethical, and unsuited for a free society.

To consider a worker's frustration in knowing how to best work with a client, see the example at the end of this chapter.

Both the ethics and effectiveness of behavior modification depend on the worker. Depending on its application, behavior modification can be a constructive growth experience or a destructive and debilitating experience. Without attempting to address the philosophical base of the individual therapist a brief description of the major techniques will be presented.

SYSTEMATIC DESENSITIZATION

Systematic desensitization has been widely used to alleviate maladaptive anxiety. The technique usually combines deep muscle relaxation with imagined scenes depicting situations that cause the client to feel anxious. It is assumed that a client who can learn to relax while imagining the anxiety-causing situation can also face the real situation with less anxiety.[48]

Systematic desensitization has reportedly been effective with patients having phobias of animals, driving, heights, flying, water, taking tests, and behavior disorders such as frigidity, compulsive exposure, sexual deviations, and alcoholism have all responded to systematic desensitization.

Behaviorists maintain that systematic desensitization has not only been proven effective but also requires less treatment time than traditional therapies. "The large scale case history reports indicate a median number of sessions (involving actual desensitization) of sixteen to twenty-three depending on the therapist."[49]

Some students may have been exposed to part of the systematic desensitization treatment if they have taken relaxation courses frequently offered in health and physical education departments or university counseling centers. The basic premise of muscle relaxation techniques is that muscle tension is related to anxiety; a person will experience a reduction in anxiety if she can relax her muscles. Alternately tensing and relaxing voluntary muscles in an orderly sequence induces mental and emotional relaxation.

Simple muscle relaxation techniques are an example of systematic desensitization.

ASSERTIVENESS TRAINING

Assertiveness training is designed to increase the client's ability to engage in honest and straightforward expression of feelings and behavior. It is appropriate for people who are afraid to say or do things that are reasonable and proper. When fear and inhibitions prevent individuals from satisfying personal needs, they usually become frustrated and function less effectively. Assertiveness training also helps people who express their needs and desires in socially unacceptable ways (temper outbursts or aggressive and demanding behavior, for example). Individuals can learn to express personal needs in socially acceptable ways.

Assertiveness training helps an individual understand the reasonableness of asserting and gratifying her needs and interests so she is not afraid to be assertive and can develop the communication skills to satisfy felt needs. and provides knowledge of socially acceptable ways to accomplish this.[50]

Wolpe uses five questions to assess the assertiveness of the client.[51]

1. If after buying something in a store you find that your change is a dollar short, what do you do?
2. After returning home from a store you find that something you have bought is slightly damaged. What do you do?
3. When someone goes ahead of you in a line, for example, at the movies or at a sports event, what do you do?
4. When you are in a store and the clerk waits on someone who came in after you, what do you do?

Assessment is an important part of the social work process regardless of the method used.

5. What do you do when eating out and the food is not the way you ordered it?[52]

Once the therapist establishes what anxieties and fears are most troublesome, she then uses techniques like practice statements, role playing, and assignments to bring about the desired change.

OPERANT CONDITIONING

Operant philosophy stresses the importance of reward and punishment in the acquisition, maintenance, and extinction of human behavior.[53] A positive reinforcer is an event, behavior, or material object that will increase the frequency of any behavior upon which it is contingent. A negative reinforcer is any event whose contingent withdrawal increases the rate of performance of a response. The kinds of consequences that increase the rate of response are positive or negative depending upon whether they reinforce when they appear or disappear.

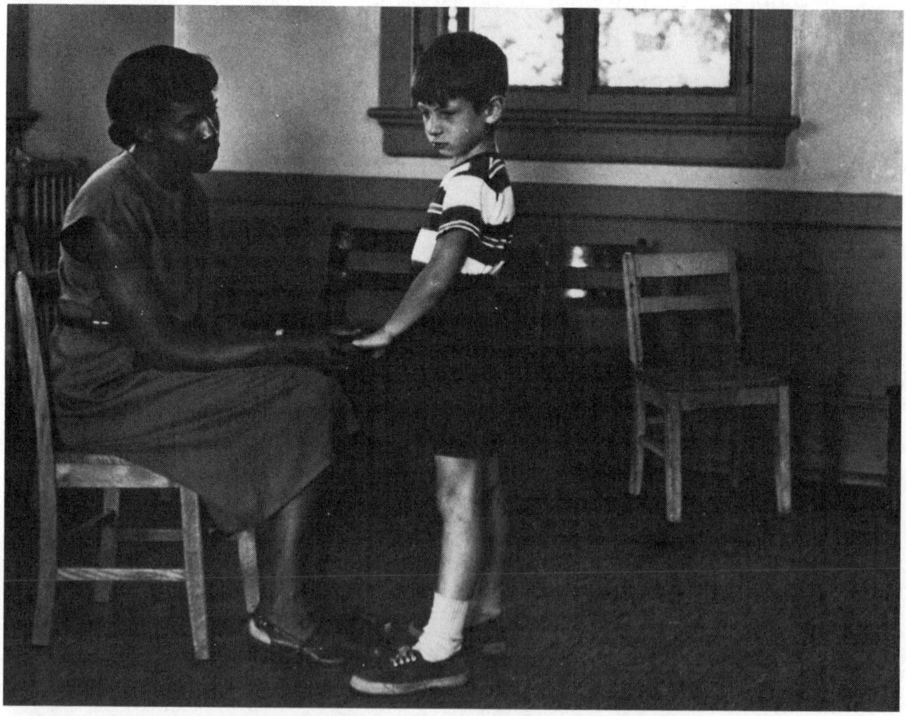

Understanding human behavior is a key element that affects the nature of the work done with clients, whether adults or children. Photo courtesy of Social Welfare History Archives, University of Minnesota.

Operant conditioning has been used to discourage temper tantrums and enuresis (bed-wetting), and to teach learning disabled children. If a child throws a temper tantrum and receives a great deal of attention (love or punishment) then the frequency of tantrums is likely to increase. If the behavior is ignored then the likelihood of tantrum behaviors decreases. When an individual wets the bed, an aversive shock can discourage that behavior. The most frequent examples of operant conditioning come from programs dealing with mentally impaired children. Positive reinforcements such as M&Ms have been used to teach words to children whose previous speech had been limited to unintelligible words. Anyone who has taught her dog to come, sit, speak, or roll over has grasped the basic principles of operant conditioning.

Summary

This chapter has addressed three important psychological theories: Freudian, self, and learning theory. While none of these theories is used by all social workers, each has had a profound effect on social work practice.

Psychoanalytic theory has made us aware of the role of the unconscious in human behavior. Psychoanalysis is not a commonly employed technique among social workers, since it involves intensive specialized training. Only a few social workers are also psychoanalysts with training beyond the traditional MSW. In the 1970s Freudian theory was simplified and repackaged as transactional analysis. Transactional analysis made some components of Freudian theory more useful for social workers.

Self-theory propositions permeate social work literature and practice. The assumption that the individual contains an inherent capacity to grow and change is a basic tenet of social work practice. The concepts of congruency, empathy, and genuineness are central characteristics of the social work relationship. Self theory provides guidance to the social worker as enabler and teacher.

Learning theory has also been used by many social workers in the enabler and teacher roles. Many social workers have used assertiveness training and behavior modification effectively. One of the qualities of behavior therapy that lends itself to social work practice is that it is a time-limited intervention. In contrast both Rogerian therapy and psychoanalysis tend to require long term treatment periods. Systematic desensitization sometimes helps patients with intense phobias, but it has also proven effective with minor disorders such as test or math anxiety. The relaxation technique developed through systematic desensitization principles has gained wide applicability. Social workers are likely to use this treatment on themselves as well as their clients.

This chapter has analyzed some theories of personality and how they apply to social work practice. An excerpt from *A Solitary Dance* (a novel by Robert Lane) illustrates how these theoretical principles may apply to practice.[54] The novel presents the story of an eight year old named Michael hospitalized for schizophrenia. Although Michael has been in the state hospital for three years, none of the staff has been able to establish a relationship with him. Patrick McGarry, a student intern, has been assigned to work with Michael and is becoming frustrated with his inability to establish a relationship with Michael. The following exchange takes place between Patrick and Scott, the chief psychologist and Patrick's supervisor. Scott begins.

A Solitary Dance*

ROBERT LANE

"Beginning therapists like you are always in such a hurry, always expecting immediate success. You're so ingrained with the American ethic of quick results for little effort—of instant change when it suits you—that you can't stand the thought of little or no progress, no overnight success stories like in the movies!

"It takes time to build a relationship, Patrick, to gain an understanding of the patient's psychodynamics, to earn his trust. It's taken little Mike eight years to get to where he is now. How can you expect him to change it all in a few months? Especially when you're clambering over the mountainside for only four or five hours out of each week? If it were truly that simple, don't you think someone around here would've stumbled on that solution and helped Mike long ago?"

Still, in spite of Scott's lecture, I was rapidly approaching my wit's end. Three months in the trenches were getting to me. All that time I had been chasing that kid, and he still wouldn't come a jot closer, talk to me, or for that matter, even recognize that I was any different from one of the rocks he liked to rest on. Except that he'd get closer to them. . .

"Well at least you're getting in shape," Scott commented.

"I'm afraid the little guy has really got my number, but good."

"Want to give up? Try one of the other kids? Lots of other possibilities around here—"

"Of course not! I'm just getting started. I can be just as stubborn . . . no, more stubborn, than Mike. But what I haven't been able to figure out yet is how to break the pattern—how to get him to relate to me."

"Maybe it's time you went back to square one."

"What do you mean?"

"Perhaps you should begin to put some of your knowledge of psychology to use: instead of allowing Mike to call all the shots, you start calling some of them."

"I still don't follow, Scott. I've been trying to do that all along, and I can't think of any other way than I've already tried."

"What exactly have you been doing up to this point?"

"Well, I've been trying to do what Rogers advocates—provide unconditional positive regard, acceptance, empathy. The emotional symptoms and distress are supposed to subside as the innate forces within the person strive for psychological balance. That's the theory, anyway. And it seems to work for Rogers . . . "

Scott smiled. "Have you seen any evidence that it's working with Mike?"

"No, not really. Maybe a look from him here and there, but I can't even be sure of that, especially at a distance of twenty-five feet."

"Okay, now. Are you ready to consider the notion that perhaps one theoretical approach is just not

*From *A Solitary Dance* by Robert Lane (New York, Signet). Used by permission.

enough to cover all therapeutic situations? That there is no one method of therapy that is going to be applicable to every single patient we encounter?"

"I suppose." It was a grudging admission for me. Scott had broached the subject before, without much success.

"Boy, you're not kidding when you say you're stubborn! Patrick, do yourself a favor and ease up a bit. You've admitted that several months of work with Mike have gone nowhere, so you've got nothing to lose by considering other possibilities, have you?"

"I'm not sure. What do you have in mind?"

"You know how I feel about Rogers'approach. It's an excellent attitude to have toward the people you work with, but there are some patients who need much more than an interested, supportive listener. I suspect Mike is one of them." Scott gave me a wry smile. "As a fellow humanist I can wholeheartedly agree with the sentiments behind Rogers' ideas, the fact that his concepts are based upon a deep respect for the person and his or her life situation, and that the therapeutic relationship is then constructed upon that premise. But remember, self theory falls far short of being a universal explanation of human behavior."

"What's the alternative, then?" I said, sensing what was coming. "You don't think behaviorism is the answer, do you?"

"Not entirely. But the principles of learning and conditioning have been demonstrated very nicely in studies, especially those by B.F. Skinner.

"Behaviorism does have its uses and some very good techniques. In spite of what you might think. Of course, it has its limits of usefulness, too, like any other theory. But we know that in certain situations positive and negative reinforcement work extremely well in changing specific types of behavior patterns. So you don't want to disregard learning theory simply because it may be anathema to your humanistic notions.

"Psychoanalysis, too. Many of Freud's concepts—such as the unconscious, the defenses—have certainly withstood the test of time. The empirical data may not have supported some of the major hypotheses of his theory, but the fact remains that many of the psychodynamic constructs, as well as the therapeutic techniques, have proven extremely useful."

"Scott, it's our same old argument!" I broke in. "I'm a dyed-in-the-wool humanist because I can't buy either the behavioristic view of people as mechanized creatures of reflex or the analysts' notions of unconscious motivation, that behavior is ruled by base instincts. I really believe in the integrity of the individual, and that each person has a choice. Anyway, I'm familiar with the principles of the various theories you've mentioned—that's the easy part. The problem is that I can't apply the techniques of any of these theories to a little buzz bomb named Michael Harris who runs up and down hills like a mountain goat and won't let me near him!"

"All right," retorted Scott. "The problem is that you have yourself prematurely committed. There are no absolute applications of any of the theories yet—that's why they're still theories. Psychology as a science is, to put it mildly, in diapers. We have a lot of promising leads, some well-conceived studies, some good data, and the start of a body of knowledge. But we are a long way from fully understanding human behavior, much less predicting it with one-hundred-percent accuracy."

"That's for sure. I'm beginning to wonder why I spent so much time in graduate school."

"Well, it's not as hopeless as it may sound. But when you make the jump from the rudiments of science to applied work you have to stay loose, flexible, and accept the fact that you're not always going to be perfectly on target. What the theoretical framework does is increase your chances; it allows you to be objective, to plan, even to predict what should happen during the course of psychotherapy. What I'm advocating you do with Mike—with anyone you work with professionally—is concentrate on understanding him and assessing the situation. And be open to using any of the theories that might seem appropriate. So when you first start working with a person, begin by picking out the theory that seems to fit the individual's dilemma best, whether that theory is called self, behaviorism, psychoanalysis, whatever. Use those explanations, but be ready to look elsewhere when they don't seem to account for what's going on. Or when there doesn't seem to be any progress. Stay loose, flexible, open to anything.

"That's what sets true professionals apart: they draw upon their knowledge of science, using their skills to objectively evaluate what is needed, and then they choose a course of action. It's rarely very clear precisely what that should be; sometimes several treatment alternatives would be appropriate. One simply has to make a choice and, if things don't work out, be prepared to switch to another approach.

"And remember, Pat, all the while the patient may very well sense what is best: the Wisdom of the Mind, if you will. Some people, for example, need to dig back into the trauma of their formative years and work through unresolved issues and long-buried troublesome feelings—as the psychoanalysts advocate—while others simply blot out the past and deal with learning a more adaptive style of living that is future-oriented. More along the lines of a behavioral approach. But most, the majority I would say, want a combination. You have to learn to mold yourself, to shape yourself to whatever will best help your patient—an accommodation between what you sense they need, and what you think they sense they need, and what therapeutic approach will be most suitable for that purpose."

I was shaking my head by this time, but Scott pressed on.

"What I'm suggesting therefore, Pat, is that you be more eclectic. Be aware of the value of trying different things instead of being locked into one theory and approach. Mix a little Rogers with some Skinner and maybe add a dash of Freud. Okay?"

"At best I think I see what you're getting at, Scott. But I still don't see how using a goulash of theories and techniques is going to help me know what to do with my particular little id kid."

"You like challenges—that's another one for you. Think about what I've said, then try to put it to use."

References

1. Robert Lane, *A Solitary Dance* (New York: Signet, 1984), 58. Used with permission.
2. Herman Borenzweig, "Social Work and Psychoanalytic Theory," *Social Work* 16, no. 1 (January 1971), 7.
3. Arthur Noyes, *Modern Clinical Psychiatry,* 2nd ed. (Philadelphia: Saunders, 1939), 370.
4. Sigmund Freud, *On the History of Psychoanalysis* (1914) 116, quoted in Fine, "Psychoanalysis," 3.
5. Reuben Fine, "Psychoanalysis," in *Current Psychotherapies,* ed. Raymond Corsini (Itasca, Ill.: Peacock, 1973), 7.
6. Ibid., 14.
7. Ibid.
8. Roy Lubove, *The Professional Altruist* (New York: Atheneum, 1971), 89.
9. Ibid.
10. Fine, "Psychoanalysis," 7.
11. Alfred Baldwin, *Theories of Child Development* (New York: Wiley, 1968), 375.
12. Donald Brieland, Lela Costin, and Charles Atherton, *Contemporary Social Work,* 2nd ed. (New York: McGraw-Hill, 1980), 189–219.
13. Carl Rogers, *On Personal Power: Inner Strength and Its Revolutionary Impact* (New York: Delta, 1974).
14. Bernard Davies, "Toward a Personalist Framework for Radical Social Work Education," in *Theory and Practice in Social Work,* ed. Roy Bailey and P. Lee (Oxford: Basil Blackwell, 1982), 171–187.
15. Carl Rogers, *On Becoming a Person* (Boston: Houghton-Mifflin, 1961), 28.
16. Carl Rogers, *Freedom to Learn* (Columbus, Ohio: Charles E. Merrill, 1969), 276.
17. Rogers, *Becoming a Person.*
18. Rogers, *Freedom to Learn.*
19. Carl Rogers, *The Clinical Treatment of the Problem Child* (Boston: Houghton-Mifflin, 1939).
20. Carl Rogers, *Counseling and Psychotherapy* (Boston: Houghton-Mifflin, 1942).
21. Otto Rank, *Will Therapy* (New York: Knopf, 1936).
22. Betty Meador and Carl Rogers, "Client-Centered Therapy" in *Current Therapies,* ed. Raymond Corsini (Itasca, Ill.: Peacock, 1973), 121.

23. Carl Rogers, "The Necessary and Sufficient Conditions of Therapeutic Personality Change," *Journal of Consulting Psychology* 21, (1957): 95–103.
24. Carl Rogers, "Client-Centered Therapy," in *American Handbook of Psychiatry,* vol. 3, ed. Silvano Arieti (New York: Basic Books, 1959), 196.
25. Meador and Rogers, "Client-Centered Therapy," 130.
26. Ibid., 131.
27. Carl Rogers, *Client Centered Therapy* (Boston: Houghton-Mifflin, 1951), 172.
28. Lawrence Shulman, *The Skills of Helping* (Itasca, Ill: Peacock, 1979), 40.
29. Beulah Compton and Burt Galaway, *Social Work Processes* (Homewood, Ill: Dorsey Press, 1979), 168.
30. Meador and Rogers, "Client-Centered Therapy," 12.
31. Ibid., 127.
32. Compton and Galaway, *Social Work Processes,* 170.
33. Carl Rogers, "The Actualizing Tendency in Relation to Motives and Consciousness," in *Nebraska Symposium on Motivation,* ed. Marshall Jones (Lincoln, Neb.: Univ. of Nebraska Press, 1963), 1–24.
34. James Whittaker, *Social Treatment* (Chicago, Ill.: Aldine, 1974), 206.
35. John B. Watson, *Behaviorism* (New York: Norton, 1925).
36. John B. Watson, "The Place of the Conditioned Reflex in Psychology," *Psychological Review* 23 (1916): 89–116.
37. Calvin S. Hall and Gardner Lindzey, *Theories of Personality* (New York: Wiley, 1957), 421.
38. Ibid., 421.
39. Neal E. Miller and John Dollard, *Social Learning and Imitation* (New Haven: Yale Press, 1941), 1–2.
40. B. F. Skinner, *Science and Human Behavior* (New York: Macmillan, 1953).
41. Joseph Wolpe, *Psychotherapy by Reciprocal Inhibition* (Stanford: Stanford University Press, 1958).
42. David C. Rimm and John C. Masters, *Behavior Therapy* (New York: Academic Press, 1974), 82.
43. B. F. Skinner, *Walden Two* (New York: Macmillan, 1978).
44. D. L. Avila, A. W. Combs, and W. W. Purkey, *The Helping Relationship Sourcebook* (Boston: Allyn and Bacon, 1975), 50–51.
45. Barbara Okun, *Effective Helping* (Belmont, Calif.: Wadsworth, 1982), 123.
46. Rimm and Masters, *Behavior Therapy,* 6–17.
47. Alan Goldstein, "Behavior Therapy" in *Current Psychotherapies,* ed. Raymond Corsini (Itasca, Ill.: Peacock, 1973), 220.
48. Rimm and Masters, *Behavior Therapy,* 43.
49. Ibid, 45.
50. Marvin Kahn, *Mental Health Practitioners* (Cambridge, Mass.: Winthrop, 1981), 202.
51. Joseph Wolpe, *The Practice of Behavior Therapy* (New York: Pergammon Press, 1969), as quoted in Kahn, *Mental Health Practitioners,* 202.
52. Marvin Kahn, *Mental Health Practitioners,* 202.
53. Rimm and Masters, *Behavior Therapy,* 277.
54. Lane, *Solitary Dance,* 53–60. Used with permission.

CHAPTER TWELVE

Social Policy: Codification of Social Values

"In numbers disproportionate to the rest of the population, minority women—particularly blacks and Hispanics—are becoming one of the largest groups living below the poverty line . . . between 1970 and 1981, the number of female-headed households in the United States increased by 97% (2.8 million). In 1981, 68% of blacks and 67% of Hispanics lived below the poverty line in households headed by women with children under the age of 18."[1]

Understanding the process and the outcome of social welfare policy is critically important to social work professionals. Social policy is an essential component of the context in which social work practice takes place. To study social policy is to study the history, politics and economics of social welfare, social services, and other societal decisions that directly affect people. Social workers need to understand policy both as a process by which a society sets a course of action to accomplish social goals and as a product of that process. Social policy can serve as a means of promoting change or reinforcing the status quo; it can support existing power structures or redistribute power.

Role of the social worker

No professional group is more directly affected by social policy, particularly social welfare policy, than social workers. Salaries, working environment, availability of jobs, and resources for clients are all provided through and limited by social policy. Whether social workers choose to be involved in the policy process or not, they will directly experience any changes in social policy. In

Social workers need to understand and at times disagree with social policy which affects their practice. In 1968, for example, social workers protested against U.S. involvement in the Vietnam War. Photo courtesy of Social Welfare History Archives, University of Minnesota.

addition to the social worker's self-interest in policy, there is a professional obligation to be informed and to contribute to the formation of humane policy. The social work profession has identified social policy as an area of expertise, and it is reasonable that legislators and the public look to social workers for leadership in formulating policy. Progressive social change is enhanced by the empowerment of both the social worker and the client in the policy-making process.

The NASW Code of Ethics (Chapter 7) states that a social worker has an ethical responsibility to support the development and enactment of social policies of concern to the profession.

Understanding the process

Understanding the nature of politics and the process of policy making is a source of power. Even in our democratic structure most people do not understand the process. The more people are informed about how decisions are made, the more likely they are to have an impact on decisions. Understanding the basis of the decision also allows anticipation of the effects of the policy.

Freedom requires an informed citizenry; to engage in the effort of policy change is to give testimony to the power of an informed citizenry. Social workers can empower clients by helping them understand how the needs they experience relate to social policy, what can be done about social policy, and how it can be done. Understanding the causes and consequences of social policy is a prerequisite to prescription. If social workers are to inform clients and make policy recommendations, these recommendations must be based on careful analysis. Policy advocacy requires knowledge of the political process in addition to the social work skills of rhetoric, persuasion, organization, and activism.

Study of social policy

Summaries of models to study social policy are presented over the next few pages.

Political scientists develop political models to simplify the policy process and to suggest explanations for political events and outcomes. Different models have directed the study of social policy, and each of these models has contributed to a better understanding of the political process. But political science, like social work, has yet to find a model that is fully predictive. Institutionalism, group theory, elite theory, systems theory, incrementalism, conflict theory and rationalism have all been used to study social welfare policy.[2] A brief comparison of the basic assumptions of some of these political models suggests the richness of the debate between theorists.

Institutionalism. Early political scientists limited their study to describing specific governmental institutions without systematically inquiring how the attributes of these institutions influenced policy. Understanding the structure of government and policy making institutions is essential to social work practice, but this model by itself is not conducive to prediction. Institutionalism helps social workers understand the context in which policy is made and administered.

Group Theory. Also called pluralism, group theory describes the political process as an interaction among groups. Public policy at any given time is the equilibrium that is reached in the group struggle; lawmakers are responsible for assuring and protecting that equilibrium. The group model suggests government must be responsive to the people because groups can and will organize to remove legislators from office if they do not meet the desires of their constituents.

Elite Theory. Elite theory suggests that public policy reflects not the demands of the general population but rather a small well-informed elite. The public is generally apathetic and uninformed. Public policy changes as a result of the redefinition by elites of their own values; civil rights legislation is often cited as an example of how an elite group may promote change in spite of popular sentiments. Elite theorists suggest that the general population was not in favor of civil rights legislation and may have actually been opposed to it. They argue that the move toward protection of civil rights was led by an educated minority of elite whites, and without this leadership (or at the least support) the civil rights marches would have been much less effective.

Incrementalism. "New" policies are actually variations upon already existing policies. In 1978 for instance, President Carter talked of "comprehensive" welfare reform, but his proposed Programs for Better Jobs addressed less than 5 percent of the total categorical grant programs. Incrementalists suggest that social policy is too complex and supports too many vested interests to allow comprehensive change. The incremental nature of social welfare policy—the addition or slight modification of programs on top of existing programs—is one of the explanations frequently cited for the "welfare mess." The basic social welfare policy framework was set with the Social Security Act in 1935, and since that time we have been adding social welfare programs in a piecemeal fashion inconsistent with any rational overall plan.

Systems theory. Public policy is a response of a political system to environmental forces. For a social system to maintain itself and fulfill its functions people adjust their own functioning to meet the needs of the larger system. When policies fulfill the individual's needs no problem exists. The task of the policy maker is to identify the needs of all persons and systems to create new policies that meet most of the needs of most people and systems.

This model could be compared to general systems theory applied to social work practice in Chapter 1.

Rationalism

All of the above models contribute to the understanding of social welfare policy, but rationalism is perhaps the ideal model. A policy is rational if "the ratio between the values it achieves and the values it sacrifices is positive and higher than any other policy alternative."[3] This analysis must take into account both financial costs and social values. The ideal of rationalism "involves the calculation of all social, political, and economic values sacrificed or achieved by a public policy."[4] DiNitto and Dye suggest rational policy-making demands that

1. Society must be able to identify and define social problems and agree that there is a need to resolve these problems.
2. All of the values of society must be known and weighed.
3. All possible alternative policies must be known and considered.
4. The consequences of each policy alternative must be fully understood in terms of both costs and benefits, for the present and for the future, and for target groups and the rest of society.
5. Policy-makers must calculate the ratio of benefits to cost for each policy alternative.
6. Policy-makers must choose the policy alternative that maximizes *net* values—that is, the policy alternative that achieves the greatest benefit at the least cost.[5]

Examining these criteria suggests rationalism is limited in its ability to reflect the reality of the policy process. First of all it assumes agreement on societal values; it also assumes comparative and predictive knowledge not available for social policy. In spite of these acknowledged limitations, however, the rational model does suggest a useful framework for analyzing social welfare policy. While it may not achieve the level of explanation desired, it does provide important insight.

Policy analysis

The questions suggested by the rational framework can be useful in analyzing an existing policy or in guiding the development of new policy. Following these steps provides the student with an organizing tool to analyze present social policy.

The steps in analyzing a social policy are presented here. Compare these to steps in the problem solving process in Chapter 3.

1. Develop a Clear Statement of the Problem. To analyze a policy it is necessary to understand the problem to which the policy responds. A clear statement of the problem must dictate both the severity and the incidence of the problem (that is, how many people are suffering from this problem and how much are each of them suffering). It is unlikely that public policy will respond to a problem that is widespread but not serious, or serious but only affecting a small number of people. For example, a certain percentage of students has always completed their education without being able to read and write—a serious problem for those individuals. On a policy level, however, their problem received little attention until recently when its magnitude became apparent.

2. Identify the Causes of the Problem. If the policy is going to "cure" the problem, it is important to understand and remove the cause of the problem. A frequently told story illustrates the importance of this step. Once there was an extremely sharp turn in a mountain-side road. People missed the turn so frequently that the village below set up an emergency hospital to deal with the accident victims. The village dealt with the problem without removing the cause. Recognizing the cause of the problem would have led the people to change the road instead of building a hospital. Similar mistakes occur in social welfare policy. It does no good to spend billions of dollars on job training if there are no jobs for the trainees. If a policy is to deal with unemployment, it is necessary to determine whether the cause of the problem is lack of training or lack of jobs.

3. Identify Policy Goals. To evaluate social welfare policy, the social worker must know what the policy is designed to achieve. This analysis usually addresses the intended effects or the manifest functions of the program. It also identifies the unintended consequences as well. Medical Assistance and Medicare are interesting examples to study. Clearly the manifest intent of this legislation was to provide health care for the indigent and the elderly. An unintended side effect has been that the costs of health care have risen exponentially in comparison to the cost of other commodities. Today the elderly are paying a higher portion of their income for health care than they did before the implementation of Medicare.

4. Identify Related Theories. In setting up a strategy to deal with a problem, it is important to predict what the outcome of the proposed policy will be and why. If one were to develop a policy designed to decrease crime, he would need to understand what the major theories of punishment (the utilitarian, the rehabilitative, the retributive, the deterrent, and the social justice) would predict about the results of the policy or program. The policy analyst must make some judgments about the relevance of the related theories.

5. Identify the Target Population. Define the segment of the population for whom the policy is intended—women, the elderly, the sick, or others in need. For example, to formulate a policy intended to change the economic status of the poor the term "poor" must be clearly defined. Social Security guidelines define fewer people as "poor" than the guidelines in the Older American's Act.

6. Identify the Predicted Effects of the Policy. Will the policy redistribute resources and power or will it reinforce the present power distribution? Will a crime bill, for example, provide increased protection for the victim or the criminal? Will it provide new benefits or rights to a particular group of people? Will it change the quality of life for any particular group? Will the changes threaten or reinforce present value systems? Will it strengthen or weaken family life?

7. Study the History of the Policy. How has (or will) this policy come about? What prompted lawmakers to sponsor this policy? What administrative decisions have interpreted the policy, and how have judicial decisions reflected on this policy? What are the legislative, administrative, and judicial forces that have acted on this policy at each level?

8. Compare the Proposal to Alternatives. Anytime a policy is developed, it is just one of many possible policies. Identify some alternatives and compare the positive and negative potential of each. Lawrence Friedman suggests social welfare policy should be judged on the basis of administrative cost, target efficiency, allocative efficiency, lack of stigmatization, consumer vs. taxpayer sovereignty, and flexibility over time.[6] But when these concepts are applied to a particular policy other concepts need to be understood. Neil Gilbert and Harry Specht identify these elements as dimensions of choice.[7]

Dimensions of choice

One dimension of choice is the question of whether or not everyone should benefit from a specific policy.

Figure 12–1 summarizes the dimensions of choice involved in public policy making.

Who Benefits? A primary decision in social policy development is who will benefit? Should benefits be allocated on a universal or selective basis? In a universal program benefits are available to an entire population as a social right. Some of the universal benefits in our society are public libraries, public schools, parks, and immunization clinics. Most industrialized countries include children's allowances and health care in their universal programs, but the United States provides medical care and children's allowances based on financial need. Both Medicaid and AFDC have income eligibility requirements as well as work-related requirements. Alfred Kahn and Sheila Kammerman have analyzed the European system of social welfare policy and argue strongly for the benefits of a universal system.[8] Others argue that by making benefits universal, we would actually give the poor less. This important policy issue is being studied in the United States particularly as it relates to the Older Americans Act, which has many universal dimensions, and the Title XX Amendments to the Social Security Act, which increased services available to the middle class. Although the data are not conclusive, some are concerned that the poor received fewer services after these amendments than before. The total number of services provided remained about the same, but more middle class individuals were eligible for those services, and fewer lower class people were served.

Later in this chapter a discussion of the food stamp and commodities programs illustrates the difference between cash and in kind benefits.

What Will the Benefit Be? Another choice dimension is whether the benefit will be cash or in kind. AFDC and SSI (Supplemental Security Income) are examples of cash programs. Clients are given the money and the responsibility to provide for themselves. In kind programs provide things such as housing, clothing, jobs, or opportunities. If a person is provided low income housing this certainly helps the budget, but since housing is not a saleable benefit, the client's choice is limited. Another example of an in kind benefit is the extra points veterans receive on civil service examinations. The veteran may or may not choose to take advantage of the opportunity, but it has no exchange value.

Equality, equity, and adequacy can be applied to "Poverty Hits Minority Women Hardest."

Will Benefits Be Equal, Equitable, or Adequate? The goals of social welfare programs sometimes conflict with each other. Equality, equity, and adequacy are three goals that are often in conflict. To pursue the goal of equity, a policy is likely to sacrifice equality and adequacy. The term equality itself presents potential conflict. We may be talking about numerical equality—the same treatment for everyone, or proportional equality—the same treatment for similar persons. If we would pursue numerical equality, we would develop programs that equalize resources and benefits available in society. What we actually do is design programs that more closely adhere to the proportional equality goal. We determine what groups should be given assistance and then attempt to treat those groups relatively equally. Attempts to equalize benefits can be seen in the Aid for Families with Dependent Children and Food Stamp programs. The Federal reimbursement for AFDC is higher in the poorer states. Further, recipients who live in states with low AFDC benefits are eligible for a higher food stamp allotment. Even though equality is frequently discussed as a goal of social welfare programs, we do not have any truly redistributive programs; in fact, equality is in conflict with the basic values of our economic and social system.

Equity prescribes that individuals should receive benefits based upon their contributions to society. Only those people who cannot help themselves should receive help. Equity is clearly related to our economic system because rewards or benefits are designed to reflect a person's contribution to the economic system. Programs most obviously designed on the basis of equity are Social Security and Unemployment Insurance. The whole concept of equity goes back to the English poor law's principle of less eligibility. No one receiving assistance should achieve a better standard of living than the lowest paid worker.

Policy ideas borrowed from the English poor laws are described in Chapter 4.

By definition adequacy conflicts with equity. Adequacy suggests it is desirable to provide a decent standard of living for all people apart from concerns about whether the benefits are equal or merited. This policy stance assumes that there is a minimal standard of living below which no one should fall. Standards of adequacy vary over time. When President Reagan came into office the Food Stamp policy allowed a family of four with an income of $14,000 to receive food stamps. Reagan felt this standard was too high and lowered the income limit for a family of four to $11,000.

As a general rule social welfare policies related to income tend to respond to the equity issue. Education and health care policies, at least in theory, address the equality issue. Policies designed to meet the goal of adequacy are frequently in kind rather than cash programs.

Who Pays and Who Decides? How are programs financed, and where does the decision making power rest? Most social welfare programs receive a substantial portion of their financial support from the federal government. Until the election of President Reagan there had been a gradual but continual shifting of costs from local to state to federal levels; the Reagan administration has at least partially derailed that trend. His proposed state federalism would have given both the cost and the decision making power back to the state and sometimes the local decisionmaking bodies. While this trend has received considerable support from Republicans, particularly conservatives, clear evidence suggests clients receive both fewer benefits and more stigmatized services the closer the decision making is to the people. Members of Congress are less threatened by irate opponents of welfare programs than are mayors. Further, there is a real benefit to states to bring federal money into the state, and one way to do this is through welfare programs.

Issues of choice are of course more complex than a brief discussion can indicate. Our purpose, however, was to provide a flavor of the ongoing debate, and it is to be hoped that we have accomplished that purpose. Applying these concepts to the food stamp program and the commodities programs should help clarify some of these concepts.

Dimensions of social welfare policy: An application

Most people know what the food stamp program is and have at least a general idea of how it operates. Many students, however, will be unfamiliar with the surplus commodities program that ceased to exist over a decade ago, although current cheese distribution programs are reminiscent of the now defunct commodities program. The present surplus of farm commodities coupled with the ideological perspective of the Reagan administration make it increasingly probable that a commodities program will be reintroduced. The commodities and food stamp programs provide an excellent opportunity to illustrate the choices

A food commodities program was a forerunner of the food stamp program and was seen by some as inefficient and demeaning. Photo courtesy of Social Welfare History Archives, University of Minnesota.

available to deal with hunger while supporting the agricultural industry. Not only can these programs be analyzed in reference to the choice dimensions outlined by Gilbert and Specht,[9] but also they may be studied in light of the desirability dimensions defined by Friedman.[10] Together the food stamp and commodities programs offer striking contrasts on these related variables.

The food stamp program provides individuals and families with actual stamps they can redeem for food. Food stamps are valid for food purchases but may not be used to purchase paper items, soap, cigarettes, beer, or cleaning supplies and various other nonfood items. If the amount of the stamps is greater than the purchase, the user can receive cash as change. The number of stamps a family receives is determined by its income and the number of people in the household.

The commodities program on the other hand actually distributed surplus food the government had purchased from producers. Food was ordinarily distributed monthly. Families or individuals were allotted a certain amount each month. Some of the surplus items included Karo syrup, bulgar, flour, butter, cheese, canned meat, powdered milk, and corn meal. Each family or individual was assigned a specific pick up point and could receive commodities only at that location. Typically, surplus commodities were transported to the distribution point in an old converted bus, and clients went to the window, showed their card, and were given their allotment of food (commodites).

Administrative costs

Administrative costs include all the expenses incurred in operating a program that do not directly benefit the client. It is logical that policymakers would like to see as few program resources as possible spent on administrative costs. Both the commodities and food stamp programs have staff costs and overhead expenses, but the food stamp program requires fewer staff. The commodity program required staff to certify the recipient's eligibility, issue the certificate, and actually distribute the goods. In addition there were staff costs in delivering the food from producer to county, storage by the county, delivery to the client, and bookkeeping at the national and state level. The food stamp program is less labor intensive at the county level. Periodically clients must renew their eligibility, but once they receive the stamps, they are responsible for locating and purchasing the food. Storage and distribution costs are minimal. On the national and state level the bookkeeping costs are probably similar to the commodity program. The actual cost of the food clients buy or the commodities they receive is not considered an administrative expense. The amount of the stamps or the commodities is directly related to client benefits.

Target efficiency

There are two facets to target efficiency. Vertical efficiency refers to the degree to which the benefits reach only the target group, the intended beneficiaries.

Horizontal efficiency relates to the degree to which all of the target group is served. The commodities program would probably rate highest on vertical efficiency. Since the method of obtaining commodities was at least inconvenient, if not demeaning, few people were likely to stand in long lines through the heat of summer and cold of winter to obtain surplus commodities they did not need. There was considerably less concern about the "unworthy" getting surplus commodities than there is about misuse of food stamps. Food stamps probably rate higher on horizontal efficiency as a higher percent of those eligible are more likely to participate in this program. Food stamps allow people choice without requiring them to be in a certain place at a certain time. It also allows them to buy what they need rather than what happens to be in surplus. One group (the elderly) consistently refuses to benefit from the food stamp program in proportion to their eligibility; the elderly tend to view welfare as signifying a loss of independence.

Allocative efficiency

What kind of incentives does a policy contain? Social policy in general tends to view allocative efficiency as it relates to the work ethic, pro-natal incentives, and integration. Will the income maintenance program encourage people to quit their jobs? Will AFDC encourage people to have more children? Will affirmative action or educational policy facilitate racial integration? The food programs under discussion relate primarily to the allocative decisions about work both for the recipient and the producer. Many people believe that welfare recipients will not take low income jobs if they can receive food stamps. But food stamps help the economy in general because they put more money into circulation; most free market enthusiasts prefer food stamps since they believe it encourages competition. Farmers and agribusiness leaders prefer commodity programs since they provide a large dependable market for their surplus produce.

Stigmatization

Social workers tend to feel that benefit programs should not stigmatize beneficiaries. They assume that poverty itself is demeaning and that social programs should improve rather than destroy the individual's self-concept. While many clients have been embarrassed by derogatory comments at the supermarket checkout, using food stamps is less demeaning than lining up at a bus to collect surplus commodities. Conservatives tend to feel that the more demeaning the program the higher the program will be on vertical efficiency: stigmatization will screen out all but the neediest. In practice it appears that the more difficult benefits are to obtain the less likely the elderly, the sickly, and mothers with small children will take advantage of the programs designed to help them—a situation clearly related to target efficiency.

Sovereignty

Who should have the choice in setting up programs? Should the client be able to choose the kind of food he buys or spend some of the change from his food stamps on non-food items? Or should the taxpayer be able to limit what food the recipient is able to receive? The commodities program is clearly high on taxpayer sovereignty. Although individual taxpayers do not decide what clients will receive, it is assumed that government policy reflects the taxpayer's choice because taxpayers elect the lawmakers.

Food stamp programs give the consumer greater sovereignty. The client determines what he will buy; if he chooses to buy steak with his food stamps, he can do so, even if he may then be unable to buy other food products. Although it is illegal to do so, recipients who get into a financial bind can sell food stamps more easily than commodities. Social workers tend to support consumer sovereignty but it is not clear that the general population does.

Flexibility

The policy making process takes time, and often by the time the policy is finally passed, changing social and economic conditions have already outdated it. COLA (Cost of living adjustment) has become a buzzword in both social welfare programs and wage settlements. Particularly in times of high inflation benefits must reflect the inflation rate so that the buying power of the beneficiaries is not eroded. Social Security was one program in which the benefits increased as inflation increased. However, in 1982 the Reagan administration used a deferral of the COLA (in addition to numerous other cuts in social welfare benefits) to help offset the federal budget deficit. In the same year, A.F.D.C. recipients in Wisconsin had their COLA deferred from July to October to help decrease the state budget deficit. These are just two cases that illustrate flexibility over time; usually when policy makers discuss flexibility over time, they are addressing responsiveness to client needs. In the cases cited, however, flexibility over time has been related to the needs of the state and federal governments.

Summary

In developing social welfare policy many decisions must be made. On what basis will benefits be distributed? What will the benefits be? How will the program be administered? How will it be financed? The answer to each of these questions has implications for administrative costs, efficiency, choice, stigma, and flexibility. These decisions will also determine the extent to which the goals of adequacy, equity, and equality will be pursued. The following figure illustrates how decisions relate to choice and desirability dimensions.

CRITERIA	BASIS		NATURE		STRUCTURE		FINANCING		
	Universal	Selective	Cash	In-Kind	Central-ized	Decentral-ized	Federal	State	County
Administrative Cost									
Target Efficiency									
Allocative Efficiency									
Non-demeaning									
Sovereignty									
Flexibility									
Adequacy									
Equity									
Equality									

Programs may be analyzed in reference to both choice and desirability dimensions.

Social policy is an integral part of the knowledge base of social work practice. Social policy affects the social worker and his clients daily. Social workers can be more effective by becoming active participants in the policy making process. Participation in this process also holds promise for the empowerment of clients. Adequate policy knowledge includes understanding the interests and actors involved in policy making, the traditional interpretations of the political world, and finally the formal procedures, rules, and institutions that constitute the authoritative structure of government.[11]

The insert from *Womanpower,* a newsletter of the National Association of Social Workers' Committee on Women's Issues, analyzes how work and welfare programs affect women. It also identifies variables frequently overlooked in analysis. You will be able to see how some of the questions we have addressed in this section actually operate in practice.

Poverty Hits Minority Women Hardest

The recent report of the National Advisory Council on Economic Opportunity, "Women and Children: Alone and In Poverty" documents the dramatic trend toward the "feminization of poverty" that occurred in the 1970s and explores its causes and possible remedies. It also points out the differential impact of this trend in the composition of the poor on minority women and their families.

The report is uneven in its discussion of minority women and children in poverty. Much of its minority data concerns Blacks alone, augmented by some on families of Spanish origin. There is no data on Asian-Americans, Native Americans or other minorities. Incomplete as the discussion on this aspect of poverty is, it still makes clear that women and children from ethnic minority groups make up a disproportionate percentage of poor women and children. It is not clear on the reasons for any disproportionate impacts between minority groups where its limited data suggests that these exist.

From *Womanpower,* a newsletter of the National Association of Social Workers Committee on Women's Issues, July 1982.

Between 1969 and 1978, a pronounced shift in the composition of the poor from male to female-headed families occurred. Poor families with male heads dropped from 3.2 to 2.6 million while those with female heads rose from 1.8 to 2.7 million. In 1978, 9.1 percent of all families were poor, but 31.4 percent of all families headed by women were poor while only 5.3 percent of all families headed by men were poor.

In 1978, more than half of all poor families were maintained by women, and more than half of all minority families headed by women were poor. The number of minority families in poverty was considerably higher than the number of poor white families. Of all families in poverty, 27.5 percent were Black and 20 percent were of Spanish origin, while only 6.9 percent were White.

The median income of White families was $21,521, of Spanish origin families, $12,570, and of Black families, $11,648. This was in sharp contrast to the median income of single mothers. White single mothers made almost one-third more than Black single mothers, but both made substantially less than the income of intact families. The median income for White single mothers was $9,933, for Black single mothers, $6,907.

In the seventies, there was a remarkable increase in the number of families without an adult earner. White families showed a 34 percent increase, families of Spanish origin, a 29 percent increase, and Black families, a 50 percent increase. This partly reflects the increase in the divorce rate and the increase in out-of-wedlock births.

The dissolution rate of marriages is almost exactly what it was a century ago, about 34.5 per 1000 marriages per year. But dissolution now comes much more through divorce than through widowhood, and more women who head households now are young mothers with children to support. The number of divorces has tripled in the last twenty years. Between 1970 and 1980, the percentage of female householders with children under 18 increased by 82 percent in all families and 92 percent in Black families.

The number of single parents who were never married has soared to 109 percent chiefly because of teenage pregnancy. The report also points out that Black women tend to remain single, in part because of the excess of Black females compared with males at the ages when most people marry.

Despite gains made in the income of individual Blacks, the report says that the Black family has decreased in relation to that of non-Blacks. It attributes this to the decreasing numbers of Black families with multiple earnings and the increasing numbers of Black families headed by women.

The report argues strongly that the causes of women's poverty are different from those of men's poverty. It maintains that women's poverty springs from two sources: the fact that women chiefly bear the burden of childrearing, and the fact that there are limited opportunities available to women in the labor market. When these two factors interact with minority status and youth, the report states, there is an even greater likelihood of being poor.

According to the report, the situation has not been much helped by welfare and job programs such as WIN and CETA that assume a job alone is the answer to women's poverty, as it usually has been for men. The evidence is that most men (one study says more than 95 percent) who work can support themselves and their families. This is not nearly so true for women who must support families by themselves.

More than a quarter of the working mothers heading households with children less than 18 years old in 1978 had incomes below the poverty level. Twenty-four percent of those on welfare worked, while half of the long-term recipients of AFDC were employed during the year. Yet, they were still poor.

Once a women is able to get a job, poor skills, education and socialization plus occupational segregation that confines women to low paying jobs with little or no upward mobility account for most of the failure of jobs to lift her out of poverty. Lack of child care which is accessible and affordable often leads her to abandon even low-paying jobs. Those women who avoid the female job ghettos encounter sex discrimination and sexual harrassment and this is worse for minority women.

References

1. Civil Rights Commission, "A Growing Crisis: Disadvantaged Women and Their children." A Report of the Civil Rights Commission released 4/11/83.
2. Thomas Dye, *Understanding Public Policy,* 3rd ed. (Englewood Cliffs, N.J.: Prentice-Hall, 1972), 19–40.
3. Ibid.
4. Ibid.
5. Diana DiNitto and Thomas Dye, *Social Welfare Politics and Public Policy* (Englewood Cliffs, N.J.: Prentice-Hall, 1983), 5.
6. Lawrence Friedman, *Dimensions of Social Welfare Policy* (Madison, Wisc.: Institute for Research on Poverty, University of Wisconsin, 1974), *3.*

7. Neil Gilbert and Harry Specht, *Dimensions of Social Welfare Policy* (Englewood Cliffs, N.J.: Prentice-Hall, 1974), 32.
8. Alfred Kahn and Sheila Kammerman, *Not for the Poor Alone: European Social Services* (Philadelphia: Temple University Press, 1975).
9. Gilbert & Specht, *Dimensions.*
10. Friedman, *Dimensions.*
11. Robert Morris, *Social Policy of the American Welfare State* (N.Y.: Harper, 1981), 181–202.

CHAPTER THIRTEEN

Organizational Theory

"One poignant message of the past decade, and perhaps decades before that, has been the power and pervasiveness of big organizations. To many of us they seem to dominate and control our lives. . . . . . . If some control over organizations is to occur, then we first need to understand the hows and whys of organizational behavior. . . . . But beyond the idea of simple protection is another reason why the study of organizations is essential: most of our major objectives are accomplished in the context of one or more organizations."[1]

For a personal account of how one person became a public administrator, see Part VII.

Social workers learn how to be enablers, facilitators, brokers, mediators, resource developers, and even teachers. One role they are seldom academically prepared for but will have to fill is that of bureaucrat. Social workers, particularly educators, resist the role of bureaucrat and fail to prepare students to fill this role effectively. When bureaucracy is discussed in the social work literature, it is usually in the context of conflict between professional and agency goals or the relationship of bureaucracy to professional burn-out.

This attitude toward bureaucracy and organizations in general creates a serious void in the preparation of social workers. Effective social work practice requires the ability to deal effectively and efficiently with organizational demands—a task as demanding as any of the other social work tasks. Pruger defines a skilled bureaucrat as a person who can manage the organizational environment in a manner that maximizes her ability to meet the requirements of the professional role.[2] In spite of what we might like to believe, formal organizations are necessary for a human service delivery system, and actually our whole life is entangled with many different formal organizations. Therefore, it is wise for social work students to acquire a theoretical and empirical basis for understanding organizational life.

This chapter presents select theories of complex organization and illustrates how integral this knowledge is to social work practice. Specifically these pages address bureaucracy, agency structure, coordination of services, and interorganizational relationships. Sociology has led in the development of organizational theory. Psychology, business, and political science have also contributed to this important area of study.

The influence of the other social sciences on the social work profession is described in Chapter 10.

Bureaucracy

> Bureaucracy is more than a matter of structure. The quality and capabilities of the people who do the work are part of the equation. They can be more or less influential depending on how well the organizational environment is understood. Unfortunately, little serious effort has been given to the task of defining the needed expertise. . . . With good reasons many people distrust complex organizations, but to behave ineptly seems hardly more praiseworthy or useful. If social workers must be bureaucrats—and they must—they might as well be good ones.[3]

All organizations must have order—a means of making actions within an organization predictable. Without organization, we have chaos. Different kinds of social organizations have different ways to keep order. The structure and control mechanism that works successfully in a family would not work well in a social welfare agency. Those different means are called structure and control mechanisms, but whatever the type of organization there must be a process which creates a structure, that is, predictable actions. "These predictable actions must be interlocked in such a manner that the operation of the units and the pattern of linkages between units produces a predictable desired outcome."[4] Within a social welfare agency structure must provide for predictable unit activities and predictable relations within units. In other words, the intake worker needs to be able to predict how each unit will respond to the referrals they receive. The receiving unit also needs to know what the expectations are or how it will handle referrals it receives.

Max Weber, the intellectual father of bureaucracy, argued that the bureaucratic structure would survive all other forms because it was more efficient. There is some evidence of truth to this statement particularly in the evolution of service delivery systems.[5,6] While traditional (custom) or charismatic (personal trust) authority may have been adequate in pre-industrial times, they could not provide adequate structure for formal organization that evolved with industrialization. At the turn of the 19th century the great man theory had to be replaced by a system that could make operations more predictable and systematic. The bureaucratic structure was more efficient than systems based on custom or trust, and it often improved conditions for employees as well. Before the rise of bureaucracy managers had absolute power;

Max Weber (1864–1920) was a German sociologist and political economist who first described the model of bureaucracy.

workers had no recourse to any other authority. As jobs became more complex, workers gained power and made demands. Rather than being a curse upon the work force, bureacracy was a movement toward rationality and predictability; rules protected as well as guided workers. The essential characteristics of the ideal bureaucratic organization developed by Weber encompass six major components—a specific division of labor, hierarchy, centralization, and formalization; in addition, the officeholder is an employee, membership constitutes a career, and hiring and promotion are based on merit.

Division of labor

First, the duties of each office are to be clearly specified. The division of labor between office holders are to be clear; individuals assigned a limited number of tasks become specialists in a limited area. A social service department may be split into a number of units: child welfare, income maintenance, older adults, foster care, etc. Social workers in these units would be expected to have a thorough knowledge of their own special problem area but not necessarily of the other problem areas. Specialization is functional in terms of knowledge and skill development; the social worker has a limited area in which to keep current and so can handle assigned cases more efficiently. But specialization may also lead to a lack of coordination since each worker is a specialist. The development of a new specialization—case manager—has been one response to this problem.

Hierarchy

The second characteristic of Weber's ideal bureaucracy addresses the means of control. Bureaucratic control is hierarchical. Rules and regulations for every position specify in varying degrees how individuals in each position are to behave. Workers know the limits of their position and to whom they may take their problems. Clients or workers who receive unfair treatment can, at least in theory, appeal to a higher authority. Of course hierarchy can also provide workers with an excuse for not delivering requested services. For instance, a worker may stall by telling a client she would like to meet her special request, but a supervisor will need to approve it. Other times a worker may truly be immobilized by having to get service plans approved by a supervisor. The development of community care for the elderly programs exemplifies how bureaucratic structures were misused and therefore caused inefficiency. The basic premise of these programs was that older people could be kept out of nursing homes if the social service agencies could respond quickly and imaginatively to their problems. The program planners recognized the importance of services being delivered promptly, but as the program developed so did dysfunctional bureaucratic procedures. Social workers made the needs assessment promptly but then had to have their plan reviewed by one and some-

An example of how these services were provided for the elderly can be found in Chapter 20.

times two levels of supervisors. By the time the plan was approved, it was frequently too late to respond to the problem.

Hierarchy also implies that each worker is subject to discipline from a higher office. Weber stressed that this discipline related to work duties only; the private life of the worker was outside the purview of official authority. But in fact there is some question about whether an individual's personal and professional life can be totally separated. Clearly, every code of ethics presumes that professionals lead personal lives consistent with their professional goals and ethics.

The NASW Code of Ethics is in Chapter 7.

Centralization

Hierarchy assumes a centralized locus of decision making, and centralization introduces questions pertinent to the practice of social work. Who will authority be vested in? In a social service agency the locus of decision making often changes depending upon the decision being made. Workers make task decisions about how to handle client cases every day. On the other hand social workers are seldom involved in making strategic decisions about how the organization will relate to other organizations or what new programs the agency will adopt; these strategic decisions are made at an administrative level. Recent organizational literature reflects a tendency to reestablish workers as an integral part of the decision making process. It is still unclear to what extent social agencies will adopt this approach.

Merit, recruitment, and selection

The next three characteristics provide the rationale for the merit, recruitment, and selection function which is performed by personnel divisions in the state and federal government. Characteristics three, four, and five are: 3) the officeholder is an employee. 4) The "means of administration" are attached to the office not the officeholder—no personal rights to the office can be gained by the individual. 5) Membership in the bureaucracy constitutes a career with distinct ladders of career progression, and hiring and promotion are to be based on competence which is determined either by professional training or testing. Merit systems then are designed to provide state agencies with highly qualified staff, place employees in working environments that promote and reward quality performance, and protect the civil service system by assuring that promotion and hiring are based on qualifications of the individual and needs of the agency. One of the main purposes of the merit system is to protect the bureaucratic hiring process from influence extraneous and irrelevant to the qualifications being sought.

Most social workers encounter a merit system at some point. The federal government hires all its social workers through a merit system; so do many states. To work for the federal government or one of these states the social worker must apply for the position and then take an exam (written, oral, or written and oral). Some civil service tests also have performance components that test skills like typing, but social workers are not often required to take them. There is also some question about the effectiveness of the paper and pencil tests in identifying social work skills. Many social work positions are filled using a variety of testing procedures. It is not unusual for an applicant to have her work history scored for experience, education, and references, take a written exam, and finally an oral exam. In fact this is the usual procedure for filling upper level positions.

The merit system makes the application for employment more cumbersome but is designed to limit the impact of partisan politics, provide fair competition among job seekers, and ultimately to protect the employee from firing on political grounds. Although the merit system has been credited with occasionally protecting deadwood, few people would like to replace it with political patronage and nepotism.

Formalization

The final characteristic of an ideal bureaucracy is impersonality or formalization. Formalization is the rules and procedures designed to direct workers to handle contingencies faced by the organization. The less complex the task, the easier it is to formalize the procedures. The more complex the task, the greater the need for formalization, but the more difficult it is to accomplish. While social workers frequently complain about the innumerable rules they must follow, most would greatly appreciate having clear guidelines on how to approach the most difficult situations such as child neglect. While there is general knowledge in this area, it is certainly not developed to the point where it can be routinized and written down—social workers are constantly in the position of having to make professional judgments.

Complexity

Since Weber was addressing the movement toward routinization taking place in the 19th century, he of course could not address the tremendous task that social workers must face today. To address organizational structure in a meaningful way for modern social workers, we must include the concept of complexity. Complexity refers to the number of different tasks an agency performs, how predictable those tasks are, how much discretion in decision making is required, and how many different professions (cognitive orientations) are involved. Prior to acquiring responsibility for Blind Aid, Disabled Aid, and Old Age Assistance (now known as Supplemental Security Income or SSI) the organization of a typical local social security office was relatively simple. Workers were required to deal with minimal variation in clients and the intake process was highly routinized; a limited number of people were eligible for benefits and eligibility standards were relatively clear. When SSI was added, social security workers were then forced to deal with public assistance clients in addition to social insurance beneficiaries. Social workers not only facilitate the collection of insurance premiums, but they also determine eligibility for financial assistance. Although the types of programs and clients have increased the complexity of the Social Security Office, it still remains much less complex than social service offices that deal with a much greater variety of economic and social problems.

Summary

To summarize organizational structure (bureaucracy), it can be said that in theory structure is designed to minimize or at least regulate the influence any one individual can have on an organization. It is also an important means by which individuals are made to conform to organizational needs. Structure is the setting in which power is exercised, decisions are made, and actions are carried out. There is not just one type of structure as suggested by Weber's "ideal" type. Different types of organizations require different types of structure.

Social workers frequently find themselves working in agencies with a visible bureaucratic structure. There is a clear division of labor between administrators, supervisors, social workers, income maintenance workers, and clerical staff. In some agencies the social workers themselves will specialize in protective services, older adults, or families, for example. The hierarchy is usually well defined and frequently discourages any exchange between the lower and upper levels without "going through channels." Social service agencies tend to be complex; the formalization does not always simplify procedures. Writing in the 19th century Weber visualized assembly line industries and less complex governmental agencies than today's social service agencies. Although Weber identified the importance of structure and the distribution of power in an organization, he was unable to address these variables in a manner that can guide the worker in the current multi-purpose social service agencies.

"Good bureaucrats"

Even with its flaws bureaucracy in an adapted form has survived. Weber was correct: to date we have not developed a more efficient structure to replace it. Since this is the situation, social workers can benefit by becoming "good bureaucrats." Robert Pruger offers social workers some concrete, constructive suggestions for combining effectiveness with survival in formal organization. In this section we will draw heavily upon his work to help prepare "good bureaucrats.[7]"

Staying power

The first requisite of a good bureaucrat is staying power. There is no way a social worker can achieve her goals if she does not stay in the agency long enough to bring her ideas to fruition. While it may give her a sense of power and righteousness to resign in protest, it also removes the power to make change. Though resignation may sometimes be in order, it should only be used when other avenues have been exhausted.

Often the worker may fail to realize how much power and discretion she actually has. Some workers deal with the complexity and strain of their job by believing and acting as if there were no choice involved—only rules to follow. Formal organizations tend to tolerate this behavior, and so it is up to the individual to preserve and enlarge the discretionary aspects of the position. Complex organizations can provide workers with an excuse to become mere bureaucrats with little creativity or pressure to challenge or effectively use the organization to meet service goals. One of the real threats to creativity is that the merit system will protect the individual who even minimally fulfills her function but may not provide the same protection for someone who is willing to risk.

Pruger provides a prescription for workers to preserve their options and expand their career. The first step is to understand legitimate authority and organizational enforcement. On the most basic level, this suggests avoiding behavior that would lead to dismissal. Nearly every organization has a manual of published rules, laws, job descriptions, and work schedules. The statements define behaviors that are prescribed, permitted, and proscribed. Since these rules govern a variety of potential situations, they are by necessity general. Most dimensions of a social worker's job are beyond advance specification; it is not only undesirable but also impossible to tell social workers in advance what decisions they will have to face or what interventions will be most effective.

Organizations are also limited in their ability to observe an employee's behavior closely, because close supervision is costly. And even if an agency could afford excessive supervision, it would be unlikely to do so because of the potential demoralization of staff. The more professionalized the staff, the more negative the effect of inappropriately close supervision. Professionals are trained to use professional judgment and resent incursion into their domain of expertise. Since the limitations of surveillance on staff is a fact of organizational life, most workers do have choices and can make discretionary decisions. The good bureaucrat can make the most of her potential for achievement if she understands legitimate authority and how the organization can or is likely to enforce authority.

Conserving energy

Pruger also suggests the good bureaucrat will conserve energy. Two ways workers waste energy are feeling sorry for themselves as being overworked and underpaid, and wasting energy complaining about what they see as needless paperwork. Successful organizational members do not expect their actions to be noted and rewarded but instead develop an internal reward system that provides reinforcement in the knowledge that the job was well done. The worker who disciplines her need to win recognition from higher officials increases her freedom to take initiative, promote ideas, and generally engage in creative behavior which keeps the individual vital.

The typical caricature of the bureaucrat is a faceless person buried in a pile of paperwork, shuffling papers from one pile to another without reducing the size of the pile. Everyone knows of at least one social worker who spends more time bemoaning the amount of paperwork than she does processing it. The good bureaucrat recognizes that for the agency to function she must collect data and report to the appropriate funding sources. On the other hand an ineffective worker may actually bury herself in the red tape of form completion or she may become excessively emotional and let the work accumulate. Forms must be complete; effective organizational survival requires completing reports with dispatch and not expending unnecessary energy on resentment.

Indispensability

Two final suggestions from Pruger include making oneself indispensable to the agency and not yielding unnecessarily to the requirements of administrative convenience. Workers become indispensable when they have a skill or competence needed by the organization. This could be proposal writing, community organization, political acumen, budgeting, or any other skill essential to effective agency functioning. Related to these skills is the necessity to make certain the skill is used to fulfill the organizational mission and not just to benefit the organization. Particularly in times of fiscal constraint, agencies suffer from goal displacement—the survival needs of the agency tend to overwhelm and steal the efforts that should be expended toward the organization's mission. Robert Scott relates how this happened in a sheltered workshop for the blind. The workshop got caught up in turning a profit and started competing with private industry for the best blind workers when they were supposed to be helping the unemployed blind acquire skills to gain employment.[8]

The human element in bureaucracies

Thus far we have discussed characteristics found in formal organizations and offered some suggestions on how to be more effective working in a bureaucracy. This is a sound basis for the beginning social worker, but it is important to address at least briefly the human element in organizations and what decision makers need to know about dealing with workers. Social workers who become either supervisors or industrial social workers will need to study these questions in considerable depth. But every worker can contribute to making the work setting more supportive of individual growth. This brief discussion of the human needs in the bureaucracy is meant to make the student a more effective and more empathetic co-worker in whatever setting she chooses to use her skills.

The existential perspective suggests that one can only be happy in a job that one sees as being meaningful.

One of the most basic needs in a work setting is a need for meaning, a need addressed in psychology by theorists such as Frankl.[9] Since working, especially for professionals, encompasses so much of one's life, it would be difficult for a professional to have a sense of meaning in life without experiencing a sense of purpose or direction in the workplace. The degree to which one's professional work creates meaning for life is reflected in how frequently professional and personal relationships overlap. It is not unusual for doctors, lawyers, or social workers to prefer to socialize with other members of their profession. Much to the dismay of spouses, professional talk frequently permeates social gatherings. Though outsiders may be bored to tears, such shop talk reflects the degree to which an occupation or career gives meaning to life.

In Chapter 1 we discussed the concept of equifinality, i.e., the idea that there is more than one way to achieve a goal.

People also desire a sense of control over life and particularly over work tasks. The need for control can be met by providing workers with options on how to achieve the outcomes expected by the agency. Allowing the worker to choose the method to be used can increase his sense of control. Even as co-workers we can reinforce an individual's sense of control by respecting and appreciating methods different than our own. Keeping things simple despite the pressure to complicate matters also increases a sense of control. As we move deeper into the computer age, there is overwhelming pressure to gather data that may be useful since it can be easily stored and retrieved. To the social worker interested in dealing with human problems unnecessary paper shuffling can decrease both the sense of control and meaningfulness of work.

We all need to view ourselves as winners. Label a person a loser and he will begin to act like one. Too many administrators feel that people, especially bureaucrats, are lazy and will only produce if we design the system to punish them for inactivity. One of the most well-grounded principles of behaviorism is that people are more likely to respond to positive than negative reinforcement. In spite of this many work settings concentrate on punishing errors and ignoring success. While Pruger is correct in suggesting that social workers should not waste energy feeling low because their accomplishments are not recognized, they may profitably spend some time building their own reward mechanisms and providing reinforcement for co-workers.

Summary

The role of bureaucrat is one of a number of roles a social worker plays. Students need to be aware of the inevitability of taking on the role and also to prepare themselves to be good bureaucrats. Our discussion drew upon Weber's structural theory to illustrate the principles that underlie bureaucratic structure. We briefly examined some of the pros and cons of formalization, centralization, complexity, hierarchy, and specialization. We borrowed from the work of Robert Pruger to develop practice principles that can help students become good bureaucrats. We ended this section with a brief overview of the human needs of individuals within organizations. For students who go on to administrative specialization, this knowledge will constitute only a minute portion of what they will come to know about organizations. For those who go into direct practice, this may be their only exposure to the organizational literature unless they take it upon themselves to pursue this area. Accreditation standards do not presently stress the importance of understanding organizations.

Coordination of human services

It is important to examine formal organizations from another perspective—how they affect clients and client services. Understanding bureaucratic structures improves the professional's ability to increase the responsiveness of the service delivery system. Bureaucratic organizations present opportunities and obstacles for the professional, make possible a broad array of services for clients, and create considerable frustration for many clients. As professionals it is our obligation to decrease this frustration by making service organizations responsive to client needs.

Providing social services requires a service delivery system: a set of organizations that can obtain resources from the environment, transform those resources into programs and services, and deliver them to the client. Few people truly believe neighborhoods and churches can provide for the social and economic needs of our society. If we were to have a totally integrated service system, it would be sufficiently powerful to generate adequate resources and deliver them humanely and efficiently to all those in need.

Benson and others suggest several important attributes of a coordinated service delivery system.[10]

1. A coordinated system provides legally available services with minimal delay and red tape. Clients receive services to which they are legally entitled without undue waiting and stigmatization.
2. Services should not be denied because of inefficiency or rigidity of the service network. Interagency squabbles or lack of cooperation should not reflect on client services.
3. Clients should get the full range of entitled services and expertise regardless of where they enter the network. For instance, if the mother enters the service network through a referral to protective services for leaving her children unattended, she would still receive the child care services even though it requires going to another agency. This same mother may also need a different job. If she started out at Job Service they would

An example of how a coordinated service delivery system might operate is presented.

Bureaucratic units usually have specifically assigned duties.

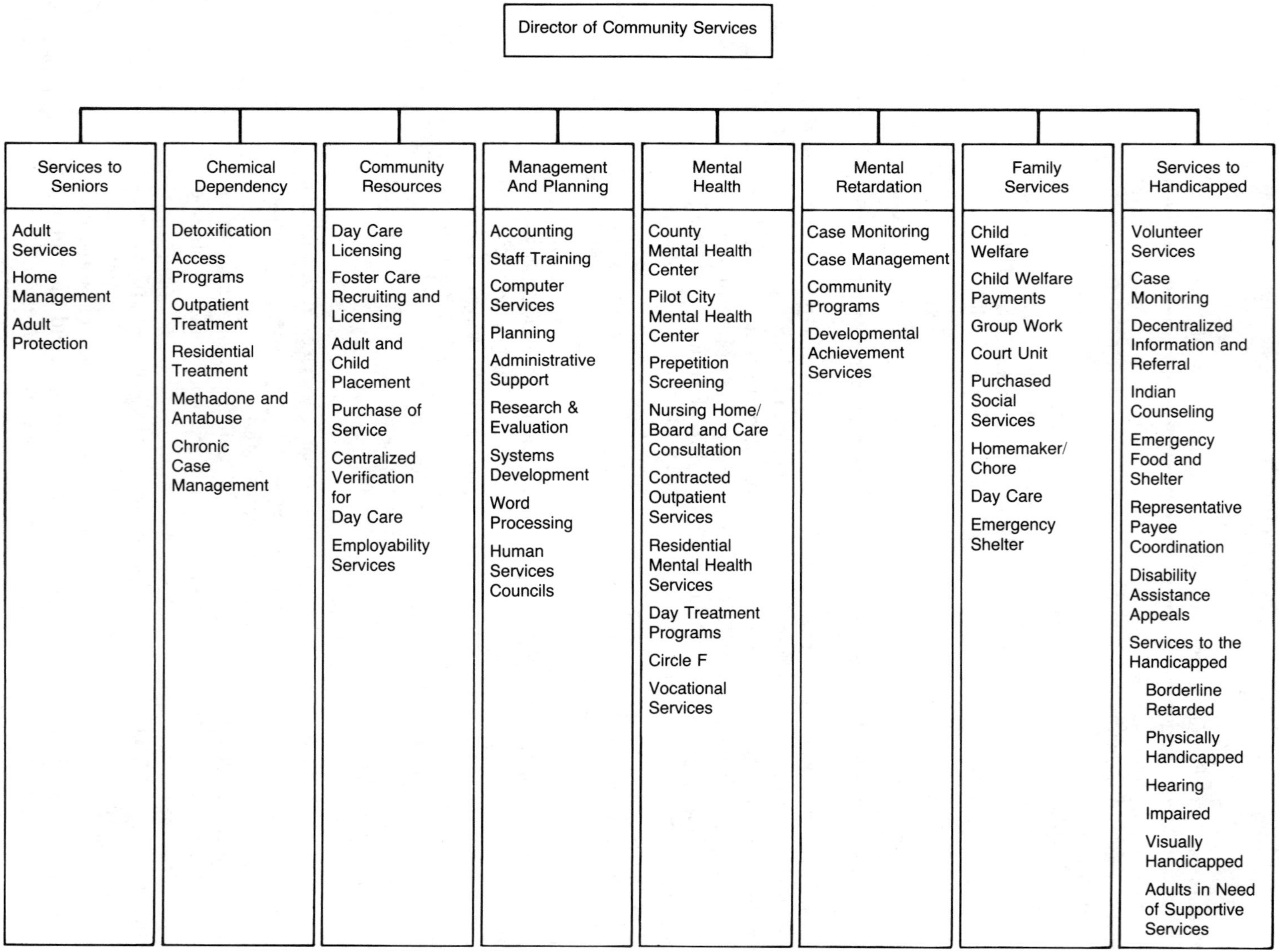

A bureaucracy is typically hierarchical and centralized.

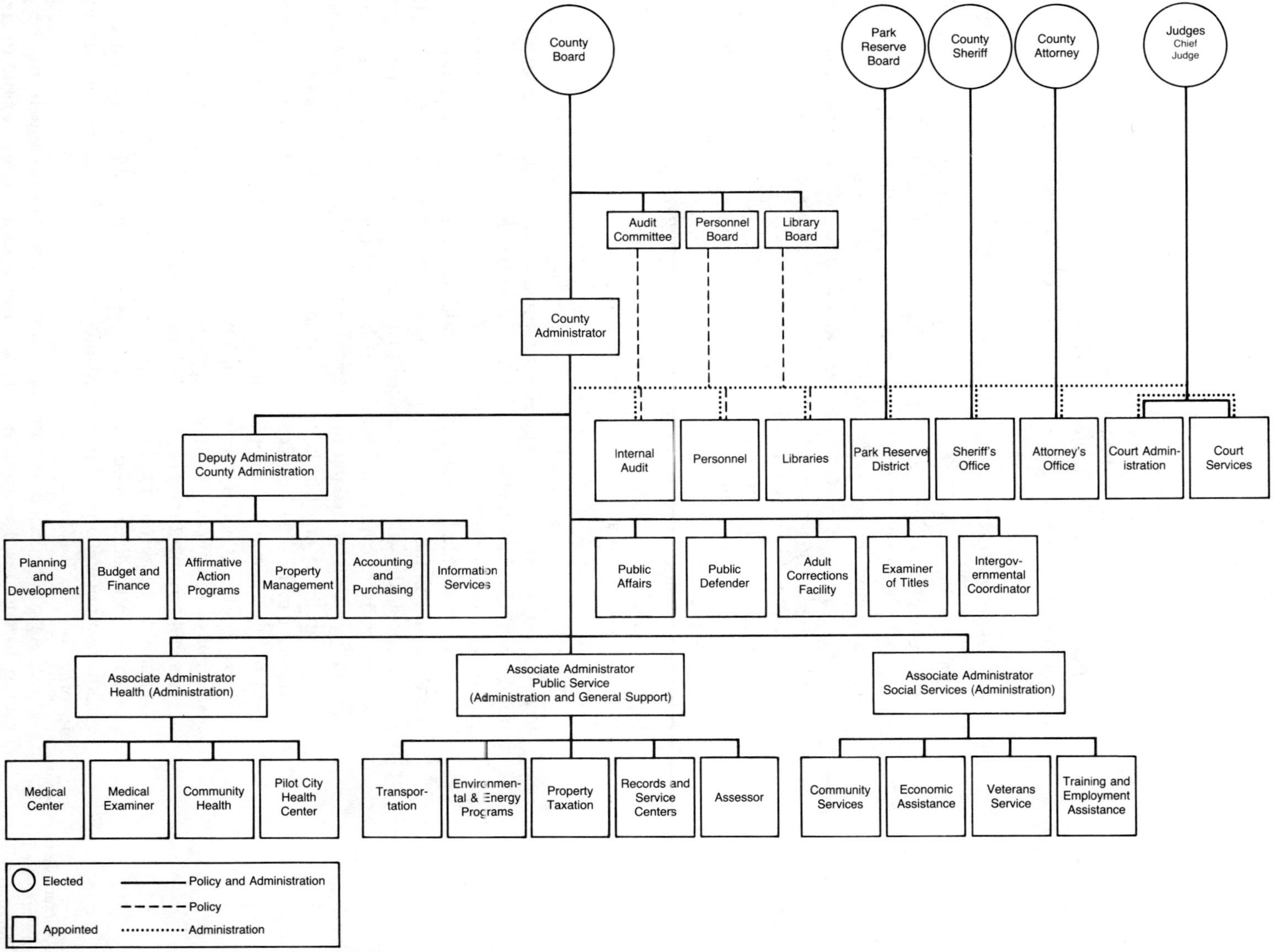

look at available employment. In a coordinated service delivery system, all of the necessary services would be made available regardless of which agency made the first contact.

4. Problems should be handled comprehensively and coherently. In addition to providing all the necessary services, services need to be delivered in a manner and sequence that the client understands.

Obstacles clients may face

In contrast serious gaps in the delivery system tend to occur, and some of the most needy go unaided. Service gaps tend to arise from four primary sources: lack of coordination, unclear program articulation, inflexibility of program requirements, and absence of needed services. Conditions necessary to overcome the gaps in service and to develop a coordinated network of services include a high degree of interaction between agencies, clear articulation of the services and boundaries of each program, and a certain degree of flexibility between agencies and programs. The service delivery system requires a high degree of interaction since a large portion of each agency's clientele are receiving services from at least one other agency. Variance in individual agency rules and requirements make it difficult for the client to coordinate services between programs. Lack of coordination takes many forms. For example, a mother may find that her AFDC grant is reduced when she receives money from another agency such as the Division of Vocational Rehabilitation.

Clear program articulation is helpful for professionals who must work together but is even more critical for clients. What the agency does and does not do and who may receive its services must be clear. If the referring professional does not understand the receiving agency's program, inappropriate referrals are more likely to take place. In addition, an inapproprate referral may put the client in the position of receiving incompatible and even contradictory services or at the very least services that seem unrelated to the problem the client is trying to overcome. Poor articulation of programs puts an unfair burden on the client by making the client the principal link between agencies.

Flexibility is another key component of a coordinated delivery system. Flexibility can be lost by excessive formalization of relationships. Personnel need to have some adaptability and flexibility in making judgments. When workers must rely on an overly complex set of rules, they are more likely to lose sight of the client's unique problem. Inflexibility occurs when programs are available to meet the client's need, but clients are denied the benefits due to eligibility requirements. This happens frequently when parents are employed and a family member has expensive medical problems not covered by health insurance. To get the needed medical care, the family must forfeit its income.

An example of program planning for the rural elderly is described in Chapter 20.

Absence of services is a problem that varies considerably from one community to another. The rural elderly, for instance, are often unable to receive services because they lack transportation.

Obstacles professionals may face

Barriers to services occur on an individual level for the client, but practitioners also face barriers—organizational and professional. Aiken and others list some obstacles practitioners face in providing services.

1. Fragmentation of services
2. Inaccessibility of services
3. Lack of accountability of service agencies
4. Discontinuities of services
5. Dispersal of services
6. Wastefulness of resources
7. Ineffectiveness of services
8. Short term commitment of services[11]

In addition even more fundamental barriers tend to interfere with coordinated service delivery. Professionalism itself creates some of these barriers, for example, organizational autonomy, conflicts between client groups, and conflict over control of resources.

ORGANIZATIONAL AUTONOMY

All organizations strive for autonomy. They fiercely protect their organizational boundaries and defend their domain; they vigorously resist control from other agencies. Organizations are threatened by other agencies providing similar services to their clientele. Each agency strives to decrease any other agency's control over them and any competition in services provided. This striving for autonomy fragments problems and creates almost insurmountable obstacles to coordination of services. The vested interests of administrators and programs take precedence over any desire for interorganizational cooperation. To develop a coordinated service system there must be a way to force organizations to cooperate. The hold-out problem is likely to occur when organizations have the autonomy to reject system-wide proposals.[12]

Autonomy refers to the ability to function independently without control by others.

Professions have always claimed the right to be autonomous. Since professionals are dedicated to public service, they claim the right to formalize their own values, identify objectives based on these values, codify their own knowledge base, and translate these components into specialized knowledge and techniques. Professionals believe they should be self-monitored and protected from intervention by outsiders not oriented to public service or knowledgeable about the complexities of providing professional services. This characteristic is functional in creating group cohesion to work for social reform, but professional autonomy also introduces distinct problems. The most obvious would be the move toward elitism and self interest. The same power that can be mobilized for social change can also be used to protect the interests of the professional. At worst professional autonomy may be used to gen-

Chapter 7 discusses the attributes of a profession.

erate or perpetuate professional and personal privilege rather than improved welfare services.[13]

Realistically if present programming has provided a comfortable existence for the professional and the agency, both will be reluctant to undertake new programs that might interfere with this position. The agency will also exert pressure upon other agencies whose practices tend to be disruptive of program requirements. Every agency strives to build a domain that is exclusive, autonomous, and dominant. The more exclusive, autonomous, and dominant the agency is, the greater the power to hold and obtain funds and authority.

CONFLICTS OVER IDEOLOGY

Ideological consensus is the degree to which professionals agree about service methods and goals. If members of the aging network, for instance, agree the most efficient, effective, and humane way to deal with the chronically-impaired elderly is in nursing homes, then there is ideological consensus. With this general agreement, other service providers in the network would refer the chronically-impaired for nursing home placement. In reality, however, there is no such consensus. Alternative programs challenge this approach. Since professions tend to view problems differently, they will pursue different intervention strategies, and the more professions involved with a client, the more likely the client will be a victim of conflicting strategies. Nursing home residents sometimes get conflicting messages from nurses trained in the medical model and social workers operating from a social model. This conflicting ideology can be a source of creative problem solving or conflicting messages to clients.

CONFLICTS BETWEEN CLIENT GROUPS OVER RESOURCES

Conflict between client groups can also be a barrier to coordinated services, for example, when race specific programs are developed with the assumptions that all native Americans or all Hispanics have the same needs and desire the same services. An Indian health program was organized so the clients themselves could determine how program money was spent, but since the money was limited, committee members favored members of their own tribe over others who were sometimes in greater need. It is unrealistic to expect clients not to look out for their interest group when that is the way the rest of society operates. Clients are no more and no less capable of rising above self interest in distributing resources than anyone else.

Control of resources also has a profound effect on the service delivery system. Robert Magill has found that the more decentralized (community control) the control of resources, the less progressive or humane the service delivery tends to be.[14] Therefore, the greater the centralization (federal control), the more money there is likely to be available. On the other hand, federal control means more red tape to get the money.

Finally, no agency wants to deal with difficult clients. Particularly in an age where accountability and efficiency are equated with processing numbers, there is little pay-off personally or professionally for identifying and serving those most in need of services. In its most blatant form, this failure to serve the most needy has been called "creaming of clients." While few professionals would admit to supporting such practice Paul Adams and Nancy McDonald illustrate how workers use professional rationalizations to "cool-out" clients.[15] Instead of dealing with professional ineffectiveness or turning clients away, some professionals convince clients they did not really want the service in the first place. For the client the result is the same whether they are rejected as ineligible or "cooled-out" of the system.

Goals of service delivery system

Having discussed the barriers to coordinated service delivery systems, it may be useful to clarify what goals should guide a humane delivery system.

The goals of a service delivery system include accessibility, coordination, compatibility, cooperation, efficiency, effectiveness, accountability, and comprehensiveness.

Accessibility. No matter how potentially effective the service, clients can not benefit unless they can gain access to the service. Different states and even different counties within states vary tremendously in how accessible they make client services. Satellite offices in poor and rural areas where transportation is a problem help address this problem. Making agencies or meal sites accessible to the handicapped by removing physical barriers also helps. Sometimes it may be necessary to have bilingual staff to communicate with groups that do not speak English. Accessible services are services that are obtainable.

Coordination. Coordinated services treat the client as a whole person. Fragmentation of care is avoided. Case-management is one technique that has been effectively used to assure coordination of services—notably in community care programs for the elderly and the "fixed point of referral" for the developmentally disabled. For a chronically impaired older person to remain in his home, it is frequently necessary to use the resources of many agencies—nutrition programs, visiting nurses, county social service agencies, day care centers, etc. In community care programs the case manager works with the client to determine what programs he needs and then arranges contracts with appropriate agencies to provide those services. The case manager makes certain that all of the services the person receives are compatible with each other and with the client's needs. Without a case manager the individual might be scheduled for many social activities on one day and none for the rest of the week or may be scheduled for social activities and have her health needs overlooked.

Compatibility. Services to clients need to complement each other. Clients need to experience services as making their lives more harmonious not more complicated. The welfare mother who is told by her protective service worker that she must be home more because her teenage children need supervision will be confused and frustrated when she is told by the income maintenance worker that she must accept employment or lose eligibility for the AFDC program since her children are over six years of age. If services are to be appropriately linked and sequenced, they cannot be standardized and routinized; they must remain flexible. Linkage must be achieved by cooperation and coordination. Inappropriate standardization of programs creates no-win situations for the complex problems clients must face.

Cooperation. While coordination deals with a quality of the system, cooperation speaks to the quality of relationship of actors within the system. Cooperation takes place when professionals involved share goals and values, accept a mutual understanding of the problem, and have the ability to work together on a common task. The less conflict clients experience between helping professionals, the more confident they will be that the service plan is sound. Professional ideological differences should not be fought over at the clients' expense. Cooperation and coordination should also lead to increased efficiency by obviating unnecessary duplication of services.

Efficiency. An efficient service delivery system is organized in such a manner that no other way of organizing the system would produce greater output (benefits) for the amount of input (resources) expended in the process. Efficiency is a term borrowed from the business literature, and it continues to be much easier to measure when dealing with profit-oriented organizations. The more efficient a business is the more profitable it is. In the human service area efficiency is equally important but much more difficult to measure. Efficiency is usually achieved by routinization. Any part of the process that can be standardized provides at least the possibility of increased efficiency. One recent attempt at efficiency in hospitals involved having patients fill out their own medical history by responding to computerized questions. Early results seem to indicate this approach is cost efficient; whether this approach is conducive to improving the patient's overall health is still under study. If the computer system fails to get all the pertinent data or causes undue anxiety in the client, the efficiency of the system is decreased.

In addition to viewing efficiency as the relationship of inputs to outputs in the human service, it has also been defined as the ratio of service extended to results produced. Whichever way one defines efficiency it is basically related to such things as personnel, time, money, materials, and equipment. Rino Patti lists some ways efficiency has been viewed in the human service arena.

1. The costs associated with units of program output (e.g., placing a child in a foster home, or delivering a treatment interview).
2. The costs entailed in achieving program objectives, with specific information regarding the component costs attributable to personnel, material, or equipment.
3. The relative costs of different services or approaches used in achieving the same outcomes (e.g., the comparative costs of chore and homemaker services in preventing institutionalization of the elderly).
4. The expenditure entailed in delivering a program compared to the monetary nature of the benefits realized (e.g., the costs of a training program for welfare clients in relation to the savings achieved as a result of reduced welfare benefits).[16]

Effectiveness. Effectiveness is traditionally defined as the degree to which the program meets its objectives, but this definition assumes consensus on program objectives. In reality funders may have one set of objectives, professionals another, and clients still another. For instance, a jobs program could be set up to get people off the welfare rolls. Policy makers would review the program's effectiveness according to how many fewer people received welfare. The professional would address a more complex measure of effectiveness and would look at both costs and benefits to clients and society. The client would view the program as effective if it improved his standard of living or quality of life. As administrators or providers of service, social workers cannot afford to overlook any of these assessments of program effectiveness. The indicators of effectiveness identified by Patti have a different emphasis than the indicators of efficiency.

1. The extent to which the program objectives have been achieved, including, for example, whether changes in client behavior, skill, attitude, or status that were expected to occur as a result of program interventions have, in fact, occurred. Client satisfaction with services received are also sometimes used as indicators of program effectiveness.
2. The extent to which treatment or service objectives established for individual clients have been attained. These are outcomes particularized to each case and are generally more specific than program-wide objectives. For example, the latter may focus on the reduction of recidivism among all delinquents served in a program, while individual treatment objectives might be targeted at the acquisition of certain social skills or a reduction in parent-child conflict for specific cases.
3. The variable effects of different kinds or levels of service on subgroups of clients. Such comparisons might involve the relative success of two methods of treatment—e.g., behavioral vs. milieu—or the same method applied for varying periods of time to two comparable groups in an institution for delinquents.
4. The differential impact of services on clients with different characteristics. A uniformly administered service, such as job counseling, may prove to be more effective with some clients (e.g., those with prior employment history) than others.
5. The comparison of outcomes for clients exposed to a program, with those for similar persons in the target population who have received no services.[17]

Accountability. Both efficiency and effectiveness are related to the goal of accountability. In discussing the different views of program effectiveness we have already alluded to some of the different groups to which we are accountable. Traditionally social workers were accountable to their agency and their profession. The client movements of the 60s made workers more aware of the importance of client satisfaction. The late 1970s ushered in a new era of accountability that all but ignored client satisfaction and professional concerns and instead stressed cost efficiency. Agencies hired individuals with academic training and experience in business rather than services. Many simplistically hoped that these managers would make the welfare system as efficient as the private sector. What has become increasingly clear is that the private sector is not nearly as efficient as we would like to believe and that efficiency is only one of the many goals human service agencies strive for.

For social workers being accountable means responding to the goals of the client, the profession, the agency, and larger society while providing services as humanely and efficiently as possible. While the social worker cannot ignore any of these constituencies they must recognize that there will be conflict between constituencies. A system's accountability will include policy makers, various professional groups, agencies within the system, clients and potential clients, and taxpayers. Whether accountability is viewed from the level of the individual social worker or of the service delivery system, the lack of agreement on what objectives to be accountable for remains. In spite of this disagreement, however, program administrators and social workers must continually strive to make services and programs more accountable.

Comprehensiveness. Comprehensiveness addresses the goal of developing a system that meets all the client's needs. A job paying $25,000 a year will not help the mother of two-year-old twins unless she can obtain adequate child care for her children. Becoming an ace welder is not going to take a person's family off welfare unless a welding job is available. Generous scholarships will not help an underprivileged minority if he has not received the basic education required for successful college work.

Comprehensiveness has sometimes been equated with cradle to the gravy security. A humane and comprehensive system certainly would remove the fear of economic insecurity and want, but it could never remove all of the problems associated with medical problems, learning disabilities, handicaps, etc. Presently our society would not even consider offering such a comprehensive array of services. In reality the goal of comprehensiveness is limited to providing enough services so that what we do provide has maximum effect. The penal system, for example, is (at least in theory) comprehensive. It provides punishments that range from fines with complete physical freedom to probation with supervision to many graduated levels of security all the way to maximum isolation away from the rest of the population. Prisons also have a range of programs from hard labor to receiving a college education. Of course our prison system is not necessarily an example of a coordinated comprehensive delivery system, but it does suggest how complex a comprehensive system would be if client, institution, and societal needs were addressed.

Summary

This discussion of the service delivery system was designed to illustrate briefly present gaps in the service delivery system, to demonstrate the barriers that face service providers, and to identify the goals service providers strive to achieve. This brief overview is not meant to immobilize students by making problems seem insurmountable but instead to increase their potential effectiveness by identifying areas of knowledge they can pursue to strengthen their preparation for practice. While administrators will become specialists in service delivery, all social workers can contribute to making the service delivery system run more efficiently and effectively.

References

1. Koya Azumi and Jerald Hage, *Organizational Systems* (Lexington, Mass.: Heath, 1972).
2. Robert Pruger,"The Good Bureaucrat," *Social Work* 18 (July, 1973) 26–32.
3. Ibid.
4. Curt Tausky, *Work Organizations* (Peacock: Itasca, Ill.: 1978) 6.
5. Max Weber, *The Theory of Social and Economic Organization* ed. and trans. A. Henderson and Talcott Partsons. (New York: Macmillan, 1975) 328.
6. Max Weber, "The Essentials of Bureaucracy," in *Reader in Bureaucracy,* ed. Robert Merton (New York: Free Press, 1967) 21–22.
7. Pruger, "The Good Bureaucrat."
8. Robert Scott, "The Factory as A Social Service Organization: Goal Displacement in Workshops for the Blind," *Social Problems* 15, no. 2 (Fall 1967) 160–175.
9. Viktor E. Frankl, *Man's Search for Meaning* (New York: Washington Square Press, 1963).
10. Michael Aiken, Robert Dewar, Nancy Ditomaso, Jerald Hage, and Gerald Leitz, *Coordinating Human Services* (San Francisco: Jossey Bass, 1975), 1–12.
11. Jerald Hage, Michael Aiken, and Cora Bagley Marrett, "Organizational Structure and Communications," *American Sociological Review* 36, no. 5 (October 1971) 860–871.
12. Howard Aldrich, "Centralization versus Decentralization in the Design of Human Service Delivery Systems," in *The Sociology of Organizations,* ed. Otto Grusky and George A. Miller (New York: Free Press, 1981) 375.
13. Ronald Frederico, *The Social Welfare Institution,* 3rd ed. (Lexington, Mass.: Heath, 1980) 323.
14. Robert Magill, *Community Decisionmaking for Social Welfare* (New York: Human Sciences Press, 1978).
15. Adams and McDonald, "Clinical Cooling Out of Poor People," in *Things that Matter* ed. H. Rubenstein and M. H. Bloch (New York: Macmillan, 1983) 139–145.
16. Rino Patti, *Social Welfare Administation* (Englewood Cliffs, N.J.: Prentice-Hall, 1983) 180.
17. Ibid.

PART
V

FIELDS OF PRACTICE

"Social work may be said to be traveling towards maturity as a profession when it is capable of assimilating knowledge and skill from many sources without loss of integrity; . . . it has achieved consistency between its goals and its methods and is willing to subject itself to self imposed standards of conduct; it recognizes its sphere of social responsibility [fields of practice]; it evolves methods for merging its empirical and theoretical knowledge; and it is able to recruit its candidates from the higher levels of intelligence."[1]

Where do social workers work? Social work offers services in nearly every area of human life where social stress and dysfunctioning are found. With such a wide range of areas of social concern, the profession has continually had to address how to describe and how to amalgamate its diversity. Social work service patterns have traditionally been differentiated by the specific locations or settings (e.g., hospitals, mental health clinics, public welfare departments), the general areas of concern or fields of practice (e.g., child welfare or health care), and the characteristic methodologies used in day to day practice (e.g., casework, groupwork, and community organization).

Shortly after the turn of the century when social workers were nearly exclusively associated with programs of public and private welfare, a movement was begun to separate practice into specific fields of practice. General welfare was joined by efforts in child welfare, family services, general medicine, psychiatry, and recreation. In the 1920s and 1930s social work concerned itself with elaborating the differences between those who worked in the various settings. After World War II, social work became preoccupied with developing specializations based not only on the specific work place and methodology but also on the theoretical orientation of the work being done. Developing these specializations was part of a general strategy to increase the profession's prestige. By narrowing its focus social work could build respect as a profession in its own right rather than depending on medicine and law. While people helping people is as old as the human race, professional social work, as a disciplined and skillful method of helping people, is less than a century old.

In 1957 the Council on Social Work Education delineated nine areas of practice for social work. Designated as "fields of practice," this list included public assistance, family social work, child welfare, corrections, psychiatric social work, medical social work (including public health), school social work, group service agencies, and community planning. By using the concept of "field of practice" it was hoped that the tendency to measure specific practice activities by attributes found outside the actual practice could be avoided, thus leaving the door open for evaluation of the social work tasks. This assumes that significant variations should be found in the social work process itself and not in the environment in which it takes place.

While the profession pursued these efforts, interest was being rekindled in explicating a more comprehensive and inclusive view of social work practice as a whole. Much of this rekindling was being fueled by the rapidly changing social and political scene at that time. Civil unrest and pressure on the government and on the providers of social services to improve general conditions of living resulted in the launching of the war on poverty.

Many new programs and expanded traditional services employed social workers. Areas of concern and concomitant fields of practice expanded rapidly in the 1960s, reinforcing the profession's need to identify the common elements of practice that could then be applied to work done in specific fields and settings. This was a major focus of the professional literature into the 1970s. In the 1980s the breadth of concerns addressed by social work practice is in the public view once again. This time economic distress coupled with changing social and political attitudes and cutbacks in funding of social programs has emphasized the recurrent dilemma of expanded social needs coupled with severe limitations in the ability of social welfare institutions to meet those needs.

To identify current fields of practice relevant to social work the dimensions developed by Harriet Bartlett in the early 1960s can be applied: the problem (or condition) of central concern, a system of organized services, a body of knowledge, values, and methods, the particular sociocultural attitudes in society that surround a problem or concern, and identifiable characteristic responses of those providing services.[2] This section introduces the primary fields of social work practice—family welfare, communities, health, and criminal justice—along with some special fields that fall under those general areas.

The chapter on family welfare includes public assistance both because strengthening the American family is a major goal of such programs and because public assistance programs are an important aspect of family functioning in many social work clients. In American society public assistance programs are only available when a family is not capable of supporting "its own."

The communities chapter combines various fields of practice generally in neighborhood settings. The first example examines community action in an urbanized setting. The discussion then turns to community action in rural settings and looks at how different resources and norms require different interventions. A natural corollary to these community actions is the self-help movements. In all community interventions the social worker is dependent on community cooperation to achieve intervention goals. The social worker's role in the self-help setting is quite different; typically she sets up a self-help group but then serves as a resource person rather than a leader. Social workers also use existing self-help groups as a resource for their clients.

Business and industry were included in the communities chapter although they might have been included in the health or family section. Many social workers work in employee assistance programs and help clients with problems related to alcohol and other drug abuse. Including industry under community programs was designed to present a more systematic view of the social worker's role in the economic well-being of a community. Prevention programs may be more effective in combatting alcoholism than many specifically designated chemical abuse programs.

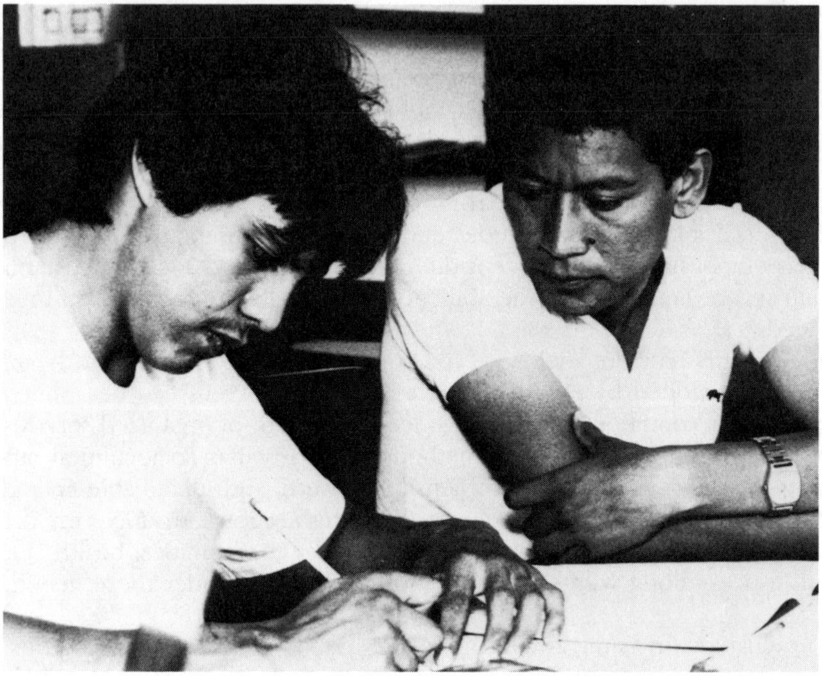

An example of the self help movement: one man helps another in a Chicano Center. Photo courtesy of Student Support Services Publication Center, University of Minnesota.

The health chapter discusses the social worker's role in physical health, mental health, and educational settings. Including educational settings in this chapter is based on the reality that most social workers in such settings deal with individuals who suffer from either physical or mental disabilities that make learning a problem for the student and educating a problem for the teacher. P.L. 94–142 (1975) greatly extended the obligation of public schools to educate handicapped children. Prior to passage of this legislation school social workers dealt primarily with truants and discipline problems. This law extended the role of the social worker to identifying, advocating, and evaluating children with special problems. In addition the traditional role of liaison between the school and family has intensified.

The criminal justice system has many arenas in which social workers are involved—correctional institutions and prisons, community corrections, probation and parole, and the more recently developed area of social work in legal settings. Value conflicts between the advocacy role and client self-determination come into sharp focus in this setting. The professional boundaries of the advocacy role have not been adequately defined by the profession. This lack of clarity leads to dissonance for many practitioners.

It is to be hoped that this collection of vignettes provides a colorful, if limited, view of how social work knowledge, skills, and values are translated into action in specific fields of practice. The selection of experiences provides an opportunity to view social work practice from a conservative social control stance of a correctional administrator to a liberal community organizer developing a day care center to a radical community organizer fighting for increased recreational facilities in the Bronx.

References

1. Eduard Lindeman, "Social Casework Matures in a Confused World," paper given at the annual meeting of the New York State Conference on Social Work, 1946 (Albany, New York: 1947) 51.
2. Harriet Bartlett, *Analyzing Social Work Practice by Fields* (New York: CSWE, 1961) 15.

CHAPTER FOURTEEN

Family and Child Welfare

"The growing emphasis on the prevention of need and the desire to conserve human as well as physical resources made it increasingly apparent that every effort to achieve what was termed social and industrial justice (indeed, all movements for social betterment) was directly related to child welfare. What was for the welfare of the community was for the welfare of the family and for the welfare of its children—and vice versa."[1]

The preceding quote taken from Trattner's description of late eighteenth and early nineteenth century child welfare activists continues to express both the attitude toward and importance of child and family welfare today. Child welfare is concerned with the well-being of individual children, family functioning, and the rights of children and their parents. Child welfare includes all those activities and services by public and private agencies for the benefit of dependent, neglected, or delinquent children.

Providing services to children has been part of social work practice from its very beginning. Rescuing children from almshouses and indenture; fighting for adequate budgets in orphanages and other care institutions; advocating for legislation to limit exploitation in the labor market, to provide compulsory education, to establish personal rights for children, and to dispel the view that children are mere chattels; and working on adoption procedures, foster home protocols, and programs to provide family income for basic support are social work efforts well documented over time in the literature.

The breadth of family and child welfare makes selecting a single intervention example difficult. An unplanned teenage pregnancy complicated by incest and a day care intervention exemplify the cases workers may encounter.

Terry: A Mother Too Soon*

GAYLA FAUBERT

Terry hesitated at the clinic door. Then with a surge of bravado she pushed it open and strolled into the waiting room. From my seat on the far side I watched her look over those waiting with an almost uncontrolled sense of panic. At fifteen, dressed in typical jeans, sweater, and running shoes, she looked like any of the several hundred of her high school classmates—physically mature but with the eyes of a child. "Over here," I called, and motioned her to come and sit beside me. As she continued strolling in my direction, a question came to mind: Why is it so many social workers, particularly as they are just getting started in practice, are drawn to working with kids? In reality it can involve many hours of thankless work, late night calls, confrontations with angry parents, hassles in court, and heartbreaks. A victim of sexual abuse in her own family, Terry, like so many adolescents, was caught between the fantasies of childhood and the harsh realities of becoming an adult. So here we are, waiting for an exam to determine the state of her suspected pregnancy. I've always thought "incest" an ugly word. At this moment, its consequences are even uglier.

Charles Loring Brace, where are you now? When you gathered children off the streets of New York and put them onto trains headed West, you were severely criticized. Even now students of professional history ask how you could have been so callous, so insensitive to the personal and emotional needs and separation trauma of the young. Were you an activist working towards alleviating the miserable conditions of homeless children or merely facilitating the needs of the rural labor force? I'll leave the answer to that one to the students of history; right now my concern is Terry.

The examination didn't take long. As I joined Terry and Dr. Vanhusen in the examining room, her expression gave the verdict. ". . . About ten weeks I'd say," was the doctor's comment. "You haven't much time for decisions. By the way, does your family know?" The question, along with bewilderment in Terry's eyes sent my mind racing. "No, they don't," I replied, filling the silence following the doctor's question. "Well, you can talk here for a while. If you need me I'll be down the hall." The sound of the door closing was in my head like the sound of the gates of San Quentin in an old movie. Terry's voice brought me back to the clinic room.

"Now what?" she asked rather nonchalantly.

"Well," I said as I pulled out the doctor's stool and sat down facing her, "I think we'd better look at all the angles."

*Case example from student social work practice, Wisconsin, 1980.

How do all past efforts to develop services and programs come together for Terry? Medical assistance will pay the clinic bill, the school may have a special home-bound program, there may be funding available for an abortion, but who pays the price of this childhood nightmare? Who is to make the decisions about what happens next in Terry's life? Providing social services to children is one of the most baffling, conflictual, and dilemma-producing fields of practice. It is a continual balancing act between legal issues (who has the right to decide?), and professional ethics (acting from values of human

Charles Loring Brace (1826–1890) developed a number of child welfare services we use today—summer camps, industrial schools, foster care, and children's shelters.

concern) that makes one wonder why anyone would choose to work with children.

The pattern of child welfare services seen today has been influenced by several recent events: the passage of the Child Abuse and Treatment Act in 1974[2]; the Juvenile Justice and Delinquency Prevention Act of 1974, which has served to divert some youth from the courts and penal systems into the welfare service system; the movement toward deinstitutionalization, which has forced community agencies to develop local treatment and substitute care services; an increasing willingness of parents to turn hard-to-handle adolescents over to public social service agencies; the trend in many school systems to push out youth who do not achieve or conform and are therefore disruptive; sky-high teen unemployment rates, particularly among urban black and Hispanic youth; and the growth of the child advocate movement.[3]

> Child advocates (including social workers) . . . address themselves to a broad array of issues. In addition to advocating the extension of constitutional guarantees to young people, they lobby for the passage of legislation through which special programs for children will be created and funded, intervene on behalf of children to see that they receive needed services, and engage in other activities . . . to advance the "children's cause."
>
> Impetus for growth of the advocacy movement in the 1970's came from many directions. It came from documented evidence of social neglect of children, including physical neglect and abuse of youngsters in substitute care settings where they had been placed for protection; the drift of children into unplanned, long term foster care; the abuse of educational and treatment programs, the need for which was said to justify depriving young people of their liberty by confining them to institutional settings; and evidence of the deleterious effects of assigning perjorative labels to young people. The advocacy movement grew, not only to advocate children's rights in specific areas, but also to act as a 'watchdog' on social and judicial agencies whose actions often seemed less benign and effective than they pretended to be.[4]

It is difficult to consider child welfare practice and concerns without attending to the area of family services, particularly if attention is paid to current definitions of child welfare. "Child welfare is concerned with the well being of individual children, the strengths of family life, and the rights of all children and young persons."[5] In the United States the welfare of children has been a traditional and primary concern of family groups. In the past, families relied on each other, friends, the church, relatives and intimate communities when there were times of stress or need. In the complex and mobile society of today these informal resources are frequently not available. Many families must rely on a variety of social agencies in times of stress and need. Social agencies have in response developed an array of services: family counseling, therapy, child guidance clinics, protective services, homemaker service, nutrition and financial counseling, parent skills training, income maintenance, permanency plan-

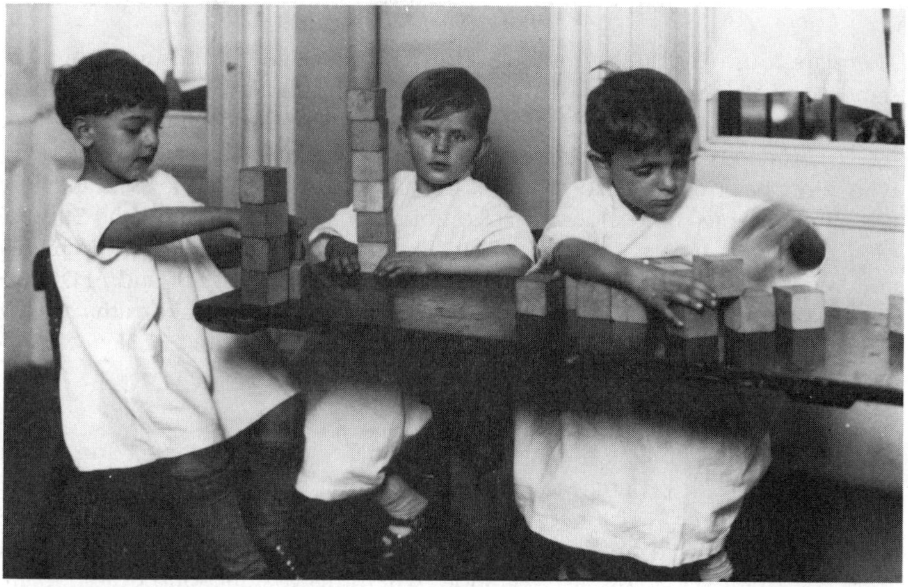

Play therapy in child guidance centers developed as one method of working with children during times of family stress. Photo courtesy of Social Welfare History Archives, University of Minnesota.

ning, and day care. Initially many of these social agencies grew under private or voluntary auspices, affiliation with religious organizations or with broad based community support. Public agencies became more prominent after the Depression of the 1930s, and federal legislation paved the way for governmentally supported family programs currently in place.

In 1976, for example, 268 out of 1,044 federal programs related to family functioning. These 268 programs carried a price tag of over 818 billion dollars at that time.[6] Administered through sixteen different governmental units, these programs affected families of all sizes, ages, incomes, and races. The enormity of the programs prompted a call from national leaders for the development of a national comprehensive family policy that would establish the direction in the future for all governmental efforts for families.[7]

The framework for understanding family policy is located in Chapter 12.

The purpose of family policy is closely tied to how 'family' is defined. The traditional perspective holds family policy to be a means of strengthening the nuclear family. At the other end of the spectrum is the idea that all types of significant human relationships should be treated equally. The traditionalist view believes family types other than the nuclear family are deviant. The egalitarian perspective validates the diversity and pluralism of our society and the idea of self determination.[8] Social work supports the concepts of egalitarianism and self-determination, and therefore family practice must reflect this approach.

Public assistance and income maintenance

Aid to the Blind (AB), the Elderly (OAA), and the permanently and totally disabled (APTD) were combined into one program—Supplemental Security Income (SSI) in 1972.

There are four major public assistance programs designed to insure a minimal standard of living for the "worthy" poor (i.e., the blind, the disabled, the elderly, and children). Aid To Families with Dependent Children (AFDC) is both the largest and the most controversial of these programs. The purpose of AFDC is to allow poor children to be cared for in their homes. Public assistance for the blind, disabled, and elderly was combined into one program—the Supplemental Security Income (SSI) program—in 1972; SSI eligibility requirements and benefits vary from one group to another. Recipients of SSI and AFDC are also eligible for medical assistance designed to insure adequate health care for the poor.

AFDC

AFDC (previously ADC) was part of the original Social Security Act and meant to be a short-term program to care for the children of widows. Architects of this program never envisioned that it would eventually serve a divorced clientele. Clearly, they did not feel that they were setting up a program that might even contribute to family disintegration. When this dysfunction became manifest, the Aid to Dependent Children of Unemployed Parents (ADC-UP) was adopted. The name was changed in 1962 from Aid to Dependent Children to Aid to Families with Dependent Children to emphasize the policy commitment to families. Since the beginning of the ADC program social workers have been involved in administering the program. With the 1962 Amendments to the Social Security Act, social workers became more involved in providing services to AFDC clients, and in fact the 1962 Service Amendments came about largely through the efforts of the profession. Social work leaders argued that providing professional casework services could cure the problem of poverty. Since both Congress and the President were committed to eliminating poverty, this amendment passed. The amendment provided federal funds to educate and employ professional social workers to work with AFDC clients. What social workers quickly found out was that no amount of individual counseling could make people employable unless there were jobs available. Since social workers had suggested a psychological remedy for an economic problem, they met with little success. When professional intervention failed to solve the problem of poverty, Congress turned to a jobs approach to decreasing the welfare roles. With the 1967 WIN amendments to the Social Security Act, the emphasis changed from professional services to job training and placement. Recognizing that single parents pursuing employment would face special problems, the amendments provided special funding for WIN social workers and day care. The bulk of the funds, however, were controlled by the Department of Labor rather than the Department of Health, Education, and Welfare (the predecessor to the Department of Health and Human Services). Whereas the Service

Amendments of 1962 made social work the primary profession dealing with public assistance clients, the 1967 WIN amendments made the social worker's role secondary to that of job developers and counselors. With both of these amendments the social work role was integrally related to preparing welfare recipients for employment. The movement away from professional services to public assistance clients culminated in a 1972 Department of Health, Education and Welfare mandate to separate social services from income maintenance. States were required to submit plans for separation by October 1 and were to implement these plans by January 1 of the following year. Although the order was rescinded in 1975, most states continue to separate aid and services. Subsequent poverty proposals such as the Comprehensive Employment and Training Act (CETA) of 1973, the Carter program for better jobs, and the Reagan job training partnership act all down play the contribution of services and emphasize job placement.

Supplemental Security Income (SSI)

The SSI Supplemental Security Income program was created in 1972 when Congress federalized blind aid, disabled aid, and old age assistance. Aid to Children (ADC), Aid to the Blind (AB), and Old Age Assistance (OAA) were all part of the original Social Security Act. In 1950 Aid to the Totally and Permanently Disabled (ATPD) was included. OAA, AB, and APTD were referred to as adult categorical assistance programs and each state could choose to participate or not to participate in any or all of these programs. All states eventually adopted the OAA and AB programs; some rejected APTD. The federal government set guidelines for these programs and shared costs. The states set eligibility requirements and administered programs. Benefit levels and eligibility requirements varied considerably among states. In 1972 the Federal government took over the adult categorical programs. The SSI program is now administered by the Social Security Administration; states can supplement payments but have no administrative responsibilities for the program.

The 1972 mandate to separate aid and services applied to all these public assistance programs. In theory the separation took place to remove any source of coercion for clients. Some argued that requiring recipients to accept service gave social workers undue power over clients. Others argued that eligibility determination did not require professional competence and it would be more cost effective for paraprofessionals to conduct eligibility determinations. Norman Wyer's is among those voices questioning the consequences of this decision. His editorial provides an excellent summary of the issues of the public assistance and social work relationship.

The question over the separation of eligibility determination and the offering of specific services continues to be debated.

Unanticipated Consequence of Policy Change*

NORMAN WYER

The field of income maintenance has been neglected by social work during the past decade, perhaps partly because many social work functions have been downgraded in the wake of separation. Only in the past several years have some social work observers begun to engage in analysis of possible problems that have resulted from separation. These problems, largely unanticipated in 1972 on the eve of separation, include deprofessionalization of income maintenance workers throughout the country; loss of organizational status and professional respect experienced by service workers; conflict between social service and income or eligibility staff; and increasing rates of staff turnover and "burnout" by service workers. Indeed, some suggest that income maintenance and eligibility determination are highly complex tasks that cannot be performed adequately by clerks or untrained technicians.

More research and evaluation are needed in the immediate future to explore various models of providing services within public assistance settings. It is premature to advocate return to the merged model. But it is likely that many consumers, often those from desperately impoverished families, need a host of advocacy, social referral, educational, and preventive services that appear to be denied to most of them within current public assistance programs. Some have argued that social workers are steadily "disengaging" from the poor. Not to develop research and policy positions relevant to low-income consumers who receive public assistance, positions that articulate methods of humanizing programs by supplementing income with social services, is to abdicate a traditional and important social work function.

* From *Theory and Practice of Social Welfare Policy* by Bruce S. Jansson. © 1984 by Wadsworth, Inc. Reprinted by permission of the publisher.

The case of Mary Olson was chosen to illustrate both the potential creativity of social workers in public assistance settings and the inherent relationships between public assistance programs and child welfare programs. In general it follows the model of social work practice described in Chapter 3. Similar interventions may also occur when aid and services are separated.

Day Care

Mary Olson had been working in the county social services department for three years when the Work Incentive Program (WIN) was introduced to the agency. Since Ms. Olson had always had an interest in employment opportunities for women, she asked to be transferred to that unit. As Ms. Olson worked with WIN clients, it became clear that child care was the most serious problem these women faced. Neighbors or relatives often cared for their children, and in some cases this worked well; but for most women child care seemed to be a constant hassle. It became clear that if these women (all single parents) were to succeed occupationally, they needed to have quality reliable day care.

PHASE I-PROBLEM ASSESSMENT

Day care options available included family day care, a number of very small but expensive private day care centers, and one nonprofit day care center that received financial support from the United Way and the local community action agency. The nonprofit center had been operating for about six years and in spite of receiving considerable support was in financial distress; it appeared that this center could benefit greatly by an influx of children from the Work Incentive Program. Since the federal government reimbursed 90 percent of the child care costs, paying for care of the children was not a problem. It soon became evident that the problem was that almost every "welfare" child placed at the center failed to "fit in" so the mother was encouraged to find family day care. Further investigation of the center revealed that although a major portion of the budget was provided by the local poverty agency, most children being cared for were from two parent families well above the poverty level. If the WIN mothers were to become employed, it was clear that either a day care center responsive to their needs would have to be developed or the practices of the present center would have to be changed.

PHASE II-NEGOTIATION OF THE CONTRACT

The first step taken by Mary Olson was to get the Director of her agency to have her named to the board of the nonprofit day care center. Once she had established credibility with the board, she brought individual cases to the board to discuss why they had been denied access to the center. Once elected vice president of the board, Ms. Olson had greater freedom to visit the center frequently. As a social worker she viewed the center not only as a resource for working mothers but also as a respite for potentially abusive mothers. Ms. Olson supervised placement of these children closely and arranged to have the mothers volunteer at the center. Although consistent with the stated goals of the center, parental participation in day-to-day activities was in direct conflict with how the center had operated.

As board support for these services blossomed, the incumbent director lost interest in the center; she began to argue that the center was not financially feasible and should be closed. Joan Allen, a public health nurse and president of the board, was committed to providing quality day care to low income women. Together she and Mary Olson presented a proposal to the board to set up an alternative nonprofit day care center to provide employment for low income women and quality day care for working women or women in need of respite child care. The board suggested instead that the resources of the present center be used. The staff of the center resigned. At this point the contract was clear: the board supported the type of day care center that the nurse and social worker proposed; even though it had many questions about whether the plan was practical, the board felt it was worth trying. Some board members resigned because they did not have the energy necessary for this new venture.

Having received the endorsement of the board of directors, Olson and Allen went to the county social services board to get support. (The social services board had to approve day care rates.) Finally they secured influential community activists to serve as board members. New board members included the chairperson of the United Way, an attorney, an accountant, the president of the League of Women Voters, and the wife of a local minister. After considerable community work, Olson and Allen felt their contract to develop a day care center had the endorsement of clients, agency personnel, and the community.

PHASE III-SECURING OF RESOURCES

The actual equipment owned by the center was adequate, but the setting was undesirable. Three major needs had to be met: a different building, new staff, and financial backing. Through one of the board members, an excellent facility was obtained. The new building had three rooms so children could be grouped by age, and each room had child-sized sinks, toilets, blackboards, tables, and chairs. The rent was equivalent to what had been paid for the previous facility. Financial backing and staff recruitment were related. Through the WIN program welfare mothers were hired to operate the center. All women working at the center were single parents; two had degrees in early childhood education. The Work Incentive Program was able to provide support in a number of ways. Women with previous work experience were given on the job training contracts that reimbursed the center for half of their salary up to six months. Women without previous work experience were placed in the work experience component; they worked for thirteen weeks at no cost to the center. Instead they received their AFDC check and incentive pay directly from WIN. Those women who wanted to work at the center following this training period were hired. Two women chose to set up family day care centers in their homes; they were able to because they had received forty hours of classroom training in the Work Experience Program.

PHASE IV-PROGRAM IMPLEMENTATION

This program was licensed to care for thirty-five children between the ages of six months and two years. Center staff were all low income women, and the program offered them training opportunities while providing quality child care for other working mothers. One problem was high staff turnover as the employees moved to higher paying positions. Child care paid for by the county agency was charged at the full rate. Women who had reduced incomes but were ineligible for child care payments paid a reduced fee supplemented by scholarship money from the United

One of the earliest forms of day care was the kindergarten classes that were held in settlements such as this class at Hartley House. Photo courtesy of Social Welfare History Archives, University of Minnesota.

Way. (United Way supported the program since scholarships were given to individual children rather than a lump sum of money to support a program. This appeared to be a tangible contribution and one that received wide support.)

This program also became an important resource for social workers working with abused and neglected children. Mothers who found taking care of their children for twenty-four hours a day overwhelming could get respite by enrolling their children in the center—both a less expensive and a more constructive alternative to foster care. Center staff also worked with these mothers to provide support and teach parenting skills; since abusive and neglectful parents almost always donated time to the center, they were able to learn constructive ways to deal with behavior by talking with other adults and observing their behavior.

PHASE V-EVALUATION

Evaluation takes many forms. Perhaps the most pertinent to a day care center is the mothers' assessment measured by the length of time they use the center. A high percentage of these children graduated from day care into kindergarten. At the request of working mothers an afternoon program was developed specifically for kindergarten children. Fall enrollment has been another measure of success. There has always been a waiting list for this center. Developed to respond to needs of low income women, the center continues to serve this clientele first although families of various income levels also use the center. Finally the center is periodically evaluated by the state licensing agency. Its reports have repeatedly cited the center for its exemplary program.

Summary

The only professional social services which predate child welfare are poverty programs. Historically interest in child welfare evolved from trying to prevent pauperism. In the 1850s Charles Loring Brace felt training children for productive citizenry and ensuring their safety could best be accomplished in a family setting. However, he did not feel the family setting should be the biological family if it was unable to be self supporting. Brace administered a program that sent thousands of children from New York to farm families in the West. Only with the Progressive Era did social workers come to believe that the child's family was the best place for the child to grow. The relationship these reformers perceived between poverty and child welfare is reflected in a statement of Julia Lathrop, the first chief of the Children's Bureau: "Children are not safe and happy if their parents are miserable, and parents must be miserable if they cannot protect a home from poverty."[9]

Family Welfare programs continue to be a primary field of social work practice, and in fact, public assistance and child welfare are the two fields where social work is clearly the primary profession. In no other field of practice is the domain of social work so clearly established. The opportunities and challenges in family welfare will continue to expand as society moves into the postindustrial era.

References

1. Walter Trattner, *From Poor Law to Welfare State* (New York: Free Press, 1979) 110–111.
2. Alfred Kadushin, *Child Welfare Services,* 3rd ed. (New York: Macmillan, 1980) 156.
3. Theodore J. Stein, *Social Work Practice in Child Welfare* (Englewood Cliffs, N.J.: Prentice-Hall, 1981) 264–270.
4. Ibid. 259.
5. Community Services Administration, HEW, *Annual Report* (Washington: GPO, 1979), 1.
6. Ibid.
7. Office of Economic Opportunity, HEW, *Annual Report* (Washington: GPO, 1979), 22.
8. Community Services Administration, HEW, *Semi-Annual Report to Congress,* Oct. 1, 1979; March 31, 1980 (Washington: GPO) 2.
9. Jane Addams, *My Friend, Julia Lathrop* (New York: Macmillan, 1935) 172.

CHAPTER FIFTEEN

Communities

"The community serves as both a context and a target. . . . The community is experienced as a complex and fluid social configuration, but we find it useful for analysis and practice, to select certain variables which are functionally important, accessible, and manipuable. We view a community in terms of the types and numbers of primary groups and formal organizations and their patterns of interrelationship. Practice consists of interventions that enhance, sustain, or sever existing linkage patterns between these social units and establish new linkages or units."[1]

When the Office of Economic Opportunity (OEO) was created by the United States Congress, its official purpose was "to eliminate the paradox of poverty in the midst of plenty in this nation by opening to everyone the opportunity for education and training, the opportunity to work, and the opportunity to live in decency and dignity."[2] Community wide programs targeted toward the poor and the disadvantaged were not the invention of the war on poverty, but with the federal initiative established in the 1960s the funding and range of available programs was unprecedented. By creating "comprehensive opportunity" both Congress and the President thought poverty could be abolished.[3] The OEO and its successor, the Community Services Administration, were seen as the administrative means by which that goal could be achieved. The objectives developed at that time to meet the goal were:

President Lyndon Johnson signed the Economic Opportunities Act, which created the OEO in 1964. Ten years later, the program was dismantled.

1. To act as the voice and advocate of the poor within the government, to make their needs and aspirations known to policy makers and to mobilize both public and private sector resources on their behalf.
2. To promote the development and strengthening of community-based institutions which represent the interest of the poor and to devise and carry out programs responsive to their needs.

3. To undertake research and experimentation to expand knowledge of poverty problems and to develop and test innovative solutions.
4. To develop and support local programs which meet the critical service needs of the poor and provide permanent improvements in their living conditions.[4]

The community action agencies that came into being to deliver the programs and services to meet these objectives have been funding and/or operating programs in manpower and employment, Headstart, education, health, day care, housing, consumer affairs, general social and family counseling, youth services, migrant labor concerns, and economic development.[5] The basic technique in establishing these programs was the combined use of federal, state, and local funds. Community programs were organized, operated, directed and overseen by locally selected boards.[6] Although not intimately involved in the conception and legislative enactment of most OEO and CSA programs, social workers became active in developing and providing many of the resulting services.

The excerpt from Mark Naison's article, "Sports and Community Organizing," shows the creativity of some workers.

The ability of the many new programs to affect poverty and its associated problems was, however, not as great as envisioned. Even with the support for community wide services provided somewhat later through the enactment of Title XX of the Social Security Act in 1975 impact has been disappointing. The resulting response of the federal government through both Congress and the Office of the President has been to withdraw support and dismantle many programs instead of considering the possibility that they were based on a faulty premise from the very beginning (poverty results from the lack of an individ-

One of the earliest types of community action programs was organized sports activities for children after school. Photo courtesy of Social Welfare History Archives, University of Minnesota.

ual's opportunity without attending to particular economic issues) and revising the programs accordingly. With the discontinuation of the Community Services Administration early in the 1980s programs that had not gained local credibility and financial support were discontinued. Continuing community action programs and agencies are supported through local resources with limited state and federal block grant allocations; migrant health and education services are examples of such programs.

Though the 1980s will no doubt continue to be difficult years for the poor, some individuals are finding creative means to mobilize communities and develop resources. Mark Naison and his Sports for the People group have identified the unlikely area of sports as a force of integration for the dispossessed.

Sports and Community Organizing: Hope for the Eighties[1]

MARK NAISON[2]

For America's poor, the 1980's promise to be a difficult time. In older industrial cities, concentrated in the East and Midwest, persistent fiscal crises have cut public services to the bone, crippling school systems, hospitals, transportation, and recreation programs that serve the working class and the elderly. Simultaneously, the deteriorating international position of American capital, along with rapid technological change, has undermined employment prospects for the semi-skilled and unskilled, producing a "normal" unemployment rate of upwards of seven percent. As competition for jobs has intensified, so have racial tensions; in the last two years, neo-Nazi and Klan groups have proliferated, antiblack violence has increased, and ghetto disturbances have occurred in several American cities. Worse yet, the issues of racial polarization and the living standards of the poor did not even enter into the recent presidential campaign, which was dominated by debates over military preparedness, public morality, and the role of religion in politics.

Given the levels of human suffering in the inner cities, the absence of serious programs to create jobs or improve public services from the platforms of all three presidential candidates was striking. Not only did it reflect the weakness of the left and minority-group organizations, but it suggests a thorough depoliticization of America's poor. Unlike the late 1960's and early 1970's, when inner city communities were hubs of protest and cultural ferment, political elites have been able to make such communities the main victim of their austerity measures without courting major resistance. Many explanations have been offered for this: the systematic elimination of radical Black and Hispanic leaders; the absorption of remaining leaders into the corporate and academic world; the withdrawal of media support from oppositional activity; and the decline of the organized left; but the result is clear. In most cities, the poor have been so depoliticized and isolated from one another on the basis of race, age, and language that private capital and elected officials can ride roughshod over their interests with impunity.

Those of us concerned with the human consequences of the marginalization of America's poor have for some time sought ways of rekindling movements to force the integration of the dispossessed

[1] This article originally appeared in *Catalyst*, no. 11 (1981): 15–20. Reprinted by permission of the author.

[2] Mark Naison is the Director of Urban Studies at Fordham University and the Chairperson of the Board of Sports for the People in New York City.

into the mainstream of the urban economy and civic culture. Protests against red-lining and landlord profiteering, campaigns to protest school and hospital closings, and movements to improve police protection and public transportation have begun to occur with increasing frequency in American cities. But one of the most successful community organizing efforts of recent years, one which has simultaneously established a base in the nation's most deteriorated ghetto and built a citywide coalition crossing ethnic and generational lines, has been generated around issues of sports and recreation. I will describe this experience and reflect briefly on its significance, because I am convinced that people involved with sports have a special role to play in regenerating humane community values in an increasingly balkanized and class-divided society.

First, let me give you some idea of the dimensions of the group I'm discussing. At the present time, Sports for the People runs a community center in the heart of the South Bronx employing fifteen full staff and sponsoring ten men's and women's teams, a senior citizens' fitness center, and a sport and skill program that uses sports to teach basic literacy and principles of city government. Once a year, we sponsor a senior citizens' sports festival that brings programs into more than one hundred senior citizens' centers and mobilizes over 2000 senior citizens for a one-day program of competition, recreation, and instruction in diet and exercise. We head a citywide coalition of recreation groups that has successfully fought to keep after-school centers open and assure high school coaches of back pay they were promised. And we are currently launching a center for athletes' rights which aim to create a national sports lobby. This lobby will work to insure that college athletes get professional tutoring and remediation and that college sports are placed under faculty supervision and control.

Significantly, none of the group's founders originally anticipated that it would attain these proportions. Sports for the People started six years ago as a discussion group of radical sports journalists, college professors, and competitive athletes. It did not envision itself as a power in city politics or as an organization providing services in a minority community—given its size and racial conposition (fifteen people and nearly all white), such a vision would have been the height of intellectual arrogance. Our first concerted action (typical of intellectuals) was to call a conference of people pursuing innovative approaches to sports and recreation. While successful enough to keep the group going, it hardly seemed like the start of a major protest organization.

The key move for us, the thing that taught us that our concerns had far greater resonance than we had ever imagined, was our involvement in a campaign against the diversion of public monies into the rehabilitation of Yankee Stadium. Initially, the Yankee Stadium project was to have been accompanied by a major influx of funds into surrounding neighborhoods, including funds for the rehabilitation of parks and playgrounds, but by the time the stadium had been completed, all those funds had disappeared. Several Bronx organizations were protesting this, and we offered them our services as publicists and organizers. In the process, we discovered two things that surprised and excited us: first, that South Bronx activists welcomed whites willing to help them (something many people on the left thought would never happen) and second, that deteriorating recreation space was an issue that aroused extremely strong feelings.

The outcome of our collaboration was a "People's Opening Day" at Yankee Stadium held in a park across the street from the stadium that attracted 1500 people. Even more important, this event marked the beginning of a permanent political relationship between members of Sports for the People and several leaders of South Bronx organizations, including Gilberto Genera-Valentin, a radical attorney soon to wage a campaign for the City Council. These relationships not only changed our group into a multi-ethnic organization, but also provoked a fundamental rethinking of our goals and objectives. Without renouncing our longstanding commitments to ending sports contact with South Africa and developing a sports research center, we decided to concentrate our energies on the question of the distribution of sports resources, which we expressed through the slogan "Sports as a Right." As the Yankee Stadium issue made clear to us, recreation facilities available to the city's working class and poor, already limited, were deteriorating rapidly due to mass layoffs and cuts in maintenance, while tens of millions of dollars were flowing into private sports franchises and sports clubs serving the upper middle class. Baskets without rims, empty swimming pools, glass-littered diamonds, benches without backs, fountains without water—all stood as glaring reminders of the deterioration of parks and playgrounds in the world's richest city.

But equally important, this was one injury that people, once aroused, were not willing to accept passively. It is a truism of community organizing that protest flows out of confidence—defeated, frightened people rarely demand their rights. One of the great tragedies of the 1970's has been the success that the media and political elites have had in convincing poor people that their conditions are hopeless, that they are trapped where they are because of their own inadequacies. But this demoralization, so visible to those who work in the public schools, has not extended to sports. Sports is one sphere of life in which the poor, whether black, Hispanic, or white, participate with confidence, where they feel they are better, tougher, and more skilled than those with more money and better opportunities. Seeing sports as an art form and a way of being, as a ship in a stormy sea, they squeeze every ounce of time out of the meager facilities available to them. No more poignant image exists of life in the city ghettoes than that of youngsters shooting baskets in a lamplit schoolyard on a freezing November night. The Tony Archibalds and Julius Ervings of the National Basketball Association flow out of that harsh world.

To demand better, to insist on the forbiddden luxury of a weight room or an indoor track, of lockers and showers and decent equipment and coaching or even that the drafty old gyms in the public schools be open at a decent hour is to give political expression to a thousand private thoughts. To give people the weapons to fight for this, and to win, is to open up a new world. Two years ago, when five million dollars were cut from the city schools' budget, closing afterschool centers at seven p.m., we asked people to take to the streets in protest. They came and they won. The coalition we created then still exists.

What we did with youth we were able to do with senior citizens. Three years ago, some physical educators in our group proposed that we run a sports festival for senior citizens in the Bronx. We got a small grant to do this—six thousand dollars—and set to work. Once again, we found ourselves face to face with deep feelings that had rarely been given political expression. Seniors we were in contact with felt enraged at the enforced passivity of their lives, at the expectation placed on them to be inactive, at the dangers they faced in using parks and streets. To tell them it was healthy to be active, to teach them exercises they could do, to give them opportunities for competition not only expanded their feelings of well-being, but also gave them a sense of entitlement that decisively counteracted the social pressures that confine America's elderly to the margins of our culture. Our Bronx festival was a joyous event, bringing senior citizen activists into our inner circle and generating plans—which we implemented—to make the program citywide. Now, each year thousands of New York seniors participate in our instructional sessions, and we have trained large numbers of teenagers, many of them black and Hispanic, to perform this work.

Our acquisition of the Clemente-Robeson Center flowed out of our work in providing services for youth and seniors. With the help of Genera-Valentin, now a city councilman, and the support of the large numbers of senior citizens and recreation groups that had participated in our various campaigns, we managed to raise over five hundred thousand dollars to rehabilitate an abandoned building and turn it into a multipurpose recreation facility. In operating the facility, we never separate sports from the vision of political change that motivated us in the first place. Every young person using the facility must sign a contract to do at least one day of community service per week and to attend classes on community problems and city government. The result appears in the atmosphere at the facility—no graffiti on the walls, no vandalism, no portable tape decks, no major thefts—and this is the most decayed and abandoned urban neighborhood in the entire United States.

What has happened to Sports for the People—and it has indeed happened to us, we didn't plan it—dramatizes the opportunities, and responsibilities, facing those who possess an extensive sports background and a commitment to a more just and equitable society. Because so many other avenues of achievement are increasingly monopolized by the middle class, sports is probably the only participatory cultural institution (other than religion) which consistently inspires affirmative feelings among the dispossessed of America. When used as a focus of agitation, as a symbol of entitlement and opportunity, it gives organizers the potential to reach young and old, men and women, and blacks, white, and Hispanics. At a time when elites are taking great pains to divide us in order to protect their capital, their power, and their privileges, it is to our advantage to use sports issues to dramatize inequities in our society and to look to the creation of programs which recreate a sense of common purpose among the working people of the nation.

What does this mean concretely? We, of course, would love it if more Sports for the People chapters were organized. But whether under our auspices or not, there is no reason why you cannot develop sports programs for senior citizens in your community and fight to have them funded; create multi-ethnic coalitions to fight for more parks and indoor gymnasiums; demand that employers provide sports at the workplace; work for the enforcement of Title IX; or fight to create governance structures that protect the rights of college athletes. Such efforts promise to expand considerably the potential constituency for community activism and add force to the efforts of those already fighting for better housing, schools, health care, and employment opportunities.

The irony of this particular strategy will be readily apparent to those familiar with the history of American sports. The corporate elite, not clothing itself in the rhetoric of "declining expectations" was once a major force behind the construction of parks, settlement houses, and community centers. Worried about autonomous centers of working-class resistance, they hoped that the construction of sports facilities would divert workers' energies away from politics and crime and instill civic virtue. Now, however, caught in a squeeze between rising oil prices and competition from other capitalist economies, they have increasingly abandoned the facilities they have constructed and ended the pretense of trying to incorporate the poor into the American mainstream. The burned-out shell of the Miami ghetto and the rubble-strewn lots of the South Bronx and Brownsville, stand as eloquent testimony to the consequences of their political vision. In the name of democracy, in the name of justice, in the name of racial harmony, we have to reclaim what they have given up, and define sports as central amidst an array of human rights that transcends class privilege and the pursuit of profit.

Rural programs

Sports for the People is an urban program. However, community action programs have also been of particular benefit to rural areas. Often overshadowed by the enormity of complex urban problems, rural America presents no less need; in fact, it often demonstrates a disproportionate share of needs with fewer resources available to meet those needs. Rural areas currently account for 32 percent of the nation's total population, while 41 percent of those considered to be in poverty are rural dwellers.[7]

Since the establishment of the Country Life Commission under the administration of President Theodore Roosevelt in 1908 advocates for rural Americans have worked for the extension of social services into rural areas.[8] The proliferation of programs through OEO and CSA made services available in rural areas that otherwise would never have been available. Services were provided through community action agencies and county social service departments; with the withdrawal of federal support rural Americans are experiencing a proportionate decline in available services.

Community action is a concept that goes beyond the developments just discussed. Expanding and building issue-oriented coalitions and community networks to address problems of need and resource development are seen across the country. Late in 1981, for example, the Southern Rural Women's Network was launched in Montgomery, Alabama. Co-sponsored by seven local, state, regional, and national organizations, it addresses such concerns and issues as the allocation of block grants to rural communities, women's employment and training, voter and community education, preservation of arts and culture, and adolescent pregnancy and parenting. Since 1982 a group constituted as the Mississippi Human Rights Coalition has been working to develop strategies to combat the impact of federal budget cuts on the poor, the handicapped, and mentally ill. By aggressive lobbying, developing position papers, bringing in congressional speakers, and meeting with the governor's staff, the coalition has been pressing for public participation in creating a state block grant administration and for renewed attention to the plight of low income people. Whether the issue is where to draw the "poverty line," availability of reasonable and safe rental housing, or groundwater contamination, community action efforts continue. More often than not social workers participate in community action efforts by acting as advocates, organizers, and concerned citizens.

These community action programs illustrate the technique of community organization presented in Chapter 6.

Social workers in rural areas need to understand the informal service networks already in existence. Building on existing strengths is not only more cost-effective but also essential with the limited service money presently available. The following practice example illustrates how one agency that serves day care providers first identified strengths in existing day care providers and then tailored its services to enhance the informal system.

Rural Family Day Care

In urban areas a parent is likely to have a number of day care choices that range from franchised day care centers to nursery schools to family day care homes. Rural parents have fewer choices. Typically they must depend on a neighbor who is willing and available to care of their child. Recognizing the reality of rural day care, are there services that a county supported day care coordinating agency could provide? A study (needs assessment) of all the known (n=45) rural family day care homes in the community was conducted to answer this question. A questionnaire was developed to obtain information about the experience, role perception, activities, fees, and record keeping of these providers.

One clear impact of rural living is that day care providers are chosen by reputation rather than licensing. Only 55 percent of the day care providers in the study had ever advertised. Further since rural day care providers charge considerably less (over 50 percent less) than their urban counterparts, it is unlikely they would seek licensing. In fact, most rural providers see themselves as helpful neighbors rather than day care professionals.

Some day care providers had taken some continuing education in child development, but these providers charged no more than their unschooled counterparts. Eighty-four percent of the sample said they taught skills to the children. Only 13 percent (n=6) said they babysat primarily for money. Most said they cared for children either because they like kids or because they wanted to help out. Their low rates seemed to support their claim.

On the basis of these interviews it was decided to offer training in areas such as health care, accident and injury information, discipline methods, and teaching techniques through public radio, television, and correspondence courses. In addition a slightly more formal support system among providers themselves was set up. Providers formed their own group to exchange ideas and equipment. One important outcome of this group was setting up back-up arrangements when the providers were ill or had to be away. The key to successful development in this community was voluntary participation and local control.

Self help

Another way people have worked to address common concerns has been through the development of self-help groups. In the last decade the number of community groups (ranging from small independent local groups meeting in members' homes to chapters of national organizations with thousands of members) has grown to half a million in the United States. Self-help groups deal with a broad range of social, psychological, medical, and environmental problems. Social workers have helped many groups grow by providing material support, serving as a link to the wider community, contributing needed professional knowledge or technical assistance, or initiating or developing new groups. By expanding their relationships with self-help groups social workers establish closer links with an informal helping system that serves an estimated fifteen million people.

Alcoholics Anonymous is one of the best known self-help movements active today. Although organized by and around the individual alcoholics rather than helping professionals, AA is a prominent resource in the practice of social work. Make Today Count is an example of a self-help group for people with terminal illnesses. Established as a psychosocial adjunct to medical services, the group meets frequently to provide information and support to its participants.

See Chapter 5 for examples of black self-help groups.

Minorities have historically had to rely on self-help groups as the formal service network frequently excluded them. Today, racial minorities continue to have strong self-help groups. One example of such a group is La Casa de Esperanza, an Hispanic self-help group from southern Wisconsin that has been very effective in providing opportunities for its members. Their successful efforts in establishing day care programs, job placement programs, active community centers, and a strong political subgroup have merited growing recognition as reflected in an editorial from the Milwaukee Journal on June 10, 1981.

> The fact that Waukesha has the largest proportion of Latino residents of any city in Wisconsin offers that community both a stiff challenge and a great opportunity. . . . Waukesha has a chance to be a laboratory in bilingual education and in the development of programs to combat unemployment among the city's essentially youthful Latino population. Some efforts underway in those areas, while not without criticism, must be recognized as positive steps.
>
> There seems to be a need to foster a greater sense of involvement on the part of the Latino community in planning and operating such programs. Commendably, Waukesha's school system has begun a "needs assessment" to get parents' views on what steps might more effectively serve students.
>
> In Waukesha as elsewhere minority youth unemployment remains a problem. A particularly impressive effort to deal with that challenge appears to be a job counseling program operated by La Casa de Esperanza—Waukesha's principle social service agency for Latinos. The program focuses on work experience and training in job interview techniques. Significantly, the young people in the program are encouraged to seek work in the private sector, rather than in government subsidized jobs.
>
> In sum, Waukesha presents a picture of a community beset with problems but struggling to overcome them; a community conscious that progress will require greater effort and more money. If Waukesha finds answers to the problems of its Latinos, it can point the way for the state.

Involvement in community activities has long been a part of the social work tradition. Even though at the present time the fate of many community action agencies and and programs is unknown, the idea of community development, of local areas marshalling resources and developing programs, coalitions, and helping networks, has demonstrated its effectiveness in working towards solving community problems. Through community organization and development activities, social workers continue to support, promote, and be involved in collective activities that involve people in improving their own lives.

Industry and business

Florence Kelley (1859—1932) was head of the National Consumer's League for over 30 years and fought for regulation of women's and children's hours and wages.

The recognition of the importance of the work place to individual adjustment is not new to social work. Mary Richmond and Bertha Capen Reynolds were both well-known for their concern about the effects of the workplace. Other social workers such as Jane Addams, Julia Lathrop, and Florence Kelley were involved in removing children from factories and improving work conditions for adults. Social workers were involved in fighting for eight hour days and forty hour weeks. Safe and healthy working conditions continue to be a concern of social workers. However, the "post-industrial" age has introduced additional problems into the work-place. The computer revolution has drastically altered the nature of work and the relationship of the worker and the employer. While this revolution may improve production and even work conditions, it is also likely to create unique problems. What is the impact of the "factory of the future" on the workers? A report presented by Dr. Paul R. Mills at the 1984 Annual Program Meeting of the Council on Social Work Education in Detroit, Michigan suggested some answers to that question. We draw from his presentation to exemplify social work issues in business and industry and how some social workers are meeting the challenge of the computer age in industry.

The Factory of the Future*

Mills' report was based on a cooperative project at a sub-asssembly plant manufacturing carburetors and carburetor kits. In spite of the plant's profitability, high productivity, and high quality control, the parent company announced plans to close the plant and move the operation to another location. In response, the chamber of commerce, the local university, the union, and the plant workers decided to develop a plan to save the plant. An agreement between these groups and plant management resulted in the creation of an applied research laboratory to improve manufacturing procedures, energy usage, and management skills. The school of social work proposed a demonstration and research project designed to provide employees with services and to evaluate the contribution of social work to a "factory of the future."

This project required creativity in assessing what the factory of the future would look like and what human problems would be found in these plants. Mills outlined some of the problems identified in this project.

1. *Displacement*. With the introduction of robotics, there is likely to be a radical reduction in the number of workers needed in the plant. Some speculations suggest that only 10% of the current workforce will be needed.
2. *Higher standards of quality and quantity*. High technology is usually related to greater productivity. Robots can work twenty-four hours a day and, with appropriate monitoring, are essentially error free. And so, though fewer workers are needed, those workers often require a greater degree of integration with their work. Workers may well have to become problem solvers rather than assemblers. This change may in turn change the whole culture of the factory. Traditionally management made decisions and workers implemented them. Problem solving on the assembly line may require the workers to use more of their analytic abilities. With a greater emphasis on quality control, workers may face less freedom in the workplace and greater physical and emotional stress.
3. *The meaning of work*. Work may be redefined in the new industrial plant. Some may feel a sense of pride and accomplishment in being selected for a particular job, but for others the fear of unemployment and personal failure is just as real. Substance abuse, sabotage, daydreaming, absenteeism, and other forms of reaction may result as the meaningfulness of work decreases. Some workers will incorporate change into their identity without problems; others will need professional assistance to adjust to and incorporate these changes. This is an important point of social work intervention.

*Based on a CSWE Conference Paper, 1984 APM.

The "factory of the future" presents new challenges for social workers. Here Paul Mills talks with two mothers about how problems with childcare affect working parents. Photo by Ricky Yanaura.

4. *High technology—high touch.* As high technology reduces human contact, workers will search for other means of human interaction. Management and unions may assist the majority of employees to meet these needs. Employees who experience serious depression or anxiety may need specialized social work services.

In the plant where Mill's project was based social workers basically tried to help individuals adjust. Some social workers assisted management in planning alternatives based on human needs, but most assisted individual workers to increase their adaptative abilities. (In a systems approach social workers are more involved in management decisions.) Social work intervention in Mill's project had three phases.

1. *Assessment.* Social workers assessed the technology being introduced and predicted the impact on the employees. Technology was often introduced in stages to facilitate adjustment. Social workers assessed the stage of innovation and level of acceptance to identify points of stress in the plant. Creative programs were developed to decrease this stress. At the individual level, assessment involved examining the worker's ability to handle stress and his adaptability to change. Assessment of previous responses to change helped identify potential problems the worker would encounter. Those who needed special assistance were identified early and provided selective preventive measures.
2. *Program development.* Preventive programs were initiated through funding provided by

employees. At the beginning of the project, employees agreed to deposit $50.00 a month into a research fund. For some this was a financial stress. The social work team responded with a program in personal finance. This program facilitated the social work team's entry into the plant culture.

The social work team used plant teams to assess employee's social service needs, to monitor the effects of innovation on employees, and to provide supportive networks when necessary. Plant teams were viewed as a major vehicle for future preventive programs.

The social work team had a monthly column in the plant newspaper entitled "Take Home Tips". dealing with human problems. Articles on rumor control and stress management identified means of reducing and handling stress. This column also introduced the employees to a lunchtime series on stress management. Individual counseling around work or personal problems was also provided by the social work team. The personnel office, the plant nurse, and plant team leaders were important sources of referral.

3. *Evaluation phase*. In this setting social workers were faced with a new type of accountability. Profit margins were the bottomline. Social work had to demonstrate its role in containing costs. At this plant a number of cost-effective measures were instituted. Where possible the traditional Employee Assistance Program measures were used to control absenteeism, tardiness, accidents, health insurance usage, and costs related to employee turnover.

Industry estimates a twenty-five percent loss of productivity caused by employees' personal problems. The percentage of employees who use social services provided by industry range from fifteen to eighteen percent of the work force. Costing the benefits of social work programs is difficult. Many preventive programs do not result in measureable results. Whenever possible, the extent to which individual change takes place is being recorded.

Dr. Mills and his colleagues have identified some important issues that social work education and practice need to address. The "factory of the future" presents both challenges and opportunities for creative social work practice. To what degree the profession will meet this challenge is yet to be determined.

Summary

This chapter has stressed the importance of the community to individual well-being and has identified community interventions that have had a significant effect on the quality of live for the people involved. The roles that social workers have played in each of these interventions have varied considerably. In Sports for the People example the social worker was a facilitator engaging in social action strategies. In the rural family day care example the social worker used both research and planning skills to study the needs of the community and develop an appropriate response; resource development and linkage were important contributions made by the social worker. In the discussion of self-help examples the social worker worked less as a leader and more as a resource person. In the University of Alabama project social workers developed research, planned, connected people and resources, and developed resources. Given the social status of the corporations involved, it is far more likely that higher status university faculty will have more access to decisions makers in the community. Given the status present the methods involved consensus and cooptation in contrast to the neighborhood group who dealt with the New York Yankee ownership through social action/conflict strategies.

Each example illustrated that communities as a field of practice present a range of problems and many and varied possibilities for intervention, and demand of the social worker considerable knowledge of people, group behavior, community structures, and creativity.

References

1. Fred Cox, J. L. Erlich, J. Rothman, and J. E. Tropman, eds., *Strategies of Community Organization,* 2nd ed. (Itasca, Ill.: Peacock, 1974) x.
2. Emelia E. Martinez-Brawley, *Seven Decades of Rural Social Work: From Country Life Commission to Rural Caucus.* (New York: Praeger, 1981).
3. M. I. Anson, "Southern Women from New Network," *Rural America* (Jan.–Feb., 1982): 28.
4. R. W. Toseland and L. Hacker, "Self Help Groups and Professional Involvement," *Social Work* 27, no. 4, (July 1982): 341–347.
5. Frank Baker, "The Interface between Professional and Natural Support Systems," *Clinical Social Work Journal* 5 (Summer 1977): 139–148.
6. Alan Gartner and Frank Riessman, *Self Help in The Human Services* (San Francisco, Calif.: Josey-Bass, 1977).
7. Toseland and Hacker, "Self-Help Groups," 343.
8. Ibid., 348.
9. Paul R. Mills, "Social Work in the Factory of the Future," presented at APM, Council on Social Work Education, Detroit, Michigan, 1984.

CHAPTER SIXTEEN

Health Care

"All good team-work arouses my enthusiasm. Football, part singing, machine politics, even house-breaking are admirable so far as team-play is manifest in them. But of all the forms of medical team-play to which the spirit of our time is leading us, none seems to me so fruitful, so full of efficiency and of promise, as that in which doctor and patient get together against their common enemy—disease.

This union the social worker can do much to promote and to develop."[1]

Environmental tragedies include Love Canal, New York and Times Beach, Missouri.

The health care system is the largest human service industry in the United States. It is the most costly one to maintain. In 1975 over 118 billion dollars were expended in providing health care—8.3 percent of the gross national product for that year.[2] Health care has become the second largest industry and now represents about 10 percent of the gross national product. Final figures for 1983 totaled more than $320 billion.[3] Lack of effective market controls point to limited ability for any one sector of society (such as the federal government) to control costs that even now continue a rapid upward spiral. Costs, lack of organization, emphasis on disease care rather than prevention, holistic concerns for the individual, and environmental tragedies of increasing magnitude are all part of the task of meeting health care needs in this society.

Social workers have been involved in health care since before the turn of the century. In Boston at the Massachusetts General Hospital, "medical social work" was officially begun with the hiring of a full time social worker to

> cooperate with . . . . physicians in the dispensary, first in deepening and broadening our comprehension of the patients and so improving our diagnoses, and second in helping to meet their (patients) needs—economic, mental or moral.[4]

One of the most important roles of the medical social worker is teacher and provider of important information. Photo by Mary Hagler, for Riverside Methodist Hospital.

Since that time hospital social workers have become an integral part of health care teams that include doctors, nurses, and other specialists. They advocate patient rights, plan for discharge into the community, and participate in planning home care or other continuations of medical services. Social workers are also active in rural health departments, in public health agencies, on Indian reservations, in migrant and inner-city clinics, and in community agencies working to eliminate health risks and hazards and to prevent disease. The National Association of Social Workers estimates that about one-third of all social workers known to them are employed in health related settings.[5] A case example describes a joint intervention by a nurse and a medical social worker.

One of the first organizations of social workers, the American Association of Medical Social Workers, was founded in 1918.

Social Work and Nursing: A Team Approach

ANN BUCK*

After a call from a concerned anonymous caller I requested assistance from the adult social service worker. She had also received several calls from nameless friends and one distant relative of a ninety year old man reported to be neglected and/or abused. Complaints varied, but in general it seemed he was not fed enough, was left alone for hours on end, although totally bedridden, and had massive sores on both legs.

My first attempts brought no access to the home, but finally a friend of the family agreed to escort the social service worker and she was admitted to the home. The house outside showed years of neglect. Inside was almost complete disorder. The social worker felt 'abuse' might be too strong a description, but that 'neglect' was most probable. She arranged with the daughter, caretaker, to have me accompany her on a second visit the next day.

We were greeted rather sullenly by the daughter. The man, however, seemed glad for 'company.' He was very thin and lay curled in bed in an almost fetal position. He could see very little, but was quite alert and cooperative. Vital signs were in the normal range. The only remarkable finding was the heavy scabs covering most of the anterior surface of both feet and legs. These crusted areas were thick, dark and rough, extending past the knees. I explained that we could provide nursing services but hospitalization would be necessary to start with. This brought protests from the patient as he saw this as a one-way street to a nursing home. The daughter objected because of potential financial difficulties. While I explained the hospitalization procedure to the patient, the social worker calmly and reassuringly talked with the daughter about her emotional and financial concerns. They eventually reached a financial solution that relieved the daughter's fears.

Because of the past history of rejecting medical care, we returned the next day not only with the ambulance for transportation to the hospital but a court order to remove the patient. We did not need the court order as the family physician, with whom the daughter consulted after our departure the previous day, urged the family to accept the hospitalization.

Three weeks later, after debridement of the areas on the legs, the patient was returned to his home. A hospital bed was provided from the health service loan closet and arrangements were made for noon meals to be delivered. A nurse was scheduled to provide wound care and personal care twice a week. The social worker, maintaining a case management function, agreed to maintain regular contact with the daughter.

Ann Buck, R.N., is Director of the Waushara County (Wisconsin) Nursing Service. Her story, as related to Lucy Rowley, is used by permission.

Medical social workers practice in diverse health care settings—hospitals, clinics, nursing homes, and halfway houses, and with in-home care.

Katherine Kruse has identified six major areas of practice for medical social workers from the health care literature: social services to patients and families, program planning and policy formulation, participation in development and liaison with other community social and health programs, consultation to other professional personnel, social research, and social services administration within medical settings.[6] Other social workers in the field have also identified outreach and casefinding as important contributions social workers make to promoting health care. All these functions emphasize the humanistic traditions of the profession and the interpersonal skills of its practitioners.[7]

Social workers often serve as case managers and coordinators of community support systems. Of the 763 federally assisted comprehensive community mental health centers, more than a third have executive directors with social work degrees. Social workers attempt to enhance the quality of life by facilitating healthy interaction between individuals and their environment, and the main thrust of social work practice in the field of mental health is prevention. Social workers interested in prevention and treatment of mental illness work in various settings and intervene in different ways.

Mental health

Social workers work in mental health settings ranging from day treatment programs to hospitals to community mental health centers and residential community facilities.

Primary prevention aims at eliminating the causes of mental illness so that disorders do not occur in the first place, but mental health professionals do not always agree about the causes of mental illness. Social workers often believe poverty and inadequate nutrition are responsible for many disorders. Emotional problems are naturally exacerbated by economic stress; the incidence and severity of mental illness tends to rise with the unemployment index. Diet is another factor increasingly discussed as a contributor to mental health or mental illness; research on the relationship between diet and mental health is being conducted with adult probationers and hyperactive children.

The aim of secondary prevention is to decrease the client's exposure to the causes of the disorder. The social worker identifies vulnerable groups within the population and gives special help early to decrease their exposure to the supposed causes. Secondary prevention strategies include providing informational programs to help people recognize danger signs, providing information on available help, and sometimes even changing people's attitude toward mental illness. Accessibility to service and responsiveness of the service are keys to effective helping. It is important to get help early before symptoms become serious.

Tertiary care is the term used in the field of mental health for treatment; tertiary care provides rehabilitation for those who have mental health problems and prevents their situations from becoming worse. The goal of treatment is to help individuals function again and resume productive roles.

In most mental health settings social workers are part of a treatment team that usually includes psychiatrists, psychologists, or nurses. The social worker may engage in psychotherapy, but most frequently he functions as a caseman-ager and family and community liaison. All members of the treatment teams are likely to be skilled therapists, but social workers are uniquely qualified to develop the resources necessary to retain the patient in or return him to the community. To participate effectively on a mental health treatment team requires that social workers know psychiatric jargon, be familiar with psychotropic drugs, be effective team workers, and be familiar with mental health legislation and the effects of the social environment.

The case of Mrs. R. illustrates how the social worker's professional knowledge and expertise contribute to the treatment of emotionally disturbed patients.

The Case of Mrs. R.: Reframing a Problem*

GARY ROSENBERG

Mrs. R., 48 years old, white, Jewish, married, mother of one child, and bearing a history of chronic paranoid schizophrenia with multiple psychiatric hospitalizations had been admitted to a general surgical service for repair of bleeding hemorrhoids. Diagnostic tests had been completed for this "routine" procedure when Mrs. R. unexpectedly refused a final pre-op blood test and became loudly and verbally abusive to nurses and house staff. Mrs. R.'s resident physician reacted angrily and discharged her on the basis of noncompliance and the nonemergency nature of her illness just as the social worker arrived on the floor. Yet, three weeks later, Mrs. R. was readmitted by mutual choice to the same service to undergo surgery successfully.

This change did not happen magically! Rather, Mrs. R. offers a nice example of the delicate balance between meeting patient and staff system needs. Borrowing the technique of positive reframing from the field of family therapy enabled the social worker to accomplish this task. Positive reframing attempts to place a symptom or behavior in a different light, connoting it positively. Thus, it changes the cognitive and perceptual view of the symptom.

To Mrs. R., whose habitual tendency had been to view the world as hostile, the prospect of surgery with its aggressive, painful, and visible effects seemed unacceptable at first. For a person with little sense of control, losing more control risked going out of control. It can easily be forgotten just how much patient status alone implies heightened dependencies. For surgical patients undergoing general anesthesia, it implies total dependency. The first effort, therefore, was to learn from Mrs. R. what her primary concerns were. It was assumed that she wished for treatment whether or not she could presently tolerate the stress of receiving it (an attitude that immediately and helpfully separated the social workers from other staff and permitted the engagement of Mrs. R.). Though at first she regarded the worker with skepticism, the social part of the service won out! She agreed to talk and identified her physical pain, her mistrust of physicians and other strangers in the hospital network, the long delays in completing a diagnostic work-up, her loneliness for husband, son, home, and her clearly articulated fantasies (even conviction) of death or mutilation as surgery proceeded under general anesthesia. Most of all was her repetitive worry that she had failed to be a "good" patient as evidenced by her discharge. It was from her own perception that the worker molded her main intervention. Her "failure" to comply could be reframed; perhaps she and staff could both benefit. By the end of the first discussion (interrupted by her husband who thereafter participated in her treatment), it was agreed to try for a series of meetings over the next few weeks. These appointments would include, at times, a liaison psychiatrist attached to the service, her attending surgeon, resident surgeon, anesthesiologist, and various persons in the preadmission and admission offices who proved most cooperative re: room and floor assignment as well as date and length of readmission. These meetings allowed Mrs. R. to receive psychotropic medication under psychiatric guidance in order to diminish her anxiety, and to review again the surgical procedure planned and the type of anesthesia to be used. These issues were now discussed in a clinical setting, and therefore, were much less threatening. It was arranged for her to be readmitted to the floor best known to her and for a deliberate less-than-usual time, that is, 48 hours.

In working with staff, the social worker helped nurses and doctors to depersonalize Mrs. R.'s earlier attacks and to understand her behavior as defensive and a regression (particularly her low frustration tolerance and mistrust of strangers). Seen in this way, Mrs. R.'s first admission and "failure" to comply was newly and usefully reframed to staff and Mrs. R. as a

From Gary Rosenberg, "Practice Roles and Functions of the Health Social Worker," in *Social Work Issues in Health Care,* Miller and Rehr, eds., © 1983, pp. 167–168. Reprinted by permission of Prentice-Hall, Inc., Englewood Cliffs, New Jersey.

"rehearsal." Second admissions, routinely endorsed on a pediatric service, are less acceptable (although occasionally as necessary) for those persons who are chronologically older.

The interventions outlined were chosen primarily for the following reasons: as a more neutral staff member, the social worker's agenda for Mrs. R. differed from both the nurse's and physician's. Mrs. R.'s submission to authority was not required, only her alliance in gaining good care. The thrust was, therefore, chiefly towards heightening her self-esteem, self-control, and autonomy. Knowledge of the mechanisms of defense permitted explaining Mrs. R.'s initially belligerent and aggressive behavior as a mask for much deeper fears to staff less familiar with such a perspective.

Finally, Mrs. R. illustrates the point that there is no such thing as a "routine" surgical procedure since each patient anticipates in a unique manner based on his personality and character structure, prior experience, and a host of other internal and external variables. There are also real limitations to the expenditure of time and energy involved in helping a Mrs. R. through a surgical experience. For each success story we ought not forget the very real number of patients who are either lost to care or whose silence (unlike Mrs. R.'s roar) is mistaken for trust, but they may be hurting just the same.

The case of Mrs. R. illustrates what a difference effective social work practice can make for a patient with a history of mental problems as he faces routine decisions. Through preventive intervention, the social worker helped Mrs. R. avoid what might have been a serious breakdown.

See Chapter 11 for another example of intervention in a mental health setting.

Education

Educational settings, particularly the public schools, have long been considered important points of access for personal and social services provided to children and their families. Lois Taber, writing of the involvement of social workers in education, states:

> The public school more than any other social institution presents the most strategic setting for the effective use of social work for the purposes of both prevention and treatment of problems experienced by children. . . . It is regrettable that this great potential has not been realized more fully, inasmuch as the schools reach nearly all children daily and continuously from kindergarten through high school.[8]

Explaining the reasons this potential has not been realized within school programs is not within the scope of this discussion, but to understand that it has not is important since it suggests an important potential target of change for the profession.

Involvement of social work to any appreciable extent in schools and other educational programs was a development of the late 1950s and early 1960s. Intervention efforts have generally been directed toward children experiencing difficulties with the educational structure. Social workers in the schools function in various roles: counselor for children and parents; consul-

School social work began in the twentieth century as a result of specific laws such as compulsory school attendance.

tant to teachers, support personnel and administrators; liaison between school and community; and referral agent for specialized services outside the school setting. Social workers may also be involved in planning and staffing alternative educational opportunities for students unable to learn in the mainstream of public education. Lucy Rowley describes some typical teenagers whom social workers might be called upon to "treat".

> Tom, fourteen, sat slumped low in the chair in the school office slowly kicking at a wad of paper with his toe. He avoided the gaze of the police officer speaking to him: "Three fights this week and now stealing!"
>
> Mary, fifteen, hated school. Staying home with Mom was much preferable. This was the third time this week the principal had called her home because of absences. "Why can't they just get off my back," she thought, "I'll be sixteen next month, and who needs it!"
>
> "I can't do a thing with Ray," explained his stepmother to the school counselor. "He takes absolutely no initiative around the house. He doesn't pay any attention to me or to his father. He stays out late and I think he may be into booze or drugs."
>
> Jim was a muscular fifteen. In the eighth grade he could barely read and could not add one digit numbers. He was scheduled into a prealgebra class where the teacher routinely called on each student to come to the board and work out mathematical problems. "You don't know how that makes you feel," Jim stated to the social worker who had been called in from juvenile court to investigate the complaint that Jim physically threatened a teacher.

These incidents are not surprising to many parents and school officials today. Many public schools, however, cannot deal effectively with these kinds of situations. Alternative programs developed over time to provide remediation and support for children like these may exist within the school organization, but more than likely they have developed separately in the community. An example of such a program is the Lost River School.[9]

Lost River School

The goal of Lost River is to take an individual functioning at a minimal level and work with them socially and academically so that they can return to and succeed in a regular school environment. Lost River does not supplant the regular school system; it is a supplement. With a farm setting and a small student population the regular academic program takes on a new perspective. No two students have exactly the same daily program and with a student-staff ratio of 4:1, individualization and personalization are daily fare. The advantages of this are immediate. Students may be doing things they do not want to do, but they are never asked to something they cannot.[10]

In the years that Lost River was in operation, children referred to the program were returning to the regular school setting with some degree of academic and social success.[11] Both the success and demise of this creative approach to education were reported in the *Milwaukee Sentinel.*

"Special School Dies for Lack of Funds"
Dateline: Wautoma, Wisconsin.

Lost River School, a day care school for teenagers with special learning problems will close August 27th because of lack of money spokesmen said. . . An administrator of the school said the school would continue to serve the 17 pupils now enrolled until it closes. Lost River was started in 1971 to accommodate youngsters from 12 to 15 years old who because of their academic, behavorial or educational difficulties could not succeed within the structure of a regular classroom setting. The school received operating funds from federal, state, and local agencies as well as individuals, organizations, and businesses. Funding from some sources became more restrictive and the school could not qualify. Lost River was the only facility between many students and a state institution. . . . About 84% of pupils who attended Lost River had been able to return to normal school situations and function well. About 100 pupils have been enrolled . . . since the school opened.

In higher education social workers are found staffing student personnel units, working in counseling and advising positions, and in supervising residence halls. They may also work with foreign students in international and exchange programs and with disadvantaged students in special support units. Social workers are teachers in graduate and undergraduate social work programs and a variety of human service and medical programs.

The economic crises currently felt in education in this country has had and will continue to have the effect of suppressing expansion of many social services provided within the school context. Social workers could have an important role in planning and developing cost effective special services. Presently educators, teachers and administrators, and the National Education Association (NEA) have a tight grip on what happens in the school of our country. Whether social workers will be part of meeting this challenge remains to be seen.

References

1. Richard Cabot, *Social Service and the Art of Healing* (New York: NASW, 1915, reprinted 1973), 188.
2. M. Kristein, C. Arnold, and E. Wynder. "Health Economics and Preventive Care" *Science* 195, (Feb. 1977): 458.
3. Rosalind Miller, and Helen Rehr. *Social Work Issues in Health Care.* (Englewood Cliff, N.J.: Prentice-Hall, 1983).
4. Richard Cabot, *Social Work Essays on the Meeting and Growth of Doctor and Social Worker* (New York: Houghton-Mifflin, 1919), 25.
5. "The Many Career Opportunities in Social Work" (Silver Spring, Maryland: NASW, 1983).
6. Katharine Kruse, "The Health Field and Social Services" in V. Johnson, editor.
7. Leona Grossman, William Harrell, and N. Melarned. "Changing Hospital Practice and Social

Work Staffing." *Social Work* 24, no. 5 (Sept. 1979): 411–415.

8. Lois R. Taber, "School Social Work," in *The Field of Social Work*, 6th ed., ed. Fink (Winston, NY: Holt, Rinehart, 1974), 170.
9. "Lost River: An American Psychiatric Association National Award Winner," in *Milwaukee Sentinel* 2 August 1976.
10. Ibid.
11. Ibid.

CHAPTER SEVENTEEN

Criminal Justice

"Deviance is profitable for those who study, prescribe, manufacture, and exercise social control techniques. Deviance supports an "enormous enterprise"[1] that includes at all levels of government police, judges, prison guards, probation officers, sociologists, psychologists, and doctors; in addition to private security firms, manufacturers of weapons, drugs, uniforms, vehicles, and so on. Deviance control is a sufficiently large industry with adequate political clout to ensure that its business will never decline substantially for want of offenders—real or imagined. If, as Erikson[2] states, the amount of deviance found in a society is closely tied to the size and the complexity of its social control apparatus, American society should not want for deviants in the foreseeable future."[3]

Law enforcement and corrections

A discussion of social control was presented in Chapter 10.

Law enforcement and corrections are frequently called the criminal justice system since together they cover an array of services with different but related missions. The criminal justice system presents a wide range of possible professional roles for the social worker. The most common and probably most debated role for the social worker is that of social control agent. Whether the social worker is a probation and parole agent, prison social worker, or treatment specialist in a corrections institution, she is expected to be a force for social control. Some social workers argue that social control is inconsistent with the social work value of client self determination. Others argue that social work's values of individual dignity and self worth make them uniquely qualified to perform this function. Still others argue that social workers in correctional settings are mere handmaidens of a capitalistic society. The diversity of the criminal justice field makes each of these statements accurate for some roles in which social workers function.

Prisons

See Chapter 3 for an explanation of the role of enabler.

Social workers perform various tasks and roles in prisons. Social workers enter the federal prison system as officers; only through internal promotion can they assume the normal duties of social workers.

Most commonly social workers in the prison setting are counselors or enablers. Many prisoners are incarcerated for long periods of time and social workers help prisoners adjust to their environment. Clinical social workers may be involved in psychotherapy programs (although such programs are usually offered in special institutions) or they may be assigned to a unit such as clinical services where they deal only with referred clients. Some even pursue administrative positions within the prison setting. The prison social worker is often an important link to the prisoner's family and outside resources as the prisoner prepares for release. In this role problems are addressed on an individual level.

Other social workers in the prison setting take a systems approach to correctional social work and take on the additional role of planner and program developer. The following case study illustrates system wide social work intervention to improve the therapeutic milieu of a minimum security prison setting.

Officer Training

PRESENTING PROBLEM

The entry level for minimum security prison officers is the Officer III level. This means that new staff entering the minimum security system have received their training and experience based on assumptions inherent in a maximum security setting. At the request of the superintendent of the camp system the social worker assessed the training needs for minimum security staff.

ASSESSMENT

The social worker proceeded by analyzing the components of the work requirements and training programs for maximum security staff and then determined how the basic assumptions, skills, responsibilities and actions of a minimum security officer differ or contradict this prior learning. This analysis suggested certain special training needs for minimum security staff.

1. Minimum security officers require more training and education in understanding human behavior, communication skills, and human relations. Maximum security prisons are highly centralized, and few decisions are delegated to either staff or inmates; but in contrast the minimum security prisons require staff to make frequent on-the-spot decisions guided by personal judgment and general policy guidelines.
2. Minimum security officers need training in approaches to problem solving. Maximum security institutions are more stratified; the role of the officer in maximum security settings is primarily one of control. On the other hand the minimum security officer must not only assure control but also provide the inmate some room to develop sound judgment and help prepare the inmate for release. Effective work with inmates preparing to leave is enhanced by problem solving skills rather than an authoritarian control. Many officers need to be retrained to incorporate more participatory problem solving skills into their previous professional values.
3. Minimum security officers need training to prepare them to deal with the role conflict inherent in the complexity of the role they fill. Roles are less well defined in a minimum security setting. The officer cannot limit his/her role to that of controller. Minimum security prisoners are given more freedom to prepare themselves for release and officers must constantly weigh what is in the best interest of the institution and what is in the best interest of the inmate. When these interests conflict, the officer experiences conflict.

INTERVENTION

This assessment led to the conclusion that special training was needed for minimum security officers. The social worker was in an excellent position to provide this training since many of the identified skills were skills and knowledge the social worker possessed. A training program was developed so officers would receive training in understanding human behavior, interpersonal skills, and assertiveness training. They were also taught group and leadership skills such as brainstorming, synectics, basic group techniques, and group facilitation.

EVALUATION

While no formal evaluation of this program was completed, the effects of this training caused a change in the methods of hiring officers and transferring them to different security levels.

Probation and parole

The history of probation work is traced to John Augustus who voluntarily worked with offenders in the Boston courts in the 1840s.

Perhaps the most important task the probation or parole officer serves is preparing presentence investigations. The presentence investigation provides a history of the offender to assist the court in sentencing. This role requires skills in interviewing, problem assessment, and writing. The social worker needs to understand human behavior to assess the potential danger to society and to the individual; she must make a knowledge-guided prediction of future criminality. Knowledge of criminal law and correctional institutions is also necessary for a professionally sound report. Throughout this process the social worker must weigh the best interests of both the client and society. Following the court's decision to incarcerate or place on probation, the same social worker is likely to find herself in the position of social worker to the "criminal" and his or her family. There is an abundance of unresolved debate about whether it is possible for the social worker to be both judge and rehabilitator of the client. Nonetheless, whether in the adult or juvenile system, social workers frequently fill both roles. One day the social worker may be involved in intensive counseling and the next day she may need to revoke the client's probationary status.

Legal system

The legal system has recently developed new employment opportunities for social workers, and increasingly there is a need to identify their professional responsibilities and limitations in this setting. The difficulty of these issues was identified in a paper presented at the 1984 Annual Program Meeting of the Council on Social Work Education. A summary of the pertinent issues described in that paper suggests the role of social workers in the the legal setting and the complexities they face.

Social Work in a Legal Setting: Conflicts and Constraints*

Recent economic, social, and political changes have forced social workers to work under new constraints and in agencies that may call on the social worker to perform roles which conflict with traditional social work roles. This concern is evident in the literature especially as it relates to the advocacy role in agencies such as the Public Defender, Legal Aid, and Night Prosecutors. Social workers are left with conflicting messages about what constitutes ethical practice in such settings.

Clarification of these issues and guidance from the professional body is critical. To answer the issues surrounding this debate is to answer the most basic questions of all: Does social work have a unique expertise and frame of reference or is our expertise and role dictated by the organization/agency in which we work? Is the social work frame of reference something we follow in all settings or only when social workers are the primary professionals in the setting.

The 1978 NASW Ad Hoc Committee on Advocacy suggested that based on the Code of Ethics, the social work professional is ethically bound to take on the advocacy role if he or she is to fulfill their professional responsibility.

Beginning with the definitions themselves there is a lack of consensus on what advocacy is. The Ad Hoc Committee on Advocacy did not clearly define advocacy but identified two definitions that appear in the literature: 1)"one who pleads the cause of another", and 2) "one who argues for, defends, maintains, or recommends a cause or a proposal." There are very different and conflicting interpretations and the Code of Ethics provides no resolution to the problem. It is important to understand that practitioners from both ends of the continuum ("best interests" or "pure advocacy") believe their practice flows directly from the Code of Ethics.

* From "Social Work Advocacy: Conflicts and Constraints," a paper presented by Mary W. Macht, Jose Ashford, and Melissa Mylym at the Annual Program Meeting, Council of Social Work Education, Detroit, Michigan, 1984.

The following quote from Compton reflects the "best interests" view.

> Advocacy in social work differs from that found in law in that the social worker is often involved in protecting people from actions of their clients. Thus, the worker does not become an advocate for the client in situations in which doing so could result in hurt to others. The attorney stands for the client; the social worker stands between the client and other social systems and must be concerned with the totality of the situation.[1]

Consistent with this view is the idea that social workers are professionals and as such have a unique expertise and value base that is neither dictated nor compromised by the setting in which practice takes place but rather emanates from the norms, values, and the code of ethics of the profession.

Another view of the social work role is reflected in the "pure advocate" approach. This stance has been taken by some social workers involved in the court system. Reflecting this view Dickson suggests that if social workers are to be effective in the legal setting they must be "prepared to disregard loyalties to agency goals, social work theory, and ideologies that run counter to the client's goals."[2] In a similar vein, Miller sees the social worker as an equalizer for the client in dealing with agencies and others who control resources.

> The sanction of the advocate to act must come from the person whose position s/he is advancing. The advocate must be accountable solely to the client; s/he cannot and should not take a position without the informed consent or authorization of the client. The ability of the social worker to be a client advocate is shaped by the nature of his/her employment. The worker in a setting where there are conflicting sanctions or interests cannot be a true advocate. . . . The advocate needs autonomy from constraint, pressures or responsibilities to any person or authority other than the client.[3]

Joseph Senna studied social workers in the public defender's office and represents a more central position on the "best interest"/"pure advocacy" continuum. He suggests that social workers face conflicts of interest and professional ethics in such a setting. For example, the attorney's goal is winning the case; the social worker's goal is evaluating the offender's behavior. While Miller's view seems to imply that the social worker works to help the client "beat the rap" or at least get the lightest sentence possible, Senna suggests her real situation is more complex. Social workers in his study felt the goals of the agency (in this case the public defender) determine the direction and content of the evaluation, and yet they also felt that social workers must exercise independent judgment. Their primary concern was to maintain integrity and at the same time use their professional skills competently. This introduces a strong potential of going against the client, the attorney, and the agency.[4]

Since the pure advocacy position is less familiar and questions many assumptions basic to the social work profession, the issues underlying this position need to be addressed. To understand the pure advocacy position, however, it is necessary to understand the legal system—a purely adversary system in which there are always at least two sides, a plaintiff or petitioner and a defendant or respondant. One of the most fundamental tenets of this system is that every person is entitled to legal representation, "and to have his conduct judged and regulated in accordance with the law, to seek any lawful objective through legally permissable means, and to present for adjudication any lawful claim, issue or defense."[5] If the attorney does not exercise every legitimate effort in her client's behalf, then she is betraying a sacred trust.

According to their professional code of ethics, social workers are obligated to become advocates, but two major factors limit social workers as advocates. First, social workers generally lack the orientation and technical skills necessary to be effective advocates. Secondly, social workers are often employees of agencies and organizations that do not support advocacy. The pure advocate stance suggests that a social worker practicing within the legal system must not only fulfill her obligation to become an advocate, but must also overcome the two major factors that act as constraints to advocacy. The social worker must gain the orientation and technical competence needed to become an effective advocate and must work to encourage the legal system itself to support the advocacy effort.

From this perspective, then, the social work advocate can benefit both social work and the legal profession. For the social work profession new avenues of practice will be opened and social workers will be better equipped to meet their obligation to become advocates. For the legal profession social workers can perform valuable services for which they have more training and experience than attorneys. For example, social workers generally have more training and expertise in interviewing and accessing community resources than do attorneys—an expertise that would be valuable to legal programs and attorneys practicing criminal law or family law. By gaining technical competence in legal areas, many social workers may very well expand their advocate role.

Without a thorough understanding of the legal system, it may at first appear somewhat antithetical to other human service agencies and organizations where social workers are traditionally employed. In most social work settings the social worker seeks to improve the functioning of clients; regardless of her practice approach, the social worker always seeks to promote the "best interests" of the client and society.

When an attorney makes a decision in regard to handling a legal matter, she must always act in the best interests of the client. However, the decision to follow a particular course of action has to be the decision of the client. If the attorney feels the client's course of action is not in the client's best interests, the attorney must inform the client and may request him to forgo such action; but ultimately the decision rests with the client. The attorney or lay advocate represents the client and the client's position regardless of the advocate's personal or professional opinion of the client's bests interests.

For example, an attorney may feel it is in the best interests of a client charged with a criminal offense to enter into a plea bargain and may advise that client there is little probability of prevailing if the case goes to trial. If the client pleads guilty to a lesser charge, he might be placed on probation rather than incarcerated. If the client pleads guilty to the charges originally brought against him the client could face several years in prison if convicted. The attorney has a duty to inform the client of the options and possible ramifications of each option and to advise the client accordingly. If the client still insists on going to trial after having been advised, however, then the attorney must comply with the client's desires even if they work against what the lawyer believes are the best interests of the client.

Social workers rarely participate in actual litigation of a case. Their role is usually limited to the preparation, submission, and/or presentation of a presentence or other court report. From the pure advocacy perspective, irrespective of any mandates social workers might have from the social work profession, they are nevertheless an employee of the attorney or other legal services provider. As such they are an extension of the attorney or provider and must comply with the attorney's code of ethics. In addition to the assumption that the attorney will abide by the client's decision, there is the assumption that any supportive staff within the agency will also act in accordance with the client's judgment. Moreover, the attorney is required by the *Code of Professional Responsibility* to exercise due diligence and control over her employees to prevent them from disclosing confidences or acting in a manner inconsistent with the client's wishes. The attorney is responsible for the actions of employees perceived as extensions of the attorney and thereby subject to her code of ethics. Given the very nature of the legal system itself then, the conflict involves not so much the social worker's choice of ethics but rather her choice of employment.

Because of the relationship between employer and employee the social worker could very easily be placed in a position of making some difficult ethical choices. For example, the social worker in a public defender's office preparing a presentence report may feel the client would benefit from mental health services. Bringing this to the court's attention may put constraints on the client's freedom, and the social worker knows that as an employee she is expected to prepare a report in a light most favorable to the client. Should she prepare a favorable report or inform the court of what she feels is in the client's best interest or the best interests of her family? However, even this kind of conflict is not without resolution.

In the legal or adversary system each party presents her side in the most favorable light. It is not within the attorney/advocate's purview to embark upon a course of action they see as in the client's best interests except in a purely legal sense. Determining a client's best interests is, afterall, no more than a subjective opinion. It is the court and jury's responsibility to determine which side will prevail and what is in the best interest of the plaintiff, the defendant, and society. The social worker in any legal setting need not concern herself with deciding what is in the best interest of the client. In more traditional human services settings the social worker may act as judge and jury, but within the legal system that is the exclusive jurisdiction of the court. The social worker (as well as the social work profession as a whole) must develop a basic trust and faith in the legal system so she can relinquish this territory and eliminate potential conflicts of ethics.

The potential of social workers acting as pure advocates raises several questions. Can the social worker legitimately stay in the advocate role in situations that require professional judgment? Can a social worker be an expert and an advocate simultaneously? Is it appropriate for a professional practitioner to serve the exclusive interest of the client while acting as a professional consultant? What are the limits of the pure advocacy role in the legal setting? How do professional concerns for the client's total environment and particularly individuals in the client's immediate environment limit the social work role?

As it is now, there are no simple answers to these questions. The NASW Code of Ethics is vague and ambiguous in setting social workers clear guidelines for making ethical choices. As social workers increasingly find employment in legal agencies, the profession must accept the challenge of developing a comprehensive and clearly defined and delineated code of ethics. Only then will social workers be able to make decisions about the ethics of other professions. In the meantime social workers in legal settings are left to their own professional judgment as to their appropriate role.

REFERENCES

1. Beulah Compton, *Introduction to Social Welfare and Social Work* (Homewood, Ill.: Dorsey Press, 1980), 119.
2. Donald T. Dickson, "Law in Social Work: Impact of Due Process," *Social Work* 21, no. 4 (July, 1976): 274–278.
3. Jill Miller, "The Social Worker as Client Advocate," presented at the Council on Social Work Education Annual Program Meeting, Los Angeles, California, March, 1980.
4. Joseph Senna, "Social Workers in Public Defender Programs," *Social Work* 21, no. 4 (July, 1975): 271–277.
5. *The Code of Professional Responsibility and Code of Judicial Conduct* (Chicago, Ill.: The American Bar Association, 1977), 32.

References

1. S. Palmer, *The Prevention of Crime* (New York: Behavioral Publications, 1973), 76.
2. K. T. Erikson, *Wayward Puritans* (New York: Wiley and Son, 1966), 24.
3. Craig Little, *Understanding Deviance and Control: Theory, Research, and Social Policy* (Itasca, Ill.: Peacock, 1983) 272–273.
4. Mary Wirtz Macht, Jose Ashford, and Melissa Mylym, "Social Work Advocacy: Conflicts and Constraints," paper presented at APM, Council on Social Work Education, Detroit, Michigan, 1984.
5. Ad Hoc Committee on Advocacy, "The Social Worker as Advocate: Champion of Social Victims," *Social Work* 14, no. 2 (April 1969): 23–32.

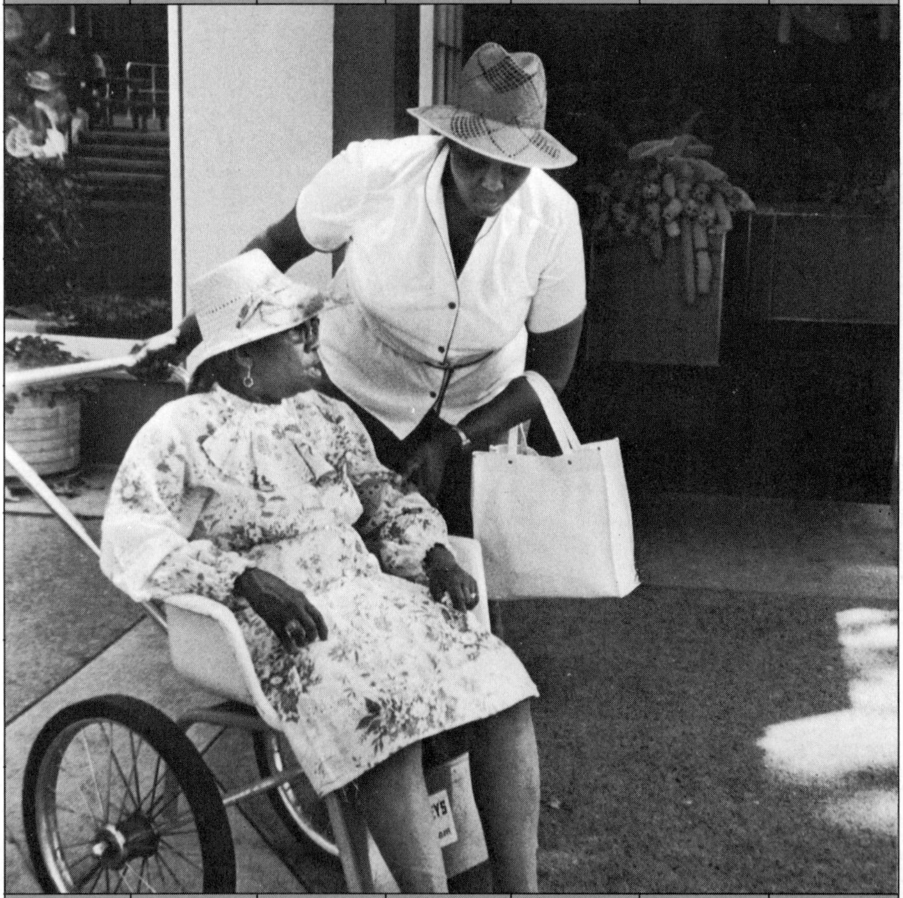

PART VI

SPECIAL POPULATIONS/ SPECIAL ISSUES

"Social work is a by-product of an unequal and imperfect society. . . . Social workers have to operate not only from where the client is at but also from where the society is at. And neither . . . ever stand still. [Social workers are essential] because of the frailties of human genetics and the aging body, because of abberations of human behavior, because plans go wrong and people die, because all political and economic systems produce victims and label them deviants, because human nature and human life are occasionally vicious, and because people . . . sometimes fight with and hurt each other. Social work has emerged as one of the twentieth century's attempts to cope with such problems as best it can"[1]

In the United States, the amount of money you have is almost the sole determinant of your standard of living, access to resources, services, and amenities. Virtually everything in our society is treated as a commodity to be bought and sold. Health, education, nutrition, and safety are all dealt with as if they were wine or blue jeans. The one with the most money gets first choice; the one with the least gets what's left over—if anything is left over. So, because everything one needs or wants must be bought, inequality of income automatically produces inequality in all other areas of life.[2]

But though wealth and income are generally distributed unevenly in American society, specific groups consistently have a smaller share, and their lack of financial leverage is rooted deeply in societally defined roles. For years minorities have been severely limited to the secondary work force that frequently pays less than a living wage and does not carry benefits like sick leave and health insurance. In fact racial discrimination has been documented so extensively that both the courts and the legislative branches of government have attempted to respond by ordering affirmative action. Women, Vietnam veterans, homosexuals, and the elderly have also been systematically discriminated against to a degree that has led to legislation outlawing discriminatory hiring practices affecting these groups. Social work is one of the human service professions working to overcome such oppression.

The minorities chapter includes case studies from ethnic sensitive social work practice, an individual life experience of growing up black in America, and one black social worker's suggestions on how to make social work education more responsive to minority needs.

The women's issues chapter first identifies the structural reasons women are economically discriminated against, and extends this analysis to the effect of social role definition on rural professional women. Finally the chapter looks at the problem of sexism as it relates to social work education and practice.

The elderly are becoming an ever larger portion of our society. Issues on providing for the elderly range from what to do with social security to how to strengthen family supports for the elderly. In this chapter two community programs are presented. The first example follows the social worker through the needs assessment stage of program planning and identifies problems unique to serving this population. In the second example a social worker combines her knowledge of gerontology, communities, and social welfare policy to develop a community alternative to nursing home care that allows chronically impaired elderly to remain in the community.

A relatively unrecognized client group has been the Vietnam veterans. This group has not only suffered severe economic problems but has also experienced severe unrecognized emotional problems frequently exacerbated by alcohol and other drug abuse. This chapter addresses the severity of the problem, presents one couple's method of coping with the problem, and provides some diagnostic clues and treatment suggestions for social workers dealing with this population.

The final group to be included are gays and lesbians. Historically, social work has been an accessory to the oppression of this group. Recently, the Council on Social Work Education has been increasingly proactive in requiring sexual diversity content as an integral component of social work education. The politics of defining behavior as deviant is addressed, and a case example is presented in which a thirty-two year old lesbian benefits from a gay and lesbian counseling service developed by social workers. An article by Lou Ann Lewis discusses both the knowledge and value system necessary to work with lesbians. In spite of social work's professed commitment to sexual choice, many agencies and individual professionals have not yet applied this commitment to practice.

References

1. Martin Davies, *The Essential Social Worker* (London: Heineman Educational Books, Ltd., 1981) 208.
2. William Ryan, *Equality* (New York: Pantheon Books, 1981) 190.

CHAPTER EIGHTEEN

Minority Concerns

"The generic formula of Blaming the Victim*—justifying any quality by finding defects in the victims of any inequality—has been retained, but in a much wider, more malevolent and dangerous form, particularly in the resurgence of ideas about hereditary defects in Blacks, the poor, and working people in general."*[1]

Two examples of personal reactions to racism appear at the end of this chapter.

Social issues and needs raised by minority groups are as diverse as the groups represented. Differences in race, ethnicity, language, gender, sexual preference, age, locality, illness, and handicapping conditions are all of current concern. Racial minorities suffer double jeopardy because social problems they face are exacerbated by racism. So what of social work's responsibility to contribute to solutions of the problems raised in minority issues—the problems of those who have been disadvantaged or excluded from participating in the mainstream of society?

In many ways minority groups have historically provided their own social services. **See Chapter 5.**

Providing social work services for minorities is a task requiring technical knowledge and skill, community strength and resources, and a commitment to political and economic "empowerment" within the group. In almost any setting social workers choose to practice, they will be confronted with issues of racism. On a societal level racism takes the form of higher unemployment and higher poverty rates for minorities. On an individual level social workers deal with the psychological damage suffered by individual minorities. Whether the group consists of inner city Afro-Americans, southeastern Hispanics, migrant farmworkers or refugees from southeast Asia, the hardships of economic discrimination are similar. The type of individual discrimination suffered varies somewhat by group.

The Cuban Resettlement Program (1980) provided a particular challenge to Nancy Kelley. She describes her experience.

My involvement in the county-funded Cuban Resettlement Program was in the last year of a two and one half year period. Two objectives drew me as a social worker in private practice into a highly politicized program. The first was a desire to counter the negative images and consequent withholding of community resources, especially private housing, that was escalating with each police related incident involving a Cuban. The second objective was to stabilize the network of services and resources available to this group of 300 individuals, knowing that federal dollars and county sponsorship would end abruptly at the end of the contract period. Seven months was all the time we had from contract award to termination.

By the end of the seven months, housing services, beginning with apartment hunting and continuing through mediation, were being provided to a total of sixty clients; forty private housing managers/owners had made units available under continuing leases; two formal assessment reports were completed to detail actual distribution of Cuban entrants in the county and their performance as tenants; and a program proposal to United Way had been submitted to continue services. Today funding has been provided to a new Hispanic organization that provides English language, job training and development, housing, personal counseling and outreach services.[2]

Minority groups are a consistent element in the fabric of American society. Appreciating our national diversity has consistently been a tenet of social work, particularly as minority groups fall prey to society's progress. In addition

It is important that professional social work education include experience and information in preparing workers for ethnic sensitive practice. Photo courtesy of Social Welfare History Archives, University of Minnesota.

to understanding the discrimination individuals have suffered as members of a minority group, the social worker needs to be congnizant that group membership itself adds to the difficulty of coping in American society. Wynette Devore and E. G. Schlesinger define minority groups as "the underprivileged in a system of ethnic stratification and people of low standing who receive unequal treatment."[3] These same authors have contributed immensely to the social work knowledge base in their recent book *Ethnic Sensitive Social Work Practice* by translating how societal discrimination and ethnicity need to be addressed in social work practice; an excerpt from their work illustrates ethnic sensitivity in practice.[4]

A definition of "minority groups" is presented here.

The Model for Ethnic-Sensitive Practice

WYNETTE DEVORE AND E. G. SCHLESINGER

It might seem that, in this massive system burdened by rules, regulations, and procedures, ethnic-sensitive practice would not be possible—not only is it possible, it is *urgent.* The large number of ethnic minority recipients has been recognized. At times when they are most vulnerable, without power to control events about them, a social worker who is attuned to the impact of the ethnic reality and its various dispositions is important.

THE ROUTE TO THE SOCIAL WORKER

To be a recipient of AFDC suggests failure in a society that expects self-sufficiency. Eligibility for assistance requires that there be an absent parent; if both are present, then one must be disabled or unemployed. In each instance there is deficiency, an inability to provide for children in the expected way. Given this requirement, who wants to be on public welfare? The route may be called voluntary, yet the circumstances suggest pain from illness or failure. Husbands and lovers walk away, leaving women to ask, "Why?" Death comes to a young father, leaving his wife and children alone. An unfortunate automobile accident leaves a mother physically handicapped. Each of these events may create eligibility for AFDC, but who would invite such pain? The trip to the agency is a response to the need to provide food, clothing, shelter, and medical care for the children. Applicants do not choose a relationship with a social worker—it is part of the procedure. Social workers must recognize this as a possibility when recipients seem to be "uncooperative." Unnecessary coercive activity must be avoided if the rights of recipients are to be respected. The directive which insists upon pushing adults to work makes this difficult to achieve. In the cases which follow there is an undercurrent of coercive activity that appears to be unavoidable due to agency policy. Nevertheless, social workers must be aware of the values and assumptions of the model for ethnic-sensitive practice as well as the layers of understanding. Whenever possible, attempts must be made to work simultaneously through individual and systemic change.

The Case of Marie and Hector Padilla

> Marie and Hector Padilla are a young Puerto Rican couple with a 6-week-old baby girl. They are eligible for Aid for Dependent Children (AFDC)because Mr. Padilla has been on strike.
>
> They do not want any services offered by the agency, only the grant.
>
> Although they are polite, friendly, and straightforward in their answers to questions, they do not respond to any attempts to discuss any problem areas such as child care, particularly because the

> baby is so young, nor do they have any interest in training programs. Mr. Padilla insists that they have no problem other than the fact that he is not working

After the company went on strike Mr. Padilla asked his family, his friends, neighbors, and *compadres* for help before he applied for public assistance (Ghali, 1977). The welfare department was his last resort. He needs to maintain his *machismo,* authority role, as husband and father; unemployment has put a strain on those relationships (Papajohn and Spiegel, 1975). However, if he does not present this potential stress as a problem, it is inappropriate for the social worker to assume that it must exist or that they are unable to care for their child. To insist that they "accept" counseling is viewed as coercive. Lack of cooperation may threaten eligibility. A large family network is available for support in child care; in fact, as their daughter grows she will be disciplined, when misbehaving, by any number of relatives, with her parents' approval (Papajohn and Spiegel, 1975). The strength of this ethnic family system is available to Marie and Hector. The model for ethnic-sensitive practice suggests that this strength be recognized and counted as an available resource. No further direct efforts are called for, except for the continual payment of the monthly allowance of $336.* Considering the inadequacy of this allowance, it is suggested that the social worker give considerable thought to entering into alliance with other social work professionals, community service agencies, the Urban League, Puerto Rican Action groups, and any others who may choose to join. These professionals, along with the recipients, may organize to work toward legislation that would increase grants to a level which allows for a standard of living with some dignity.

One of the tasks assigned to welfare social workers is to assist clients in the management of their finances; often recipients are accused of irresponsibility because the money never lasts a whole month. One AFDC mother explains how she budgets each month:

> I get $336 each month. First I pay the rent. I never keep the money from the landlord. Then I buy the food with the food stamps, I pay the phone bill and the electric. Last month my son needed sneakers. . . . No sneakers. . . . I take anyone's leftover furniture and even curtains. If they don't fit my window I may give them away or keep them in case I move to another apartment. We eat good at the first of the month but by the end it's really bad. Sometimes I have to borrow money from a friend.

*AFDC grant, June 1980, New Jersey Department of Public Welfare.

The Case of Sally Jackson

> Ms. Jackson is a burden to her social worker. No matter how she tries, Ms. Jackson is never able to learn how to manage her money. She is always running out. She is always on the brink of disaster. Like other recipients she receives her grant of $386 for her family of four, plus food stamps and Medicaid, but she still cannot seem to manage.
>
> Sally Jackson is Black and a recipient of Aid for Dependent Children. Her eligibility is based on the fact that she has three minor children. She was married at one time, but her husband deserted after the birth of their first child. Soon after she established a relationship with Ray Evans, and they began to live together. They had two children. He had been employed in a local factory. Unfortunately, he was abusive and Sally left him, taking her children with her.
>
> She is 32 years old. Her children are 12, 10, and 8 years old. On occasion Ms. Jackson works as a cleaning woman in a hospital. When she works her grant is reduced in relation to her income. The procedure is very complicated but in the end she seldom has more than $386 and so she does not pursue work heartily, although she enjoys being away from the house and with other people during the day. Work, the desired activity, is not worthwhile.

If Ms. Jackson were to work full time her income would be marginal, and she may lose her Food Stamp privileges as well as Medicaid benefits, so important when there are growing children subject to colds, contagious diseases, and broken limbs. As Ms. Jackson attempts to change her life, she finds her efforts fruitless. She feels powerless and impotent. This feeling of powerlessness may be found in Blacks at all social class levels, as society places *all* Blacks in the same single category regardless of attainment or income. The fruits of the impotence Ms. Jackson feels are a "loss of autonomy, a diminished sense of self-worth, and low self-esteem," which are even more debilitating at her underclass level. Leon Chestang

(1972) in a discussion of "character development in a hostile environment" adds that the emotional effects originating from impotence are feelings of fear, inadequacy, and insecurity. Again and again the literature alludes to the history of Blacks in this country as an experience of degradation and humiliation which affects present attitudes of society and the availability of education and occupational experiences.

The model for ethnic-sensitive practice calls for attention to Ms. Jackson's problem in the present, recognizing the effects of the history of Blacks upon her situation. But like Mr. and Mrs. Padillo, Ms. Jackson's problem is financial. As she looks to her siblings for support, as is often the custom in the Black underclass, she finds that they too are struggling with barely enough to cover their own needs. Her tenth-grade education limits her job opportunities (Willie, 1976); she is "stuck" in the welfare system.

It is primarily through systemic change that Ms. Jackson's life will become less oppressive. The change must provide a reasonable income, employment with dignity, and training programs which do not carry a coercive overtone. These changes come about slowly and Ms. Jackson's problems with money are overwhelming today. But, the problem is not hers alone. The monthly allowance is not budgetable, yet families seem able to survive; how do they do it?

A group of AFDC mothers who meet together regularly may be able to share their "survival techniques" with Ms. Jackson; indeed, she may have some to contribute herself. Such a gathering recognizes the strength in families and provides an opportunity to visit and be among friends. Ms. Jackson's attempts at employment were largely motivated by a desire to be among other adults. While efforts are made toward systemic change, Ms. Jackson's need for immediate help in making the money last as long as possible can be found among other AFDC recipients.

The grants Ms. Jackson and others receive are provided to give support to dependent children, a powerless, helpless group. They remain powerless and helpless as the program responds continually to the problems of adults (Federico, 1980). Social workers must not forget that the assistance is for children and must begin to organize for change that affects their life more directly. This effort may be as small as negotiating with the neighborhood school administration to open the gymnasium for a few hours on weekday evenings and on Saturday mornings, thereby providing a recreational resource previously unavailable for Ms. Jackson's sons and the other children in the neighborhood.

The Case of Marie Santangelo

> Marie Santangelo is 37 years old. She receives Aid for Dependent Children for the support of her son Mike, who is 17 years old. He is a high school senior and will graduate in a few months.
>
> They have lived with Jerry Rossi for most of Mike's life. Jerry is unemployed but receives social security disability benefits due to a work injury. He is 40 years old.
>
> Their life together has been one of striving to make ends meet. Mr. Rossi says that he would marry Miss Santangelo but it would be too expensive; the grant from AFDC would be decreased. In a few months, however, Mike will be 18 and no longer eligible for assistance. When it is suggested that Miss Santangelo begin to consider employment, Mr. Rossi becomes very agitated, claiming that it is not right for her to work away from home. Both Miss Santangelo and Mr. Rossi are Italian.

The reality of lost income is a threat to the Santangelo-Rossi family. But, the eligibility criteria are clear. Children are eligible for AFDC from "birth to eighteen or to twenty one if in school, college vocational or technical training."* Mike's eighteenth birthday and graduation from high school are only a few months apart. He expects to find employment in one of the small industries in the area. His earning will no doubt exceed the $255 that his mother receives for their support, but neither will be eligible for food stamps or Medicaid any longer.

Adherence to the model for ethnic-sensitive practice will alert the social worker to the possibility that Mr. Rossi's agitation when employment is suggested for Miss Santangelo may be the response to an ethnic disposition. The family has continued to be the central focus in Italian interpersonal relations. Women are expected to "take care" of their men. A majority of Italian women in Krause's study (1978) agreed that women do best as wives and mothers and that *true* women are happiest with their husbands and children. If this is the feeling of Miss San-

* New Jersey Department of Human Services—Department of Public Welfare. July 1978.

tangelo as well, then resistance to employment is not as irrational as it seems in a system that is beginning to consider the employment of women to be a major determinant of worthiness.

The dilemma may be compounded. Miss Santangelo, like the respondents in Krause's study, may feel that women are too emotional for some jobs and that they are different from men. If this is so, then social work efforts to steer Miss Santangelo toward training and/or employment may meet with minimal success.

Miss Santangelo does have two resources immediately available—her son and Mr. Rossi. Is it possible that they are willing to assume the responsibility for the support of their "wife" and mother. Since Mr. Rossi insists that work is not appropriate for his friend, then he must recognize the consequence of his position. He has been a part of this family for most of Mike's life; his discussion of marriage suggests a commitment to Miss Santangelo. To insist that she enter training or find employment is coercive activity which does not take into account the wishes of this AFDC family.

A study of community resources may reveal social service agencies, churches, or women's groups that will be able to assist the Santangelo-Rossi family when the AFDC grant has been discontinued.

In our present society it does not seem to be unreasonable to expect high school graduates to seek employment if they do not intend to continue their education. Mike, in fact, looks forward to the independence that will come with a job. As an Italian male adolescent moving toward emerging adulthood, he has become more involved with friends at school and in the community. He has done without many of the "extras" that are important as children grow, but he now looks forward to independence.

Solutions that please the system are not always forthcoming. The social worker must respect Miss Santangelo's decision not to work and provide her with knowledge about community resources which may be helpful to her in the future.

Special Program Example: The Indochinese Refugee Program

Among the special programs supported entirely by federal funds is the Indochinese Refugee Assistance Program introduced to provide financial assistance to individuals and families from Vietnam, Cambodia, and Laos. This new group of refugees has problems with language, employment, and adaptation to a new country. Special centers have been established to aid them as they learn to speak English, seek employment, and learn to solve problems in a strange environment. They are eligible for public assistance programs as individuals, couples, or parents with children.

The Case of Mr. and Mrs. Dinh Nguyen

> Mr. and Mrs. Dinh Nguyen are Vietnamese. They have a 4-month-old child. Mrs. Nguyen's brother Pao lives with them. They are all quite young. Mr. Nguyen is 24. His education in Vietnam was extensive and he holds what could be called a baccalaureate degree. At present, however, he is not employed but attends the county vocational school to learn new skills. In the evening he attends an adult program for newly arrived refugees from Indochina.
>
> Pao is 19. He is employed as a maintenance person in a local supermarket. In the evening he too attends school to learn English. Some evenings he goes to the vocational institute to learn a new trade. In Vietnam he was a factory worker.
>
> Mrs. Nguyen is 25. Her primary task is to take care of the baby.
>
> The family was sponsored by a local church. The congregation assumed responsibility for locating housing when they arrived. The house was furnished with secondhand and new items supplied by the church. Members have assisted with shopping for household supplies and food. They were most helpful when the baby was born, providing the necessary clothing and furniture.

The family receives public assistance. Their grant of $336 is based on AFDC allowance standards. Months before the Nguyens arrived, the church began its efforts to sponsor a Vietnamese family. Contacts with the denomination headquarters and Church World Service led to the assignment of the family. The congregation agreed to help in the ways described earlier and have continued to do so. This initial institutional response to need is supported by the legislation which gives financial support to the Nguyens and Pao.

As social workers apply the model for ethnic-sensitive practice in work with the Nguyen family they realize that history has had an immediate impact upon their lives. Past and present history of war and its aftermath have caused their migration to a new country. Their ethnicity causes immediate strain as they confront an entirely new environment in which they are dependent upon the church and the welfare system for support. Strength and support may be found in relationships formed with members of the church, but the most comforting are found among other participants in the refugee assistance program. The bilingual and bicultural counselors understand the tensions that are present as the Nguyens and Pao find their way.

In the public agency workers must be aware that Asian recipients are most responsive if at initial contact agency functions, services, and the kind of assistance available are made very clear (Ho, 1976). Ho suggests that short-term service with concrete goals is usually needed. This has been the experience of social workers in public agencies who have worked with Vietnamese families. Their experience suggests that Mr. Nguyen and Pao will complete their training programs, find employment with the help of the refugee assistance program, and request that assistance be discontinued.

The system has designed a special program to meet the needs of this special group of Asians; however, there are countless Asian Americans who are without the many resources available to new arrivals. Elderly Japanese, Chinese, and Koreans are hidden in many "Chinatowns" of our urban centers. Japanese families have problems with alcoholism, mental illness, and retarded children, as do other American families; yet there is a negative attitude toward mental illness in the Japanese community (Mass, 1976). Chinese youth are faced with the tensions common to adolescence as well as cultural value conflicts that may arise with their Chinese-born parents (Chen, 1970). At each stage of the life cycle Asian families are in need of various services, including public assistance. The need for systemic support is evident but is lacking. The tendency of Asians to hide problems because of their sense of shame and pride makes work difficult, but efforts must be pursued. Chen (1970) has presented steps which need to be taken in working toward change in the Chinese community. They are useful in other Asian communities as well: (1) inform the general public and the Chinese community; (2) develop community resources to cope with the existing problems by initiating social programs; (3) promote social action; (4) initiate constructive legislation; (5) develop leadership; (6) educate bilingual social workers; and (7) conduct research and surveys into the changing Chinese American family structure. These steps enable the ethnic-sensitive worker to move in an organized fashion toward change in neglected Asian communities; the effort may well begin with an Asian recipient of public assistance.

SUMMARY

This chapter has considered the application of the model for ethnic-sensitive practice in the public welfare setting. We recognize that recipients for the most part do not wish to be a part of this system. They are continually negatively viewed for behavior that is acceptable at other social class levels. There is continual coercive activity which provokes a sense of powerlessness, and a budget allowance which barely meets minimal requirements for survival. Many recipients are women and their children; often they are members of ethnic minority groups and are judged more harshly than other recipients. The ethnic-sensitive worker must recognize these factors and work continually for systemic change that will support voluntary employment training programs and provide grants to enable parents to provide their children with nutritious meals all month, appropriate clothing as the seasons change, and a few of the extras that make childhood a joyful experience.

REFERENCES

Brown, Sam Ervin. 1974. From "Poetic expressions of a white urban family." Submitted in partial fulfillment of course requirements for the Urban Family, Rutgers University School of Social Work. Fall.

Chen, Pei-Ngor. 1970. "The Chinese community in Los Angeles." *Social Casework, 51*(10), December.

Chestang, Leon. 1972. "Character development in a hostile environment." Chicago: The School of Social Service Administration, The University of Chicago.

Federico, Ronald C. 1980. *The social welfare institution—an introduction.* Lexington, MA: D. C. Health and Co.

Ghali, Sonia Badillo. 1977. "Cultural sensitivity and the Puerto Rican client." *Social Casework,* October.
Harrington, Michael. 1962. *The other America—poverty in the United States.* Baltimore: Penguin Books.
Ho, Man Keung. 1976. "Social work with Asian Americans." *Social Casework,* March.
Kitano, Harry H. L. 1976. *Japanese Americans* (2nd ed.). Englewood Cliffs, N.J.: Prentice-Hall, Inc.
Krause, Corinne Azen. 1978. *Grandmothers, mothers and daughters.* New York: American Jewish Committee.
Lowenthal, Martin. 1972. "Work for welfare clients: a nonreform." *Urban and Social Change Review, 5*(2), Spring.
Mass, Amy Iwasaki. 1976. "Asians as individuals: the Japanese community." *Social Casework,* March.
Mauch, Joan. 1972. "Voices never heard/faces seldom seen." *Public Welfare, 30*(3), Summer.
Mencher, Samuel. 1967. *Poor law to poverty—economic security policy in Britain and the United States.* Pittsburgh: University of Pittsburgh Press.
Morales, Armando, and Sheafor, Bradford. 1980. *Social work—a profession of many faces* (2nd ed.). Boston: Allyn and Bacon, Inc.
Murillo, Nathan. 1970. *The Mexican American family.* In Hernandez, Carrol, Haug, Marsha J., and Wagner, Nathaniel N. (eds.). *Chicano—social and psychological perspectives,* St. Louis: The C. V. Mosby Co.
Papajohn, John, and Spiegel, John. 1975. *Transactions in families.* San Francisco: Jossey-Bass, Inc., Publishers.
Peretti, Peter O. 1973. "Enforced acculturation and Indian-White relations." *The Indian Historian, 6*(1), Winter.
Reid, William J., and Smith, Audrey D. 1972. "AFDC mothers view the work incentive program." *The Social Service Review, 46,* September.
Rein, Martin. 1972. "Work incentives and welfare reform." *Urban and Social Change Review, 5*(2), Spring.
Sermabeikian, Patricia. 1975. "What's so bad about being poor." In *A little piece of the world.* Submitted in partial fulfillment of course requirements for the Urban family, Rutgers University School of Social Work, Fall.
Time Magazine. *The American underclass.* August 29, 1977.
Wilensky, Harold L., and Lebeaux, Charles N. 1958. *Industrial society and social welfare.* New York: Russell Sage Foundation.
Willie, Charles V. 1974. "The Black family and social class." *American Journal of Orthopsychiatry,* 44(1), January.

Some minorities suggest that whites cannot adequately understand racial discrimination since they have never experienced it. Professional education assumes that education as well as experience can prepare students for ethnic sensitive practice. Janet Williams, a black social worker, has agreed to describe her personal feelings of how discrimination affects the life and well-being of minorities. Having graduated with honors from an accredited BSW program, she has yet (three years later) to find a professional social work position. She presently works as a receptionist in a Salvation Army Office. Janet's very personal sharing of her experience provides insight that can be generalized to many individuals who find themselves in powerless positions in our society.

American Racism

JANET WILLIAMS

The best way for me to describe or talk about my feelings on discrimination, race prejudice, and racism is to talk about my own personal experiences growing up black in America. I can vividly recall how I felt about being treated unfairly as far back as four years old. This is one of the reasons I strongly reject the notion, too often expressed by white adults, that children are color blind. Although my consciousness was not as fully developed as it is now, I was very aware of color differences in people and gradually learned how these differences could so affect a person's destiny. My trusting and innocent view of the world was shattered quite early.

What does it feel like to be the target of discrimination in a racist society? It is like calling out in the middle of the night with your voice left unheard. It is like being chained to a curse which had its foundation well laid before your birth. It is like living with a disease which you know the cure for, but treatment lies outside yourself and in the hands of other people. It is over four centuries of coping with a problem when mental health "experts" say if you have been coping with the same problem for a year that is too long. It is turning around and finding yourself in the same predicaments as past generations—a spot you never really thought you would be in, because you convinced yourself you would be so much more in control of life forces. It is having your stomach muscles tighten while you grope for the words to explain irrational white hatred to your preschooler, who you desperately want to grow up positive and healthy in a hostile society. It is being hungry knowing if you were white there would be less chance of it being so. It is sitting and listening to white liberals tell you all about your culture and your history as if whites are smarter about you than you are about yourself—the ultimate insult by white intellectuals. It is being angry and in a cage. Paul Laurence Dunbar, the noted black poet, says a lot about black people's frustrations in *We Wear The Masks* and *I Know Why The Caged Bird Sings.* Blacks have been slaves in this country for a long time. And, while a lot has changed—a lot more has not or has merely taken a different form.

Naturally we are all unique individuals, shaped by the experiences we have lived. It should go without saying, blacks are no different. It is interesting, however, that blacks have been pushed into the position of having to qualify themselves first as human beings before they can move on to any other social level. It does something to a person having to qualify first as a member of the human race, before moving to square two. It fills me with indignation when I am placed in that position. When it is a one-on-one interaction then at least I can confront my offender. When it is hidden behind a tangle of policies, rules, and laws, it takes a longer time to confront. It is so much more difficult to figure out exactly who is attacking or restricting your freedom to be a human being when the culprit lies hidden behind traditions.

Before I entered kindergarten, I was curious about everything. I could not wait to read so I could understand all the words bouncing off the walls around me. A white woman screamed the word nigger at me one day for peering at her red faced, squealing infant in a stroller. I truly did not understand the full weight of the name she selected to assult me with, but I knew it had something to do with her being white and me being black. I was so hurt and then angry for the obvious reason—I had done nothing to deserve the attack. My eleven year old brother was also in the playground. He saw this woman screeching obscenities at me at the top of her lungs. He quickly grabbed my hand, cursed her back loudly and took me home.

The black parent's job is not an enviable one. It is not easy explaining prejudice or countering racism. I remember my sense of disbelief upon learning I could expect similar scenes (like the playground scene) and worse as well as things too complicated for me to fully understand. It all seemed so stupid. It did not make sense. It was a bad joke, unfair, and painful. Could skin color be that important? I was confused. It did not seem possible that color was a valid reason for hating an entire race of people and relegating them to an inferior rank.

I thought that by learning more about black people, my people, I could learn the deep, dark secret or terrible thing we had done to bring about what appeared to be a social curse. I went to the dictionary for a definition very early in my elementary school education. The dictionary described a Negro as one of the black race with negatively described physical characteristics such as flat noses, kinky hair, big lips, etc. rather than broad noses or curly hair or full lips. Negatives surrounded me.

During this period of my childhood, a teacher selected me to read the paragraph about blacks in our social studies reader. For several weeks we had studied about the different states, the fascinating people who made this country strong and brave and beautiful. Then we came to the era of the Civil War. I wanted to die as I read about Negroes and that all they did was pick cotton as slaves and make themselves a burden and source of trouble by setting off a Civil War. I did not know whether to believe this shocking bit of information, but I was furious with the teacher for having me read it in front of all my white classmates. I have no doubt that she did it to humiliate me. I hated her and hated white people for making my people slaves and then I was angry at my people for being slaves. I grew more ambivalent.

It was a mixed bag of sitting in back of classrooms, false accusations, being ignored or given the wrong kinds of attention. One teacher patted my head and then had the nerve to tell me she was dying to see what my hair felt like. She was surprised it was soft. I wondered what she expected—barbed wire? I resented this form of recognition. I know too well what it is like to sit in a class and starve for positive attention.

Name calling and rejection by teachers became a pattern. I developed a sixth sense for who cared and who didn't. Too often they did not care. The few who did care helped sustain me. I grew less passive and more rebellious, rejecting adults in general, whites in particular. I developed defenses to shield me from all the negative information I was receiving about myself (always thankful for caring parents and friends). I saw the ugly light whites persisted on casting on me reflected on them. I was not the animal—they were. I was not ugly—they were. I was not dumb—they were. And so the defenses grew.

By the time I was in junior high school, I was angrier, but I began to learn just how unhappy and miserable life could be if you do not have choices or options. Because of a zoning law, I was left with no alternative, but to walk well over a mile to a ghetto school where the majority of students were both black and poor. It took little time to understand why our books were outdated, torn and defaced; why the school was infested with roaches and the teachers were terrible. One teacher kept a vodka bottle in his briefcase and sipped out of it all day long. Another teacher hung a child by his feet outside a window. There were some so apathetic and burned out it did not make any difference whether they came to the class. It was a nightmare. I felt helpless—totally victimized. What could I do? I was only twelve years old. My parents did not seem sure whether to believe my accounts of a typical day at school. I was enraged, but frightened by what I saw. When my parents finally realized what was happening (we were new to the city), and saw my fears were based in reality, I felt it was almost too late. A whole school year had gone by and I was cheated out of a seventh grade education, which was very important to me. Not that I was such a scholar or loved school so much, but I believed then education was the only way I would achieve social and economic equality. This was being denied to me. My family, the black community, my black role models had stressed getting the "white man's education."

I was also confused by the messages I got in school such as you deserve straight A's for being mannerable and well dressed. It did not seem to matter what the quality of my work was. Nobody cared whether I learned anything. By the time my parents were ready to accept the financial burden of sending me to a private school (at great personal sacrifice), a new zoning law was passed and I was bussed to a suburban school which was in a much safer and better maintained environment.

It took over half of the next school year for me to be placed in a classroom that provided any learning. As my dear racist guidance counselor explained twice, since I was from an inferior school and of minority background I belonged in the lower half of the eighth grade class. I resented her assumption, but was glad to finally be at a "real" school. Before the end of the year I was finally placed in the advanced class. Imagine the shifting around and adjustments for an eighth grader merely because of skin color.

This school also assumed that all black children needed to talk to a special counselor. Are your parents living together? Is your home noisy? Do you have a place to study? Much later, in college, I was required to read the results of these findings in social science courses. I was a subject for the cultural deprivation theorists of the sixties. A white girl, who sat behind me in homeroom said, "I've never seen a black person before." Fourteen years old—I had been looking at them, learning their ways all my life, and she was going to tell me she had never seen a real live one like me before. I told her that was her problem and it must be sad to be so stupid. My tolerance had come to an end. Evidently the other black children's patience had also worn thin, because they were openly hostile to not only the white students, but the teachers as well. There were fist fights every other day. The school administration did not know what to do with us. They did not know how to talk to us. They did not know how to teach us. We rebelled. A black face was always in the principal's office, including mine.

I brought some poems to social studies class. The teacher had suggested we share poems of social relevance. They were poems by Don L. Lee. One began . . . "A rat done bit my sister Nell and Whitey's on the moon." These poems were confiscated from my locker and I was called to the principal's office. The social studies teacher, whom I will never forget, came out of the principal's office blushing. In a phony voice he said, "How in the hell did they find out"? I knew how they found out. This teacher had come across so supportive, so liberal and so encouraging. He taught me to mistrust in a way more profound than words can express. A "militant" tutor, a black college student, who wore mini skirts and a large Afro, said "I told you so; you can't trust white folks ever. Now let that nice liberal be a lesson to you." She had warned me and he was a lesson to me. And, it all became sort of a game of risks and survival.

High school proved to be more of the same but on a different level. It was 1969, and I was not only questioning the education system, but white America as a whole. I was fully aware of the double standard—one for blacks and another for whites. I hated the hypocrisy around me. I did not like the unrealistic expectations. I needed space to grow and make mistakes. It was as if a black person making a mistake, being less than perfect, was evidence of inferiority. It was like being measured against a foreign set of ideals that the foreigners themselves could never measure up to. It was enough to make people sick in the head, but survival was primary.

Why did we not have black teachers? Why were we not taught black history? Where were the black counselors? Why were we punished for doing the same things as white kids, while they went free? Why were we unheard? Ignored? We were fed up. We boycotted classes. Tensions rose. Violence increased. Black students were arrested. Police were in the schools checking for weapons. There were skirmishes in the city. Racial tension was the name the papers gave it. Curfews were set. Anger took center stage.

After a couple of deaths, and numerous injuries, the city began negotiations with black community leaders. We wrote up a list of demands—not requests as our parents had urged—and presented them to the Superintendent of Schools and the Mayor. I will never forget that confrontation as long as I live. Our voices were finally being heard. What do you people want? This was the question of the hour. It seemed so hollow. What did they think we wanted. We wanted to be treated as human beings.

Well, we got a black history course, two black teachers, one black counselor and an Afro-American studies club. My energy focused on seizing the time, placing my creativity in directions other than hatred. I directed a play about religion, drugs, and the black community. I danced African dances, wore African clothes, and had a wonderful time being my black kinky headed self. But, the redundancies in being black and being female began to hit me. I'm not a chick, a broad, a ho'e, or a hammer, I screamed. The more things changed the more they remained the same. If we do not learn from our history we are destined to repeat it.

All I wanted was to get out of high school, my hometown, and my parent's home. By the time I stepped on a college campus as a full fledged student, it was being said my generation caught the tail end of the action that had gone on at campuses across the nation. Boston University did have a solid Afro-American Studies program, the Martin Luther King Center, black fraternities and sororities, Afro-American Orientation week, and a black student government organization. I became involved in both white student government and black student government. I began to see how I had to play a game in order to get through the system. Do what I had to do to retain my dignity and identity, but conform to white folks ways of doing things to get what I wanted. I began to see how blacks and whites really have different values and ways. Basically nonconformist, I struggled with conformity. There was so much to learn about how to figure the mess out, live my life, and be happy.

I searched for answers to the problems of race—being black in America. The more I searched the more I ended up right back where I started. I am a black woman who made it through white America's education system, but I did not make it through in one piece. I have had to compromise too many of my true values and ideologies, and that has taken a little something away from me. But one thing white America will never take away and that is my dignity and human spirit—they did not give it to me. You cannot take back what was never yours. While I may have some semblance of sanity, the inequities around me put me in a headset of preparedness to kill or be killed. I still get called nigger. Sometimes by little children, but mostly by men in fast moving cars. I am immune. They reinforce what I have known for a long, long time. Bigots have no guts just blind hatred. I am a product of American socialization. I manage my emotions very well, but it is inevitable I will have hypertension like my father. I carry stress in my back. There is a price to pay for being so called educated by white schools. I am so tired, but will never give up the cause. The cause for freedom for every black woman, man and child in these United States of America.

P. S. If you should feel that this struggle is part of the past, let me relate a recent incident to you. I was asked by the local University Department of Social Work to be a respondent to a panel presentation on Racism in Field Placements. Although I am very tired of being the resident minority in this community, I felt obligated to do what I could to make education more accessible to minority students. I was told that four field supervisors would do short presentations and I would be asked to respond. From the outset it appeared that the agenda was very different than what I had been told to expect. Much to my surprise, the panel deferred to my "minority" status and allowed me to give the first presentation. Swallowing my feelings of betrayal by the organizers, I extemporaneously addressed race issues in field placements. As I feared, the panel of "experts" then went on to say they could not relate to race discrimination but they wanted to address discrimination against the elderly, the mentally handicapped, and the learning disabled. My anger was further exacerbated as I had to sit and listen to the local professionals relate their difficulty in hiring minorities in this area. Here I was an honors graduate of this social work program, qualified to speak as an expert on racism in field placement but unable to secure a professional position in the community in spite of endless interviews and applications. Strangely, I could muster no sympathy for their efforts to recruit black professionals. It seems the only function I served was that the Social Work Department could now document that it sponsored a full day conference to deal with issues of racism. I am sure the Council will be impressed with these efforts. After all, isn't that what affirmative action is about—effort not results. Racism marches on!

One of Janet's classmates, Toby Ferrell, has also experienced the frustrations and discriminations Janet shares. Based upon his research, education, and experience, Toby has developed the following proposals for social work educators. While Toby would not suggest that all black social workers would agree with his stance, he feels his suggestions need to be addressed. Toby provides some provocative ideas worth considerable class discussion.

Farrell's description of racism in social work can be compared to Cummings' description of sexism in the profession in Chapter 19.

Modifying Social Work

TOBY FERRELL

Social work as a profession has not responded to the needs of the black population. This must not be allowed to continue. There must be fundamental change in the social work curriculum, practice, and thought if we are to be effective in moving blacks into the mainstream and advantages of our society.

One of the reasons conventional social work methods have been ineffective in the black community is the setting in which it developed. Settlement Houses, Youth Agencies and other early forms of social services were appropriate for white immigrants and poor whites who were only in need of financial assistance. They were of little use to blacks who were seeking to gain acceptance as human beings.[1] There is no service capable of remedying this problem.

Another reason social work has been ineffective in responding to black need is its inherent function in the present political and economic system. Social work has been given the mandate to make our society more humane. In order to do this social workers most frequently function as social control agents keeping things rolling along with minimal change. For blacks to become equal, major change must be not only allowed but facilitated. Capitalism as an economic system is dependent upon low wages. Low wages occur only if there is competition for jobs. Therefore, there must be fewer jobs than people, requiring a segment of the population to be unemployed. Over the past 200 years, this segment has been the black population. Therefore, any agency or profession in the business of maintaining such a system will come into direct conflict with black equality.

REDEFINING THE BLACK IMAGE

The black's role in the labor force presents conflict for blacks from a very early age. The urban black child is lectured by social workers and teachers to attend school, study, work hard, etc. The values upheld by white society are drilled into their head but the avenues upon which to achieve them are not open to these children.[2] The inner city school which the child must attend is frequently substandard; as he gets older jobs that are available will most likely be at substandard pay and the cycle will be repeated with the next generation. Social work must share in the responsibility for stopping the perpetuation of this cycle.

To uphold its share, social work must first revolutionize its thought patterns toward black clients and practitioners. One of the prerequisites for being a social worker has been the ability to view people from a "color blind" perspective. This is an error. Black clients must be viewed as black clients with problems and causes distinctly different from those of other racial groups. For instance, black children have a totally different lifestyle than white children. White kids enjoy a carefree childhood while black children are preparing themselves to enter the adult phase of life—the maturing process is much quicker in the ghetto than in suburbia. This should not be viewed as a fault or weakness in the black family. Social workers need to understand and appreciate the strengths of the black family. Early maturity is a means of survival in the ghetto.[3]

Finally, if radical change in the analysis of black problems is to occur, there must be a re-analysis of black history. This is a history of frustration and betrayal by white institutions in which blacks have placed trust. Now the white social worker comes into the black community offering ideas and methods that sound faintly similar to those of the white missionaries who came to Africa years ago; they brought the bible but took the land.

Social work must also re-analyze its relation to black history. What assumptions have programs and services to blacks been based upon? Most services were given with the basic belief that blacks were lazy, subhuman and in need of patronage by the superior white race. This negative concept must be changed to a positive concept of blacks. Black poverty is not genetically inherited, but environmentally and socially thrust upon blacks. As Malcolm X once said, "We didn't land on Plymouth Rock, it landed on us!"

The history of blacks must be appreciated as a history of struggle and survival.[4] The strength exhibited by blacks ability to survive, and in fact "progress," should be viewed as a positive characteristic. Social workers should recognize and value the undeniable strength of the black race.

SOCIAL WORK CURRICULUM

To allow this reversal of attitude toward the black race, social work curriculum must be "blackened," i.e., the black experience "must be incorporated in social work curriculum and practice.[5] The black experience is translating all occurrences and events and how they impact on the black community. It is an increased emphasis on black culture, black heritage, and the basic realization of what it means to be black.[6] This is a condition which is remarkably absent from social work but it is a situation which can be rectified.

There are three basic components of the social work curriculum: human behavior and the social environment, social welfare policy and services, and the practice sequence. Each of these can be injected with the black experience. The human behavior sequence should examine the idea that it is socio-economic factors such as institutional racism that cause stress in the black community and decrease the chance of blacks receiving either a good education or job. Human behavior should stress the black experience as unique to overcome the long held view that sees blacks as inferior. It is also necessary to look at the social controls that manage to keep blacks "in line," such as law enforcement agencies, educational systems, and the pacifying profession of social work.[7]

Social policy should emphasize the impact profit, power and privilege have on policies, and that since blacks are scarce in these categories the cycle has consequently been able to sustain institutional racism.[8]

Social work practice courses should train students to be able to work in the black community. This must start with studying the history of black culture, black religion, family development, marriage patterns and customs, etc. Students should be taught how to study and learn to understand the individual black communities. The political, economic, and social institutions and their impact on black development must also be included in this analysis.[9]

It is essential that social work thought and curriculum be blackened to the extent that the problems of blacks are accepted as unique and different from those of any other group. Only then can social work methods be revised to effectively attack these problems and their causes. Current methods are too passive. Social work needs to be more action oriented. Services must be taken to the people. It is not important how attractive the office is but how much it can help people.[10]

The advocacy role should be more widely adopted. This can take the form of participating in boycotts, pickets, and if necessary fear-inducing and violent tactics. Social workers can also be responsible for monitoring the programs in their agencies that are funded for a specific purpose to insure that the funds are appropriately used.[11]

BLACK VS. WHITE ROLES

There is one thing to remember when examining all these changes that should take place. *The bulk of the work for black liberation must be done by blacks, not whites!* Whites are to be responsible to themselves because the problem is not a black problem but a problem of white racism. Social work is but one of the many societal institutions that can contribute to the remedy.

REFERENCES

1. Eugene Perkins, *Home is a Dirty Street: The Social Oppression of Black Children* (Chicago: Third World Press, 1975), 114.
2. Ibid.
3. Charles L. Sanders, *Black Agenda for Social Work in the Seventies* (Georgia; Atlanta University School of Socail Work 1971), 21–22.
4. Ibid., 36.
5. Ibid., 1.
6. Ibid., 4.
7. E. Aracelis Francis, *Black Task Report: Suggested Guides for the Integration of Black Content into the Social Work Curriculum* (New York: Council on Social Work Education, 1973), 6.
8. Ibid.
9. Ibid.
10. Sanders, *Black Agenda,* 22.
11. Ibid., 32.

References

1. William Ryan, *Blaming the Victim,* rev. ed. (New York: Vintage, 1976), xiii.
2. Nancy Kelley, interview with Lucy Rowley, 23 July 1983.
3. Wynette Devore and E. G. Schlesinger, *Ethnic Sensitive Social Work Practice* (St. Louis: Mosby, 1981) 11.
4. Ibid., 228-236.

CHAPTER NINETEEN

Women's Issues

"I felt, then, as I do now, that women students were largely ignored. That is, faculty members nurtured the intellectual and professional growth of male students, while female students were largely left alone (benignly, without malice) to find their own way. I believe this same relationship persists after the degree is awarded with "patronage" and concern with the development of former male students' careers continuing while female students are forgotten and ignored."[1]

While social work has been called a "woman's profession," female workers have not paid particular attention to the issues of women as clients.

From the earliest days of the Charity Organization Society, social work has been concerned with the poor and powerless. Originally the poor and powerless recipients of social work efforts were immigrants, unemployed men, and widows. It is only within the last twenty years that social work has recognized women as a substantial part of the poor and powerless and further that their poverty was rooted in the institutional structure of our society.

Elaine Norman and Arlene Mancuso identify three sources of discrimination against women:

1. the denial of equal access to the opportunity structure of the society;
2. the stigmatization of women by definitions of them as inferior to men and then the use of that stigma as an explanation and rationalization for the denial of equal access to the society's opportunity structure; and,
3. the sense of helplessness in women created by this stigma, which translates into behaviors that suggest lack of confidence, ability, or capacity to effect changes in themselves or in the systems that oppress them.[2]

The historical patterns of inequity in education, employment, and salary have made women much more dependent on welfare than men. Women are

Historically, women have organized to be better informed and to be able to inform others about issues affecting women. The League of Women Voters is an example of a conservative organization that sees women's issues as part of larger societal problems. Photo courtesy of Social Welfare History Archives, University of Minnesota.

six times more likely than men to be poor. Thirty-five percent of female headed households are poor while only six percent of male headed households are poor.[3] Diana DiNitto and Thomas Dye identify eight reasons why women earn less than men.

1. Traditionally, many women have not been the major wage earners in the home.
2. The wages of working women have been considered as secondary to their husband's wages.
3. Women have been considered temporary employees who would leave their jobs to marry and have children.
4. Women's paid work has been considered as extracurricular activity to fill free time.
5. Women have had fewer opportunities for education that would lead to better-paying jobs.
6. Women have been forced to accept jobs that do not conflict with family schedules.

7. Career-oriented women have been thought of as selfish or neglectful of their families.
8. "Women's work"—cleaning, child rearing—are not wage-earning jobs.[4]

Some problems are unique to rural women. "Rural Professional Women" suggests strategies to empower rural women.

Rural women experience the discrimination of women in general but also have particular difficulty entering into the male hierarchy in argricultural communities.

Rural Professional Women*

LUCY ROWLEY AND MARY MACHT

There is little doubt that job differentiation within occupations takes place on the basis of gender. This is particularly true in the attainment of upper level hierarchical positions. Whatever the field, the participation of women has been found to decline as the power and prestige of the positions increases.[1] Explanations for this phenomenon vary considerably and range from the inner personal psychological traits of women to the broad social context within which we all live and work. Horner's "fear of success" theory which has been translated into women's "will to fail" is probably the most frequently cited.[2] This reinterpretation of an important social psychological concept reflects a problem inherent in many psychological "theories." Psychology looks for inner traits rather than looking at social context. This paper suggests that social context is a more useful and important predictor of women's successful attainment and fulfillment of upper echelon, managerial positions than the inner traits suggested by many psychologists. We will develop this view by examining role theory and the socialization process as it specifically relates to both the success and frustration of women managers in rural settings.

Starting from the premise that social context is a critical variable, we will begin this discussion by defining what we mean by rural and then develop how that context produces a socialization process and role models that impede the upward professional mobility of women.

The term"rural" is one that has received much attention and debate. There is consensus that the term reflects in some degree a place of residence, an indicator of occupation, a psychological set, and certain demographic data. The U.S. Bureau of the Census defines municipalities of less than 2500 population as "rural" and areas of under 50,000 population as "non-metropolitan." Even though a nonmetropolitan area may have municipalities of over 2500 population the term is becoming synonymous with a rural area. Our interest in rural women is not related to population figures but rather the influence of the traditional occupations of the community.

Rural occupations have traditionally consisted of those identified with farming, ranching, mining, and the lumber industry. Now, however, with manufacturing going rural to some degree and agriculture going "agribusiness," the occupational distinction of rural residents has become blurred. Without attempting at this point to specify all the details this might include, it is important to recognize that just as migration to the cities by rural residents a generation ago produced social and psychological problems due to conflicts in cultural and psychological set, the reverse migration now being seen, even with some blurring of differences may evidence failing of urban psychology and culture in the country. However, diversity remains and even though accomodation and assimilation takes place with each migration, many

* Presented at the NASW Conference entitled "Empowering Women for Social Change," held in Minneapolis, Minnesota, May 1982.

rural traditions and influences tenaciously persist in influencing social roles and the concommitant socialization. Our goal is to analyze role theory related to women managers in areas which are predominantly agricultural. The preponderance of agriculture sets up a unique social context and some specific role expectations which are related to the wife-manager position typical of women in agricultural areas. We suggest that the wife-manager role facilitates women's entrance into the work force but impedes her ability to move up the hierarchy into managerial positions. A brief review of role theory and the process of socialization into roles will be followed by an analysis of how this theory particularly applies to rural women and how this theory can be used to develop strategies to make the necessary role transition for rural women more successful and less stressful.

Zaniecki has defined social roles as:

> . . . a set of mutually interdependent social relations between a "social person" and members of the person's "social circle." The role's functions are performed through "patterned duties" on the part of the person toward the circle in general or toward any segment of it, and through the "personal rights" its members grant in the form of action, facilities or permission to carry out one's part. The role provides the pattern from which the individual acts in a particular situation.[3]

Rural communities have unique sets of social relations which lead to patterned duties for women inconsistent with achieving formal power and prestige.

Socialization is the process through which individuals acquire the knowledge, skills, and values that enable them to participate effectively in the social interactions of the group. It is also an important mechanism of social control.[4] These processes combine, we suggest, to in fact limit women's occupational choices. Women have, due largely to the socialization process, accepted certain secondary roles as right, just, and to be expected. These are roles with typically little prestige and power, roles that are concentrated in the home and family and in the lower echelons of the work place, whether in rural areas, in agriculture or not.

To understand the process of socialization is to see the development of self as a process, continu-

Living in a rural environment can strongly affect the roles that women perform. Photo by David Strickler.

ously created and recreated in each social situation one enters. Each entry is affected by and related to one's past experience. This transition is in itself part of the socialization process. New roles are taken up, expectations learned and identities assumed, with identity itself being socially bestowed, socially sustained, and socially transformed.[5]

To become involved in a social role a person must develop relationships with other people in the social circle. Hence the social circle itself is instrumental in achieving successful role performance. To understand the social circles surrounding many professionals in managerial positions held by women in rural areas, some consideration must be given to the rural agricultural communities in which these positions are created and exist.

A rural community is, among other things, a geographic area with which the community members identify and within which they spend the better part of each day. This community life is a combination of intimate family-to-family association with the neighborhood and an increasing number of both personal and impersonal contacts spread over a much wider area. As modern living in rural as well as urban areas requires a wider range of social and economic services, new and ever-expanding patterns of interpersonal associations, i.e., the social circle develops both formally and informally. The informal groupings have a profound influence on the formal organizations which provide services. The socialization process which has helped define appropriate role expectations, limitations, and sanctions becomes apparent.

Of concern in this paper are the rural influences reflected in the regions that are primarily agricultural, where the preponderance of agriculture sets up a specific social context. Within that context, certain role specifications and expectations for women are established. Of particular interest are those role expectations related to the farm wife-manager or housewife/homemaker-manager roles typical of women in these agricultural areas. We suggest that the existence of this wife-manager role facilitates women's entrance into the work force in rural areas, but impedes their ability to move up the hierarchy into managerial positions.

Our analysis of the impediments to rural women are only slightly different than those identified by Lopata in a study of suburban housewives conducted in the late 50s and early 60s. A great number of patterned expectations relevant in her study population appear to hold today, particularly in agricultural communities. Lopata found:

> Women limit their definition of feminine behavior to a concern with popularity; they work in traditional fields without any strong commitment to them and a career is viewed only as an intermediary state between education and homemaking. Living in a highly vocationally oriented society, women have not developed a strong vocational orientation toward such future roles. In spite of their low commitment to fields of knowledge or work, or for that matter to other spheres of societal life, young women do engage in a complex of social roles away from the home, roles requiring large stores of information, skill, and relational ability. . . . Not only at school and at work but in all her youth the American urban woman is being provided a variety of types of knowledge and skills enabling behavior in complex social situations. She learns to interact with many categories of people in circumstances calling for a great range of actions, feelings, and levels of involvement requiring understanding of complicated situations. She must learn to use different sources of information and to modify her behavior frequently. She participates in a multiplicity of groups within many spheres of societal life, thus learning and acting out multidimensional involvements. . . .[6]

What better description of a professional managerial position might we devise? The elements that remain to be specified are those of technical information required for a particular position, the description of the span of control the woman holds, and the size of the social circle affected.

Every role also has attached to it a certain identity. Individuals tend to become habituated to certain identities (e.g. farm wife, housewife) so that even when the social position changes such as taking on employment in a managerial capacity, previous role expectations linger. As the learning of new roles occurs in the interaction within the social circle, role identity is not something "given" to a person such as an honorary title, but is bestowed in acts of social recognition.

Berger suggests that every social structure (rural, agricultural communities in this case) selects those persons it needs for its functioning and eliminates in one way or another those that do not fit.

Maintenance and support of a person in a particular role by the members of the social circle may, therefore, be interpreted as success, and expulsion as the exercise of socially controlling sanctions could be interpreted as failure. Thus a critical variable in the socialization of women into managerial roles in the rural community is not so much the woman's view of herself but the acts of social recognition demonstrated in the relevant social circle.

The role of the farm wife-home manager is a common one in rural communities. Characteristics of this role include childbearing and rearing, housekeeping, household management, budgeting and financial accounting, animal husbandry, agronomy, machinery and equipment operation and repair, and community relations. The span of control is the homestead.

Professional and managerial roles held by women in rural communities whether in business or human services tend to be lower echelon positions and have limited responsibility and influence. Such positions include teachers, nurses, social workers, administrative assistants, staff bookkeepers, accountants, office managers, etc. We might ask ourselves at this point whether the location of women in these roles, as opposed to those of principals, nursing service administrator, social service director, program director, certified public accountant and business executive support the contention that women accept certain secondary roles based on their own socialization process? Or, does this phenomenon support the view that the social structure selects those needed and eliminates those not needed in particular role positions. We must further question whether the person selected is the most qualified or the most like the predecessor or traditional office-holder. Part of the selection of "those needed" tends to be very closely related to the maintenance of the status quo.

In either case an inherent and increasingly apparent stratification process is at work—one that moves to discourage women from expanding their span of control and moving beyond certain circumscribed roles, i.e. that of wife-manager. To be able to break out of this role set and to be able to increase the span of control for women the long range goal must be to change the social context. However in the short run women can increase somewhat their potential for success by developing the following professional areas:

1. specialized education, background knowledge.
2. technical skills associated with the particular higher level position
3. persistence and success in breaking into the "old boys" or in this case "old farmers" network.

Breaking into relevant networks usually places an unfair burden on women attempting to achieve success in managerial positions—a burden not usually felt by men in equivalent positions. An individual woman cannot address the issue of fairness and must concentrate on developing her own skills.

The problems addressed in this paper were identified in interviews with women in management positions in rural central Wisconsin. The sample for this study was very small since the very nature of the problem assures that there will not be large numbers of rural women in management positions. Nine women were interviewed in depth and while these numbers are not significant, there were clearly recurrent themes that arose in each of the interviews. Two significant themes that emerged were technical skills and roles and role isolation. This isolation parallels again our contention regarding the farm wife—as manager role with limited span of control and lack of the farm support—a circumstance that appears to be reinforced in the social context of the rural agricultural community.

The management roles held by these rural women fall into three general categories: human services and education, business, and self employed professionals (attorneys). The specific occupations were Mental Health Program Director, Developmental Disabilities Program Director, two executive directors of Sheltered Workshops, COA Director, Agriculture Program Coordinator, Nursing Service Administrator, School Principal, Executive Director of the Chamber of Commerce.

Within these diverse positions there were recurrent themes around span of control.

1. Six of the nine women felt their salary was less than a male would have been offered.
2. All nine women were required to report to male dominated boards.
3. All had a sense that male boards clearly circumscribed their role in a way they would not had they been males.

4. Each woman felt the effects of "role isolation." Each position was one of a kind (for women) in the community and there was no obvious peer support system.
5. All nine women experienced continual stress in maintaining credibility. Regardless of how many successful projects they developed, they were required to again prove themselves with each new project. They did not see their boards as placing this burden on male counterparts.
6. These women clearly felt limited in their abilities to expand their role.
7. None of these women were from the community originally but were hired directly into their managerial position. This fact itself suggests the difficulty of role change for rural women.

This paper has suggested that women are victims of social circumstances which seriously circumscribe their potential for power and influence in a rural community. While it would be most desirable to remove the social impediments to women's advancement, this is beyond the capabilities of this endeavor. Even though the woman professional is not the cause of the problem, we suggest there are strategies she can use to increase her success in expanding her span of control.

The first step in expanding one's power is to understand the structural resistance women experience rather than internalizing rejections; the next step is to thoroughly analyze the community itself, i.e., identifying individuals, organizations, and informal groups active in community decisions and development. Most individuals quickly discern the formal decisionmaking bodies but tend to overlook informal decisionmaking systems which are usually more powerful than the formal system in rural areas. Access to the informal power structure is critical to successful program management.

In terms of the women's professional and technical qualifications, it is important to recognize the added burden that will be placed on the woman in a rural area. Wheras these community people are comfortable with men making decisions based on their membership in the "right" sex, a woman needs to have management credentials to offset her membership in the "other" sex.

Recognize that each new project undertaken requires gaining sponsorship from a new group of people (those directly concerned), while maintaining the support of the community elite. Women cannot assume continuing support which is available to their male counterparts.

Learn to recognize where gaps in decisionmaking exist. Step into these gaps as the opportunity presents itself. Use structure and decisionmaking opportunities that naturally exist within the community to build credibility in your special area of interest. The rural woman in management does not have the luxury of concentrating only on her own program and letting the community take care of unrelated issues. In rural communities issues that might be totally separated in urban areas are very interrelated.

Establish linkages with other agencies. Since these agencies are frequently controlled by men, the woman (particularly if she is new to the community) will not have the benefit of the "old boys" club. Since the woman will need a different framework to operate from, it may be helpful to consider "social exchange" theory. Rather than developing support through friendship, the woman manager might develop relationships by providing resources or expertise to male managers. As male managers see it to their benefit to exchange support, the barriers will be decreased. If this exchange relation becomes valuable to the male manager there is the possibility that his social circle will provide a potential source of support.

On a personal level it is important for the woman to build a support system. While continuing to develop social skills to deal with the male establishment, it is important that the woman also develop a personal network to provide the nurturing and caring necessary for her own ego development and security. The most effective antidote to organizational or professional battering is a personal support system that provides unconditional positive regard at the end of a long hard day. One rural professional manager suggested that since she was unable to find other professional women who understood her frustration without running her telephone bill to gargantuan proportions, she had developed the habit of finding solace in the refrigerator and had managed to add ten pounds per year to her original weight of 110 lbs. Her five foot frame must now carry 170 lbs. Clearly, we would not suggest eating as solace. But this example does illustrate both the importance and the difficulty of building the necessary support networks.

Not surprisingly, women in professional-managerial positions in rural areas have tended to meet with less resistance the closer the positions they take parallel the farm-wife role in rural agricultural areas. However this is a very limited role, and as a result of this inability to move upward, the role isolation is compounded by the frustration of limited upward mobility.

As socialization and learning are ongoing processes, there is potential for change within the social circles that limit these roles that women hold. While dealing with this problem on a societal level is a life time process, we contend on an individual level a woman can maximize her span of control through the strategies we have identified. Granted these may be only pebbles with which to fight the giant, i.e., the social context in which rural professional women must operate. We have not addressed other equally important interventions such as policy change and networking. This is a limited view of what can be done but hopefully one to which women can relate.

REFERENCES

1. Epstein, 1970; Roni, 1971; Henning and Jardin, 1976.
2. Matina Horner, "Fail: Bright Women," *Psychology Today* 3, no. 6 (1969).
3. Zaniecki, quoted by Helena Lopata in *Occupation Housewife* (Oxford University Press, 1971).
4. Jo Freeman, "The Building of the Gilded Cage," in *Crisis in American Institutions,* 4th ed., ed. Skolnick and Currie (Boston: Little, Brown, and Co., 1978).
5. Peter Berger and Brigitte Berger, *Sociology: A Biographical Approach* (New York: Basic Books, 1972).
6. Helena Lopata, *Occupation Housewife,* 31–32.

The Rowley and Macht paper looks at structural impediments for rural women. Joan E. Cummings analyzes the position of women from a radical perspective. She suggests that sexism is a problem within the profession as well as a problem the profession needs to address. In addition to delineating the structural causes of sexism she identifies some strategy for social change.

For a review of the radical perspective see Chapter 2.

The Parameters of Sexism in Social Work*

JOAN E. CUMMINGS

Where might we begin to seek a vantage point from which the sexist realities just described become visible without distortion? Probably the most central fact of our data needing interpretation is that within and beyond social work there is both a dominant sex and a dominant form of labor which has been appropriated by the dominant sex. A starting point for our theoretical discussion, then, is with the social division of labor into men's work and women's work; with the domination of the former over the latter; and with the societal sources of both. Our vantage point will need to encompass the complexities of these phenomena.

Conceived in its most elementary form, the sexual division of labor has assigned the socially necessary work of providing for society's material needs (the productive sphere) to men; and the equally socially necessary work of providing for its own continuation through the bearing and rearing of chil-

* "Sexism in Social Work" *Catalyst* no. 8, 1980. Cummings' theory is based on data collected from the Atlantic Social Service Project funded by the Welfare Research Program, National Welfare Grants, Social Service Programs Branch, Health and Welfare, Canada. Dr. Cummings is a professor of Social Work at the Maritime School of Social Work, Dalhousie University, Halifax, Nova Scotia, Canada.

dren (the reproductive sphere) to women. While throughout history, women have always been held primarily responsible for child rearing, prior to the advance of industrial capitalism they had been central to production as well. It was not until the emergence of a factory system, which centralized and so sharply separated production from the home, that women as a group were consigned to the reproductive sphere, and denied a place in the mainstream of production. Indeed this separation of production and reproduction was so complete that each sphere became dominated by a set of institutional characteristics antithetic to those of the other. Angela Miles has called these the separative masculine and integrative feminine principles respectively, as they have come to embody the prototypes of male and female character structure. (8) As such, they provide a double standard for judging male and female behavior which has functioned not only to reinforce separation between the two spheres, but to perpetuate male domination in both.(9)

There is little dispute among theorists of any persuasion that a highly systematic sexual division of labor does in fact exist. The debate has been about the origin of this; and about how one sex and one form of labor came to so totally dominate the other. Theoretical explanations have generally fallen into three categories: the biological, the cultural, and the economic. Because of the very different assumptions on which they are predicated, the three have spawned quite different conclusions and directions for action.

It is not so long ago that biological theories occupied a position of unchallenged centrality.(10) Men, the physically stronger sex, were better equipped to meet the harsh and competitive demands of material production. Women alone, on the other hand, could bear children. Further, while limited by their biological functions (menstruating, gestation, and lactation), they were nonetheless highly suited to providing the intimacy and compassionate components essential to the nurturing role. In potent justification of woman's consignment to reproduction, then, the biological theorists argued that the division of labor was, after all, a "natural" one, and must therefore be accepted.

Cultural theories have buttressed and even largely replaced biological ones.(11) Children are socialized from early infancy to internalize a culture which not only exaggerates the differences between the sexes, but which defines appropriate male and female behavior (and the values to be attached to them) on the basis of these exaggerations. The social division of labor continues because we believe that it is men's basic responsibility to provide through material production, and women's to support and nurture. If beliefs and attitudes could be changed, presumably through reeducative strategies, the behaviors would follow and change would occur. When women and men truly believe themselves equal, then women will seek and be allowed full participation in production, and men in nurturing. While the cultural theories have persuasive aspects, they fail completely to address some basic issues. They do not explain, for example, why the division of labor came about in the first place; why socially necessary reproductive labor came to no longer qualify as "real" work; and especially why women have so long accepted their subjugation in the reproductive sphere, and their marginalization from the world of "real" work.

Theorists working in a Marxist tradition have come closer to dealing directly with the latter questions.(12) Marx and Engels broke sharply with not only the biological explanations, but with a central assumption held by all theorists preceding them. This was that social life is an outgrowth of individual life and traits. Social inequalities were to be explained on the basis of inequalities among individuals with respect to particular capacities, character, orientation, and other human attributes. Marx and Engels argued instead that social life, as well as individual character and consciousness, is fundamentally determined by the material conditions under which people must labor to provide for their sustenance and survival. It was their view that inequalities arise from the fact that some people dominate others, thereby preventing them from gaining access to control over the means and fruits of production. They charged that in providing erroneous alternative rationalities, political theory had functioned historically not only to justify inequalities, but to obscure the material conditions giving rise to them. They undertook to provide a true account of the dialectical processes through which social forms arise and change. They undertook as well to offer a positive vision of future social organization under changed relations of production.(13)

That Marx and Engels did take enormous strides towards exposing the oppressive nature of woman's place in society is undeniable. Besides opening the way to recognizing the social origin and material basis of such oppression, and the ideological role of theory in obscuring these, they developed a theory of individual and collective consciousness which has made it possible to conceive and continue to develop a strategy of liberation through collective action. All of these contributions are of direct relevance to the current analysis.(14)

Despite their major contribution, however, Marx and Engels cannot be said to have been free of the very error with which they charged their fellow political theorists. While on the one hand they were able to take up the vantage point of those engaged in wage labor, and thereby to place in working-class hands a strategy which allows them to remain subjects in their own action, they were clearly less capable of comprehending the vantage point of women. By accepting the male definition of "real" work as that which has an exchange value, they forced women in the wake of their enormous influence and despite their considerable compassion, to continue to comprehend female experience through a framework which made invisible and fragmented female reality. In conceiving class inequality, class consciousness and class liberation in the context of the relations of production, without a central focus on the relations of reproduction, Marx and Engels condemned women as a group to a marginal position in that strategy; to somehow bending our experience once more to fit the male perspective.

Several feminists working in a Marxist tradition have argued that both woman's oppression and her consciousness have been fundamentally determined by her relationship to reproduction, rather than by her relationship to production.(15) This is true not only for women engaged solely in reproductive labor, but for those engaged in production as well. Less clearly spelled out is the nature and source of the existing relationship between production and reproduction—the domination of one by the other, and the dynamic of male dominance in both spheres. This, it seems to me, is a theoretical issue central to explaining the specific phenomena described earlier, and to conceiving a strategy for women in social work which acknowledges the real substructure of sexism within the profession. The recent works of both Lorenne Clark and Angela Miles have been particularly helpful in this respect.

In her highly persuasive critique of Marx and Engels, Lorenne has pointed to what she considers the most significant faults in Marxist and neo-Marxist theory.(16) They have failed to comprehend fully and unambiguously that not only the relations of production, but those of reproduction as well, are social and conventional rather than "natural."(17) Accepting the basic Marxist premise that it was the emergence of private property which provided the material basis for both class and sexist society, she criticizes Marxism for confusing the relationship between the two. They viewed sexism as superstructural; as helpful in maintaining but not essential to the development and maintenance of class society. She argues, however, that it was (and is) not just a system of private property, but a system of private property under exclusively male control which makes up the specific character of the productive sphere. By the time capitalism began to flourish, women as a group had already been marginalized by men as a group from any form of "real" work, and therefore been barred access to private property in the form of control over the productive surplus. Their consignment to the reproductive sphere, therefore, as well as their conversion into a form of private property available for the ownership of men, was and is *essential* to the maintenance of exclusively male control over the surplus of production. Sexism, then, is a part of the substructure on which this specific character of the productive sphere depends. Following on this reasoning, Lorenne argues that women were in fact the first class (even within a Marxist definition of the term) though Marx and Engels did not acknowledge this. The implication of this conclusion is that contrary to the predictions of substantive Marxism, sexism will not disappear with the elimination of class society. Indeed women cannot be the equals of men in relation to control over production until men are equals of women in relation to the responsibilities of reproduction.(18)

Angela Miles has carried this same conclusion one step further. In her view the dynamic for progressive change resides in the gradually changing relationship between reproduction and production. The former is becoming increasingly important vis-a-vis the latter; and there is mounting pressure toward reintegration of the two spheres, as embodied in a heightened demand for a more human and less alienated existence. On the basis of her historical analysis, Angela has concluded that society is ripe for (i.e., now has the material basis to support) efforts that foster and even accelerate the growth of the integrative feminine principle; and particularly for its application to production. This is an important key to progressive change. She explicitly rejects as non-viable a strategy which would imply pressure group tactics directed merely at being let into existing definitions of humanity based on the separative principle, or into existing definitons of "real" work.(19)

Returning now briefly to the particular sexist phenomena described earlier, what have these notions about biology, culture, and economics, to do with our analysis and strategy formulation? They do, I think, provide a four-pronged framework for thought and action which acknowledges both the complexities and the political nature of the struggle involved. To recapitulate briefly the four basic elements, they include: (1) a pervasive and enduring sexual division of labor which, by means of the double standard it has generated, has assigned greater value to men and to their "real" work; (2) a cultural mechanism which recreates and then justifies in the everyday lives of individual women, this exploitative pattern of social organization; (3) an individual and collective female consciousness rooted in enforced consignment to and domination within the reproductive sphere; and (4) a dialectic struggle between the sexes, in which potent economic forces have thrown their weight on the side of the masculine separative principle (and the prototypical male character structure), but in which the stark violations of humanity inherent in the overdevelopment of this principle have created a dynamic shift toward reemergence of the integrative feminine principle. With these basic ingredients of the political strugle identified, then, we can now reflect more specifically on the realities as well as on the change potential within social work.

In light of the sexual division of labor and its double standard, the differential pay, structural location, and job content of women and men in social work make sense. The profession appears to have incorporated quite directly the male definition of what constitutes "real" work; and what is merely supportive of "real" work but not an integral part of it. Administration, supervision, staff training, policy analysis and research all involve, directly or indirectly, control not only over other forms of labor, but also over those performing it. They qualify therefore, as the "real" work that gets paid and valued more. As the more valuable form of work, they are the prerogative of the dominant and more valued sex. Direct practice, on the other hand, involving largely helping and caring interpersonal relationships with people who are in a dependent state, qualifies instead as the supportive work which is paid and valued less. Women are fully participant in this work, but it is carried out mainly under the control of men.

In social work as elsewhere, the double standard functions to maintain the separation between "real" and supportive work. Embodied in the separative masculine and integrative feminine principles, the double standard exerts pressure to keep social work women in their "place" and to draw men towards theirs. Women who abdicate their traditional professional roles to take up "real" work typically find that they must somehow overcome their "intruder" status. They must establish their legitimacy by demonstrating not only the attributes embodied in the integrative feminine principle (i.e. that they are not masculine) but also a job competency significantly beyond that ordinarily required of men, whose legitimacy is assumed.

The cultural mechanism through which the sexual division of labor finds concrete expression in our daily lives, and through which that expression is justified and thereby reinforced, will vary somewhat from one specific context to another. In its essence, however, it will involve those organizational forms which participate most significantly in discharging five functions: (1) communicating organizational norms and evaluative criteria; (2) defining the work and deploying people to it; (3) establishing control over the organization's resources; (4) allocating organizational rewards; and (5) justifying the practices of the organization. It would clearly be impossible in this paper to undertake a detailed analysis or even an inventory of these structures within social work. A few illustrative ones, however, will hopefully be helpful in clarifying what types of structures are typically participant in giving expression to the sexual division of labor in an organizational context. From the vantage point of social work practice, one might point to such structures as the following: recruitment and promotion criteria and practices which reserve the higher paying and more prestigious jobs for those best schooled in the separative principle (often symbolized by an overreliance on credentials assumed to be at least a necessary, and often a sufficient condition for performance of the "expert" role); or formal job definitions which characteristically fragment the implementation of service plans with clients (direct practice) from their formulation and control (administration, supervision and so forth); or salary scales which characteristically provide very limited career ladders for direct practitioners, thereby limiting the rewards they can claim while in that role, however well they perform it; or the application through service practices of diagnostic and outcome criteria which assume traditional roles for women, and which pathologize, penalize, and stigmatize women clients who refuse to conform to these traditional roles; and so forth.

From the vantage point of social work education, the structural communication of sexism is no less striking. Classic among curriculum structures is the fragmentation of classroom work (which is typically oriented to the turning out of tangible products) from field work, particularly that of direct practice students (which is typically oriented to direct interpersonal engagement with clients in a service context). Even within classroom activity itself, there is a consistent tendency to package courses in such a way as to fragment content pertinent to "real" work from the pertinent to people-facilitation through interpersonal engagement (direct methodology courses). Even more striking is the content of theory courses characteristically used in social work education. The theories given to students to guide their practice, and on which are based the diagnostic and outcome criteria they will later enforce in their jobs, have almost universally been borrowed from other disciplines such as psychiatry, psychology, sociology, economics, etc., where they have been developed by men out of a male perspective derived from male experience. They are often highly discriminatory to women, assuming for them the traditional role to which men have consigned them, and providing the pathologizing concepts and conceptual categories which justify a deviant status for non-conforming women. These theories, like those which Marx and Engels challenged, are potent instruments in the concealment and perpetuation of the domination of women by men within and beyond social work education and practice.

Organizational structures within social work education are generally complementary to curriculum structures. Some are perhaps even more illustrative as structural repositories of sexism. Classic are the tenure and promotion structures through which are allocated the formal rewards of the system. Tenure criteria almost universally favor faculty whose research and publication record is impressive, even when their teaching record is not. Outstanding teachers, on the other hand, if they have had to apply their energies to facilitation of student learning without sufficient opportunity for concentration on research and publication (though they may have freed others to do so), stand typically at risk when it comes time to jump the tenure and promotion hoops. The burden of proof rests heavy upon those (and they are often women) whose primary contribution has been the people-facilitation which does not count as "real" work. And finally, the organizational arrangements by which faculty and students in most social work schools sort themselves into working groups (usually in streams or other ways that reflect some version of the split between direct practice and "real" work) are direct expressions of the sexual division of labor. Indeed this streaming is frequently accompanied by competition between the streams for legitimacy, power and prestige. Many of these struggles are, in their essence, sexual struggles.

The existence of structural forms which justify and bring the sexual division of labor into our day-to-day interactions is a necessary, but not a sufficient condition for its survival. An individual consciousness which has internalized the justificatory ideology, and a collective consciousness which reinforces it, are also necessary. In Margaret Adams' view, the individual character structure as well as the collective consciousness of social work women has typically tended to embody an overemphasis on some of the integrative feminine principle to the exclusion of a functional balance with separative attributes: namely an emphasis on other-directedness which precludes sufficient attention to self; a submissiveness which stifles assertive action; an emphasis on the intuitive and emotional which inhibits analysis; and a personal engagement in other people's experiences which acts as a blinder to objective conditions. She refers to this internalization of cultural expectations as the "Compassion Trap." She considers it to be one of the most powerful forces inhibiting the ability and willingness of social work women to act decisively upon the structures they experience.

> The main target of my concern is the pervasive belief amounting almost to an article of faith that Woman's primary and most valuable social function is to provide the tender and compassionate components of life . . . Woman's supposed social strengths have been gradually turned to her disadvantage, and now are used to blunt her protest and to bar her escape from the confused role that their exclusive exercise has forced upon her. Women in social work have been restrained from uncompromising or threatening action on their own behalf, for fear of negative repercussions on other individuals towards whom they stand in a protective role. Because of their ambiguous status . . . they find it very tempting to be designated the person or group relied upon to smooth away difficulties and reconcile warring elements; and to remain the willing repository for everybody else's unsolved problems.(20)

The female tendency to shrink from uncompromising action came out quite strikingly when Atlantic social work students were asked their views on what approaches to achieving change they would consider legitimate in extreme circumstances (i.e., when other means had already been tried and failed). Male and female responses showed predictable differences. Table 10 gives the relative frequency with which male and female students indicated that they would consider each approach legitimate. Male students more frequently than females defined as legitimate every measure listed.

The dialectical nature of the sexual struggle has thus far defined and maintained differential access to control, influence and reward for women and men. It is thus within a discriminatory power structure that the political struggle must be played out. As more women achieve greater consciousness, however, of the contradictions between our ascribed and our felt worth, we will be less willing to be ruled by the existing structures. What forces will be called in to play by our attempts to escape our bondage? It is important to look at what the forces working against change are and where they derive their power.

It is easy to confuse two levels of vested interest that might be threatened by the change efforts of women in social work. At one level, any significant challenge to the existing male-dominated definitions

Table 10 Beliefs of Male and Female Students About What Selected Ways to Achieve Change Would be Legitimate in Extreme Circumstances

N = 166 Means in Extreme	% Male	% Female	% Total
Using group social pressure to change attitudes	85.7	75.8	78.3
Taking the problem to the political arena	73.8	54.8	59.6
Taking the problem to the news media	71.4	58.1	61.4
Informing clients of conflicts internal to the agency	47.6	41.9	43.4
Defying, ignoring or circumventing agency policy	42.9	14.5	21.7
Work stoppage	38.1	18.5	23.5

of humanity and of "real" work, might be threatening to most men. At least, such redefinitions would eliminate the competitive advantage they enjoy on the basis of superior schooling in the now prevailing norms, but beyond this level of immediate vested interest, there would be those men who, despite their competitive advantage (and perhaps because of it), will have experienced an oppression different from, but analogous to our own. There is within the grasp of these men a consciousness of common interest with us—a desire to escape from social definitions that inhibit, distort, and contain individual potential. In a political struggle, these men and we could pursue common goals.

By men whose consciousness does not pose fundamental contradictions between their own individual needs and the external structures, the threat would likely be seen as greater. From them can be expected the more powerful resistance to our change efforts. But their power is not in themselves. It lies in their greater containment by and appeal to the culturally prescribed role stereotypes that define greater worth and a privileged status for men; and in their ability to reawaken in us the vestiges of our own internalized prisons constructed of these same definitions. More fundamentally, their power lies in an appeal to higher and higher levels of institutional and societal power for their own legitimation and for our delegitimation. At the pinnacle of this power are those men whose fundamental economic interests, supported by the means to market them, are tied up in maintaining the sexual division of labor and thereby their own control over the productive surplus. When we vigorously resist the sexist behaviors of men in our midst, we are recognizing them as the institutional instruments of these powerful vested interests. In the final analysis, however, even their power depends on our willingness to continue playing the roles they have assigned to us, and on our failure to demand a definition not only of "real" work but out of humanity itself within which we and they stand as equals.

SOME THOUGHTS ON STRATEGY

By now it will be apparent that I view sexism as a highly complex phenomenon; one which grips us in a strangle hold in our concrete daily realities, but which derives the strength of its grip in realities seemingly far removed from our own. I have no simple recipe for change. So I will try only to outline very briefly some of what I think are important parts of the change process.

Like the problem itself, our solutions must touch the myriad dimensions in which sexism is manifest: our concrete realities; our cultural and internalized consciousness about them; and the societal and institutional power structures within which the dialectic between the sexes is played out. The solutions cannot imply a linear change process. Whatever action we may undertake will need to recognize the organic nature of the multi-dimensional problem; and we will need to know that intervention in any one dimension will likely stimulate reaction beyond its immediate target.

Let me start with some comments about building our consciousness. Those of us who are living the contradictions of sexist realities bear, I think, a very special responsibility to understand them; to locate the common bondage we experience as women, whatever our differences might be in other respects. Beyond this, I believe, we need to grasp the similarity of our bondage with that which is being experienced by people bearing other devalued labels; by Blacks and Indians, by the handicapped, and by many men. For all of us, the bondage consists in its essence of our being forced to live realities that have been first created and then defined for us by others; defined in ways that exclude us from full participation, and from deriving equitable benefits from both the productive and reproductive spheres of society.

I believe that this consciousness-building process entails two quite distinct stages. In the first stage, we women need to purge our consciousness of the images and labels that strip us of our equality, identity, and dignity as human beings. This, I think, we need to do together, and without men. I say without men only because I believe the habits of our heritage as men and women are so ingrained in our day-to-day interactive patterns that the reality of what would ensue in their presence would almost inevitably reinforce rather than purge the old images. It is when we have gained the strength to be consciously self-defining as women that we can look beyond our differences to what we have in common with men.

It is in the second stage of our consciousness building that we will, I think, meet our mightiest challenges. Here we will need to comprehend and confront the most powerful forces of inaction; the fragmentation of consciousness resulting from society's complex and intricate labeling system. By means of this labeling system, we are persuaded to become instruments of each other's bondage and devaluation, even when we share a reality and a partial consciousness of it. This stage, then, will undoubtedly provide the acid test of our capacity to respect and tolerate our real differences while seeing beyond the images of difference that divide us. We will need to locate our common interests.

In more concrete terms, and often before we feel ready to do so, we are called upon to take action in relation to our unequal realities. Like consciousness, and in dialectical relationship to it, action also moves in uneven stages. There are two basic kinds of action, both of which are essential. The first involves resistive action; a refusal to participate any longer in playing out the images that have been defined for us. The particular priority targets for resistive action in our environment may well vary from one social work school to another, or from one agency to another. What is important is that the choice of targets be rooted in the experiences and consciousness of those who will undertake the resistance. We must together locate in our particular context the specific structures which are most significantly involved in communicating sexism. Out of the process of locating these structures, priority targets can be set. Whatever is chosen, two conditions need to be met. First, the scrutiny of structures and criteria must be vigilant and rigorous, and the exposure of sexist bias thorough and direct. Secondly, action needs group sanction to arise out of group consciousness and support. To whatever degree resistive action is successful in rooting out and confronting sexist structures and practices—whether these involve pay checks, work assignments, the shape of our organizational service, and curriculum structures, the content of our diagnostic and methodological tools—to that same degree the individuals involved in the resistive action are likely to find themselves subject to an activated cultural press. This will be wielded by the threatened power structure and will seek to fragment and invalidate whatever collective consciousness has been achieved. Unless group consciousness and support afford an alternative to the asylum previously provided by submission to the demands of the label, individuals will be sorely tempted to retreat to the shelter of the stereotype, however cramped the space inside it.

Resistive action, then, is necessary. It is by itself, however, not sufficient. Creative integrative action is required as well to provide the alternatives; to replace sexist structures with egalitarian and growth enhancing ones. It is in the concept of creative integrative action that we encounter must fully the complexity of the sexist phenomenon. Our schools and agencies host but a small fraction of the concrete realities wherein sexism affects each one of us. Creative action, then, requires not only that we act upon the many faces of sexism wherever we may find them, but that we build bridges to those who, through social manipulations comparable to sexism, are forced like us to live realities of economic and social exclusion.

The significant challenge to each of us as individuals, I think, is to position ourselves with respect to both resistive and creative integrative action; to determine in what arenas we can best pursue our individual and collective change goals; and then to find the courage to take the risks inherent in positive action.

NOTES

8. According to Angela's historical analysis, there has been a tendency over many thousands of years to associate particular characteristics with men, and their antitheses with women. The core distinction has been in relation to the relationship of each gender with nature. Women have typically been associated with harmony with nature; men have tended to define humanity, however, in terms of the degree of separation from nature (transcendence over it). Her choice of the terms "separative" and "integrative" are based on these enduring associations of characteristics with one sex or the other. She uses the separative masculine and integrative feminine principles as a structural metaphor to help situate the processes of change in late capitalism (and Marxist analyses of them) in their broadest historical context.

The individual and institutional characteristics which have come to dominate production under capitalism, and which now symbolize masculinity and make up the prototype of the male character structure include individualism and pursuit of self-interest, aggressiveness, fragmentation, emphasis on the analytical, objectification of experience, orientation to the material, artificiality (man-made), hierarchical relationships, and specialization. It is these institutional characteristics which Angela has defined as the separate principle. The antithetic characteristics which have been dominant in the reproductive sphere, and which now have come to be the prototype of femininity and the female character structure include an emphasis on the collective, other-directedness or nurturing, submissiveness, integration, intuitiveness and affectivity, personalization of experience, orientation to the spiritual, natural, democratic relationships, and holistic synthesis. Miles has graced historically the assendency of the separative principle and the subjugation of the reproductive sphere to the demands of production and the separative principle. Indeed the history of civilization is the history of this ascendency, with separative principle domination reaching its height with the emergence of simple labor power. See Angela Miles, *The Politics of Feminist Radicalism: A Study in Integrative Feminism.* Doctoral Dissertation submitted to the Ontario Institute for Studies in Education and the Department of Political Science, University of Toronto, 1979.

9. In her critique of current radical feminism, Angela has analyzed the forces which have unleased the separative masculine principle, and constrained the integrative feminine principle over the course of civilization, and particularly in late capitalist society. By the time capitalism had moved to the emergence of simple labor power the separation of man from nature had become virtually complete; "and except for temporary infusions of the feminine principle, production had come to dominate over reproduction; aggression over nurturing; competiton over cooperation; instrumental over affective; individual over collective; hierarchical over consensual; partial over holistic; rational over intuitive; ends over means." *Ibid.,* p. 19.

10. Two sources in which there are reviews and critiques of the biological theories and of empirical, historical and cross-cultural research relevant to them are: Naomi Weisstein, "Psychology Constructs the Female," in *Woman in Sexist Society,* edited by Vivian Gornick and Barbara K. Moran, (New York: Basic Books Inc., 1971), pp. 133–144; also Pat and Hugh Armstrong, *The Double Ghetto,* pp.98–110.

11. There is an almost inexhaustible supply of literature on the role of culture in sex role stereotyping. Some sources which I have found quite useful because they are succinct, and because the summarize and critique are: Pat and Hugh Armstrong, *ibid.,* pp.111–132; Alice Russel Hochschild, "The Sociology of Feelings and Emotions: Selected Positions," in *Another Voice,* edited by Marcia Millman and Rosabeth Moss Kanter. (New York: Anchor Books, 1975), pp. 280–377; and Vivian Gornick and Barbara K. Moran, eds., Part II, "Woman is Made, Not Born", *ibid.,* pp. 133–418. The latter source contains a collection of twelve articles examining the subjects in different perspectives. Together they make a very good cross section of material on the role and impact of culture, as purveyed through a variety of social institutions.

12. Again, the sources of information on this subject are many. However, I have, in developing this article, relied more extensively on the following: Peggy Morton, "Women's Work is Never Done," in *Women Unite* (Toronto: Canadian Women's Educational Press, 1972) pp. 46–68; Margaret Benston, "The Political Economy of Women's Liberation," in *Women in a Man-made World,* edited by Norma Glazer-Melbin and Helen Waehrer (Chicago: Rand McNally, 1972), pp. 119–128; Charnie Guettel, *Marxism and Feminism* (Toronto: Canadian Women's Educational Press, 1974); and Pat and Hugh Armstrong, *The Double Ghetto,* pp. 133–175.

13. Lorenne Clark has referred to these two separate aspects of Marxism as "methodological Marxism" and "substantive Marxism." the former she defines as essentially backward looking, and the latter as essentially forward looking. She indicates that her point in making this distinction is to "separate those aspects of Marxism which are essentially concerned with describing both the real and alleged processes of historical change, and the real and alleged functions of political theory; from those aspects of Marxism which offer a positive account of future social organization under changed relations of production." See "A Marxist-Feminist Critique of Marx and Engels" a paper presented at the annual meeting of the Learned Societies, Saskatoon, June 1979, (see especially pp. 1–2, 4, and footnote 1, page 1), (mimeo).

14. Marx and Engels defined Woman's role in relation to production as that of reserve pool of labor, available to be brought into the productive labor market (and thereby into the class structure) when it is in the interests of the dominant class to do so. Marxist strategy for women was therefore essentially to bring thm into equality with men in the productive sphere. Methodological Marxism is a description of how people are organized and determined within a structure of *productive relations.* Lorenne Clark, *ibid.,* p. 12.

15. See, for example, Peggy Morton, Women Unite; Margaret Benston, *Political Economy;* and Maria Rosa Della Costa, *The Power of Women and the Subversion of the Community* (Bristol: Falling Wall Press, 1972).

16. Lorenne Clark has identified many of the inconsistencies within Marxist theory respecting women. First, Marxism defines as "labor" the expenditure of labor power which has an exchange value within the sphere of productive relations. Thus reproductive labor does not qualify as a

form of productive labor, though Marx and Engels are ambiguous on this. Several aspects of Marxism reinforce the notion that reproductive labor is not productive labor. For one thing, the fact that women in reproductive labor are considered a reserve pool of labor, and available to be drawn into productive labor, suggests that they are not already engaged in it. Secondly, the fact that women in traditional roles have no class position of their own, deriving it only from fathers and husbands who are engaged in productive labor, is also suggestive that they are not engaged in productive labor. Yet, despite the apparent contradiction in doing so, Marx and Engels do consistently refer to reproduction as a form of production. It is a form, however, which leads only indirectly to the production of surplus value; and is remunerated only indirectly through the earnings of fathers or husbands who are specifically related to production. But if reproduction is a form of production, Clark argues, then why do not reproductive laborers have a class position in their own right? And if they have a class position in their own right as reproductive laborers, why are not all women engaged in reproductive labor of the same class? These ambiguities lead to serious consequences for the ability of Marxist theory not only to analyze women in the reproductive sphere, but to project how sexism will be eliminated. Marx and Engels viewed sexism as superstructural. It will disappear, that is, with changed relations of production. But if women are not engaged in pro-duction and are simply available as a reserve pool to be brought into the productive sphere, why should it be expected that changed relations of production will or even might bring about the elimination of sexual inequality?

A second major criticism advanced by Lorenne, then, is of the invisibility of women within Marxist theory. Because Marx and Engels developed their theory and their strategy in the context of production, persons who play no role in the relations of production are invisible an immune to analysis *within that structure*. Because women have historically been denied access to the productive labor market, and because reproductive labor has been extracted from women as unpaid labor, women and reproductive labor are invisible within the basic framework of Marxist analysis. See Lorenne Clark.

17. In her paper Lorenne has documented a variety of places in *Capital.* in *The German Ideology,* and in *The Origin of the Family* where Marx and Engels have at best taken only a partially social view of the relations of reproduction. They have quite specifically and repeatedly refered to the division of labor as a "natural" one. It is particularly in this respect that Marxist theory is vulnerable to the same criticisms as were levelled against other political theorists. See Clark, *A Marxist-Feminist Critique of Marx and Engels.*

18. Lorenne Clark, *ibid.,* p. 8.

19. In pursuing her study of *The Politics of Feminist Radicalism,* Angela makes the assumption that such radical politics cannot be understood only in the context of pressure at times of social disintegration. Instead they need to be seen as a response to both pressure and the opportunities that come with social change. Her analysis therefore studies both the pressure and the opportunities that underpin radical feminism. Within her framework, the pressures derive from woman's unique relationship to production. The opportunities however derive not just from women's entry into the work force, but more significantly from a deep shift in the relationship between production and reproduction. She argues that there has been a marked increase in the importance of production vis-a-vis reproduction in recent years, and an accompanying decrease in the distinctness of the two spheres. It is these opportunities which have provided the impetus for women not only to seek greater equality with men in the traditionally male productive sphere, but also to assert the value of traditionally female spheres and characteristics. She identifies as the progressive aspects of feminism, therefore, those which fundamentally challenge the established notions of humanity that tend to exclude traditionally female activities and characteristics. It is on this basis that she rejects the liberal approach which would involve pressure group tactics to be let into established definitions of "Man."

20. See "The Compassion Trap," in *Women in Sexist Society,* edited by Vivian Gornick and Barbara K. Moran, pp. 402, 405.

For reasons of space only the theoretical and strategy sections of Cummings' paper have been reproduced; her actual text included a detailed report of empirical trends in data obtained from a large sample of social work employees, faculty, and students in the four Atlantic provinces of Canada. There was a strikingly pervasive tendency for female social service employees at all organizational levels and across all job categories to be paid less than their male counterparts. There exists a marked hierarchy of functions within social-work organizations, with much higher value (expressed in salaries) placed on "male" roles (administration, supervision, policy analysis, staff-training, planning, and research) than on "female" roles (caregiving, counseling, case management and concrete service-giving). Very few women occupied "male" roles and their salaries reflected only marginally the higher value placed on those roles. While female social work students significantly outnumbered men in social work educational institutions, a disproportionately large percentage of them were concentrated at the lower program levels (technical and undergraduate). Female students received significantly less financial assistance to undertake study than male students; the primary source of income for female students was student loans, while male students more often benefited from government bursaries, reimbursement of tuition by agencies, and sponsored educational leave. Male social work faculty tended to be concentrated at the higher academic ranks and women at the lower ones. Female social work students tended to be concentrated in curriculum areas preparatory to the less valued practice roles, where they were taught almost exclusively by men.

These trends led Professor Cummings to select particular theoretical formulations. She made a deliberate attempt to build theory and strategy to "fit" the real experiences of the social work women. Her starting point was thus experience rather than the existing dominant theory (much of which has incorporated essentially male perspectives) that has functioned to filter out rather than reflect the reality of women.

Summary

Today the assumptions about women's work being extracurricular activity have been widely challenged. Few women have the luxury of working simply for enjoyment. Most women work to support their children either as a single parent or as an essential economic contributor to a two parent family. Although women frequently take temporary jobs, this tends not to be by choice. Most women want and need jobs in the primary labor force that provide a decent income, fringe benefits, and job security.

Individual social workers and the profession itself can become involved in combatting sexism on many levels. The National Association of Social Workers sponsored a national conference "Social Work Practice in Sexist Society" in 1982. In 1983, the Association decided to hold these conferences on a regional level to facilitate greater attendance. The Council on Social Work Education has set up a Commission on Women's Issues. As practitioners it is important to support professional associations in these efforts. In addition to national efforts many social workers are in a position to develop resources on a local level that can empower women. Some social workers have been active in developing rape crisis centers, spouse abuse shelters, day care centers, and job opportunities for women. The problems women face (particularly poor women) are myriad. It is important that the ubiquitousness of the problem does not immobilize individual workers. Each service or each opportunity a social worker is able to develop for women decreases the powerlessness of the women served.

References

1. An anonymous response to an evaluation questionnaire. Study conducted by Mary Macht for the School of Social Work, University of Wisconsin, Madison, April 1978.
2. Elaine Norman and Arlene Mancuso, *Women's Issues and Social Work Practice* (Itasca, Ill.: Peacock, 1980), 3.
3. US Bureau of the Census statistics cited in *The World Almanac and Book of Facts 1982* (New York: Newspaper Enterprise Association, 1981), 250.
4. Diana Di Nitto and Thomas Dye, *Social Welfare Politics and Public Policy* (Englewood Cliffs, N.J.: Prentice-Hall, 1983), 20.

CHAPTER TWENTY

The Elderly

"We who are old know that age is more than a disability. It is an intense and varied experience almost beyond our capacity at times, but something to be carried high."[1]

Gerontology is a growth area for social work. See Chapter 1.

"America's population is aging," begins a U.S. Office of Management and Budget report.[2] Now about 11 percent of the population is 65 and over, a figure expected to double in the next 60 to 70 years. Increasing life expectancies, falling birthrates, and aging "baby boomers" are all contributing to the growing attention to services (both public and private) needed by the elderly. Gerontology, the study of the aging process and its effects, is a relatively new multidisciplinary endeavor, marked by the founding of the Gerontological Society in 1945. In 1960 the National Council on Aging was established. It was intended to become "a central national resource that works with and through other organizations to develop interest in work with older people and to design methods that can be used in programs designed to meet their varied needs."[3]

Subsequent White House Conferences on Aging have explored the role of federal involvement, legislative and policy needs, and the coordination of services across the public and private sector. The elderly have also made substantial efforts at organizing themselves to have an impact on services to meet their needs. The major organizations for the elderly include the American Association of Retired Persons (AARP), the National Retired Teachers Association (NRTA), the Gray Panthers, the National Association of Retired Federal Employees, the National Caucus on the Black Aged, and the National Council of Senior Citizens.

The major pieces of federal legislation instrumental to meeting the needs of the elderly are the 1935 Social Security Act and its subsequent amendments, particularly the Older Americans Act (1965). The Older Americans Act (frequently amended) established the Administration of Aging, through which federal funds became available through states to local governments and local agencies for assistance in the planning, development, and coordination of service programs. It also has provided for the development of services needed to bridge gaps left by Social Security, Supplemental Security Income, Medicare, and Medical Assistance, and those agencies providing elder-oriented goods and services.[4]

Social work has had substantial involvement in developing programs and delivering services to the elderly, particularly at the local level. Two case examples illustrate the kinds of work social workers do to assure a continuum of care and choice for the elderly and the various stages of program development. The first example is a generalist approach to needs assessment and program planning. The second is an example of actual program implementation. Both case examples presented here address a critical issue—how can we provide care for the elderly with current economic constraints?

Generalist Practice in a Community Setting

The social worker was contacted by the director of the community retirement center to provide program planning consultation. The director felt that the equipment and facilities of his nursing home could and should be made available to chronically impaired in the community who could use some of the services but did not require twenty-four hour care. Since a new program in the community might disrupt interorganizational relationships as its domain developed, the director felt it was important to develop this project with community involvement and commitment. Successful implementation of the program required community support. One way to increase community support was to include the professionals in the aging network in program development. The vehicle to facilitate this "ground floor" involvement was a needs assessment of the elderly in the community. The contract between the program director and the social worker was to conduct a needs assessment which accurately reflected the community need and was conducive to program development. Practice principles are evident throughout this case.

PROBLEM IDENTIFICATION

Unnecessary institutionalization of the elderly is expensive and may disrupt social relationships vital to the well-being of older persons. It also involves excessive expenditures for construction of facilities, personal maintenance, and staff support. Unnecessary institutionalization also leads to extensive depletion of personal, family, or public funds. Even more importantly, natural helping systems are disrupted and the emotional health of the individual is adversely affected. The overwhelming preference of the elderly to maintain independent living arrangements when combined with the high cost of nursing homes makes it imperative to develop programs with the potential of increasing the time the elderly can remain in the community.

GOAL IDENTIFICATION AND SOLUTION SEARCH

The goal of this project was to identify what circumstances force older people to enter long term insti-

The elderly are encouraged to participate in community senior centers where they can interact with other people in planned activities. Photo courtesy of Social Welfare History Archives, University of Minnesota.

tutions prematurely and to develop community commitment to a creative and cost effective alternative to institutionalization program. While any one agency can develop a specific program designed to meet the community care objective, it seemed clear that true dependency prevention must be a community project. With this in mind the social worker attempted to discover a solution to the problem. To do so she needed to

1. determine whether a significant number of older persons in the community could remain independent if given restorative, preventive, and/or educational service.
2. determine what services were presently available to avoid duplication and battles over turf.
3. explore the willingness of existing agencies to cooperate in a coordinated effort to promote independence in the older population.
4. explore available knowledge in this subject area.

In this case available knowledge included the literature, expertise of service providers in the aging network, and three "experts" on aging—three active senior citizens in the community. All agreed that the first step in the intervention plan needed to be a thorough assessment of the need.

DEVELOPMENT OF INTERVENTION PLAN

The model of needs assessment was designed to exploit the process to insure implementation of the program developed. An effective needs assessment would play an important role in helping communities face decisions in the distribution of resources, reveal both the extent and severity of need, reveal segments of a population inadvertently missed in the normal course of service delivery, and provide community support and acceptance of programs subsequently developed. Underlying this approach to needs assessment was the assumption that it was one step in the more complex planning process. When viewed in the context of program planning, needs assessment must blend citizen and consumer participation with professional judgment in a manner that stimulates the subsequent steps of coordination and integration of existing community services. The people who judge the results have to be involved in the development of the program—particularly in identifying which needs have the highest priority.

IMPLEMENTATION OF THE INTERVENTION PLAN

Five major steps were essential to successful program implementation: securing a commitment from the community to use the needs assessment data, developing a planning board to include potential clients, professionals, and community representatives, identifying potential funding sources, selecting the assessment technique most appropriate to the population being assessed and most likely to provide the information required by the funding source, and analyzing the many different types and sources of information simultaneously. Discussion of each of these steps will further clarify the social work process.

Step One: Securing a Commitment to Use the Data

This project began with a very specific purpose. However, if the data collected were of interest only to the program being developed it would have limited importance. In trying to determine broader community needs and priorities, a great deal of data was gathered: 266 different pieces of information from each individual. The advantage of such an exhaustive study was that the individual being interviewed sensed a concern about himself as a whole person instead of just an old person. An obvious disadvantage was the time it took to conduct the interview and the exhaustion of the party interviewed, although the interview technique was structured to prevent fatigue. Further, only data that agencies would actually use were collected. The specific techniques used to secure the commitment of the community were to set up a coordinating committee that would also serve as a planning board (all agencies that could potentially use the data generated were invited to have a participant on this committee), to have those committee members determine which questions would be useful to their agency as well as which questions could increase the general body of knowledge pertaining to the elderly, to allow the coordinating committee a chance to respond to three different versions of the questionnaire to confirm their questions had been included, to allow coordinating committee members to be instrumental in identifying the study population, to forward all requests for service to the County Coordinator of Older Adult Services who then channeled the requests to the appropriate agency, and to guarantee participants they would receive a copy of the report generated.

Step Two: Developing a Planning Board

Developing a planning board was based on the premise that any community program needs the endorsement of community members and professionals. Even though funding may be provided by an outside source, clients, staff, and physical resources come from the community. Positive evaluation by the community of the sponsoring agency and the programs are necessary, and the proper time to begin getting this endorsement is at the outset. Contributions from planning board members included expertise in program planning, community organization, financial support, public relations, and program knowledge. As community members came to share ownership in the ideas generating the program, they began to take on additional tasks. For example, sometimes in the course of an interview a serious individual need would be identified. Since the interviewers were not in a position to respond to these needs, board members took on the responsibility of finding ways to respond whenever possible. The board was committed to assuring that the needs assessment did not lead to unfulfilled expectations. While not every identified need was met, the existence of the planning board greatly increased the responsiveness.

Step Three: Identifying Funding Sources

The major purpose of the needs assessment was to support the need for a community alternative to institutionalization program. Therefore, data were needed that could meet the requirements of funding sources and local agencies. This guided the structure of the questionnaire developed.

Step Four: Selecting Assessment Techniques

Discussion with the elderly and the visiting nurses revealed that the elderly would be very threatened by random selection. The decision was made to use a "snowball" sample, with professionals and the older citizens on our planning board identifying potential respondents. These board members would then contact the proposed respondents to reassure them that the questionnaire and the interviewer were nonthreatening. Once initial participants were interviewed, they were asked to refer friends and neighbors to us. This approach paid off because organizers were able to reach many frail elderly who would not have consented to a personal visit or phone call without this prior contact. Semi-structured questions were asked by social work students especially trained in interview techniques.

Another method of data collection used was the Nominal Group Technique NGT—a structured group exercise to elicit in depth responses from seven to nine people to one specific question.[1] The Delphi Technique was also used.[2] This has the same purpose as the NGT, but is done anonymously. Individuals are asked to give written responses to a specific question. It is useful for people who cannot come together face to face. Students interested in planning could benefit by familiarity with these techniques.

Step Five: Analyzing and Synthesizing Data

Given the three different types of data collected, synthesis and evaluation were necessary. This evaluation phase addressed the quality of the data collected, but even more important to the program planning process, it documented a need for the proposed program. By following this detailed process to conduct the needs assessment, the program developed because evidence of established need convinced a funding source to support it, professionals to make referrals, and clients to enter the program. This intervention was just one phase of an extensive program planning process.

REFERENCES

1. Andre Delbecq, A. H. Van de Ven, and D. H. Gustafson, *Group Techniques for Program Planning* (Glenview, Ill.: Foresman, 1975).
2. Ibid.

Needs assessments (both nationally and locally) have consistently identified the need for increased community care option for the elderly. The next case study illustrates how one social worker was able to respond to this need in her community.

Care Program

Coordination of Alternative Resources for the Elderly (CARE) was sponsored by a small, private, non-profit agency in northeastern Wisconsin with grant funds from the Lake Michigan Area Agency on Aging. The mission of that agency, one of the oldest social service organizations in the community, is to strengthen family life in the community. The major objective of the CARE program was

> . . . to help elderly individuals examine the alternatives available for health care in the community, then assist them in deciding which option is best. Providing this central contact point for services will insure accessibility for all elderly individuals. . . . Our CARE program works with you, the elderly, to determine what helps are available for you to live independently in your own home as long as possible. We want to provide assistance to you and your family to determine the most appropriate care plan.[1]

Loss of social contact and isolation are frequent problems of the elderly. A. L. Strauss and B. G. Glaser suggest that lessened social contact and considerable social isolation are among the most pernicious effects of the aging process and chronic disease.[2] Only with hard work and some skill at making suitable arrangements can the tendency to social isolation be countered among the frail elderly. Social relationships are disrupted or tend to disintegrate under the impact of lessened energy, impairment of mobility or speech, hearing impairment, body disfigurement, and time spent on management of disease. This is particularly detrimental since most elderly or chronically impaired people are entering a stage in their life cycle when their need for supportive interaction is at its greatest.

The CARE program was designed in response to a need identified by a social worker who had been involved in the agency's home health care program for the chronically impaired. A phone call from an individual, a family member, or a community referral source would gain entry into this program. The first step was a thorough problem assessment: collecting relevant information about the individual's overall situation is an important step in helping the chronically impaired remain independent. Physical conditions and limitations, emotional strengths and weaknesses, personality, motivation, finances, and the physical and social environment in which the individual lived were all considered.

During the initial contact, the social worker attempted to get a clear picture of how the individual needing services (the client) and the primary caretaker viewed the situation and problems they faced. The caretaker's assessment was important because the client's ability to remain in the community was frequently contingent upon the caretaker's support.

After reaching a consensus on the situation and what needed to be changed, the social worker would proceed with an assessment of resources available to the client. The first step in this resource assessment was to determine what support systems were still intact and what support systems might be developed within the family or neighborhood. The social worker analyzed why they had not been developed or maintained, how they might be activated, and what would be required to keep them operating once they were established. The availability of services from local social service agencies was also evaluated. It was sometimes necessary to provide services to the caretaker or the family to enable them to continue caring for the client. Transportation and housing were two needs local agencies or organizations often addressed. A great deal of emphasis was placed on linking the client with natural and volunteer helping systems to maximize the degree to which they could manage their own lives while keeping costs to a minimum.

Once he had determined available resources, the social worker explained them to the client and family or caretaker. Appropriate services for the individual situation were then identified and referrals made accordingly. Once the client was linked with the appropriate resources, the social worker continued to monitor the situation to make sure everything was working.

In developing and working to maintain the CARE program, the social worker fulfilled four primary functions: enhancing the problem-solving capacities of the client and his family; facilitating interaction within resource systems; establishing linkages with resource systems; and dispensing material resources. The social worker helped the client and family deal with the reality of their situation by systematically examining alternatives and helping them set realistic goals. It is not unusual for families to become immobilized as the problems facing the older person increase. The social worker's support and knowledge of options helped them deal with the problems. A common phenomena in situations with the frail elderly is that family members become lax in providing care for their parents or support for those siblings providing the care. The social worker within the CARE program intervened in some of these situations to correct misunderstandings, decrease hostilities, and open up communication within the family. The elderly as a group would prefer not to be dependent on others or on what might be seen as the public "dole." With some clients, it was necessary to develop an understanding of how the program operated and to assure them that accepting referred services was an honorable choice. Some people did not have access to resources because transportation was a problem; others felt they had tried to get services but were denied eligibility. With the social worker's knowledge of service availability and eligibility requirements, the client's access to necessary services was facilitated. This program did not provide money or material resources as part of the grant received. The services consisted primarily of counseling and case management. The resources actually dispensed came from donations, friends, neighbors, social clubs, and organized social services.

The CARE program was based on the assumption that chronic impairment of the elderly leads to decreased life satisfaction and increased stress on the extended family. The involvement of the social worker was designed to intervene in this cycle to maximize the quality of life and family functioning. The physical deterioration of many elderly cannot be reversed, but the CARE program attempted to humanize the aging process for a population at risk of being institutionalized by providing accurate assessment of needs and resources and by ensuring that all systems work together to benefit the client and caretaker or family. The social worker found the generalist model of social work most relevant to this practice setting.

REFERENCES

1. Mary Wirtz Macht, *Care Project Report* (Green Bay Wisconsin: Family Services Society, 1982).
2. A. L. Strauss, and B. G. Glaser, *Chronic Illness and the Quality of Life* (St. Louis: Mosby, 1975).

References

1. Florida Scott-Maxwell, *The Measure of My Days* (New York: Penguin, 1979), 5.
2. United States Office of Management and Budget, *Data Coverage of the Functionally Limited Elderly: Report of the Intra-agency Statistical Committee on Long Term Care for the Elderly* (Washington, D.C.: 1980) 1.
3. *Encyclopedia of Social Work,* 16th issue (New York: NASW, 1971), 34.
4. Sheila Kammerman and A. Kahn, *Social Services in the United States* (Philadelphia: Temple University Press, 1976) 322–324.

CHAPTER TWENTY-ONE

Vietnam Veterans

I was a young man just full of life,
and was married and had a good wife and family.
Then I went to war and fought for my country,
where men were wounded and died so bluntly.
I was a lucky one and came back home,
but I've felt ever since that I've been alone.
Since I had a wife and raised a family,
I thought things would be fine and dandy.
Then I got sick and things were tough,
and nobody seemed to care enough.
As years went on I kept getting worse,
and I found I'd been hit by the Delayed Stress curse.
I kept hoping and praying someone would see
the bitterness and tears of my family and me.
It's not only me but thousands of others,
who found that same war that darkness covers.
We are proud to be Vietnam Veterans,
and to this day our fighting is not over yet.
Our minds are shattered and our bodies are weak,
but there's always hope for the next day and week.
The world is so ugly and is full of hate,
but to have a true friend would be worth gold in its weight.
I am forty now and feel so old,
but one of many who stand so bold.
The time will come and the public will see
what the fight for freedom has meant to me![1]

Neither our government nor the American people have wanted to deal with the aftermath of the war in Vietnam—a painful experience everyone wants to forget. However, over 500,000 veterans cannot forget. This is a conservative estimate of the number of veterans suffering from Post-Traumatic Stress Dis-

The possibility of future war and the expenses involved in preparing for it are discussed in Chapter 13.

order (PTSD).[2] The formal definition of PTSD offered by the Veteran's Administration is "a survivor reaction to catastrophic stressors experienced in war, having a prolonged effect on personality development, patterns of adjustment, coping styles, and interpersonal functioning."[3] This disorder can be acute, chronic, and/or delayed.

A personal account of a "victim" of the Vietnam War is presented in this chapter.

The actual psychiatric casualties during the Vietnam War were low compared to previous wars. Psychiatrists felt that the method of deploying and replacing men as individuals and not as units would prevent psychiatric casualties.[4] In retrospect, it seems as if this assumption was not only premature but grossly in error. The implications presented by PTSD has had devastating consequences for some veterans traumatized by the battlefield or combat experiences. The acute subtype of the disorder is synonymous with disorders labeled shell shock or combat fatigue in previous wars. Combat fatigue manifests itself earlier and generally responds to treatment. It seems that the chronic and delayed subtypes are more prevalent in the Vietnam veterans.

In spite of the many people suffering from PTSD little research has been done on the problem. This section draws on both the personal experience and research of Ron Cross and Beverly Gudex to illustrate the problems and potential strategies in dealing with victims and their families. Ron is a Vietnam veteran presently pursuing a social work degree. Bev is a hospital social worker. Bev and Ron have been married for five years. Since PTSD has had such a powerful effect on their marriage, they want to share this experience with future social workers to increase knowledge and understanding of the problems. First, Ron presents his story and the findings from his research; this research itself has been an important component of Ron's therapy. Then, Bev presents her view of this relationship. Though their accounts are personal, both Ron and Bev feel important practice principles can be drawn from their experiences.

A Personal Account of PTSD

RON CROSS

Perhaps the best way to illustrate some of the symptoms of PTSD is to describe two victims. I will describe my own experience and then my wife will describe hers. While my wife did not serve time in Vietnam, she too is a victim of PTSD as it has had a devastating effect on her life.

My story begins as a Marine in Vietnam. I spent thirty-two months in combat. After returning from my third duty in Nam, I felt the horror was behind me. Then, seven years ago I experienced acute depression:

My marriage was falling apart. I spent most of my time at home alone upstairs, my wife and children downstairs. My wife tried to tell me that she cared for me, but I got real uncomfortable talking about things like that so I would get up and leave. I would hit my wife for no reason. I didn't have any friends. My children tried to get close to me. I just wanted to get away. They didn't understand. There were times when I drove real crazy, screaming and yelling.

There were times I was so depressed that I couldn't even go downstairs. As I became more depressed, I drank more. Frequently I thought about committing suicide.

Sometimes, my head still replays some of my experiences in Nam. Regardless of what I want to think about, it comes creeping in. It's so hard to push it out. It's old friends, their faces, the ambush, the screams, their faces (tears) . . . children dying, blood, helicopters, and death. You know, everytime I hear a chopper (helicopters) or see a clear unobstructed green treeline, a chill goes down my spine—instant memory. When I go hiking now, I avoid green areas. I stay above the timberline. When I walk down the street, I get uncomfortable with people behind me. I feel most comfortable in the corner of the room, with walls on both sides of me. Loud noises irritate me and sudden movement or noise make me jump.

Night is hardest for me. I go to sleep long after my wife has gone to bed. I think of so many of my Nam experiences at night. A number of times, my wife has awakened me with a look of fear in her eyes. I'm all sweaty and tense. Sometimes I've grabbed her neck and started choking her before I realized where I was. Sometimes I remember the dream, I guess most of the time I do. It's always the war or the enemy is chasing me and I can't run anymore.

My experiences are not unusual—I know that now. One of my friends recently shared a similar experience. He had fallen asleep on the couch watching TV. He woke up sopping wet from a cold sweat. When he awoke he was in elephant grass and saw eyes, faces—they were coming and he was shooting and shooting, but they just kept coming. He didn't have enough bullets so he ran and ran and ran. When he came to, he was exhausted.

The literature on PTSD documents thousands of similar cases. Hopefully sharing my personal experience will increase your sensitivity to the agony of the Vietnam veterans who are suffering from this disorder. Personal experience provides a meaningful backdrop, but it is also important to look at this problem in a broader spectrum. Mine is not an exceptional case. For this reason I will present a summary of what is known to date about PTSD.

There is some evidence that not all Vietnam veterans with intensive combat experience are disturbed by delayed stress. The veterans who have combat-related disorders appear to have been younger men with high intelligence, high levels of education, considerable verbal ability, middle-class urban backgrounds, who may have either volunteered or been drafted but who had achieved no high rank and who have been discharged from the military.[1]

The nature of Post Traumatic Stress was different than the stressors of the previous wars as it did not emerge until after the war was over and personnel had returned to civilian life. The symptoms also differ from previous war-induced traumas. PTSD is a group of symptoms, large and small, specific and vague, and with affective, attitudinal and adjustment components. Guilt is a major component: guilt for atrocities performed, guilt over transgression of traditional morality (specifically in reference to sex, drugs, and violence), guilt for having failed buddies, and survivor guilt. In addition there are feelings of rage, feelings of betrayal by the country which sent soldiers to war, self and societal alienation, apathy, depresssion, anxiety, obsessive tormenting memories, nightmares, insomnia, sensory hypercuity, extensive use of the ego defense mechanisms of denial and suppression. Other symptoms include confusion, nihilism, ideological disillusionment, uncontrollable hostility, wanton violence, flashback experiences, drug and alcohol addiction, unemployment, lack of goal orientation motivation, reentry shock, inability to adapt to the banality of civilian life after the excitement of war, and suicidal tendencies.[2]

The incidence of psychiatric syndromes among veterans is difficult to determine from the literature. Some veterans with emotional problems have received discharges which preclude treatment services from the Veterans Administration. There have been no resocialization programs for veterans where such problems might surface. The psychic numbing or numbed guilt syndrome is more than likely to escape notice as long as it leads to no overt disruptive behaviors, and as mentioned previously the full-blown syndrome tends not to occur until after return to a civilian environment and is in some cases ten or more years later. For these reasons, the incidence of psychiatric syndromes remain difficult to estimate.

Rage is one of the more common syndromes. There are many reasons for the rage I personally feel. For me Williams sums it up best in the following words.

> Military training equated the rage with the masculine identity in the performance of our military duty. Whether in combat or not, the military experience stirred up more resentment and rage than most had ever felt. Finally, when combat was experienced, the combatants were often left with wild, violent impulses and no one upon whom to level them. The nature of guerilla warfare—with its use of such tactics as booby traps, land mines, and surprise ambushes with enemies quick retreat—left the combatants feeling like walking timebombs; the veterans wanted to fight, but their enemy had disappeared. Often they unleashed their rage at indiscriminate targets.[3]

Such experiences are much more common than most people believe. Other symptoms such as flashbacks, sleep disturbances, anxiety reactions, and survival guilt are also common. Re-experiencing feelings and experiences is especially troublesome for those of us who are still numb and attempting to avoid these feelings. For others, it is just a constant reminder of their time in Vietnam, something they will never forget.

Thus far I have presented some of the most common effects of these problems in everyday life and in interpersonal relationships. Now I would like to discuss some of the techniques that have been developed to treat PTSD.

The extent to which PTSD affects the individual varies. The variables which account for the level of disruption in the veteran's life is unknown. The best predictor of the intensity of symptoms tends to be the extent to which the veteran was exposed to actual combat.

Before the publication of Wilson's *Forgotten Warrior Project* the vast majority of the affected veterans were ultimately diagnosed as having personality disorders such as schizoid, paranoid, antisocial and so forth. The major focus was apparently on etiological factors other than the intrinsic traumatic qualities of combat.

In treating a PTSD victim, it is particularly important to be empathetic to the horrors of the combat situation. Many veterans have struggled endlessly to suppress these feelings, in part because of the refusal of society to even acknowledge their existence. Anyone involved with veterans is aware that the veteran's ability to talk about his wartime experience is diminished by fear of losing control. If professionals ignore this important issue then the veteran is harmed again. The wound caused by the professional is called the "second wound".[4]

The "second wound" connotes the delayed emotional damage that is inflicted by the hostile and insensitive responses of hospital personnel, social workers, criminal justice personnel, and even by friends and family. It is the failure to acknowledge the trauma the veteran is suffering. For this we excuse ourselves and alleviate our fear by blaming the victim, i.e. deciding the problem is caused by mental imbalance not social injustice.

Exploration of the veteran's combat experience and evaluation of how the veteran views his present affective experience is important to problem assessment. Some veterans will continue to express numbness to their combat experience and current affective issues. Yet, on close examination of present day activities, they do suffer feelings of remorse and sadness. As already described, a great many veterans with this disorder have periods of intensely violent, impulsive behavior, very often directed at close family members and friends. These veterans question their own sanity. In contrast, those veterans with personality disorders almost invariably blame something external to themselves in order to provide some justification for their behavior. They suffer no remorse or horror for their actions. This is very different from veterans suffering from PTSD.

Most veterans had minimal problems before their combat experience and were totally unprepared for the Vietnam experience. In fact, the key components in an accurate diagnosis are: a good premorbid history, an exploration of the veteran's combat experiences, and an examination of his coping skills immediately after the war and to the present time. Many veterans with PTSD also have significant problems due to multiple substance abuse. It appears that some have habitually medicated themselves and compounded their problems. Not only does the stress problem prevail, but also a dependency for substance abuse. These problems must be dealt with before any lasting treatment for PTSD can begin.[5]

Successful treatment of PTSD requires a recognition that this disorder is not an underlying psychosis or a simple or complex hysterical reaction but rather a dynamic survivor's syndrome of combat veterans of the Vietnam War.

There is growing consensus among professionals as to the etiology of the disorder. There is strong feeling that a primary cause of PTSD was the young age of the combat soldier. The average age was only nineteen—normally the time when a young man seeks personal identity and forms ideological commitments. The average young adult experiments with education, jobs, travel, lifestyle and other activities during this period. Vietnam asked too much of young men in the period of psychosocial moratorium. The soldier in Vietnam, especially the combatant, was faced with a series of moral, social, and political conflicts which resulted in a strong personal need to justify his experience and to find existential meaning in actions. Furthermore, this task of cognitive reorganization and search for meaning in the role of warrior required ideological change in order to cope with the situation psychologically while fighting to physically survive.[6]

The length of tour in Vietnam also contributed to the soldier's problems. The Army, Navy, and Air Force tours lasted twelve months. Marines stayed thirteen months. During World War II the average time in combat was six weeks. This and the nature of guerilla type warfare created a constant stress of unknown magnitude. The time element in getting to and from the war contributed further to the problem. A soldier was transported from the United States to Nam and vice versa within seventy-two hours. This left no time for preparation or debriefing.

There were no funerals or ceremonies for the dead, so friends that were present one day were gone the next. There was no time to grieve—no rites of passage. Originally the average soldier did not question his patriotic duty: in fact, the majority of the soldiers volunteered. Patriotism waned as the war dragged on. A hill was taken one day, left the next and retaken a month later. Nothing was gained and many friends lost. One goal remained constant—getting home. Personal problems were magnified by the hostile reception of the American public—they were now called baby killers. Veterans internalized these conflicts.

In addition to the causes of PTSD identified by professionals, I feel there are additional causes. One problem for the soldier was a lack of professional leadership. During the 32 months that I participated in combat, there was an officer in charge of our platoon only six months of this period. The leadership was then placed upon young soldiers untrained in leadership.

Another problem in combat was intelligence reporting. This information was often incorrect and demoralizing. A unit would be told that there were only small units of enemy forces. Upon entering the area, large units were the norm and loss of buddies was a common experience.

Finally, the lack of compassion of higher ranking officers, Members of Congress, and the public in general, during and after the war numbed and disillusioned the soldier. Only recently have people and the media begun to consider the effect of the war on the veterans.

My plea to you as future social workers is to understand this disorder. Statistics show that over 59,000 veterans have committed suicide since the war. The prison population is over 25 percent Vietnam veterans; their unemployment rate is 31 percent higher than the national average; 38 percent have divorced within 6 months of returning home; 38 percent are experiencing drug dependency.

PTSD is a reality. Unfortunately, not all veterans recognize this. Some are still stuck back where I was seven years ago. I have been lucky. I have participated in one of the few treatment programs available. I have not received any magic cure. I know dealing with PTSD is a process—I take one day at a time. Hopefully, sharing my personal experience will make you better able to help other veterans cope with this disorder.

REFERENCES

1. Charles Figley, *Stress Disorders among Vietnam Veterans* (New York: Brenner/Maxell, 1978), 1–295.

2. Tom Williams, *Post-Traumatic Stress Disorders of the Vietnam Veteran* (Cincinnati, Ohio: Disabled American Veterans, 1980), 32.

3. Ibid., 78.

4. Ibid., 87.

5. Figley, *Stress Disorders,* 202.

6. John P. Wilson, *Identity, Ideology, and Crisis: The Vietnam Veteran in Transition* (Cleveland, 1978), 1–196.

Coping With The Effects of PTSD

BEVERLY GUDEX

It always helps to know that you are not alone. I am sharing my story with the hope that some of you will understand and then try to help the Viet Nam veterans and their families.

OUR STORY

We met in January 1979; I was a naive twenty-four-year old social worker in a nursing home. He was a thirty-nine year old traveling salesman from an out of state company. When he first told me he had been in Vietnam it did not seem important.

Life was happy. I was oblivious to Ron's attempt to share his suffering. I remember one evening he asked me to read a book entitled *A Rumor of War* by Philip Caputo. Ron was a character in that book. I was simultaneously horrified and engrossed by what I read. And angry, angry at the thought that anyone had to endure such a horrifying experience. He was intensely interested in my response. He seemed to feel he was on trial as a human being.

Our first few months were happy and fun-filled. Ron was desperately struggling but I assumed this was related to his recent divorce. I thought divorce was the explanation for the deep hurt in his eyes and the detached way he spoke of three children. Whatever the cause of the pain, I thought our love could conquer it. And, just as his pain would heal, so would his employment record. He would not quit jobs and disappear.

As our relationship grew more serious I introduced Ron to my parents who immediately disliked him. As I watched my father quiz Ron, I knew the battle had begun. He saw fifteen years age difference, a divorced man with three children, a job hopper. Ron was desperately seeking acceptance. He tried to tell him of his capabilities. The harder he tried, the worse it got. To all these adjectives was added exaggerator.

After that fateful meeting, Ron was hurt and I was angry. Hard feelings and harsh words ensued: the more my parents attacked Ron, the more committed I became to marrying him. My parents finally relented.

Back home Ron and I began to socialize more with my friends. I noticed that he had no friends. I was his best and only friend. He did not understand my need to be with other people. He would not look people in the eyes. These problems seemed small and we proceeded with our wedding plans.

Ron continued to work for the same corporation doing heating and air conditioning. He traveled each week but was home weekends. The pay and benefits were good and we had frequent warm phone conversations during the week and great weekends. There was even talk of a promotion for him. About a month after we were married, he took a week's "vacation" to work on our house. After several days he announced his intentions of staying home. There was no reasoning with him. He even refused to call his boss to make a formal termination. His rationale was "I want to be home with you."

Within a couple of weeks he began a lower paying job locally. He was excited, productive and got along well with his co-workers for six months. Then, it went downhill. I knew what was coming—by spring he was laid off.

By now Ron had developed a fairly good rapport with my parents. He wanted to try dairy farming with my dad. I saw problems but Ron was as insistent upon trying farming as he had been upon leaving the other two places. Needless to say, the cycle repeated, complicated by emotions involving family. I saw the relationship gradually deteriorate. Ron was angry and hostile both at himself and my father and angry at my father. I heard the target of Ron's accusations change from my father to me—I was choosing my parents or I would not let them treat him as they did. We moved back to our own home.

Ron began to search for a job. The search was longer this time. He was tense, hostile, volatile, and depressed. This was the first time in his life he was unable to walk from one job to another. His work record, age, and the economy were against him. I began to notice an increase in his alcohol consumption. He was also beginning to admit to frequent nightmares about Vietnam.

Ron did find a job by late spring but the job was taken out of desperation. His new employers were engaged in very shady practices. Both men drank on the job and Ron followed suit. Work was not steady. When I began to find him drunk, sometimes he would try to offer an explanation, other times he would just cry and promise to quit. I was repulsed. My responses ranged from crying and self pity to anger. The promises were always broken and the behavior repeated. It was no longer just the drinking. He began to contemplate suicide. I remember coming home one night and finding a folded white note on the stove. I feared this was "the note." Fortunately it was not.

The intensity of the situation continued to grow. One Saturday morning I found a knife sticking in the floor on his side of the bed. I removed it and said nothing. He demanded it back. When I asked why he needed it the reply was "I'm not going to let those gooks kill me in my sleep."

He refused to discuss his problems other than a sentence or two about hatred of God and religion, fear of losing me, self-hatred or fantasies of retaliation against his present employer. It was now June, warm and raining. He would get tense and pace like a caged animal. "Smells like Nam, God I hate this," was all he would say.

He seemed to be in Vietnam more than he was in reality. At this time we heard about a couple of other Vietnam veterans in Fond du Lac that were beginning to organize. I made a few phone calls and found out about rap groups for Vietnam vets. Together we hestitantly walked through the door the first evening together. It was obvious that the meeting was for veterans only. I left. That night he came home almost happy. He had a pamphlet about Delayed Stress. He kept saying, "It's not just me. I'm not crazy. Look at this, it's me." The pamphlet listed the symptoms: depression, anger, anxiety, sleep disturbances and many more.

He fit all of them! At the rap group he also heard of an inpatient treatment program just for Vietnam veterans. It was one of three programs available in the country at that time. He had to go—everything was crumbling around him.

Ron entered treatment in August 1981. When I called his dad and let him know of Ron's admission, his father's voice broke. He said, "His mom tried to tell me Ronnie was not the same when he came back from Vietnam, but I did not want to believe it." At least I could talk to them about it. I had so few friends who understood.

We knew little of what to expect from the treatment program. The day of the admission I left filled with fear because the staff had treated Ron rudely and then admitted him to a locked ward with some pretty strange characters. I remember seeing real fear in his eyes as I left.

Time went fast. Ron changed. He seemed to be calming down, and he began to talk about his future. He talked of the Veteran's Administration sending him to college to study social work. He began to compare himself with the twelve vets in his treatment program. He saw himself as being a lot more together than they were and this strengthened his self-image.

Ron came home a new man. He was happily making plans to start college. He started on schedule and seemed to enjoy his classes.

But we did not live happily ever after. Initially Ron had been sent home on tranquilizers. He was a zombie. In the follow-up outpatient appointments his medications were switched often. He reacted poorly to most of them. I nagged, he quit taking them and for a while he functioned better. I was not prepared for the consequence of taking that crutch away.

His alcohol intake after treatment was minimal. Then he went on a couple binges in late spring. I called the program director frantically to ask what I should do. He told me that Ron was well aware of the fact that he should not drink—not even one. He explained that inside Ron was a trained killer and when under the influence of alcohol anything could happen. I pleaded with Ron not to drink, and told him what the director had said but he denied it.

By now Ron had established a network with other Vietnam veterans in Fond du Lac. Few of these men acknowledged that they had any problems and chemical use was common. They saw the Vietnam experience as the problem and chemical use as relief. One particular vet was always available when Ron wanted to drink. They reinforced each others' dependencies.

The worst came in early June. It was Walleye Weekend and Ron was going to help man the Vietnam Veterans booth. He went early Sunday morning. I went on an outing with my family. When I got home at 4:00 p.m. and he was not home, I was worried.

He came home with his "enabler" friend. He was highly agitated and violent. He had seen one of his most recent employers at the park and decided to "get even." From Ron's disjointed talk I gathered that he had broken into his former place of employment but decided that was not enough. He was bent on getting a coke bottle and gasoline, making a molotov cocktail and going back to the shop to destroy the building. He tried to get into the garage to get the things he needed. I tried begging, reasoning, and physical restraint. His buddy Bruce wrestled him to the ground. Ron did manage to get to the garage door and punched out one of the wooden panels with his fist. The sight of blood was no deterrent. Between the ranting and ravings about the destruction of the shop were sobs and repeated "I'm crazy." It was unreal. His behavior had regressed to before treatment times. In desperation I called the program director at home. Before putting Ron on the phone, I briefed the program director on the situation. He told me that Ron should not be allowed any more alcohol and encouraged to sleep. Because his behavior was so bizarre, the program director suggested emergency admission with treatment in the alcohol rehabilitation unit. The problem was a two and a half hour trip and he was too crazy to take anyplace safely. I could not call the cops on my own husband.

Ron talked to the program director. He calmed some, enough to consent to going for a walk. My hope was that he would get tired enough to go home and sleep. Bruce walked with us. Once we started walking it became clear that the only reason he had consented was to get another bottle of alcohol. When I objected he became violent again. As we neared the house on the corner of our block, he grabbed one of the wooden slats on the porch trim and ripped it off. Bruce restrained him from doing any more damage. We walked a couple more feet. He again pleaded for booze. I said no. Bruce disagreed with my approach and suggested I allow Ron to drink himself into oblivion. Ron then proceeded to change his mind and headed home. When he got to the house he found two sleeping tablets, took them and fell asleep.

Filled with anger and sobbing hysterically I watched him sleep. How could this man who said he loved me put me through this kind of terror! How could he show so much growth over the past ten months and regress so rapidly? Why was this happening? Was he ever going to be cured? How much more did he expect me to endure? How much could I endure?

I had two friends I confided in. They asked questions that included, "Is he an alcoholic?" I said no and repeated to them what Ron told me, namely, that the delayed stress was the primary problem and while he used alcohol it was only in response to the primary problem. One close friend who had been through some bad times with her husband, now a recovering alcoholic, said, "Bev, the bottom line is what are you willing to put up with, the cause of his drinking be dammed."

It was now summer of 82. I kept repeating the question my friend had asked: What are you willing to put up with? I began to ask myself my limitations. I was aware that my power or influence base with my husband had eroded over the past three years. I tried to evaluate Ron's situation. I saw progress in his ability to relate to people (he had even begun a few friendships of his own); he was able to complete one semester of college, was now in summer school and doing well scholastically. He no longer seemed suicidal and was less dependent upon me. He had begun to talk and write about his Vietnam experience. On the negative side I saw his irrational, sudden explosions of anger. While these were not easy to deal with, they were nothing in comparison to the combination of violence and despair that I saw during periods of intoxication. He continued to be negative and nasty towards my family. He continued to complain of a memory impairment, especially in regard to school activities. There were also times when he drew away from any intimacy for extended periods of time.

It was like living with a time bomb. I never knew what to expect. When things were good they were exceptionally good. However, the reverse was also equally true. I knew that I could not live like this forever. I again tried to find additional help for Ron because I knew that he still had not resolved a lot of things about his Vietnam experience.

Ron joined a Vietnam Vets rap group and I began to see further progress by the end of 1982. He was beginning "to blossom" at school and was elected to the student government. He began to develop new interests and more friends. The drinking decreased as did the frequency of his fits of rage.

Things were going so well that my confidence in our relationship grew. By spring of 1983, I knew we had it together now. Except for periodic, normal arguments that go with living together, things were fine.

Then he had two drinking binges in August. The violence and irrationality were at the danger limit. Then one weekend in September Ron accompanied me on a weekend "up north". I was attending a conference and planned to mix business with pleasure. When I left for my meeting Saturday morning Ron was already on the lake doing what he did best—fishing.

I came back at 4:30 p.m., to find a full bottle of Blackberry Brandy on the table and him drunk on the floor. He was barely conscious. There was no pity left in me, only anger. I told him I was leaving. He was alert enough to say "You mean you would leave me here like this?" In a flash again I knew that if I left him he would end up on the bottom of the lake. I threw all of Ron's gear into the car, gave away the fish he had caught, and went back into the cabin to collect my drunk husband. He begged me to stay there. I could not. I hated the cabin, the bar, Ron, and everything that went with this fiasco of a weekend.

It was 6:00 p.m. when I got him settled into the car and began the three hour trip home. What a trip! We were on the road for about two minutes and the terror began. I realized he was in Vietnam, not on the way home. The sun was beginning to set and he was busy scanning the horizon looking for "gooks." He kept saying, "It's too green, they're here, I can feel them." Then he began grabbing at the wheel or behind the seat, looking for his gun. When unable to grab at anything else, he would fiddle with the radio knobs until he had it between stations and had no reception. Then he began to frantically scream, "We're out here. Can't you hear us? Come in, please come in," getting even more frantic when he received no reply on the radio. For the first time I was unable to get him to realize that he was in Wisconsin, not Vietnam, and for the first time I was actually afraid of him. I stopped in the next town and got him two cups of coffee. He was better momentarily but as soon as we were on the road again he was back in Nam. Now he would not drink the second cup of coffee because he was saving it for Indian, a fellow Marine pointman in Vietnam. This scenario continued for two hours until he began to doze off. We made it home by 10:00 p.m. and then I fell apart.

That episode solidified a decision in my mind. I would take one last stab at getting help for Ron. If he refused help and insisted upon drinking, he could do so but I would not be around to pick up the pieces. I called his social worker again and told him of the problem. He was surprised because Ron never let on in group that he was having any problems. There Ron cast himself in the role of the helper and professional.

The social worker agreed to meet with Ron and me. For three Thursdays, Ron recounted in great detail his Vietnam experience. I was not shocked by what he was saying. By now I had either heard it or read it in his papers before. Once this was established, we moved on to the subject of his alcohol abuse. The social worker helped me clarify my feelings and then spell out my position to Ron. Ron saw his alcohol use like this: Bad Vietnam dreams/nightmares/thoughts + alcohol = relief. I tried to point out that the real equation was Vietnam + alcohol = temporary relief followed by long term pain and destruction. He agreed and said he would quit using booze if that made *me* happy. The social worker interceded and said the decision must be based on his needs not mine. Ron agreed to quit using alcohol. Again I thought the decision was made and life would be wonderful.

One Saturday afternoon in February I came home to find Ron and a Vietnam veteran friend smoking dope in the basement. It took me only one minute to notice that Ron had also been drinking.

After a heated emotional discussion the bottle came out from behind the washer. I did not pour it out or do any of the other things I had done in the past. This time I was ready to leave. Circumstances prevented it, but never before had I spelled out my feelings as I did then. I let him know that I loved him, had given him what I was capable of, and from then on he was on his own. If he chose to drink or to smoke pot, he had every right to do so, but if he did I would leave.

What does all this mean? What conclusions have I reached about living with a Vietnam veteran with Post Traumatic Stress? What advice would I give other women married to Vietnam veterans? I think it is extremely important for all women who have Vietnam vets as husbands to read all they can about Vietnam. Vets usually refuse to talk about Nam. This only buries the problem deeper and it does not help to work out the difficulties. Be ready to listen but do not force the issue. If one can convey warmth, caring, and understanding despite the horror stories, the vet will talk, if only in small segments. I learned the hard way that the spouse should also be extremely attuned to signs of chemical dependency. Vietnam veterans tend to deny any problem with addiction. My experience with PTSD victims is that healthy coping mechanisms develop only when the veteran stops using all chemicals. The key ingredient needed to make a relationship work is patience and strength. One must learn and accept the fact that one learns to cope with PSTD but one is not cured. The poor coping mechanisms may have been learned from childhood, traumatized during Vietnam, and reinforced thereafter. I had been expecting my husband to change behaviors that he has learned over the past fifteen years. The other thing a spouse must do to survive is to establish a strong support system of her own. This support system is vital for when things get rough (as they inevitably do.)

The ultimate decision for the spouse is what she is willing and capable of giving. The spouse can increase her capacities by developing support systems, she cannot change what her husband has suffered, she should not waste time feeling guilty about it. She must allow herself to place expectations on her spouse. While he cannot stop the terror PSTD causes him, he can stop the use of alcohol and other drugs which exacerbate the pain and spread it to those around him.

I have found pity to be destructive to our relationship. As difficult as it sometimes is, I know I can only help Ron by demanding that he remain strong and help him in every way to maintain that strength. Because I love Ron I am frequently overcome with feelings of sympathy and understanding for his destructive behavior. But I have learned that this understanding must be channeled to constructive expectations not destructive sympathy. While I am feeling confident about our future, I remain aware of the continuing threat PTSD holds over our life. We approach life one day at a time, balancing our expectations—neither allowing ourselves to despair nor anticipating the impossible dream. Life is what we make it on a day to day basis. Life is enhanced by our concern for each other, loving friends, and qualified professionals who can provide the support and guidance we need in difficult times.

REFERENCES

Philip Caputo, *A Rumor of War* (New York: Holt, Rinehart, and Winston, 1977).

References

1. Ron Cross, "The Price of Freedom."
2. John P. Wilson. *Identity, Ideology and Crisis: The Vietnam Veteran in Transition* (Cleveland: 1978), 1–196.
3. *Diagnostic and Statistical Manual*, III (Washington, D.C.: American Psychiatric Association, 1980), 309–381.
4. Tom William, *Post-Traumatic Stress Disorders of the Vietnam Veteran* (Cincinnati, Ohio: Disabled American Veterans 1980), 1–237.

CHAPTER TWENTY-TWO

Homosexuality: Deviance or Choice

"There is no doubt that people who are distressed or in trouble because they are homosexual need help. But what kind of help and who should provide it? The help provided . . . is not enough. Both individual and group counsellors must value homosexual erotic experience, and understand what it feels like to be gay. They must proceed from a felt rejection of the ideas of heterosexual superiority that permeate our culture."[1]

Analyzing societal response to homosexuality or gays and lesbians brings the potential of oppressive labeling to bear on a current phenomena. Within the last twenty-five years, homosexuality has been defined as a crime, as an illness, and as an individual's choice. As recently as the 1950s homosexuals were being imprisoned for their sexual preference. Along with this punishment they were likely to receive "treatment" for their problem. Treatment often consisted of aversive and frequently painful stimuli being presented simultaneously with homoerotic stimuli.

The term "gays and lesbians" is used in place of "homosexuals" because it focuses less on sexual behavior and more on lifestyle.

In 1963 Karl Menninger, one of the most progressive psychiatrists of the time, suggested that homosexuality was a condition that called for treatment to transform the homosexual into a heterosexual.[2] Within twenty years of Menninger's statement the American Psychiatric Association, the American Psychological Association, and the National Association of Social Work had all taken a public position in support of homosexuality as a choice.

Though social workers as a group were the last to speak out for the rights of homosexuals, they also voiced the most active commitment to overcoming the oppression. An excerpt from the policy statement adopted by the delegate assembly of the National Association of Social Workers on May 22, 1977, in Portland, Oregon, reflects the tone of the commitment.

An estimated 5 percent to 15 percent of the U.S. population is homosexual.

> The profession of social work is uniquely suited to assist American society in understanding the relationship between environmental conditions and human functioning. The burden of the eradication of homophobia—the fear of homosexuality—cannot be placed on the homosexual minority. . . . The ultimate responsibility for the eradication of discriminatory practices which impinge on the lives of the homosexual minority falls on the social work profession, together with other groups in the society.[3]

The Family Protection Act was introduced in Congress in 1979 and attacked nontraditional families, feminists, teen age sexual privacy, and homosexuality.

Since 1977 legislation has been passed to protect the rights of homosexuals from discrimination in jobs and housing, but there have also been attacks on homosexual rights by groups such as the Moral Majority. Conservative politicians led by Senator Paul Laxalt (R-Nevada) have introduced legislation, The Family Protection Act, that would define homosexuality as deviance and would condone oppression of homosexuals as individuals and as members of a group. In the following piece Craig Little recounts how societal and professional decisions are made about what is or is not "deviant".

The Politics of Definition*

CRAIG B. LITTLE

In December 1973 the American Psychiatric Association (APA) officially declared that homosexuality "by itself does not necessarily constitute a psychiatric disorder." From 1951 to 1973 homosexuality had been categorized in the APA's *Diagnostic and Statistical Manual* in the context of "sexual deviation." The APA Board of Trustees' action was accompanied by a "Position Statement on Homosexuality and Civil Rights" which clearly recognized the power of society's most potent official "labelers," especially psychiatrists to influence the lives of their "clients." In their position statement

> . . . the board deplored all public and private discrimination against homosexuals and urged the enactment of civil rights legislation to protect homosexuals and the repeal of all discriminatory legislation against homosexual behavior. It further deplored the use of "perjorative connotations derived from diagnostic or descriptive terminology used in psychiatry" as the basis for such discrimination.[1]

Almost immediately, opposition led by psychoanalysts Irvin Beiber and Charles Socorides mobilized to resist the change in nomenclature. This group circulated a petition, gathering the 200 APA members' signatures required to throw the board's decisions open to a referendum of the entire APA membership. A vote was scheduled for April 1974, with both sides campaigning strenuously during the three months preceding the vote. The issue of whether officially to classify homosexuality as a mental disorder was being politically decided by the members of a prestigious professional society in a hotly contested "election" on the issue. Over ten thousand of the APA's eighteen thousand members voted in the referendum with the Board of Trustees' decision being upheld by 58 percent.

One might rightfully ask: What's so important about a definition? Some thought on the question necessarily leads to the realization that deviance and

1. M. Spector, "Legitimizing Homosexuality," *Society* 5, No. 14:53.

*This excerpt reproduced by permission of the publisher, F. E. Peacock Publishers Inc., Itasca, Illinois. From Craig B. Little *Understanding Deviance and Control: Theory, Research and Social Policy,* 1983, pp. 73–74.

the theoretical images concocted to explain it, are very much pure matters of definition arrived at by far from unanimous agreement through intensely political struggles. Likewise, this episode directs our attention to the pivotal position of the professions concerned with human behavior, especially those like psychiatry, psychology, sociology, and medicine, as battlegrounds for issues of social control in a modern society.

Changing views of homosexuality illustrate how society defines and redefines behavior as deviant or normal. These phenomena are also reflected in changed legal and societal responses to abortion, marijuana, and mental illness. For the prospective social worker, the importance of this exercise is to be aware of the needless oppression society may be inflicting on certain groups of people. This understanding can decrease the potential of unknowingly becoming a part of that oppression. History provides a powerful lesson. The following selection illustrates how liberating practice can help overcome oppression and what kinds of knowledge and skills are needed to work with homosexuals.

A healthy developmental model for the coming-out process for lesbians is presented at the end of this chapter.

This case example illustrates a positive social work response to a lesbian client.

Gay and Lesbian Counseling Services

Kay Sullivan, 32, realized that her inability to sleep, loss of appetite, and periods of crying were symptoms of depression she had experienced on previous occasions. Now the depression seemed overwhelming and it took all her energy to make it to her job as a third grade teacher in an elementary school where she had taught for the last seven years. Kay was fairly certain about the source of her depression yet she was uncertain about who she could go to for help. Rather than talk to her friends or colleagues she looked in the yellow pages of the phone book and found an agency called Gay and Lesbian Counseling Center. She called the phone number and after a brief interview, she made an appointment for two days later.

Kay arrived early at the appointment and drove around the building several times before entering. Once she was in the waiting room, she nervously looked around her at two men and one older woman who were also waiting to be seen. Soon a small, dark-haired woman about Kay's age entered the room and introduced herself as Susan Williams—Kay's social worker. Susan spoke briefly about the purpose of the agency and the different services that were available—coming out groups, individual counseling, support groups, couples groups, family counseling and community education. Susan also explained that there were both male and female counselors as well as gay and straight counselors and if Kay would feel more comfortable with someone else, that could be arranged after the initial intake interview.

With gentle encouragement from Susan, Kay began to tell her story. When Kay was in graduate school working on her degree in education she met a woman named Elizabeth. She and Elizabeth became good friends, studied together and eventually moved in together in order to share expenses. As the two women became closer they began to engage in sexual fondling and sleeping together. Elizabeth told Kay she had been involved with two other women when she was younger and considered herself to be a lesbian. Kay was not even sure that she understood what the word lesbian meant or that she had ever known anyone who was lesbian.

Kay went on to explain that she fell in love with Elizabeth and convinced her not to tell anyone about their relationship. She and Elizabeth found jobs teaching together in the same school and bought a small house together near the school. In the past two years, Elizabeth had grown increasingly restless with her job and her relationship with Kay. She moved out of the house and began seeing other women. Kay panicked that as Elizabeth became more "out," her colleagues at school as well as her family who lived in the community might find out about her. At the same time there was a part of Kay that envied Elizabeth's openness and wished to experience new relationships too.

Susan, the social worker, allowed Kay to cry and ventilate her feelings of loss over an important relationship. Susan explained that Kay was going through a grieving process and at the same time being forced to consider her own "coming out" process. Both of these problems were contributing to Kay's depression and to periods of great anxiety. Kay felt some relief after telling the worker her problems and agreed to come back for another session.

Over the next six months, Kay was seen eight times in individual sessions, and twelve times in group sessions. Elizabeth attended one session and some old issues of anger and guilt were resolved and it seemed possible that the two could continue to remain friends. The social worker suggested that Kay join a lesbian coming-out group when she felt ready to do so. Kay found the group to be very helpful and as a result "came-out" to her parents and to a friend at work. Although her parents had some resistance to Kay's behavior, they agreed to attend a family support group. Kay has been dating other women and has made new friends in the group she attended. Although she continues to worry about some of her work colleagues finding out about her sexual preference, she is considerably less depressed and feels more comfortable with herself.

REFERENCES

Don Milligan, "Homosexuality: Sexual Needs and Social Problems," in *Radical Social Work,* ed. Roy Bailey and Mike Brake (New York: Pantheon Books, 1975), 195.

Karl Menninger, *The Vital Balance: The Life Process in Mental Health and Illness* (New York: Viking, 1963).

Bernice Goodman, "Some Mothers are Lesbians," in *Women's Issues and Social Work Practice,* ed. Elaine Norman and Arlene Mancuso (Itasca, Ill.: Peacock, 1980).

M. Spector, "Legitimizing Homosexuality," *Society* 5, No. 14: 53.

The next article describes the coming-out process for lesbians.

The importance and potential of services for gays and lesbians is illustrated in the experience of Kay Sullivan. Lou Ann Lewis suggests the values and knowledge conducive to liberating practice with homosexual clients.

The Coming-Out Process for Lesbians: Integrating a Stable Identity*

LOU ANN LEWIS

Coming out as a lesbian in the 1980s is a different process than it was 20 or 30 years ago. With the advent of the "sexual revolution" of the 1960s, feminism, and gay liberation, social roles for women have broadened. Attitudes toward being "different" and tolerance for alternative lifestyles have increased among many people. In 1974, the American Psychiatric Association removed the definition of homosexuality as an an illness from its diagnostic manual.[1] In the years since, social workers and men-

* Reprinted with permission from *Social Work* 29, no. 5 (September-October, 1984): 464–469.

It is important to fully understand the coming out process for gays and lesbians in order to work with them as unique individuals. Photo by David Strickler.

tal health professionals have needed to understand more about lesbians, but, because lesbians are both hidden and invisible as a population, it has been difficult to gather accurate information. In the 1930s, 1940s, and 1950s, identifying oneself as a lesbian and feeling good about that identity were arduous and sometimes impossible tasks. In recent years, it has become possible for some women to "come out of the closet" by going through several periods of development that integrated their lesbianism into a healthy self-concept. In this article, a model is presented of the process a woman goes through in developing a healthy, well-integrated lesbian identity.

Before undertaking this process with a client, a worker needs to examine himself or herself—to assess personal biases and comfort with homosexuality and to ascertain whether his or her own conditioning and feelings will interfere with providing good services. As Potter and Darty explain,

> to be effective in casework with lesbian clients, social workers must become knowledgeable of and comfortable with lesbianism as a sexual preference and lifestyle. Social workers must recognize that heterosexist society (one governed by both heterosexual and sexist norms) has shaped their perceptions of this sexual orientation. . . . Social workers who cannot accept lesbian clients unconditionally will be destructive to their clients' personal growth.[2]

LITERATURE REVIEW

Three articles have addressed the coming-out process in homosexuals. Cass describes a six-stage process that applies to both gay men and lesbian women.[3] The stages begin with identity confusion and move to identity synthesis. Lehman presents a five-stage model similar to Cass's but applicable only to lesbians.[4] Although it describes the process, it is not a competence-based model. Neither Lehman nor Cass describes possible social work interventions for the stages. Grace presents a competence-based model of development for gay men and addresses clinical issues for the stages.[5] However, he deals exclusively with gay men, and there are significant differences for lesbians in the coming-out process.

Several books on lesbianism include descriptions of the coming-out process or various aspects of forming a positive lesbian identity, the most extensive and relevant of which is Lewis's *Sunday's Women.*[6] This contemporary book, written for the lay reader, discusses lesbian identity formation at length and presents excellent material on lifestyle, politics, and relationships. However, although Lewis's and other popular books present valuable material, they are more anecdotal and descriptive than clinically oriented.

BEING 'DIFFERENT'

Awareness of being different may start as early as age 4 or 5. For the young girl, this awareness may manifest itself as a sense of "knowing she is somehow different." She may be able to verbalize this difference as a child, or only in retrospect, or not at all. For some women, this feeling stays below the level of awareness until adolescence or into adulthood. Because our society and its process of socialization do not include a positive vocabulary for same-sex attractions (whether emotional or erotic), many girls experience only vague, undefinable feelings of "not fitting in." If the feelings are definable, they are associated with words like "queer" and "homo," are explained away as "just a phase," and, during adolescence, are often denied or sublimated in an attempt to conform. For a young girl who cannot deny her attractions, childhood—and especially adolescence—may be periods of isolation and withdrawal, and she may wonder, "What is wrong with me?" She may be teased mercilessly by others. A young woman's sense of not fitting in may promote self-blame and self-hatred.

A social worker will rarely encounter a client dealing with this awareness who can verbalize what is going on within herself. It is important to wait for cues from the client before initiating some gentle exploration. A worker need not phrase questions in terms of sexual preference but might ask, "Who have you ever felt close to?" or "With whom have you had important relationships in your life?" If the client's answers reveal significant relationships only with women, the worker could explore further with questions such as, "Are you aware that all your important relationships have been with women?" "How do you feel about that?" A variety of responses from the client are possible, some of which may lead to further exploration of same-sex feelings and some may not. As a general rule, digging and probing extensively can be frightening to the client during this time. Thus, waiting for cues and discussing the woman's anxiety as it emerges are more appropriate.

'DISSONANCE'

As a woman connects her sense of being different with same-sex feelings, she begins to have words for her struggle. During adolescence and young adulthood sexual feelings emerge. At this time a woman may become aware that her strongest emotional and erotic feelings are in relation to women rather than men. Acknowledgment of the sexual element of being different is often accompanied with feelings of denial, shame, anxiety, and ambivalence. This is a time of great dissonance and inner turmoil. A woman faces a conflict between the process of socialization, which teaches her that she will probably marry and have a family, and her feelings, which pull her toward wanting intimacy with other women. This was aptly described by a client as having two choices: "You can be in conflict with yourself and in harmony with the world, or in harmony with yourself and in conflict with the world." Also, the woman's feelings conflict with family values and expectations, adding to the anxiety and shame. In her article on developing a positive gay identity, Berzon poignantly describes her feelings at this stage:

> I felt . . . the loneliness of alienation from the true self, as if deep in one's center there is a truth pleading for acknowledgment but lost in denial and dread of exposure to the unknown. Risking the acknowledgment of my gay feelings, the expression, the being known for what is true and so long denied, had been terrifying for me.[7]

With acknowledgment of her same-sex feelings, a woman may begin a grieving process that resembles Kübler-Ross's stages of dealing with a loss.[8] The woman may show signs of denial and of bargaining with herself. She may say or think, "I feel close and attracted to *one* woman; that doesn't mean I'm a lesbian." Or, she may refuse to admit to others or to herself any same-sex attractions. Bargaining comes with many rationalizations. She may say or think things such as "Because I'm married, I can't be a lesbian" or "If I'm a nun, I'm certainly not a lesbian" or "I know I want to have children, so that must mean I'm not a lesbian." During this time, both denial and bargaining are used to lessen the dissonance experienced and can be effective in keeping a woman from acting on her feelings. Unlike typical grieving, however, coming out means choosing to move from a socially accepted identity to a socially stigmatized one, so this progression may be accompanied with shame and anxiety. A woman may be terribly afraid of the consequences of being found out and may try to hide her feelings. This concealment may add to the shame she already feels about same-sex attractions. Unlike groups whose minority status is immediately visible, such as racial minorities, in which parents may teach their children skills for coping in a hostile world, a woman with emerging same-sex feelings has not learned these skills and is not supported by her family. Some anger may be experienced at this time, but often it is turned inward, with the woman thinking she is "bad" or "wrong." Wolf describes the pain of same-sex awareness clashing with cultural norms:

> many women describe the process of gradually realizing they were lesbians in isolation, of feeling that because of a lack of role models they were the only one in the world "like this" and of finally coming upon medical or psychoanalytical literature reflecting the norms of the larger culture in which a "scientific" description of homosexuality could only depress them and cause them deep anxiety.[9]

Continuum

For some women in their twenties, thirties, and forties who identify strongly as feminists and who were formerly heterosexual, the early phase of coming out may be different. In their important study of sexual feelings, behavior, and fantasies, Kinsey and his colleagues developed a six-point continuum as a way to illustrate the range of same-sex/opposite-sex feelings and attractions.[10] With 0 as exclusively heterosexual and 6 as exclusively homosexual, Kinsey and his colleagues studied the histories of a large sample population and rated their responses on this continuum. Results showed that the bulk of the population is a mix of same-sex/opposite-sex erotic responses and fantasies.

Many women who would fall in the mid-range of Kinsey's scale do not have a sense of being different as strongly as those closer to the exclusively homosexual end. Because of strong socialization to become heterosexual, a woman in the mid-range may fit fairly easily into a heterosexual lifestyle. She may marry and have children, yet feel something is missing. At some point, her feelings of attraction or her political beliefs may lead her to exploring same-sex attractions. If feminism becomes central to her life, she may use political values such as having an egalitarian relationship and personal independence as an ideological framework for her explorations.

Many feminists in Kinsey's mid-range who are choosing to identify as lesbians in the 1980s might have been fairly well-adjusted heterosexuals in the 1930s or 1940s. Changes in the social environment and the increasing emphasis on liberation and personal growth provided these women a less hostile and frightening atmosphere in which to try new kinds of relationships. These women are spared some of the internalized self-hatred that many exclusively lesbian women cannot avoid. They have often been spared the struggle of having a profound sense of being different, of being ostracized, and of experiencing the resulting isolation. Because they have formerly fit into expected roles and lifestyle choices, these women may begin the coming-out process with more self-esteem. Being heterosexual gives a woman cultural and family validation that is not available to her otherwise. According to Schaef, "We are taught that once we attach ourselves to a male, we can get validation and approval."[11] A woman who has been heterosexual may have more freedom to explore same-sex feelings with less suspicion from friends and relatives regarding her sexual preference. Although she will still experience dissonance and shame, starting the process with more self-esteem may aid her in moving more easily toward self-acceptance than a woman who has always felt different.

Inner Conflicts

Many clinical issues can emerge out of feelings of dissonance. Because of inner conflicts, a woman may be full of contradictory feelings and fear. This may be evidenced in an aversion to discussing lesbian feelings or in an extremely strong reaction (anger, fear, hostility) to any mention of homosexuality. Because a strong reaction in the client could come from a variety of sources, it does not always indicate an identify conflict. As before, the worker needs to be aware of the high-risk nature of this struggle and to proceed sensitively. Rather than using the label "lesbian" when doubts about sexual preference are raised, the worker can refer to the Kinsey scale and explain the idea of sexual attraction being on a continuum. Because most people are somewhere between 0 and 6, this information can serve to normalize a client's feelings and decrease her fear.

It is essential that the therapist provide accurate information about a lesbian lifestyle during this stage. This can be done by providing written material or connecting the client with various resources. Many women in the early stages of same-sex identification have all the stereotypes that the culture perpetuates. A woman may fear that she will have to make herself into a different person if she explores same-sex attractions. Thus, suggesting that she visit a women's bookstore or coffeehouse could be helpful. She could observe the women there and see how she feels, and in that way start to deal with her own stereotypes and fears.

The worker needs to encourage discussion and expression of dissonance. The client's fears and ambivalence need to be verbalized and examined openly. The therapist must work hard—whatever his or her own biases—to provide information and support that validates the client's feelings as being worthwhile. If necessary, the worker could discuss with the client the cost of not dealing with dissonance. Rather than backing down in the face of the client's confusion and distress, the worker can reassure her that the feelings are normal and help her to resolve them and accept herself.

This time is a turning point. Depending on who she is and how she handles the dissonance, a client may choose to explore the feelings further or not. This is an individual choice that deserves respect at this stage in the process.

RELATIONSHIPS

What has been an internal and verbal process may next be translated into action. Because women are socialized to have and maintain relationships, sexual exploration and experimentation often take place within the context of a relationship. Schaef says, "Women's sexuality seems more intimately connected to relationships than men's, and sex for a woman can be difficult or even unpleasant outside the context of a meaningful relationship."[12] However, lacking models and courtship experiences that felt right in adolescence, these first same-sex relationships tend to be stormy and unstable. There may be a period of many brief relationships that have a sense of being experimental. In trying to define, or redefine, what is important to her in relationships, a woman may try new behaviors. This may include multiple, nonmonogamous relationships; serial monogamy; and experimentation with roles. According to Lewis,

> The lesbian's exploration of intimate experiences with other women is an emotionally turbulent process. It is, essentially, a second adolescence, complete with many of the symptoms common to the mainstream heterosexual adolescent period.[13]

In trying to develop her own sense of what being a lesbian means, a woman may also experiment with styles of dressing. She may cut her hair short and wear jeans. According to Wolf, culturally defined masculine attire is "more strongly assumed by young women who are newly aware of their lesbianism and looking for a community. They may dress in a more extreme manner . . . in order to be recognizable as lesbians."[14] Having been socialized to dressing attractively to "catch a man," some women rebel by paying little attention to their appearance or dressing in ways that are comfortable rather than socially approved.

First relationships are difficult and may be subjected to additional stress by a lack of social support. Without a larger community and access to other lesbians, two women, whose only real compatibility may be their sexual preference, could stay together for security and out of fear of never meeting another lesbian. These isolated relationships are often dependent and enmeshed. Even if a closeted lesbian knows where lesbians meet, she may fear being seen there and losing her job. Thus, the lack of community or social support can contribute to isolation of individuals and couples. In smaller communities, the bars may be the only gathering place. This can be a factor in substance abuse and low self-esteem.

As relationships are started there may be a further withdrawal from family. A woman may need to actively hide her involvement with a lover and become even more anxious and fearful about family consequences should she be discovered. According to Abbott and Love,

> The feared break with parents epitomizes the total conflict with society. They know that lesbians who have told their familes are sometimes unable to go home again, never permitted to see the children in the family or even to claim their possessions.[15]

On the other hand, having new relationships may serve as an impetus for coming out to one's family. A woman who has some support within a relationship may find it easier to break the news to her family. In either case, dealing with family members becomes an important issue.

The search for community—a place to belong—is another important part of this process. As a woman begins to accept the label "lesbian," she needs to have a support group who validate and accept that identity. Individuals cannot feel good about themselves if they are isolated from others who are like them. Today, with the rich cultures that have developed in conjunction with the feminist movement and gay liberation, there are many ways for a woman to find a community and meet other lesbians. In Minneapolis, for example, some examples of resources are a women's coffeehouse, a lesbian survival center, lesbian softball teams, a women's bookstore, a women's theater group, and a women's chorus. Thus, a woman who is exploring attractions to women can pursue her interests and use community resources to meet lesbians.

Separatists

Many women who are coming out define themselves as separatists for a period of time, or make an ongoing commitment to a separatist lifestyle. Separatists try to minimize or avoid all contact with men and often with nonlesbian women. For some women this means living, working, and socializing, as well as being intimate, only with lesbians. Others may carry it further and avoid male salespeople and try to support only female-owned or female-managed businesses. This lifestyle has many motivations. Living completely independent of men can give a woman a sense of total acceptance for the first time in her life. She may find new avenues of self-definition when she removes herself from the oppressiveness of the patriarchal culture. She may discover strengths and skills in herself that she formerly defined as male and that were thus unavailable to her. Within the context of a separatist lifestyle, she has the freedom to express her anger and rage at men because she is no longer dependent on them. There may also be considerable fear of men. A woman may feel that she does not know how to relate to men or what (if anything) she wants from them.

As a woman goes through a process of separatism, she will be free to reevaluate her attitudes toward men and choose how and whether to relate to them. Thus, separatism can be an extremely healthy and active way for a woman to explore her own strengths, attitudes, and relationships. However, if she gets stuck there, she may be in a position of being perpetually reactive to men and never disentangle herself emotionally.

Nonseparatists

For a woman who does not like the idea of separatism, has male children, or wants to keep men in her life, there may be considerable pain, anger, and disillusionment with some community resources that are strongly separatist. This may further her isolation. She will need encouragement to keep exploring and looking for a place to fit.

While the client is finding a place to fit, the mourning process continues. The woman is usually past denying her lesbianism and is both angry and sad. For a woman who has related to men in the past there is anger at the loss of status in the culture that is called "heterosexual privilege." The woman begins to realize the loss of such large and small benefits as feeling safe walking at night with a male companion, easy acceptance at work when talking of a boyfriend, and joint income-tax returns. There is anger and sadness at the loss of an easy sense of belonging with her family. Even if she has come out to her parents and they have accepted her, there will still be pain. For both parent and child, the intergenerational bond that comes when the younger generation has children and identifies with their parents may be lost. There is also sadness regarding the woman's own hopes and dreams about marriage, children, social acceptance, and the whole package of expectations from the culture. Feeling these losses and grieving them is an ongoing process that may take many years.

The social worker can continue to educate and support the client. Information about the process she is going through and support to experiment, explore, seek a community, and define her own needs are important aspects of this phase. The client may express contradictory feelings of excitement and relief about her sexual experiences with other women along with sadness and anger about what she is losing. Often a woman will focus only on the excitement and try to deny the pain. It is important to make sure the losses are acknowledged, accepted, and resolved, or they may interfere later in the woman's intimate relationships. Also a worker needs to know that much anger and rage at men may be expressed during this phase. The practitioner must examine his or her own feelings about accepting the client's anger and dealing with it in a helpful manner. Experimentation with roles and relationships is part of a woman's search to define her own needs and wants.

A worker can help by educating the client about clear communication of needs, respecting differences, and learning to listen to oneself. Using the therapeutic relationship as a tool for teaching about honesty and expression of caring can be beneficial. At this time, a woman may have real difficulties with intimacy. She may not have had a real adolescence: While other girls were defining intimacy needs with boyfriends, she was pretending to fit in with peers or fantasizing about other girls. Thus, a developmental lag may be evident. A therapist can help a client clarify her own need for intimacy and how that balances with her need for independence. They can discuss the lack of positive role models, and the therapist can encourage the client to find and talk with lesbians who are at ease with their identity. Referral to an "exploring affections for women" or "coming out" group could be helpful. The therapist can talk about his or her own early love relationships, if appropriate, and how he or she learned to define needs. Abbott and Love write,

> Readiness to become an acknowledged lesbian seems to involve a personal and emotional restructuring of values. . . A good deal of energy goes into this process. The lesbian has to accurately perceive her motives and the consequences, and if she can get out from under the weight of old arguments and truly believe in the goodness of her love and the possibility of a rewarding personal life-style, she arrives at a new place.[16]

Family

Coming out to one's family is almost always experienced as a turning point. Women tend to do this in crisis or after having carefully weighed the pros and cons. The crisis may be a political one, such as a vote to prevent discrimination against gays, or it may be personal. The issue of coming out to one's family is frightening and difficult for many clients. However, many women work through their fears. As a woman becomes more accepting of her lesbian identity, she may grow discontent with the distance that concealing her identity necessitates and may decide to take the risk and tell her parents.

Reclaiming family relationships is an important step to a positive self-concept and an integrated identity. Clients should be encouraged to weigh the pros and cons, and to come out to family members when they are ready. If a woman has withdrawn to the extent that she has an extremely limited relationship with her family, a first step may be to get to know her parents and discuss other aspects of her life. As a bond is formed and strengthened, she will be better able to assess whether she can discuss her lesbianism with them.

A worker can be helpful by rehearsing the coming-out scenes with the client and role playing the parents' imagined responses. The worker can help the client focus on what to say and how to say it, line up support for the client before and after the event, and explore the client's worst fears and best possibilities. For most women, actually telling their parents is traumatic. However, with continued interaction and discussion, many families work things out. This is often a good time to encourage a client to invite family members in for some family sessions. It is important to help family members listen to each other's feelings and needs and learn to respect differences. Educating parents with books and pamphlets about lesbianism and referring them to a support group for families with a gay or lesbian member could also be helpful. Some women who feel certain of rejection choose not to disclose their sexual preference to their parents. This choice needs to be examined. If it is clear that the woman would lose more than she would gain, her decision must be respected. Wolfe writes,

> Many women are successfully integrated into the lesbian community, are in long-term relationships with women they love, openly identify themselves as lesbians without constraint—and still find that they cannot tell their parents they are lesbians.[17]

STABLE LESBIAN IDENTITY

After a time of experimenting and exploring, a stable lesbian identity emerges. This is accompanied by a sense of settling down that is similar to finishing adolescence. Much of the earlier dissonance, fear, and anger is resolved and the woman is more self-accepting. She is also developing a community of friends with similar values who are accepted as her "chosen family" and are people she can go to for support, assistance, and companionship. She may spend her holidays and vacations with them. Often, at this time, an ongoing committed relationship is formed. In some larger cities, lesbian marriages in which two women exchange rings and promises are becoming more common. Many women buy homes together and have a committed relationship without undertaking any type of ceremony. Within this long-term relationship, both women experience a sense of settling into what feels comfortable. They define their roles according to what each of them likes to do, rather than trying to fit into a socially prescribed role. Potter and Darty state,

> More women than men are apt to be involved in a quasi marriage marked by a relatively high degree of sexual fidelity. . . It would appear that the most viable option for most lesbians may be that of a fulfilling and relatively monogamous "marital" relationship with another woman.[18]

Along with this committed relationship may come a stabilization of political ideas and identity. Some women who had been separatists begin including men in their lives. Much of the earlier reactiveness and anger is resolved, and the woman feels she has found a niche for herself within her relationship, community, and, possibly, family.

This stabilization may take place gradually, over a period of years. A woman need not have a primary relationship to have stabilized her identity. Although lesbians may come in for or remain in treatment during this stage, the focus will no longer be on coming out. Instead, relationships or work might be the focus. Once a woman has accepted her lesbianism and found a community, she often no longer needs therapy. Rather than focusing inward to resolve conflicts, she may begin focusing outward and become involved in the community, politics, or career advancement.

INTEGRATION

As time goes on, a woman integrates her lesbian identity into a positive self-concept, a process that is ongoing. A woman accepts and feels comfortable with her sexual identity. She chooses how much to discuss her lifestyle and with whom. She often becomes more public about her identity. She continues to find ways to be positive about herself as a woman and a lesbian. Rather than looming large as it did earlier, her lesbianism becomes one aspect of her life and demands less time and energy. There will still be pain and anger about discrimination, but, rather than blaming herself, she will know that the culture is oppressive.

Although this process as described in this article has seemed linear, often it is not. Most women go through parts of the process more than once and in various orders. A woman who had reached a sense of integration might be thrown back into a time of experimenting by the breakup of a long-term relationship. Or, a move from a supportive city environment to a small town could promote the woman's returning to earlier emotional stages.

Another variation is not uncommon. Occasionally, a woman will become involved in a sexual encounter or relationship with another woman without forethought—it seems to just *happen*. In this case, there will not have been a prior sense of difference and dissonance or a search for community. If a woman in this situation decides to work to integrate her same-sex feelings into her identity, the phases of development described in this article may follow her involvement with another woman. The model has been developed in the hope that practitioners will use it when it fits and that it will expand their understanding of a lesbian coming-out process as a complex, multifaceted journey to health and self-acceptance.

NOTES AND REFERENCES

1. The current edition is *Diagnostic and Statistical Manual of Mental Disorders* (3d ed.; Washington, D.C.: American Psychiatric Association, 1980).

2. Sandra J. Potter and Trudy E. Darty, "Social Work and the Invisible Minority: An Exploration of Lesbianism," *Social Work,* 26 (May 1981), p. 190.

3. Vivienne Cass, "Homosexual Identity Formation: A Theoretical Model," *Journal of Homosexuality,* 4 (1979), p. 219.

4. J. Lee Lehman, "What It Means to Love Another Woman," in Ginny Vida, ed., *Our Right to Love: A Lesbian Resource Book* (Englewood Cliffs, N.J.: Prentice-Hall, 1978), p. 25.

5. John D. Grace, "Coming Out Alive: A Positive Developmental Model of Homosexual Competence." Paper presented at The Sixth NASW Professional Symposium, "Social Work Practice: Directions For The 1980's," San Antonio, Tex., November 14–17, 1979.

6. Sasha G. Lewis, *Sunday's Women: A Report on Lesbian Life Today* (Boston: Beacon Press, 1979), p. 19. See also Sidney Abbott and Barbara Love. *Sappho Was a Right-on Woman: A Liberated View of Lesbianism* (New York: Stein & Day, 1972); Betty Berzon and Robert Leighton, eds., *Positively Gay* (Millbrae, Calif.: Celestial Arts Publishing Co., 1979); Lehman, "What It Means to Love Another Woman"; and Deborah G. Wolf, *The Lesbian Community* (Berkeley: University of California Press, 1979).

7. Berzon, "Developing a Positive Gay Identity," *Positively Gay,* p. 2.

8. Elisabeth Kübler-Ross, *On Death and Dying* (New York: Macmillan Co., 1969), pp. 38–136.

9. Wolf, *Lesbian Community,* p. 31.

10. Alfred C. Kinsey, Wardell D. Pomeroy, and Clyde E. Martin, *Sexual Behavior in the Human Male* (Philadelphia: W. B. Saunders Co., 1948).

11. Anne Wilson Schaef, *Women's Reality,* (Minneapolis, Minn.: Winston Press, 1981), p. 32.

12. Ibid., p. 48.

13. Lewis, *Sunday's Women,* p. 18.

14. Wolf, *Lesbian Community,* p. 41.

15. Abbott and Love, *Sappho Was a Right-on Woman,* p. 230.

16. Ibid., p. 223.

17. Wolf, *Lesbian Community,* p. 31.

18. Potter and Darty, "Social Work and the Invisible Minority," p. 188.

Coming Out for Lesbians: A 5-Stage Process

	Differentness	Dissonance	Leaping into Relationships	Stabilizing	Integration
Experiences	awareness of • not fitting • not belonging internalized self-hate • as a woman • as different ↑ Kinsey 4's, 5's 6's start here ↗ Feminist midrange start here	fear/ambivalence/shame socialization . . . • culture • family —VS.— . . . awareness of same-sex attractions political motives equal relationship independence from men & sexual attraction begin process	←——coming-out to family——→ 1 sexual exploring 2 identify exploring • intimacy • relationship needs 3 search for community 4 anger 5 separatism	settled relationship or singlehood stable community stable political views	lesbian identity integrated into life as a whole
Tasks	to identify sense of differentness resulting from same-sex attractions	to lessen dissonance through coming to accept feelings as valid and worthwhile	to explore sexuality, intimacy needs; to self-define; to find a community/support system	to find ways to fit needs into lifestyle	ongoing integration of positive lesbian identity into life as a whole
Clinical Issues	1 support 2 gentle exploration 3 follow client's leads	←——family sessions——→ 1 validate same-sex feelings 2 educate about lesbianism 3 connect with resources 4 encourage exploration 5 discuss and work through dissonance 6 work through self-hatred and build self-esteem grieving process begins ——→	1 use therapy relationship to educate and define relationship needs 2 connect with resources 3 express anger 4 encourage exploration 5 encourage self-definition 6 work through self-hatred and build self-esteem	←——1 support——→ therapy may be terminated or focus on other issues	

REAGAN'S
SAY NO TO
SAY NO
SOCIAL
CUTS
MACHINISTS
JOBS NOT BOMBS

PART VII

THE END AND THE BEGINNING

"'Begin at the beginning, and go til you come to the end: then stop,' said the King to the White Rabbit."[1]

'We found social work to be an inseparable part of the society in which it grows. Our practice has its roots and finds its opportunity in the kind of concern for the well-being of people which society really has. What we social workers believe about people, then, cannot be uninfluenced by what society wants of us. Neither can the philosophy we hold and the practice of social work in our hands fail to make an imprint upon the society of our time.[2]

In the beginning of this text we presented the idea that the political economic environment is the major determinant of the practice performed by professional social workers. Throughout the text we have drawn upon the liberal, conservative, and radical perspectives to analyze the past and current state of the profession. But what of the future? It is likely that all three positions will continue to influence our practice as well as the world in which we live. But we cannot afford to heed the king's advice to the white rabbit in *Alice's Adventures in Wonderland;* we cannot simply stop because we have come to the end of this text. We must anticipate the shape of the future and design a network of services that will help enhance everyone's life.

In this final chapter we look at some visions of possible futures for our world and consider what possible responses the social work profession may have. We particularly consider the future in relation to the threat of nuclear war and consider how military spending may influence the availability of resources for social services. The current state of the profession is presented as well as some views of new directions for social work practice. In many ways the future appears hopeful for social workers and the clients they will serve.

Social work futures

In 1978 a Professional Futures Commission was created by the National Association of Social Workers consisting of fifteen participating members and twenty-one corresponding members. Four scenarios of future histories were developed by the commission based on the concepts of postindustrialism as conceptualized by Daniel Bell and on transformationalism as developed by Willis Harmon.[3, 4] Of the two post-industrial scenarios one concludes positively in an ideal technological society; the other ends as benign facism. The transformed societies also end successfully in one instance and in repressive facism in the other.[5] Social workers serve somewhat different functions in each of the scenarios. Let us briefly consider these four possible futures.

Beck, who chaired the commission, stated that the scenarios were not necessarily predictions of the future but instead were intended "to indicate events that could possibly occur in the general twenty-year period between 1980 and 2000."[6] The first scenario assumes a positive outcome of postindustrialism called "the American technological dream" in which a highly technical, scientific society emerges with a particularly efficiently managed social service network and health care system. Computer technology guides social workers into highly specialized roles, and in general the world is orderly, peaceful, and productive.

The idea of a.computerized social work profession is explored later in this chapter.

In the second scenario technology develops in a similar pattern, but it does not solve all of our problems. Major concerns include racism, unemployment, inflation, pollution, poor health care, and protests. Terrorism flourishes, and the government becomes repressive. Social service programs exist to maintain social control and reduce dissent. Social workers in this society might either enforce the government control, or as Beck suggests, "become radicalized and go underground."[7]

The final two scenarios developed from transformationist views and assume a society characterized by massive change. The more positive of these views envisions a strong environmentalist political party influencing the direction of the country and eventually gaining control. The major thrust of this society is on community development and cooperation. Bartering and exchange services proliferate, handicrafts are valued, and people begin such mutual endeavors as community gardens. Beck feels that in such a society "social workers who pride themselves on clinical skills have a diminished role because self help is the dominant mode . . . social work, as a profession disappears . . . finally, people have learned to help themselves."[8]

Unfortunately a transformed society might also result from catastrophe, terrorist takeover, or nuclear disaster. Though social workers might possibly assume a leadership role in organizing or re-building a damaged society, they might just as easily be repressed in this kind of setting. Social services would be unnecessary in a brutal, fascist society, and social work would probably not survive.

These visions of possible futures lead to many different possibilities for the social worker in the year 2000. While the nature of our society may not change as rapidly as these scenarios suggest, they do illustrate once again the impact of political and economic perspectives on the delivery of social services and the future of the social work profession.

The nuclear threat

It is interesting that only one of the futures scenarios considers the possibility of a nuclear disaster and even then assumes (perhaps naively) that enough structure would survive that social workers could help to rebuild a society. Many social workers feel that nuclear buildup is the major issue for the future if we are to have a future at all. Of course there is also a conservative argument in this debate; the point can be made that a strong nuclear defense is a necessary deterrent to war and a necessary bargaining tool in arms reduction talks. An even more conservative position is that indeed nuclear weapons are "peacekeepers" or security: a stronger defense leads to a stronger nation and all our citizens are better off when more money is budgeted for military expenditures. Both sides agree that the costs for military expenditures are staggering, and because resources are limited military expenditures drain money

Jane Addams, a pacifist, discussed the effects of resources wasted on war in *Peace and Bread in Time of War* (1922).

from other programs. Usually health and human service programs and indirectly the elderly, the poor, the handicapped, children and women (the most vulnerable members of our society) pay the price for increases in military spending.

A radical change in our priorities and a fundamental restructuring of the actions of those in power would be necessary to create a lasting world peace in which resources could be made available for improving social conditions. Social Workers for Peace and Nuclear Disarmament, a special committee of the NASW, serves as a vehicle to express the concerns of the social work profession in promoting nuclear disarmament and peace. Sister Frances Russell, the 1983 Social Worker of the Year, talks about what she is trying to do as one social worker working for peace. She makes the point that she is a private person who ultimately needed to show her anger publicly as she began to realize the connection between a nuclear arms buildup and the needs of her clients.

An example of a public issue becoming a private trouble (referred to in Chapter 1) is offered in the insert by Sister Frances Russell

The Price of Peace: Empowering Human Service Professionals*

SISTER FRANCES RUSSELL

I would like to share with you a little about me. I am a teacher and a social worker. Teaching in the elementary schools was my first professional experience, followed up by social work experience with children and families experiencing poverty, abuse, and neglect. I have worked, in addition, with the mentally ill, the incarcerated in state and federal prisons, and Indo-Chinese and Cuban refugees. Of late, I began Siena House, a Catholic Worker House in Cheyenne, Wyoming, where sheltering the homeless has been a needed and important service. Along with sheltering, I have been responsible for the coordination of a three state network of people in Wyoming, Colorado, and Nebraska who oppose the basing of the MX missile in our region. This coalition, the Tri-State Coalition, has recently become Western Solidarity, the eight-state coalition, opposed to the deployment of the MX missile system.

For my work in providing shelter to women and children and in forming state and regional opposition to the MX missile, I received the NASW Social Worker of the Year Award in 1983. I am proud of this award for several reasons. First, it helps me handle the "flak," "hostility," and "misrepresentation" I receive from the threatened publics of the west; secondly, it represents the spirit of the social work profession, a spirit which has a preferential concern for people at risk, especially the economically poor. In addition, this award represents the commitment of the social work profession to peace. It confronts this country's policies which threaten peace. Where I live in Cheyenne, Wyoming, there were two reactions to my award. One, admiration that a national organization was courageous enough to honor this controversial woman, and secondly, suspicion that a national organization (of benign purposes) publicly honored a subversive. Most of all, this award has helped me become more visible. It has enhanced my opportunities to educate, to encourage, to protest and expose political and military fallacies, and to promote a return to sanity in our social policies.

*Excerpts from a speech given in Minneapolis, Minnesota on May 16, 1984.

It is my thesis that this country is at war, that bombs of disenfranchisement, disinterest and neglect, are now falling on people of color, women, children, the elderly, the sick, the unemployed. We all fear a *future* war, a nuclear exchange, nuclear escalation. Children, the homeless, the unemployed fear today and tonight. They face a growing threat, that jobs/services/assistance will continue to be closed to them. They fear being nothing, counting for nothing. They are numbers on budgets that face increasing reductions.

To become a social worker, a change agent for people living in the contemporary war zones of our cities, will take strong and persistent commitment, a relearning of advocacy, of becoming a public voice for the poor and for their share in our public resources. All of this means opposing the makers and producers and sellers of war and weapons and promoting the causes of people. To be a social worker, a change agent, is always a challenge. To be a social worker, today, in 1984, in the USA is probably the most challenging and critical of times. When have we heard lately of our country being a country for the people, by the people? We have heard that our nations' vital interest is at stake, that interest being defined as military and strategic superiority and economic control of third and fourth world markets and people.

It is to the credit of the social work profession that government policies are analyzed and critiqued. Social workers are taught and trained to enter fully into the political process. Today, it is not by accident but by choice that curriculum planning and continuing education programs are stressing skill in social and political analysis, perceiving the connections between foreign and military policy and domestic decision making and public in our support or opposition of the same.

I am not an expert on nuclear weapons. I am familiar with them and have developed some expertise on the MX missile. The MX, called the missile experimental, has been on the Pentagon drawing boards for some 15 years.

The MX already has cost the US taxpayers six billion dollars. Completed it is estimated to cost $30,000,000,000 (30 billion) dollars. It is already obsolete in concept. It has proved to be no bargaining chip with the Soviets. Yet the President solemnly assures us that this peacekeeper is in our national interest. With this year's appropriation for the MX (5½ billion) we could retain nine major low income programs inclusive of these needed services to people; #1, Food Stamp restoration, energy assistance, and Aid to Dependent Children. This is one missile program in the defense package, remember.

The Reagan Administration plans to spend 1.6 trillion dollars in defense during the next five years. In 1981, we spent $154 billion on weapons and related defense expenditures. In 1985, we are looking at $214 billion and in 1986, 258 billion. In that year, 1986, federal spending outside of the Social Security program will be reaching 78% of our national budget.

We need to reflect on this. These numbers baffle us. They numb us. One task we learn in peace education is to confront numbness and numbers. Look at them! Ask questions of them. Eventually we have to dismantle them and convert them. When you do confront numbers, you discover important facts. You discover, in addition, connections.

A connection that I find as most significant to the issue of militarism is that of unemployment. Unemployment, present and to come, is the most serious social problem in this country. Depending on what figures are used between 10 and 14 million people are unemployed in the United States. This is the largest number of unemployed people since the depression of the 30s. Some unemployment is due to the fact that we are moving into the postindustrial era. This era is characterized as a development from labor intensive to capital intensive industries. Due to the increased mechanization of work, fewer middle and lower skill jobs will be available to people. Another reason for such high unemployment is diversion of interest and concern on the part of government to deal with the problems of unemployment. As social workers, we know these problems are massive.

Let's make a connection between the making of weapons and unemployment. First consider that of the fifty largest US industrial companies, thirty-two make or export arms. Half of the nation's engineers or scientists work directly or indirectly for the Pentagon. The making of weapons has become a permanent part of our economy. Industries that make the weapons are capital intensive. For every additional billion dollars spent on defense, we lose 10,000 jobs. When you pay for the MX missle, as a taxpayer, you literally pour thousands of dollars into those silos. Let me clarify. Imagine three tiers of people in defense industries. The designers and engineers of weapons are high salaried, specialized people. They are level one types. Impact planners, military officials, lobbyists for the Pentagon, are level two types. They earn substantial and secure pay checks and are key people in keeping this vast military machine operating. On the third level are laborers and construction workers "on the assembly line" in weapons plants. In "economic conversion" language, these same numbers of people, presently employed in defense industries, could be tripled IF the amounts of money now going into weapons making could be diverted into civilian jobs.

Another example here. In Cheyenne, Wyoming we expect to hire 1,700 workers at the peak of MX construction. These numbers may change somewhat. But the jobs offered the flow of people coming into our city will be temporary. The amounts of money needed to pay just for the impact of moving people in temporarily will be borne by taxpayers. Overall, Wyoming has to lose money on the MX project. The makers of MX will gain.

The arms race weakens the government's role in promoting and adopting progressive legislation for the unemployed. Legislators are focused on winning defense contracts for their districts. See the Wall Street Journal, July 28th, 1983, which states that fees for Congressmen from defense industry interest groups have doubled in the past year. I've been told by people in Minneapolis that have dialogued with Honeywell personnel about their potential for "conversion" from defense to civilian products that at the present time, defense contracts are the most reliable and most lucrative for them. Unemployment is not a priority for legislators or contractors who are making it very good designing and selling arms.

Besides draining the expertise of our most creative and bright scientists, the arms industries are helping to bring about a permanent underclass in this country. Diversion of energy, interest, and capital from people to weapons puts OUR clients the most vulnerable of people at risk.

From a study recently completed by Harvey Brenner of John Hopkins University, the side effects of unemployment are of tremendous concern. For every 1 percent rise in unemployment, there is a 30 percent increase in domestic violence, a 4 percent rise in suicides, incarceration and admission into mental hospitals, and a 6 percent rise in homocides. For every 1 percent rise in unemployment the feminization of poverty is enhanced, since one third of the women employed in job ghettos are heading single parent families. Collectively, what is happening to people in American society is alarming. I am not saying that defense industries have as their goal to increase unemployment in this country. I am saying that because they are a high tech, capital intensive industry, they have been integrated permanently into our economy and the result is a transference of resources away from civilian jobs to warmaking.

Additional impacts on human services include the following cuts in people programs because of the need to "balance the budget" etc. This year there have been 13,000 foreclosures on family farms, 75,000 teachers have been laid off, 700,000 thousand children have been dropped from Medicaid, 1 million people have been dropped from the Food Stamp program, 250,000 have lost day care services. Thirteen thousand small businesses have gone under and close to four million people are now living on our streets. Indeed, we may fear future wars, but for many of our clients and past clients, war is here.

Now, what to do. One thing we must do. And that is refuse to see these statistics as normal. Refuse to see or to believe that we are living in normal times. We must break through the numbness, become involved in social and political action; assist your peace groups with your interpretation, as social workers, on what is happening to poor people today with concrete examples of what we are doing to children, poor parents, women, the elderly, the homeless.

I have learned to become public. I didn't choose my role. But now, having been moved to the front by the situation in my city, I can't withdraw. I can't stop. I can only go forward. I think we all need to do this—become public, go forward, be a voice.

Sometimes the numbers being spent on what has been called the largest peace-time military buildup in our nation's history become confusing and overwhelming. Budgets of millions and trillions of dollars are hard to understand when we deal with small amounts of money with our clients. To better understand these comparisons consider what the budget for military spending means for Social Service programs.[9]

What a Trillion and a Half Dollars for the Pentagon Will Mean for You*

STEVE SOWLE, STEVE DAGGETT, AND CYNTHIA WASHINGTON

President Reagan has launched the largest peace-time military build-up in our nation's history. The billions cut from social programs to pay for this will fundamentally change government's role in our society, leaving millions of poverty-stricken and low-income Americans without adequate income and health protection. While tax cuts will bear a large share of the responsibility for the tremendous pressure on the budget over the next few years, the planned growth in military spending will add almost as much to the federal budget as the tax cuts will take away. Some of the trade-offs this military build-up will entail are: The $1.6 billion it costs to build one Trident Nuclear Submarine . . . could restore the $1.3 billion cut from FY 1982 Mass Transit subsidies. The $457 million going for 12 more F-15 fighter planes . . . could save the Guaranteed Student Loans program from a $450 million cut. The $2.1 billion it costs to build one CVN-71 Nuclear Carrier . . . could restore full funding for Medicaid (cut by $900 million), and Aid to Families with Dependent Children (cut by $1.2 billion). The $400 million authorized for development of the Pershing II missile system . . . could restore the $352 million cut from health education and training programs. Funds totaling one-thirteenth of the FY 1982 military spending increase over 1981 levels ($5 billion) could restore full funding for Food Stamps (cut by $1.7 billion), Child Nutrition (cut by $1.5 billion), and unemployment benefits (cut by $1.7 billion). The $121 million it costs to build two KC-10A Cargo Planes . . . could save the National Endowments for the Arts and Humanities from a total cut of $113 million.

*Excerpted from "What a Trillion and a Half Dollars for The Pentagon Will Mean for You" (Washington, D.C.: Coalition for a New Foreign and Military Policy, 1982).

Even with these examples we aren't always certain that the changes we see now and may continue to see in the future in our agencies are directly related to increases in military expenditures. Fewer jobs for social workers. Fewer resources to offer our clients. Agency cutbacks in personnel and programs. What are the long-range effects of such changes? We can only speculate on this point. But Betty Surbeck describes the changes as she experienced them in working with a multi-program family in a child welfare agency.

Effects of a Budget Cut in a Child Welfare Agency*

BETTY SURBECK

In the fall of 1980, the child welfare agency for which I work reduced its budget by 34 percent, cutting staff and services proportionally across the board. One service, a residential unit, was eliminated. All the county child welfare agencies' budgets in Pennsylvania were reduced by 34 percent because the state government, which had previously approved the submitted budgets through the Department of Public Welfare, refused to allocate the funds.

Before the budget cuts, protective services in the county had been provided by three separate offices. After the cuts, one office was closed, and the county was divided into two parts to use the remaining funds more efficiently. The cuts resulted in the layoff of approximately 34 percent of staff, including administrators, caseworkers, and aides, and in the transfer of the remaining workers and clients to the two offices left open.

At the time of the layoffs, the agency was committed to the philosophy of keeping the family together. This goal, which was part of the state guidelines, was initiated a number of years ago as a preferable alternative to foster home and residential placements. Our county perhaps had come closest to the state's directives. To prevent further serious abuse and neglect, which would have previously required placement of the children, intensive in-home services were provided to insure the safety of the children and to improve their family situation. These services were costly and included home aides, child aides, child welfare day care homes, transportation services, and weekly visits by social workers.

The budget cuts and layoff of staff meant that it was no longer possible to provide intensive in-home services to meet the state guidelines. The cuts also meant a reduction in the number of child placements the agency and other agencies were willing to make. Thus, the number of options available to protect children was reduced considerably.

EFFECTS ON ONE FAMILY

To dramatize the effect of the cuts, I will discuss what they meant in relation to what one social worker could achieve with one family.

> The A family was an intact white family consisting of a father, a mother, both of whom were in their fifties, and two children, a 13-year-boy and a 14-year-old girl who was five months' pregnant. The family had no extended family members. The mother had a history of hospitalizations at a state mental hospital. The father worked steadily at a good-paying job. He worked on the night shift and slept during the day. The family lived in a dilapidated twin house on a run-down street in a low-income area.
>
> The family was initially referred to the agency by a neighbor because the girl had run away from home. The father was said to be unwilling to let her come home. The school reported that both children were truant and that the girl had said her mother was behaving in a disruptive manner, that she was incontinent and screamed night and day.
>
> The father, on contact with the intake worker, requested placement for his daughter during her pregnancy. The initial intake process was about the same as it would have been before the cuts. The only difference was that the intake period was shortened and a quick decision was made not to use child placement but to refer the family to the protective unit for in-home services. Further evaluation showed that the family had long-standing multiple problems and that the agency had become involved about three years before.
>
> The mother's serious illness prevented her from assuming even minimal responsibility for the children. The father was a withdrawn person with no outlets except betting on horses. He slept all day and made little attempt to provide structure for the family. Thus, the family never ate together, few chores

were done in the house or yard (the house was filthy and the yard was piled with broken glass), there were no rules for bedtime or curfews, and supervision was minimal.

In such a situation, placement of the children is usually a consideration. Because of the budget cuts, I was told that placement was only a remote possibility. Placements were to be reserved for extreme cases, and this case was not considered extreme. Meanwhile the school put pressure on me, the worker, because in their view this was a serious situation that would have warranted placement in the past. I walked the tenuous path between two different authorities, knowing that I did not have many options from which to choose.

The parents were upset and ambivalent. The school was complaining to them, the child welfare agency was expecting something from them, their daughter was going to have a baby, and they had to make a decision about her pregnancy. The school told them their daughter should go away until the baby was born and they wondered why she could not be placed.

There is an interplay between the agency's limitations in helping and the family's ability to accept aid. The family's ability to accept services is based in part on its level of functioning and level of trust. The family has to trust enough to let a worker in the door. It must have a certain level of responsibility and organization so the worker and family will be able to coordinate their visits. Mr. and Mrs. A barely met those requirements. Their children had been raised with few restraints and little structure and were accustomed to doing what they wanted when they wanted to.

Although the father was aware that the agency would not place his daughter, placement was his immediate goal. His second goal was to get the children to go to school so he would not have to pay any more fines. My initial goals were to help persuade the father to hospitalize his wife, who was refusing psychiatric care, and to gain his trust. Although the father did not want to bother about going through the process and embarrassment of getting help for his wife, he knew she was disruptive and that she needed hospitalization. He finally agreed and helped to hospitalize her.

My goals for the A family included providing support in relation to the daughter's pregnancy and help with planning for the baby. Other goals were to help the father improve the children's school attendance and to help the father and children deal with the mother's chronic mental illness. Long-range goals included raising the children's self-esteem, helping the father to gain some authority in the family and to provide some structure in the household, increasing and clarifying family communications, and encouraging positive interactions between the parents and children.

What could have been done to help this low-functioning family before the budget was cut? To build initial trust, I would have offered concrete services, including transportation to the girl's doctor and therapy sessions, a home aide to help with household management, and a child aide to work with the children individually. I would have met with the family one to two days a week instead of every other week.

I was able to arrange four or five sessions in which the father and two children met with me and a family therapist to help improve communication in the family and to bolster the father's position of authority. However, the family was not organized to maintain appointments. Perhaps if some of the resources that were lost because of the budget cuts had been retained, more intensive treatment could have been given, and improvement in family functioning could have been longer lasting.

PROGNOSIS

What is likely to happen in this family without the services they need so desperately? The son will probably start using drugs and get involved in shoplifting and other forms of petty theft. (The son recently did get picked up for shoplifting.) The children will probably not graduate from high school. The girl may become pregnant again and end up on welfare. Having had no chance to observe basic housekeeping or parenting skills, she will probably be unable to provide them for her own children.

The reduction of supportive services is likely to become a common phenomenon in social work agencies. The services provided by our agency prior to the cuts were not great, but they were considered to be good in the child welfare field. They were never totally adequate, and the frequent turnover of social workers and direct service staff perhaps is the best evidence of the frustration felt by the workers. It is difficult and frustrating to know that those in power arbitrarily have decided that some children do not deserve full care.

I do not know any children who deserve half a chance. Children accept what little they have and are not aware of what they are being deprived of until later when society feels the effects of their deprivation, whether their anger or their perpetual dependence. If they never were able to have had a loving secure family, how are they to know what they have missed? How are they to know that is why they run away or steal? Thus, the budget cuts really mean that children will receive less of a chance to experience their birthright: discipline, security, and love.

Current status of the profession

Given the recent declines in social service spending, some people have predicted a decline in the number of workers who will be needed in the next few years. This is in sharp contrast to the growth years of the late 1960s and early 1970s. During that period a strong economy stimulated new social service programs, and schools of social work could barely keep up with the demand for new workers. In fact the pressure to educate new workers led to the NASW's expanding its membership guidelines to include persons with BSWs from institutions accredited by the Council on Social Work Education. During this period there were also numerous paraprofessional associate of arts programs developed to help meet the need. According to the U.S. Department of Labor the unemployment rate for social service occupational groups in general was about seven percent in late 1982 and early 1983, somewhat lower than the national average for all professions and occupations.[10]

A description of levels of social work practice is presented in Chapter 8.

Most recently these trends have been reversing themselves. Several graduate schools of social work have reduced the numbers of students in their programs. For example the Columbia Graduate School of Social Work reduced its enrollment from 600 to 500 students. Other schools have moved toward more areas of specialization or concentration hoping to attract BSW workers into graduate training. For example, the University of Minnesota has developed three areas of concentration: health/mental health; family and children's services and human services management. In addition, they also offer three joint degree programs: an MSW-MPH (with the School of Public Health), MSW-MPA (with the School of Public Affairs) and an MSW-MA in Family Social Sciences. Other schools are expanding their post-master's programs, their doctoral programs and their post-doctoral offerings.

Currently there are nearly ninety professional schools of social work in major universities offering the MSW degree and more than four hundred accredited undergraduate programs offering the BSW degree. While it is difficult to estimate the number of persons actually working in social work and social work-related fields, some estimates have placed the figure as high as a half million workers (according to the 1980 census). In contrast the major professional social work organization (NASW) has over 90,000 members in fifty-five chapters.

In the accompanying inserts we look at two social workers with different histories and different career paths within the profession. One is a social welfare administrator with a PhD and one is a social worker in a rural county social service agency.

A Social Welfare Administrator Reflects

KEVIN J. MAHONEY

I was introduced to social work in 1967 at Berkshire Farm for Boys, a private correctional facility for delinquent boys located in upstate New York. I had recently entered the Jesuit Novitiate, and I was assigned to work, under the direction of the chaplain, two to three partial days a week. The chaplain had a masters degree in social work as did the treatment coordinator for Sloane Cottage where I worked.

Berkshire Farms emphasized a total milieu approach to treatment. In additional to institutional staff, special social workers were assigned to work with the families and peer groups that the boys would return to. Special emphasis was given to group work; at times counseling sessions were taped so that they could be reviewed with supervisors or peers.

My own duties were modest. In addition to planning the liturgy for the Catholic service on Sunday, I worked with the cottage parents and had primary responsibility for a couple of boys. I also oversaw work projects where the boys assisted frail elderly people in nearby communities.

Like my Jesuit training, Berkshire Farm stressed the value of the individual and the importance of knowing and understanding yourself. What I learned—especially at Berkshire Farm—was the importance of dealing with the whole person—never ignoring the family, peers, or the community.

In September of 1968 I was transferred to St. Louis, Missouri to complete the last two years of my college education. St. Louis University did not have a BSW program so I majored in Sociology and Philosophy—and chose a set of courses which focused on applied Sociology. Many of my classes required papers or presentations on social problems in the community—applying basic concepts.

During 1968–9 I worked as coordinator of the Jesuit volunteers and as recreation leader at the City of St. Louis Home for Delinquent Boys at Missouri Hills. And in 1969–70 I was Program Director at a settlement house in a racially-mixed area of the near-south side. In addition to overseeing a large tutoring program—and serving as a probation officer for a number of children—I coached the local baseball team.

In 1970 I left the Jesuits and had to consider what to do with my life. My values and experiences led me toward the field of social work, but by that time I was discouraged about change to the individual or group level—unless it was accompanied by structural change. This belief grew out of my work with children and families in the inner city. Structural barriers seemed to block individuals from breaking out of poverty. So at the end of the summer of 1970 I returned to New England and entered the University of Connecticut School of Social Work in the community organization and administration sequence.

My MSW programs stressed the interplay between knowledge and practice. Classrooms relied heavily on examples from the field. Emphasis was placed on applying knowledge from all of the social sciences, but especially psychology, sociology, political science and economics.

Sometimes I wonder what exactly did I learn in my Masters level program. No doubt I was exposed to all the modes of social work practice. Whereas the University of Connecticut's program was not "generalist" in the fullest sense of the word, each student was required to have classroom and field experience in casework, group work, and community organization. The vast majority of the students were in the casework sequence, and Freudian theory was the core of that curriculum.

Because such a small number of students were in the other two sequences, a special closeness developed among the students in community organization and those in group work. The relationships formed here affected my values and influenced my life—in fact my wife, Janice, was one of those group workers.

Social work history, ethics, and values were taught in introductory classes. My first community organization course was basically a course in citizen participation and "empowering the powerless"—learning not to "blame the victim". These were times of turmoil and issues of race and war impinged on every class. These beliefs have affected my life—but I have developed more of an understanding of when and how consumer involvement works.

In my first year field placement with the State Department of Corrections, I had to write a grant and help lay the groundwork for a program to work with the families of inmates. But, before my first year ended I was called before my draft board to defend my application as a conscientious objector. The draft board approved my application and strongly urged me to finish my masters in social work. I was therefore able to do my field work, plus work full time at Connecticut Halfway House, Inc., first as a caseworker and later as the assistant director.

Counseling ex-offenders I learned to use authority as part of the treatment process. As an administrator I learned a great deal about innovation and program change. Each year I planned and organized a weekend retreat for managers, board members, and representatives of the residents. These sessions led to program revisions and an expansion of the halfway house program to include a halfway house for women and a satellite program for former residents who needed continuing support.

During my second year in the masters program I also served in the search committee for a new dean, and helped found Link, Inc., a corporation made up of faculty members and students from the University of Connecticut law and social work programs and key members of neighborhood civic associations. The purpose of this organization was to link the expertise of these professional schools with the experience and problem of Hartford's neighborhoods. The corporation leased, then bought, a home in the Blue Hills area of Hartford and a number of students (including myself) lived and worked in this community.

These varied experiences gave me a great chance to contribute and to build confidence. Enthusiasm is contagious, but I also began to learn that one can only do so much. In social work all one has is one's self. You learn to accept your limitations—knowing you can't "save the world".

My wife helped me learn this lesson. She was not willing to marry me and the halfway house—so the day after our honeymoon ended, I took a new job as the town of Mansfield's first Director of Social Services.

My first responsibility was for income maintenance programs. I ran the general assistance program, took applications for public assistance (including Medicaid, AFDC, etc.) and, after a great deal of advocacy, convinced food stamp representatives to travel the twenty miles to take new applications and reapplications on a monthly basis. I learned a lot about advocacy and even became a witness in a federal court case forcing the food stamp program to provide outreach and home applications for the frail. Working in a rural community (population approximately 20,000), I had the chance to do direct counseling and job-finding—as well as administrative tasks.

In the mid-1970s Mansfield was feeling its lack of human services; so I was able to help start a youth center, a youth/family counseling program, the housing authority, a meals-on-wheels program, telephone reassurance for the elderly, and a senior center. My responsibilities for human services brought me in regular touch with the town council. I learned to describe the town's needs succinctly and to present the options clearly and effectively.

Certainly my favorite work was with the aged. When congess authorized the Supplemental Security Income Program (SSI), I organized a group of volunteers to visit each of the approximately 800 elderly in the community. In addition to informing them about the new SSI benefits, we took the opportunity to survey their needs and to let people know about the services already available.

My interest in Gerontology was so clear that when I had the opportunity to return to graduate school to get my doctorate I knew I wanted to specialize in social gerontology. I applied and was accepted for the PhD program at the University of Wisconsin-Madison. At the bachelor's level my training focused on social problems and basic concepts/theories in the social sciences. My master's program emphasized skills and techniques. Here I learned a great deal about supervision and administration and why I did what I did. The PhD program was to prepare me for research and policy analysis. Wisconsin's program was exceptional because it forced the student to utilize the resources of the whole university. I took courses in the business school and in the Departments of Social Work, Sociology, Economics, Political Science and Urban and Regional Planning. Three of my PhD committee members were from my own department but the other two were from sociology and urban and regional planning. This was a truly interdisciplinary program.

I would be remiss if I did not mention the importance of the collegial atmosphere at Wisconsin. I received a great deal of support, encouragement, and friendship through the Institute on Aging, and I benefited greatly sharing ideas with teachers and fellow students. During the first year I had the opportunity to try my teaching skills as a teaching assistant. But in the second and third years I had the chance to be part of the research team evaluating Wisconsin's community care for the elderly demonstration program. I had major responsibility for the rural site (Barron County). This project was the basis of my dissertation (on the effects of forced coordination on organizations and clients), and the focus of many later professional papers, and even a book.

My research and experience in long term care has provided me with valuable career opportunities. After graduation I received a three month research fellowship from the National Gerontological Society. The Gerontological Society was trying to link key administration agencies with trained gerontologists skilled in research and policy analysis. I went to work for the Connecticut Department on Aging developing a model adult day care program, evaluating adult day care services, and making recommendations to the state legislature on the need for adult day care, possible standards, and future funding. At the end of three months I stayed on with the Department rising from Senior Planning Analyst to Director of Policy, Planning Research to Chief of Elderly Care. My responsibilities included work with the General Assembly, coordination with other state departments, research and program development, oversight of the state's community care program for the frail elderly, and the Nursing Home Ombudsmen and Protective Services Programs.

Certainly my PhD gave me a certain status on the job, but the main benefits of my training were a knowledge of the literature, and the ability to analyze problems, define researchable questions, and apply research.

A View from a Rural County Social Service Office

JUNE HAGLUND

As a child growing up in Duluth, Minnesota I knew some day I would be a nurse. My parents—especially my mom—always wanted me to go to college—Gustavus Adolphus—our church supported college. This would really make my mom proud.

Off to Gustavus I went to do my one year to please my family, to grow up, but after one semester I didn't want to leave. I really enjoyed being there so I had to change my plans. Almost everyone at Gustavus was majoring in education, ministry, or social work. At that time I didn't even know what social work was. Growing up in a middle income family I knew nothing about "welfare" or anything connected to it. I did know about adoption and thought I would like to do that.

Gustavus was a small college with small classes and a great deal of individual attention. Since I changed majors in midstream I was behind my peers. Our instructor used to take me individually to teach me the introductory classes. She was great—I knew I wanted to be a social worker after that. During my senior year I spent time at the local welfare office. They gave me five old age cases to do whatever I thought they needed. I loved it—felt really proud of myself after spending time with. We had several classes at the mental hospital also located in St. Peter. This really told me I didn't want to work there on a full-time basis.

Before graduation directors from county agencies came to Gustavus recruiting workers. They came from all over the state. I wanted to work in Minneapolis because I had several friends working and living there. Wonder of wonders I was hired by Hinepin County Department of Social Services to work with a case load of ADC families.

I began working in 1946. I was hired as a war probationary employee. If I remember correctly our case loads ran around 100. Most of our involvment was in the area of finances and eligibility. We saw our clients once every three months in their homes unless there was an emergency. For a period of time I worked with blind people who lived in a small hotel. I quit working in 1950 with the birth of our daughter. I returned to social work in 1968, the year she graduated from high school.

During the years I wasn't working I did a lot of volunteer work. I couldn't keep myself out of our field. I did volunteer work at Hastings Mental Hospital; I used to write discharge summaries for the social workers. I did a lot of PTA and scout work. Why I didn't go back to school and get my master's in those days I will never know. I had a close friend living by who had worked at Hennepin County with me who also quit with the birth of her first child. Each year we'd say, "next year we'll go back." She never did either.

When I was ready to return to work in 1968 we were living in Marshfield, Wisconsin. I hoped to work four years to help with college funds. Could I be hired after not working for 17 years was a big question. In order to be hired at that time we had to take a test. I was so nervous taking that test I could hardly write my name, but I made it. Marshfield is in Wood County and is a town of about 17,000 people. Wood County has two offices, one in Marshfield and one in Wisconsin Rapids. Marshfield serves about one third of the county.

I began in a very small office. I was the fifth social worker and there were two clerical staff. There is now a staff of twenty-six. I was hired as a child welfare worker, meaning that I worked with youth referred by police and sheriffs, schools, parents and children in foster care. After about two years I was offered the opportunity to become Foster Home Coordinator at the north end of the county, a new position with our agency. This meant one third of my time would be spent licensing foster homes, relicensing, recruiting, and placing—a whole new field for me. I still am Foster Home Coordinator. Our program has changed considerably since that time. I have helped our agency develop a medical foster care program which has now grown so large it has its own coordinator. I helped develop a respite care program which is short-term (two day to two weeks) care for severely handicapped children in foster care homes. Our program was first funded through a grant; later grants included our training other counties to reproduce our program. We currently have one full-time respite home and an additional home during the summer months. Our medical foster care program serves no more than twenty children at a time. Children come from all over the state; this need developed because of the Marshfield Medical Center. Other counties purchase our service when they must place a child in one of our homes.

I have been on a state committee to determine how Federal Funds should be spent to educate foster parents. I teach, twice a year, a class for new foster parents. I give speeches in the community to various service agencies to make the foster care program known and to help recruit new foster parents. I have been active in a group of foster home coordinators from the Fox River Valley. Together we have produced a complete handbook on foster care for foster parents. We arrange two workshops a year for foster parents. We work with the legislature and do all we can to better the foster care program. I began an adult foster care program in our community. We have a mental hospital in addition to our hospital and nursing homes in Marshfield, and many people who were ready to leave need homes. This program has also grown so large that another worker is now doing that program. I believe in a few years it will be as large as our children's program.

Over the years the other two thirds of my case load has changed also. I began working with juveniles, I have worked with families with money management problems, physical and sexual abuse, child management problems—almost any kind of problem. Over the years I have developed a more specialized practice—working with unmarried mothers.

Working in this area has been most interesting and rewarding to me. I have helped develop prenatal classes given at St. Joseph's Hospital. Their social worker and I planned and held the first classes. We continued this for two years then the hospital agreed to have their nurses from the new baby department take my place. These classes are still functioning. I was part of a community effort to establish a group for girls who have kept their babies—I worked with them on several groups. I now have a group that has been meeting monthly for the past year.

New areas of practice

Some of the fields of social work practice are described in Part V.

In looking to the future there appear to be many areas of growth within the social work profession. Mary Ann Quaranta, past president of NASW, defines social work as a "growth profession, despite popular thinking to the contrary."[11] As evidence for her position, she cites an intensive survey completed by 57,000 social workers in 1982. In a ten year period employment in the public sector declined somewhat but employment in profit-making enterprises increased (most clearly in the area of private practice). The largest area of practice was mental health services; in the past health services had been first. It appeared many workers were beginning to move into private practice, although there is still a need for social workers in rural areas and there is less competition for those positions than similar positions in larger cities.

One of the most prominent areas for new opportunities for social workers is in gerontology. When one considers that over 5,000 people a day become 65 years old, the demands for this ever increasing population become evident. Social workers in this area are managing cases, doing intergenerational counseling with three and four-generation families, providing specific services (transportation, meals, day care), and developing new services (for example, ethnic hot meals programs, sexual counseling, Alzheimer's disease support groups, elder abuse projects, and assertiveness and leadership training programs for older women).

If one reviews current social work journals it appears that the possibilities for social work practice may be limitless. Recent articles have appeared about such varied areas as forensic social work (helping clients to stand trial, evaluating criminal responsibility and mental status, and training social workers who need to appear as expert witnesses in court),[12] social work and optometry (working to organize outreach services to those who have no access to good eye care and helping patients understand, obtain, and use treatment that is available),[13] and social work in a veterinary hospital (working with pet

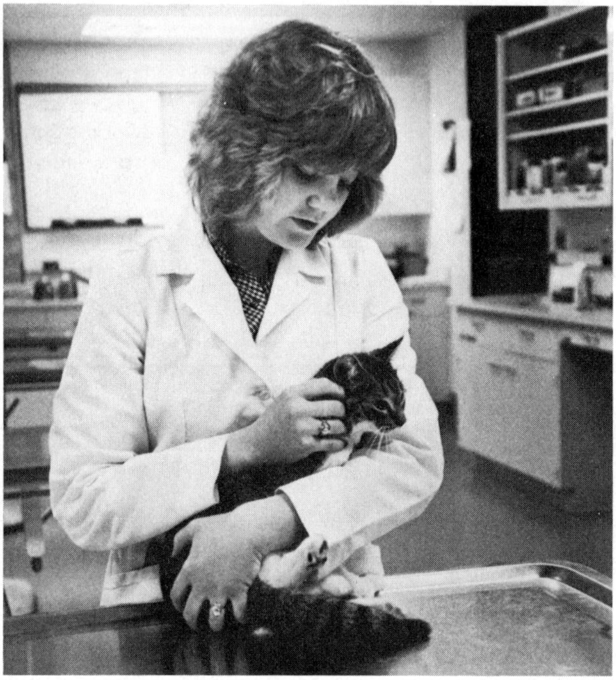

One of the newer fields of practice for social workers is counseling with pet owners in veterinary hospitals. Photo courtesy of Student Support Services Publication Center, University of Minnesota.

owners grieving over the loss of a pet which was a part of the family for many years).[14] In addition social workers who have always worked with immigrants are finding that new groups of refugees (such as the Vietnamese) require help in finding their place in a new country and building a sense of belonging for themselves and their families. Then too, we have recently seen old practice ideas applied to new populations. In the past twenty years the concern over child abuse has grown dramatically; skills developed to handle that problem are now being applied to cases of elderly people abused at a rate and frequency only slightly less than that of child abuse.[15] New areas for social work practice are limited only by our imagination and ability to creatively respond to the needs in society as they occur.

A computerized profession

One of the most innovative visions of the future is a society that fully uses the advances in computer technology. While some may argue that an increasing emphasis on technology may result in a decreasing emphasis on the humanities and social sciences, it seems possible that both areas could benefit from each other. In the 1970s and 1980s computers have been reduced so dramatically in both size and cost that most of us have access to them in our schools, offices, or homes. Software (the programs that run the computers) are made to be user friendly so that almost anyone can quickly learn how to write a letter, balance a checkbook, play a game, or organize a budget. But what uses will computers have for the social work profession in the future?

Most professional training in schools of social work is already beginning to incorporate skill-training in the use and application of computerized information systems. It is clear that computers could easily help to organize massive amounts of data regarding client histories and services offered and used. One major issue raised in computerizing client data is confidentiality. Who will have access to data entered into an agency's computer? While a variety of measures have been devised to "code" client names, it is still not possible to fully assure confidentiality in computerized data banks.

Computers offer numerous ways to better serve the needs of the client and the agency particularly in gathering initial information. Photo courtesy of Student Support Services Publication Center, University of Minnesota.

A recent text presents numerous uses of computer technology in mental health treatment settings. [16] Specific clinical applications include the automated MMPI, computer scoring of the Rorschach ink blot test, computerized psychotherapy, computer assisted behavioral and biofeedback treatment, computerized interviewing and clinical consultation, automated nursing notes, computer diagnosis and prediction, and an online patient assessment system. It is likely that in the future we will see more automated testing, interviewing, diagnosis, assessment, and perhaps even treatment.

It is possible to imagine a client entering a social work agency for the first time and being asked to be seated in front of a computer terminal. After two or three minutes of general instructions, the client is left alone to answer intake questions.

Would you please enter your full name and address and telephone number and then press return key?
What is your age? Return.
What is your current place of employment? Return.
Could you please describe the problem that brought you here today? Return.
How long has this been a problem for you? Return.
What have you tried to do about this problem? Return.
Did that help? Why or why not? Return.
Did you try anything else? Please explain. Return.
Have you ever been seen by anyone else for this problem? If so, who? Return.
Please tell me anything else that you would like us to know about you. Thank you.

In addition to simply gathering some information, this process may actually reduce a client's anxiety by having a nonjudgemental listener encourage the client to discuss the presenting problem. It is also possible that intake information could be quickly assessed and a tentative diagnosis made before the client is ever seen by a social worker. From the worker's perspective a computer could be invaluable in decision making. Through research efforts the risk factors associated with need for placement in a nursing home or possibility of child abuse can be made fairly clear. If the information system confirmed a high percentage of risk factors, the worker might be able to more confidently make decisions regarding clients' lives. Again, there are questions to be raised. What happens if the worker intuitively disagrees with the recommendation of the computer? What is a better predictor of behavior—objective criteria or a combination of objective criteria and subjective assessment? At this point the vision of a computerized social work profession may raise more questions than it answers, but the potential for fully utilizing computer systems is great.

Summary

We have repeatedly made the point that social work is a product of the social, political and economic environment in which it exists. We have analyzed various social issues as well as social work practice itself from a radical perspective, a liberal perspective, and a conservative perspective. We see these approaches clearly evident in the historical roots of the profession and in the possible futures of the profession. We also see these approaches in the knowledge base and the value base of the social work profession. It is not possible to predict the future or the role that social workers will play in the future. In our perhaps somewhat optimistic view, we see social workers playing a key role in designing our future society. Our current view of looking at people within the context of their environments is both a solid idea used by social workers in the past and a revolutionary way of trying to understand the problems of the present and the unknown issues of the future. Our message to the next generation of social workers is perhaps best stated by a quotation.

> Social workers are not oracles, but the social work focus on person-and-environment in interaction means that they cannot allow themselves merely to survive, ignore, or adjust to the future. They must help shape it. They must prepare themselves to work in the future. They must continue to work to improve the quality of life.[17]

References

1. Lewis Carroll, *Alice's Adventures in Wonderland* (New York: MacMillan, 1865).
2. Bertha Reynolds, *Social Work and Social Living* (Washington D.C.: National Association of Social Workers, 1975).
3. Daniel Bell, *The Coming of the Post-Industrial Society* (New York: Basic Books, 1974).
4. Willis Harmon, *An Incomplete Guide to the Future* (San Francisco: San Francisco Book Company, 1976).
5. Ann Minahan, "Social Workers and the Future," *Social Work* 26, no. 5 (September 1981): 363–364.
6. Bertram M. Beck, "Social Work's Future: Triumph or Disaster?" *Social Work* 26, no. 5 (September 1981): 367–372.
7. Ibid., 369
8. Ibid., 371.
9. Steve Sowle, Steve Daggett, and Cynthia Washington, "What a Trillion and a Half Dollars for the Pentagon Will Mean for You" (Washington D.C.: Coalition for a New Foreign and Military Policy, 1982).
10. Carol Kleiman, "Rural Areas Show Biggest Demand for Social Workers," *Saint Paul Sunday Pioneer Press,* 22 January 1984.
11. Ibid., 7H.
12. Dane S. Hughes, and Barbara C. O'Neal, "A Survey of Current Forensic Social Work," *Social Work* 28, no. 5 (September-October 1983): 393–394.
13. B.J. Seymour and Beverly Marston, "Social Work and Optometry: A New Partnership," *Social Work* 29, no. 6 (November-December 1984): 536–541.

14. James E. Quackenbush and Lawrence Glickman, "Helping People Adjust to the Death of a Pet," *Health and Social Work* (March 1984): 42–48.
15. Deborah Bookin and Ruth E. Dunkle, "Elder Abuse: Issues for the Practitioner," *Social Casework* 66, no. 1 (January 1985): 3–12.
16. J.B. Sidowski, J. H. Johnson, and T. A. Williams; eds., *Technology in Mental Health Care Delivery Systems* (Norwood, New Jersey: Ablex, 1980).
17. Minahan, "Social Workers and the Future," 364.

About the Authors

Mary Wirtz Macht received both her M.S.S.W. and Ph.D. from the University of Wisconsin. While a graduate student she studied under a fellowship provided by the National Institute of Mental Health. As a fellow she worked at the Center for Evaluation, Research, and Training. Prior to graduate study, Dr. Macht worked for five years in a county agency carrying a mixed caseload. She was instrumental in developing both the Work Incentive Program and a Day Care Program in that county. After receiving her doctorate Dr. Macht taught in the University of Wisconsin system and Marian College, Fond du Lac, Wisconsin for seven years. She has published articles on corrections, women, child welfare, gerontology, and organizational theory. A generalist planning perspective is the organizing link between these various substantive areas. She is presently a small business owner, real estate developer, political organizer, and sometime teacher. Dr. Macht currently serves as the Chairperson of the Wisconsin State Public Defender Board, and as a board member of the Regional Domestic Abuse Program, and the Winnebago Mental Health Association.

Jean Kathleen Quam is associate professor in the School of Social Work, an associate faculty member in the Women's Studies Department, and an advisory board member of the Center for Advanced Feminist Studies at the University of Minnesota in Minneapolis. She received her Ph.D. from the University of Wisconsin-Madison in 1981 studying social work practice and gerontology. Her dissertation was on the supportive nature of older women's friendship networks. She earned her M.S.W. from the University of Nebraska-Lincoln and graduated *cum laude* from Moorhead State University in Minnesota with a B.A. in social work.

In addition to teaching, she has worked with oncology patients and mentally retarded and physically handicapped clients and their families, and has done psychiatric social work. Dr. Quam has published widely, and she has recently completed a series of biographical essays for the revised NASW *Encyclopedia of Social Work.* She has also co-authored a special issue of *New Directions in Mental Health Services* that focuses on older mentally ill patients. In addition, Dr. Quam has presented numerous papers at national conferences. Dr. Quam cofounded Community Care Corporation, which operates two board and lodging facilities for the aged chronically mentally ill.

Name Index

Subject Index